D0431870

INDIAN LIFE
ON THE NORTHWEST COAST OF NORTH AMERICA

The motif used on the title page is from a painting by John Webber of Captain Cook's two ships, the *Resolution* and the *Discovery*. Photograph courtesy of the Provincial Archives of British Columbia at Victoria.

INDIAN LIFE

ON THE NORTHWEST COAST OF NORTH AMERICA

As Seen by the Early Explorers and Fur Traders during the Last Decades of the Eighteenth Century

Erna Gunther

The University of Chicago Press
Chicago and London

The University of Chicago Press, Chicago 60637
The University of Chicago Press, Ltd., London

Printed in the United States of America
International Standard Book Number:
0–226–31088–4
Library of Congress Catalog Card Number:
72–188822

Contents

Illustrations

Preface

The research for this study was carried out over a long period of time and involved travel to many museums and libraries. The places visited depended on the diverse nationalities of the explorers and fur traders whose journals were the main source of information and on the locations of the museums where the "curiosities" gathered on these journeys finally came to rest.

The British expeditions were so anxious about the journals of their members that they extracted a pledge from them to deliver their diaries at the end of the voyage; the information was to be published only as a carefully edited narrative. This happened with the Cook and Vancouver expeditions. The Spaniards considered the diaries of the captain, the pilot, and the chaplains the property of the government, and since the expeditions started from Mexico, the diaries were returned there. After two copies were made, the original was sent to the king of Spain and the copies were filed in the Archivo General de la Nación in Mexico City. The publication of these diaries was very slow, and many are still in manuscript form. The journals of the fur traders seem to have been regarded as personal possessions, and although some received almost immediate publication others are still waiting.

In contrast to the journals, the "curiosities" which were collected were never really considered official, and they appear in the most surprising places. They were given as presents, sold to museums and dealers, sold again at auction, or kept in family cabinets. To museums that have material from paleolithic man and ancient Egypt or Greece, a few scattered objects in materials of no great value that were collected just "yesterday" in the eighteenth century have no great importance. Even the labels, if they have any, seldom mention the historical significance which is so important to the ethnohistorian of the Northwest Coast.

The libraries having both published books and unpublished manuscripts are:

Americana Room, New York Public Library, New York City
Archivo General de la Nación, Mexico City
Bancroft Library, University of California, Berkeley
British Museum, London
The Huntington Library, San Marino, California
Massachusetts Historical Society, Boston
Museo Naval, Madrid
National Maritime Museum, Greenwich, England
Northwest Collection, University of Washington, Seattle
Provincial Library of British Columbia, Victoria, Canada
Public Record Office, London
The Sutro Collection, University of San Francisco, California

Objects collected have found places in the following museums:

British Museum, London
Hunterian Museum, University of Glasgow
Museum für Völkerkunde, Berlin-Dahlem
Museum für Völkerkunde, Munich
Museum für Völkerkunde, Vienna
Museum of Anthropology and Ethnography, Leningrad
Museum of Anthropology and Ethnography, University of Moscow
Museo Etnografico, Florence
Museo d'América, Madrid
National Museum of Ireland, Dublin
Royal Albert Memorial Museum, Exeter, England
Royal Scottish Museum, Edinburgh
University Museum, Cambridge, England

Since the staffs of these libraries and museums have changed during the long period in which this research was done, I can only thank them all collectively for their patience and their willingness to share their knowledge with me. I wish to thank Miss Mary Gormly, formerly a graduate student at the University of Washington and now librarian at the California State College at Los Angeles, for her generosity in allowing me to use her notes on the Spanish explorers and the bibliography she assembled. I also wish to thank my colleagues in anthropology in the many institutions with which I have corresponded, especially Dr. Frederica DeLaguna. At the beginning of the project, I received much aid from Frederic Douglas, of the Denver Art Museum, including a grant from the Neosho Foundation for the Study of Material Culture. I am also grateful for grants from the University of Washington Agnes Anderson Fund and the Graduate School Research Fund.

Introduction

THE DIMENSIONS OF ETHNOHISTORY

Ethnohistory can extend the knowledge of a culture beyond the reaches of ethnography, provided written records of first contacts between a native society and a literate culture are available. These records can also supplement any archaeological research which has been done in the region under study and often helps to interpret fragments of objects that alone would not be understood. The Northwest Coast of North America has had one of the richest Indian cultures in North America—and the poorest archaeology. But in compensation there are excellent written records of almost a century of contacts before white settlement of any proportion began in the area. Explorers, fur traders, and occasional travelers provided this literature, with some additions from the small hunting settlements of the Russians.

There are many aspects of native life that even extensive archaeology cannot reveal, especially in a nonceramic culture. The authors of the eighteenth-century diaries and journals used in reconstructing the culture by ethnohistorical methods saw a well-established and active society. They could observe the reactions of a native people when they first saw ships that sailed, were offered strange foods, and, too often, heard gunfire. Captain Cook walked around in several Nootka villages and described what he saw. Don Jacinto Caamaño was a guest of honor at a feast where he received a sea otter skin as a gift, and he had by that time learned enough of the etiquette of this society to make the proper response. Their accounts of the Indians they met are contemporaneous—not the fading memory of the old men from whom anthropologists in the twentieth century and even the nineteenth century have had to pry their information. When the same customs are reported by both sources, one is reassured that the twentieth-century information is well remembered and that the culture has been stable.

Ethnohistory has several kinds of documentation at its disposal: (1) published journals and diaries; (2) unpublished manuscripts; (3) artifacts collected on expeditions, now in museums; (4) contemporaneous sketches of native people and their setting.

USE OF JOURNALS

The history of a journal and its author should be carefully studied before it is used as an ethnohistorical source. Journals and diaries were based on the incidents and narrative of voyages, and travel conditions were difficult in the eighteenth century. The question arises, When were the entries in a journal made? On the day of the event? On Northwest Coast expeditions daily entries were possible when the ship was at anchor for a long period. On the other hand, if the explorers were trading with the Indians, working on the ships, or charting the coastline, time for writing was scarce. The answer is that there were short and long reports, the first written in port, the second, later at sea. Captain Cook's journals are a good example of this technique. He made daily entries regarding the weather, the position of the ships, and visits from the Indians; then when he left Nootka Sound and stood for Prince William Sound, he wrote that he would now summarize the Nootkan culture as he saw it and add details to the daily events. Others did the same while they sailed to Hawaii for the winter. This gives the ethnohistorian confidence in the material. An example of unreliable reporting is a fur trader who came to the mouth of the Columbia River in 1793, then visited the Haida in the Queen Charlotte Islands, and did not write his account until he had settled in Hawaii about 1812. He published his little book in 1820, attributing a number of items to the Chinook on the Columbia River which belong more correctly to the Haida.

THE USE OF DOCUMENTS

One formerly had to go to the archives or libraries where the unpublished documents happened to be, but with the use of microfilm and microcards this is no longer always necessary. But even documents need examination. The Spaniards, as I mentioned before, assembled their documents in Mexico City, where they were copied before the originals were sent to Madrid. The accuracy of the copy can be tested only if it is read side by side with the original. Although they are an ocean apart, they could be compared with microfilm, and this should definitely be done sometime in the near future. One great advantage of copies is that the handwriting is vastly superior to that of the voyagers.

ARTIFACTS COLLECTED ON EXPEDITIONS AND NOW IN MUSEUMS

As far as is known, no intensive study has been made of the artifacts still available from the eighteenth-century expeditions. There are several articles about the Vancouver expedition artifacts in the British Museum, two articles on the Webber collection from the Cook expedition in Bern, and a description of the Cook material in the Ethnological Museum in Florence, but no survey has been made for all the Cook expedition objects which are scattered from Dublin to Capetown. The Vancouver collections are a little more concentrated. The fur traders brought little to public institutions, though pieces that Dixon gave to Sir Joseph Banks were given to the British Museum and have been numbered with the Cook collection.

It is interesting that collecting artifacts had no place in the program of the expeditions. The fur traders forbade their crews to barter with the Indians because they wanted trade goods to be accessible only through the company's trading for sea otter skins. But, La Pérouse, who was on an exploring expedition and had no mind for trade, had to remind his crew—who were actively trading with the Indians using the buttons on their uniforms—to keep a few buttons for their return voyage. When the Cook expedition returned to England, the officers helped themselves from the accumulation of artifacts and the remainder were delivered to Mrs. Cook. She then sold them to Sir Ashton Lever for his museum in Manchester, which he then moved to London and later sold to James Parkinson. Since it was not a profitable venture, Parkinson in turn sold the whole museum at auction; it is surprising that about three hundred pieces can still be found.

To a museum-minded person these artifacts are just as important as the literature, and their historical value has not been realized. By checking the journal accounts of bartering with the Indians for the artifacts, it is possible to identify many pieces and fix the dates of the transactions. Handling these objects gives one an understanding of the technical skill in wood carving, basket weaving, and the making of weapons that had been developed in this rich culture. These pieces are also excellent examples of the stability of the art style and indicate the development of ceremonial life. The interrelation of the literature and the artifacts gives a new dimension to ethnohistory.

CONTEMPORANEOUS SKETCHES

The sketches made by the artists who accompanied the expeditions are another source of direct information, but need considerable analysis before they can be used as true examples of the people and objects they represent. We must exercise the same caution that was mentioned in connection with journals: How much was sketched on the scene and what details were added from memory? An artist who visited the Northwest later sketched Indians, details of costumes, and scenes of villages; then when he arrived at home he offered to paint pictures of Indians with any costume detail the purchaser selected. Until this was discovered about his methods, his pictures were constantly used as true examples of Indians in appearance and costume detail, and they appear in many books without any explanation of their composition. It apparently was exceedingly difficult for the Spanish artists to restrain themselves from giving the Indians Spanish faces with clipped beards and moustaches. Some northern Indians actually did have some scraggly facial hair. Like the artifacts, the sketches bring the people closer to us today.

THE PLAN OF THIS STUDY

This study was written to assemble all the information available on the Indian life of the period. The history of the voyages has been considered from the point of view of native life, and so large parts of the stories have been ignored. To establish some chronological order in these early contacts, the expeditions were not used as units. The information about places like Nootka Sound or the Queen Charlotte Islands has been used in relation to all European contacts there.

Once this material has been assembled, it will have many uses. It establishes the continuity and depth of the principles of Northwest Coast Indian life and the areal extent of certain cultural similarities. It brings personalities to these painted, singing people who approached the ships in their handsome canoes. It gives endless examples of the matching of wits between the Indians and the fur traders, often to the great chagrin of the latter. This was the living Northwest Coast, and the cultural traits of these people, partly forgotten, still have enough of the spark of life to make one hope that this great culture may inspire and guide their descendants who are facing a modern world.

INDIAN LIFE
ON THE NORTHWEST COAST OF NORTH AMERICA

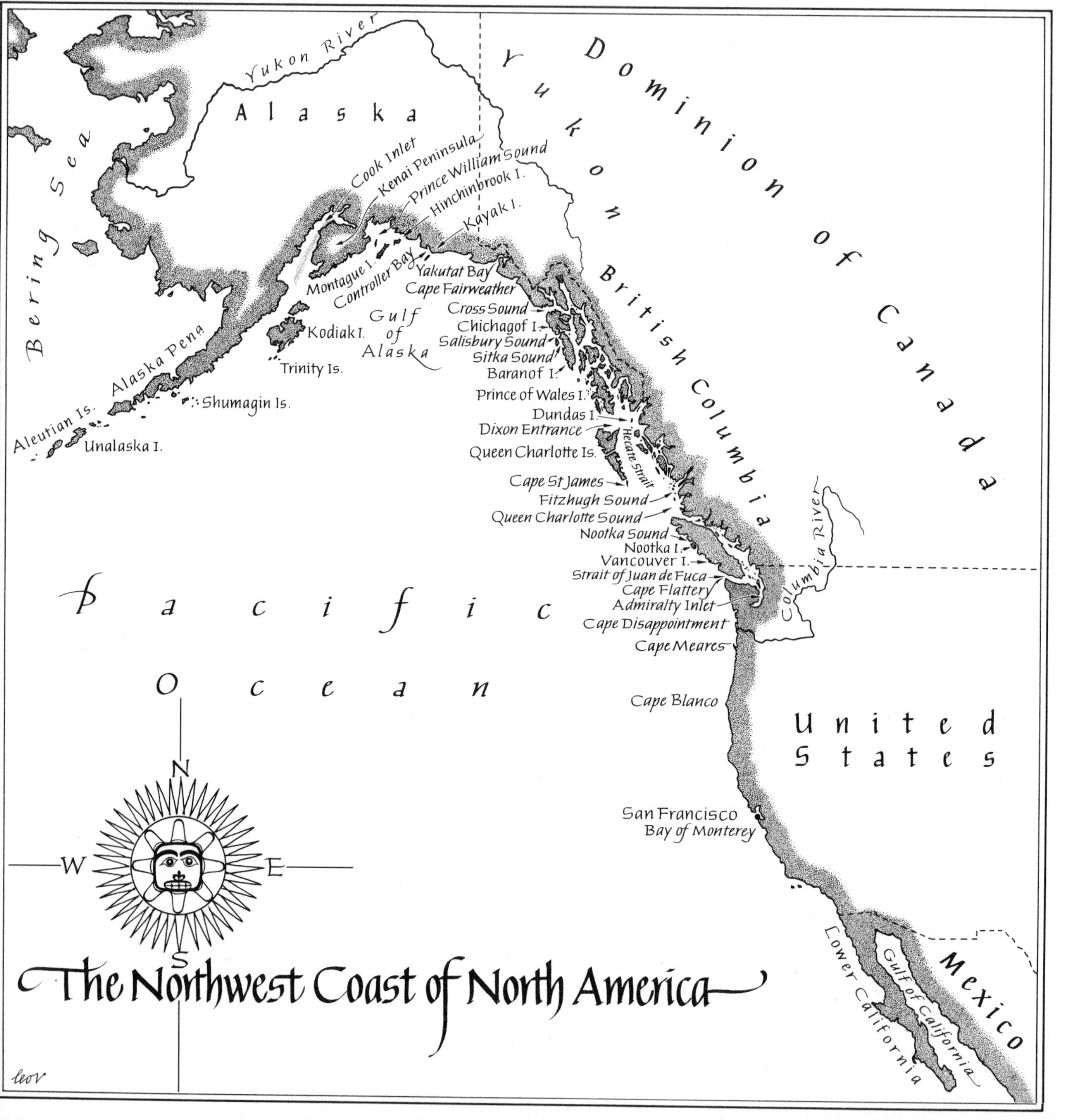
Yukon River
Alaska
Bering Sea
Yukon
Dominion of Canada
Cook Inlet
Kenai Peninsula
Prince William Sound
Hinchinbrook I.
Kayak I.
Montague I.
Controller Bay
Yakutat Bay
Cape Fairweather
Cross Sound
Chichagof I.
Salisbury Sound
Sitka Sound
Baranof I.
Prince of Wales I.
Dundas I.
Dixon Entrance
Queen Charlotte Is.
Hecate Strait
Cape St James
Fitzhugh Sound
Queen Charlotte Sound
Nootka Sound
Nootka I.
Vancouver I.
Strait of Juan de Fuca
Cape Flattery
Admiralty Inlet
Cape Disappointment
Cape Meares
Cape Blanco
British Columbia
Columbia River
Gulf of Alaska
Kodiak I.
Trinity Is.
Alaska Pena
Shumagin Is.
Aleutian Is.
Unalaska I.
Pacific Ocean
United States
San Francisco
Bay of Monterey
Lower California
Gulf of California
Mexico
N
W
E
S
The Northwest Coast of North America
leov

1

The Russians Seek the "Great Land" and Thereby Arouse the Spaniards to Reconsider the Northern Boundary of "Alta California"

In the decade when George Washington was born, the eastward movement of the Russians across Siberia had culminated in efforts to discover what kind of land there might be across the Pacific, whether America and Asia were joined, and where the eternal fogs could be penetrated to reveal the answers to these questions. Russia had tried to compete with the maritime nations of Europe to find a northeast passage along the northern coast of the continent, but the severe Arctic ice and climate proved the enemy of them all. England and Holland gave up the search, but the Russians had another approach to the east. The treasures of India and China were not as important to them as to the other European countries early in the seventeenth century; they were interested in furs. At the Ural Mountains, the eastern boundary of European Russia, salt was being exchanged for furs, and this stimulated the Cossacks from the Black Sea and Caspian Sea to move eastward. The open country was a great delight to them and they found that they did not need large armies to subdue the small kingdoms and nomad camps on the Siberian steppes. By the spring of 1628 the Cossacks had built a fort where the city of Yakutsk later stood as the capital of eastern Siberia.

As they pressed on to the Pacific they became aware of land across the sea—"Bolshaya Zemblya," they called it—with its many offshore islands. Not waiting for official expeditions to be sent out, the impatient fur traders started building ships in Kamchatka. They had only poor materials, and the workmen were unskilled, and so the Pacific storms played havoc with the crude craft and many ships and their crews were lost. At last the government sponsored an expedition to study the Russian coast northward from Kamchatka. Captain Vitus Bering was selected by Peter the Great to command a series of expeditions which proved the separation of America and Asia and gave the first glimpse of the Alaskan shore near Cape Prince of Wales.

Bering was then ordered to mount another expedition which was to approach the American shores from Kamchatka and through the Aleutian Archipelago. For this voyage he had two ships, the *Saint Peter* and the *Saint Paul*, the latter commanded by Chirikof. They left Petropavlovsk, Kamchatka, on 4 June 1741. By 20 June they encountered severe storms which separated the ships and led to the tragedy of this undertaking. For two weeks they tried to find each other without success, though they were often not more than thirty miles apart.

On 16 July and 20 July each of the leaders came into independently sight of the mainland of the northwest coast of America. Bering saw Kayak Island on 16 July, and this represented the "official" discovery of northwestern America. From there he saw Mount Saint Elias, and some scholars believe that he named it. It was here that Steller, the naturalist with the expedition, made the first ethnographic study in the region; he and Waxel went ashore and saw a recently deserted dwelling where a meal was being prepared. Steller commented on the likeness between the greens being used and those in Kamchatka. After noting all the utensils in the house, Steller left an iron kettle, some cloth, iron tools, and some beads in return for several native pieces he took with him.

At this time Bering was already too ill to come ashore, even though they had then accomplished one objective of their voyage. They next headed for Kodiak, Trinity Island, and explored for seven days in the Shumagin Islands. By this time Bering's health was so poor that Waxel, second in command of the *Saint Peter*, took over and started westward, hoping to return to Kamchatka before the winter. They became stranded on Bering's Island with a dying commander and a crew suffering extensively from scurvy. There they stayed until spring, when they built a ship out of the remnants of the *Saint Peter* and returned to Petropavlovsk.

On 20 July, Chirikof, still having made no contact with Bering, came into Sitka Sound and sent a small boat ashore with ten men, well armed, to get water. When they did not come into sight again after landing, he sent another five men to search for them. They also disappeared. It is logical to assume that they were captured by the Indians, but their fate, death or slavery, was never known. Chirikof could not afford to risk any more of his crew to rescue them, and so he stayed around for a few days in the hope that there might be some sign of them. On the first day, when the larger group disappeared, some Indians came to the shore, crying *agai, agai!*, which means "come here." Perhaps they wanted to capture more Russians or lead them to their companions. Some have felt that if they had killed the men they would not have come to the shore and tried to communicate with the ship. Many theories have been proposed, but no clue to their fate has ever been found.

Both these earliest contacts lacked personal relationships, but at least one cannot consider them hostile. The Tlingit's coming to the shore shouting what could be interpreted as a desire to make contact, and the desertion of the dwelling on Kayak Island, can be attributed to the natural fear which a large ship would inspire. Many first contacts between native peoples and Europeans were friendly, and only after some error was committed on either side did the attitude change. It is unfortunate that it was the white man's firearms that broke the charm rather than a shower of arrows.

This was not a very auspicious first contact with the new land, but the reports of plentiful fur-bearing animals, especially the sea otter, stimulated the Russians to greater activity, just as the same news which Cook's ships brought to Macao later started the non-Russian fur trade on the north Pacific coast. Soon the Aleutian Islands had been almost stripped of sea otter, and the Aleut were forced to pay tribute and to hunt sea otter for the Russians. Because of this decline the Russians looked elsewhere for more profitable hunting grounds. The expense of outfitting an expedition large enough to defend itself shut out all but the big firms who through subsidy or otherwise had government support. Larger companies were formed, but they too began a cutthroat competition, and the natives' situation became critical because of ruthless exploitation. Shelikof was the most successful of the great traders in the latter part of the 1770s. As the Russians pressed forward toward the mainland of Alaska, one group of natives acted aggressively enough to delay their movement beyond the Aleutian Islands. These were the Chugach, an Eskimo tribe living in Prince William Sound. Berkh wrote, "The fearless natives of Chugatsk who had, by their raids, spread terror among all the surrounding tribes, and especially among the inhabitants of Kodiak, were not frightened by Russian guns . . . they blocked their way to the hunting ground, trading posts and to subsistence" (Berkh 1823, p. 85).

This was the situation when the Spaniards and, later, Cook came into the area from 1774 to 1778. Cook was under orders to go north as far as possible, not exploring any area closely, but still to watch for inlets that might lead to a Northwest Passage.

The Spaniards, who were comfortably settled in Mexico and southern California, did not concern themselves about the northern boundary of their claim in North America, which was vaguely called "Alta California," until rumors were circulated that the Russians were exploring Alaska. The Conde de Lacey, Spanish minister to Russia, obtained a printed Russian map which he sent to Mexico in 1773 with orders from Madrid to organize an expedition to investigate its validity (Wagner 1937, p. 172). In 1774, Juan Josef Pérez Hernandez, a seasoned navigator from Mallorca, was ordered to sail to 60° north latitude and dislodge any Russians he found on the coast. Then he was to follow the coast south, making no settlements but taking possession in the name of the king, erecting a cross and burying bottles with documents.

For this voyage Pérez sailed in the *Santiago* from Monterey, California, on 11 June 1774, and returned on 27 September of the same year. He did not reach 60° north latitude as ordered, but he did make the first known contact with the Haida at Langara (North) Island off the northwest coast of Graham Island in the Queen Charlotte Islands. Here he met the people who occupied the archipelago, which consists of two large islands and smaller groups of offshore islands, some of which are no more than bird-inhabited rocks. Langara, or North Island, as Dixon called it a few years later, was occupied during at least some seasons of the year. The Haida live in a series of villages or towns, speak closely related dialects of the same language, and are one of the three distinguished northern groups of the Northwest Coast.

Dawson, a geologist, visited the Queen Charlotte Islands in the 1880s, and while pursuing his work he also left some excellent notes on the Haida as he saw them at that time. He recorded a legend about the first European ship the Haida saw, which may have been Pérez's. The chief thought it was a great bird and went out in a canoe, dancing, to greet it. As they approached they saw men on the deck, and because of their dark clothing they likened them to shags (cormorants), which look almost human when they sit on the rocks. They observed that when one man spoke many of the others would go aloft in the rigging until something more was said, and then they would all come down (Dawson 1878–79, p. 161).

There are three diaries of this voyage, one by Pérez, another by Fray Juan Crespi, a chaplain, and the third by Fray Tomás de la Peña Savaria, the second chaplain. Both chaplains described the Indians in great detail. There is no mention of a village at Langara or at any later anchorage, which is characteristic of the settlement pattern of the Northwest Coast; villages were tucked into quiet bays and coves, away from a direct line to the sea, to give protection from enemies. The navigators missed these sites because they were afraid to risk going far from the sea without charts. They preferred to stay where it was easy to pick up the wind if a hasty retreat was necessary. The explorers always feared attack, which was justifiable when they were surrounded by canoes as large as their ships and carrying more men than the ship's crew. For this reason village names and locations are seldom found in eighteenth-century journals.

On 20 July at 53° 58′ north latitude, a canoe came toward the ship with seven men paddling, a boy, and a man who stood up making dancing movements and throwing feathers into the sea around the ship (Crespi n.d., p. 181). Soon another canoe came out with people singing. These canoes were made of single logs except for the gunwales. The people were corpulent, with good features, fair complexions, and long hair. They wore cloaks of sea otter and "sea wolf" (a frequent European term for seal). They had hats plaited of rushes, with pointed crowns. This type of hat is shown in sketches by later explorers, but it is not known in any museum collections. The rushes, if they really were rushes, were probably cattails, but they could also have been broad bands of split cedar bark. A sailor exchanged a piece of ribbon for such a hat. For another piece of ribbon, a plaited mat was obtained. It was described as woven in small black and white checks. Plaited mats were woven of split cedar bark, which could have been dyed black, but white is difficult to explain, unless the cedar bark was overlaid with basket grass. Such a piece was not found in any collections.

The Indians exchanged some dried fish "whiter than cod" for trifles. This probably was halibut, widely used on the Northwest Coast. In the canoes were two very large harpoons for fishing and two axes. The harpoon looked "like a boarding pike" and seemed to be made of iron. We must remember that this contact was entirely between Indians in canoes around the ship and the Spaniards on the deck. The presence of iron is surprising and possibly indicated to the Spaniards that Russians had indeed been in this region, or close enough that articles could have been traded among the Indians. However, there are other sources of iron and copper which Cutter ignores in his publication of the Peña diary. According to Rickard, the Indians of the Northwest Coast had long been using drift iron, that is, iron that came to their shores in the drifting wreckage that the Japanese current brought over from the Asian side (Rickard 1939, p. 25). There was also native copper in the Copper River area of Alaska that had considerable distribution among the Indians, probably before the advent of white men. So Cutter's denial that metal tools could have been seen in the canoes at Langara and later at Bucareli Bay is not acceptable.

Cutter also states that "of course these Indians had no woolen stuffs" in one paragraph and then later describes a woman's dress as consisting of a "cape with a fringe on the lower edge and a cloth reaching to the feet, made of their own woven woolen stuff or skins" (Cutter 1969, p. 161). His second statement is correct, for in the collections, in sketches of accompanying artists, and in verbal descriptions there is constant reference to woven materials; there is even mention that the wool came from "wild sheep"—the mountain goat of the Northwest Coast.

In many instances the literature states that collections were made, but they have never been found, at least for public display. Both Crespi and Peña often mention the purchase of objects, but the statement implies that these purchases might have been by individuals on the expedition and not official, which would explain their absence in museums. Cutter has translated and published the list of items that came to the viceroy of Mexico in December 1774.

1. A cloak that appears to be a coconut burlap [this is a cloak of shredded cedar bark].
2. Another of the same made with greater ability and bordered on one side with white and black [design] and with little pieces of sea otter fur in the form of squares on both sides like a checkerboard. [The fringe was probably along the lower edge and the design directly above it. There are a number of cloaks in collections that would answer this description (see Appendix 2, weaving).]
3. A sash or belt that looked like wool, well woven, with the edges bordered in black [this is perhaps a tumpline made of split cedar bark and edged with black-dyed wool].
4. A hat woven with a great deal of ability which appears to be of fine basketry.
5. Another of the same, of Chinese style, much more beautiful because of its weaving and because it has depicted thereon the canoes which they make and made of basketry material dyed black. [The description of the design is typical of the Nootka and not the Haida. Whether such a hat could have been traded such a distance or whether it was included in the wrong collection cannot be ascertained now.]
6. A quadrangular pouch also of basketry and without any stitching, with twenty-four little sticks of wood, well carved and delicate, which they use for playing music during their dances. [This is more likely a set of gambling sticks. They did use sticks for beating time in singing but they would not be described as delicate, whereas the gambling sticks were (see Appendix 1:121, 122).]
7. A pouch or bag of very delicate basketry, very beautifully made, and on it a species of bird made of bone with its upper beak broken. Acquired from an Indian woman who wore it around her neck along with a number of little teeth, which looked like those of a small alligator. [This last assumption is of course impossible; sea otter teeth are sometimes used in such a necklace.]

This is the earliest list of specimens obtained by explorers and it is most unfortunate that these pieces did not survive their trip to Spain (Cutter 1969, p. 278).

After a pleasant visit with the Haida of Langara Island, Pérez sailed northwest and passed an island which he named Santa Cristina (Forrester Island), then came to a cape which he called Cape Maria Magdalena (Cape Muzon). Here he again encountered Haida, a segment of these people who had migrated across Dixon Entrance to the southernmost islands of Alaska—Dall Island, which ends in Cape Muzon, and Prince of Wales Island of the Alexander Archipelago, which extends far into Tlingit territory. Legend has it that this migration took place about five hundred years ago, but there is no documentation to prove it. The stories which have been told about this migration are typical of similar events among all the tribes of the Northwest Coast. Swanton was told such a story which is worth relating here because all the cultural factors involved are so basic in the distribution of Northwest Coast settlements.

> The StAstas family of Kaigani tell of a man living at Yak' whose wife was fond of dried codfish and told her husband that it was all gone, when she still had some. He went out fishing and was drowned. This woman's name was Sa'wa. She knew how to weave blankets of mountain goat wool. Friends came from DadEns to see what property he left, but when the widow brought out her husband's box, only two pieces of wood dropped out. The friends of the man were so ashamed that a man took the woman and wanted to make a slave of her because she had caused her husband's death. He took her to DadEns. She was an Inlet-born Masset. When they reached DadEns her brother's son came to see his aunt. The chief seized him, saying, "I will make a slave of you too." The chief who held this man was also a StAstas. When they reached the door the captured man drove a dagger into the chief's heart. They got ready to fight, but when the brother of the slain man came back from fishing he did not want to fight, but pay for his brother. He paid the biggest blood money ever paid. Next day he told the people to separate for a while and told some to go to Alaska. Some did so and others went to Virago Sound. They were the Up-Inlet-Town people [Masset]. Taking their wives with them involved the emigration with other families as well" [Swanton 1905, p. 88).

Here on Dall Island twenty-one canoes of all sizes came out with about two hundred persons. They sang and played on drums and timbrels and some made dance movements, like the scene they had encountered at Langara Island but on a smaller scale. These people looked like those at Langara, well made, with even, rosy faces; they had long hair, and some men had beards. This repeats Crespi's and Peña's descriptions of the people of Langara, which Cutter does not believe (Cutter 1969, p. 100). Perhaps he is unaware of the darkening effect of sunlight and also of the results of constant use of red ocher as face paint. If Northwest Coast Indians are seen early in the season and without makeup they can well fit these descriptions.

With so many people present, a remarkable variety of clothing was displayed. Many wore sea otter skins, as well as skins of other animals, all well tanned and dressed. These skins were sewn together into blankets or cloaks with stitchery so fine that Crespi said no tailor could have done better. All the Indians had the body completely covered, and some garments were said to have sleeves. This is difficult to believe, for sleeves present a difficult problem in clothing design and are seldom attempted in the primitive world; to my knowledge they were not known on Northwest Coast clothing until after European patterns were seen there. The Chilkat shirt is an example of this. Some wore a cape that came to the waist. This was probably twined of shredded spun cedar bark and generally was worn by the women (see Appendix 2, weaving). With this cape Crespi stated that they wore well-dressed skins or woven cloth of different colors in handsome patterns (Crespi n.d., p. 192).

This is one of the several references to weaving among coastal tribes in which this art was not well developed in the nineteenth century. The obvious reason for its later absence is that commercial materials replaced the native-made cloth; but it does also seem to indicate that the distribution of mountain goat wool which was added to the cedar bark was more general in the exploration period than later in their history. In addition to Crespi's statement about the "woolen cloths," he wrote about cloaks woven of wool or hair which looked like wool. It is known that the hair of lynx was used in this way (see Appendix 2, weaving).

To these costumes were added many forms of ornamentation. The women wore labrets which caused much discussion by all travelers on the Northwest Coast. Crespi wrote that they were made of wood and painted. The women also wore bracelets of iron and copper. The men painted their bodies with a fine tint of red ocher. They all wore hats woven of reeds. Whether they resembled the hat described from Langara is not mentioned, and the word "reed" could be interpreted as this or as the traditional spruce root hats which were unfamiliar to the Spaniards.

The Indians brought in their canoes a variety of household utensils, but whether they were for trade was not mentioned. Crespi listed wooden platters, well made and carved with figures of men, animals, and birds, and wooden spoons carved on the outside of the bowl but smooth on the inside. There were large spoons of horn, a variety unknown to Crespi, but in all probability from mountain sheep. All these pieces are characteristic of the Northwest Coast household, and it is interesting that they should have been in the canoes so that Crespi had opportunity to see and record them so faithfully. He must have handled them; this is especially true for his description of the boxes, made of pine (cedar), as he said. The sides were made of cedar, and instead of being nailed together they were sewn with "thread" (split spruce root) at all four corners. In these boxes, so plentifully found in all nineteenth-century collections, all four sides are made of a single piece of planking which is steamed and bent at the corners and is sewed only where the first and fourth sides meet. The box described here may be a forerunner of the later type or it may be a variation. These boxes had no hinges, because the cover came down over the inner box like that of a hamper. One finds this feature today on some of the oldest and finest boxes, often referred to as "telescope" boxes. Crespi said that these boxes were decorated with carving and painting and inlaid with marine shells. The painting was done in red and yellow. They were as much as a yard long and proportionally wide. All kinds of possessions were kept in them, and in the canoe they were used as seats while paddling (Crespi, n.d., p. 192). There is little for Peña to add to Crespi's description of the Indians, but he did include a detail about their canoes which may be significant. He wrote that they were larger, twelve to thirteen yards long, and made of a single log except for the planking on the sides. Crespi had said, "except for the gunwales." It is uncertain whether they were both familiar enough with marine terminology to distinguish correctly between these terms. There has been a question whether planking was ever used on the Northwest Coast. Peña also commented on the iron and copper bracelets of the women and children. The Spaniards were always searching for precious metals, and these low-grade products probably disappointed them (Johnson, p. 123).

The third writer of the expedition was Pérez himself, who commented on the expertness of the Indians' trading, indicating that perhaps much trade was carried between tribes and they had polished their technique in this practice. They sang and danced before they traded, a custom that irked the later fur traders because they were so anxious to proceed with business.

Pérez mentioned the beautiful woolen blankets, of which he obtained four. They are not now known in any public collection. He also noticed the whiteness of the Haida's skin and their fair hair. The women were as well built as the men, but, he said, "they gave signs of meekness and good disposition." This again was questioned in later trading. He commented on the labret and added that it was worn only by married women (Johnson 1911, p. 59).

From 22 July to 8 August Pérez sailed south to an estimated latitude of 49° 32′. Then he anchored a league from shore in a roadstead shaped like a C, He named the anchorage San Lorenzo and the northwest point Santa Clara. Two leagues to the south he named the point San Estaban, supposedly because 10 August was the saint's octavario, but Crespi declared that he named it in honor of the second pilot, Estevan José Martinez, who later played a leading role in the Spanish occupancy of the Northwest Coast. This is described in detail because there has been great controversy about where all this took place. It is argued that Pérez was not at Nootka Sound, but farther south. However, even before Cook came into Nootka Sound it was known in the Spanish world as Boca de San Lorenzo; but Cook, not knowing this, renamed it King George Sound (Wagner 1937, p. 173).

When Pérez came to this anchorage, Indians came out in canoes and motioned the ship to go away. The sailors indicated that they needed water, and the Indians brought a cupful before they realized that the ship needed more. The canoes were smaller than those in the north, about twenty feet long, but they also had several pieces of planking fastened together with cord along their sides. This planking is mentioned several times in early accounts and there must be some truth in the reports, but by the nineteenth century none of the ethnographic informants could give satisfactory information about it. The paddles of these canoes were well shaped and painted. The next day more canoes came with about one hundred men and a few women. They traded sea otter skins and hats with a pear-shaped bulb on top. This is characteristic eighteenth-century headgear of the Nootka and was often sketched in later voyages. Crespi stated that the hat was painted like the ones at Cape Muzon, but that is not correct. The Nootka wove the design into the hat, but from a distance it could easily be misinterpreted. The woven cedar bark blankets and short capes were described as cloths woven of a material very like hemp with a fringe of the same thread. These were probably the cedar bark capes of which there are many in the eighteenth-century collections. Some clothing was decorated with shells, and Crespi added that they had picked up some shells in Monterey for possible barter. These were abalone (*Haliotis*) shells, which the Northwest Indians dearly love. There had always been some trade in these, but because of the distance they were rare and expensive. With the beginning of the fur trade they became more easily accessible. Crespi's final entry was that the women did not wear labrets.

When one realizes that the historians have always considered this visit of Pérez to what may have been Nootka Sound a kind of touch and go, Crespi's report is certainly rich in detail. Many expeditions have lingered longer in Indian villages with fewer results. This is the end of the first visit by Europeans to the Northwest Coast except for the Russians in Alaska. Pérez returned to Mexico, without reaching 60° north latitude and without seeing any Russians. But the iron and copper worn by all the Indians he saw gave mute evidence of some trade going on in the north where iron and copper can be found. The Spaniards collected sea otter skins when they saw them, but did not make a great effort to get them until they realized that these could be exchanged in China for mercury, which the Spaniards sorely needed in their mines in Mexico. They did not envisage the lucrative and destructive trade that followed Cook's voyage, when the skins sold for high prices on the Canton market.

The viceroy was dissatisfied with the results of the Pérez voyage and in 1775 he sent two more ships north. The schooner *Santiago* was chosen again, this time with Bruno de Heceta as captain, and with her went the goleta *Sonora*, commanded by Juan Francisco de la Bodega y Quadra with Francisco Maurelle (Mourelle) as pilot. Both these men wrote accounts of parts of the voyage, which did not achieve the goal of 60° north latitude either, but came closer than before by sailing approximately to 58°. The two ships traveled together from 16 March 1775 when they left

Monterey until they separated as the result of a storm and an argument among the officers at 47° north latitude. Heceta wished to return south, but Bodega and Maurelle wanted to continue as ordered. When the ships were separated again in a storm about 1 August, Bodega and Maurelle made little effort to find their consort and proceeded north.

Before the ships separated they explored Trinity Bay in northern California, where Fray Benito de la Sierra, the chaplain of the *Santiago*, made notes on the appearance of the Indians. The Spaniards took possession, planting a cross which Vancouver found in 1793. When they left Trinity Bay, Heceta did not see land again until 11 July when he entered a small inlet which he named Rada de Bucareli (now Point Grenville). The first day a canoe with nine Indians approached the ship and bartered for trinkets in return for sea otter skins. They also brought fish and whale meat. The chaplain observed the likeness between the clothing worn by these women and those of Trinity Bay. Since no details were given for Trinity Bay costume, a description has been taken from Kroeber which reads:

> The women's dress consists of a buckskin apron about one foot wide, its length slit into fringes which were wrapped with a braid of lustrous Xerophyllum, strung with pine nuts. From the rear a much broader apron or skirt was brought around to overlap the front piece. This rear apron was also fringed but had considerable area of unslit skin as well. In cold weather a blanket of two deerskins sewed together was worn over the shoulders. These capes were seldom squared off for they liked the ragged effect of the neck and legs of the animal. The women's aprons were always made of dressed hide with the hair removed. [Kroeber 1953, p. 76]

It is interesting to speculate whether this comparison between Trinity Bay and the coast of Washington was exact or general, since it is likely that the skirts seen by the Spaniards at Port Grenville were made of cedar bark rather than skin. However, since the Indians of the Olympic Peninsula had easier access to hunting areas than many coastal tribes, it is conceivable that a fringed skirt of skin could have been used. Olson lists only cedar bark skirts in his ethnography on the Quinault (Olson 1936, p. 58), but Willoughby, who was with the Quinault in the early 1880s, although he stresses the cedar bark skirt, does mention the use of seal, elk, bear, rabbit, and deerskins. He illustrates his section on clothing with a sketch of a woman in cedar bark clothing, and this is copied in Olson (Willoughby 1886, p. 268).

On the afternoon of the first day the commander, pilot, surgeon, and chaplain made a quick landing and took possession of the land. Considering the Indians very peaceful, Heceta sent a longboat ashore the next day to get water and to cut a tree for a topmast. When the boat landed at the mouth of the Moclips River, the Indians attacked and killed five men. Two more were drowned while trying to swim to the ship. The Indians smashed the boat and took away every piece of iron they could find.

After this attack several Indians came out toward the ship in a canoe. They wore well-tanned and dressed skins which Fray Sierra described as white "as the Spanish soldiers' coats" (Sierra 1930, p. 228). These coats were shaped like cloaks which extended to their feet and were painted with skulls representing their victims. This was the fighting garb of these people, but in spite of this readiness for hostility, they did not attack the ship.

The use of protective armor in the Northwest seems much more widespread in the eighteenth century than it was later. This is true not only for the cloaks or jackets of hide, but also for the slat or rod armor as found among the Nootka and northward. It may be that the introduction of firearms caused the decline.

A few other random statements about dress and appearance which Sierra added mentioned the cloaks of deerskin or sea otter which they wore in winter, but otherwise the men frequently went naked. The women wore nose rings made of copper and had their ears pierced around the entire edge, and from these holes small shells of many colors were suspended (Sierra 1930, p. 226).

After the ships separated, Heceta sailed up to 47° north latitude and then turned south. He moved in toward shore after passing Port Grenville, and on 17 August he discovered the Columbia River, to whose entrance many names have been given. He called it Rio San Roque and sailed south, arriving at Monterey on 29 August.

Bodega y Quadra went north on 16 August and saw Mount Edgecumbe at about 57° north latitude. He named it Mount Jacinto. Then he anchored in a bay which he called Puerto de los Remedios and took possession. This was probably what is now Sea Lion Bay according to Wagner (1937, p. 490) which is also substantiated by Orth (1967, p. 847). Some Indians came out and took away the cross and placed it in front of their own house. The Spaniards tried to indicate that they needed water. The Indians gave them a little but were not satisfied with the beads they offered in return and threatened them with long flint-pointed lances. Bodega, whose account of the voyage is now being used, since the chaplains were both on the *Santiago*, wrote that the dress of the Indians resembled that of Trinity Bay, but was longer. They wore caps over their hair which covered the whole head. These may be some of the narrow hats of the eighteenth century which have a small brim that was pulled down and tied with strings under the chin. They could easily be called caps. This is the only description of Indians recorded on Bodega's journey north. The ship remained in the region exploring the inlets until 26

August and returned to Monterey on 7 October 1775. This is another instance of explorers' being out at sea and seeing very little of life along the shores. It also emphasizes that the Indian villages were not out on the ocean beaches (Barrington 1781, p. 506).

The viceroy was as pleased with the results of the 1775 expedition as he had been disappointed by the previous one. All the officers were promoted and their diaries were sent to Madrid, where they arrived in February 1776. The results of this expedition were considered very important by the Spanish government and a short notice was published in the official gazette. The British ambassador at the court of Madrid notified London of this, and on 28 June the *London Annual Register* for 1776 published a comment which was mainly erroneous (Greenhow 1844, p. 124). Since Greenhow did not publish the statements in the Spanish court notice, it is impossible to comment on the "erroneous" additions, but it is important that it was printed only a few days before Captain Cook started on his third voyage, which took him to the Northwest Coast. It is sometimes hinted that he also received maps from the ambassador to the Spanish court. If this is true, it is not important whether he did or did not see this notice.

Soon after this, the court of Madrid heard of Captain Cook's departure on another voyage to the South Pacific; if this was true, they were certain that he would also travel to the North Pacific to search for the Northwest Passage, for which Parliament had posted an award of £20,000. Orders were quickly sent to Mexico to outfit another northward expedition, but for lack of ships and other difficulties the voyage did not get under way until 11 February 1779, when they left San Blas, reaching Bucareli Bay on 3 May. The vessels were the *Princesa*, under the command of Ignacio Arteaga, and the *Favorita* under Bodega y Quadra. They stayed in this region until 15 June, exploring extensively. Unfortunately their journals contain very few remarks about the Indians, although many came around the ships. At one time about one hundred canoes established themselves in a cove where the ships were anchored and the relations were generally peaceful and friendly. Although this was never stated, it is thought that the detailed exploration of this area was carried out with the idea of creating a settlement at some point. Instead the settlement was later set up at Nootka Sound.

On the *Princesa* was Fray Juan Antonio Garcia Riobo, the chaplain who left the only account of the Indians encountered on this voyage—the people at Port Santa Cruz on the west coast of Suemez Island. He never stated whether these Indians resembled the people of the south end of Dall Island (Cape Muzon), which would have made them Haida, or seemed to be from the north where they spoke a different language, which would classify them as Tlingit. Their possessions and actions as described by Riobo do not help much in placing them. He begins with the following description:

> From the first day we tried to get in touch with the Indians, searching for them among their rancherias. After having hidden their women in the woods, they came to us with signs and tokens of peace, some throwing white feathers in the air from a promontory on the sea, and others standing in a line on the shore with their arms extended in the form of a cross. We gave gifts to each of them and they in turn gave us fish. The fish was of the ordinary kind, a very common species, yet as we were in great need of fresh food we appreciated it highly. From that day they continued to come to our vessels at all hours but especially at sunrise and sunset, bringing mats made of bark of a certain tree, skins of seal, otter, deer, bear and other animals. They showed us their weapons and even traded us some of them. Their arrows are very finely made; some of them are pointed with flint, some with bone, but most of them have heads of copper and iron and they are very sharp. These Indians have a kind of armor something like that of the ancients with buckler and spear; they have even protection for their thighs and legs, very skillfully made of pieces of hard wood, joined and fastened together with a kind of strong cord. On their heads they carry the figure of a ferocious beast rather skillfully and artfully carved of wood. [Riobo 1918]

The description of the helmets gives a faint clue. These were used by both the Tlingit and Haida, but as far as can be determined from museum collections there is a tribal distinction. Riobo stated that "they carry the figure of a ferocious beast." This is distinctive of the Tlingit. Even the few helmets illustrated by Niblack (1890, pl. 13) more often show the Haida headgear as a large wooden hat, the type used in the nineteenth century as a ceremonial hat. The closest Tlingit village to Port Santa Cruz known in the nineteenth century is Klawock on Prince of Wales Island, which was first noted on Russian hydrographic chart #1993 in 1853. This village started to develop its historic character with the opening of a cannery in 1878. An older site is farther north on the west side of Prince of Wales Island, Tuxekan, once the largest town of the Henya, a division of the Tlingit. When the cannery opened at Klawock, most of the people at Tuxekan moved south. From Klawock southward the island is inhabited by Haida.

Riobo goes on to repeat that the Indians were interested in acquiring copper and iron, since they were familiar with the use of these metals and preferred them to glass beads. He speaks of a small knife which women wore around their necks and used for carving wood. They made trays of various shapes. This is most unusual, for wood carving is consistently the art of men in historic times, and no other mention of this as the work of women appears in the eighteenth-century literature. The trays they carved were probably for serving food (Riobo 1918).

This expedition closed the early Spanish endeavor on the Northwest Coast, where they based their right to the indefinitely bounded "Alta California" on the Line of Demarcation and the apocryphal voyage of Juan de Fuca in 1592. War in Europe was one reason for the lack of attention to the Northwest Coast, but the area was not abandoned by the Europeans; only the nationalities involved and the areas visited changed. The chain reaction continued: the Spaniards had gone to look for the Russians and then the English came to the Northwest Coast to find out what the Spaniards were doing. The message sent by the British ambassador to the court of Madrid hastened the outfitting of the third voyage of Captain Cook. The report of his expedition led to the maritime fur trade which made the port of Friendly Cove in Nootka Sound one of the busiest on the whole Pacific Coast.

2

Captain Cook's Third Voyage to the Pacific Ocean Arrives at Nootka Sound

Activity on the Northwest Coast shifted from southeastern Alaska to Nootka Sound with the arrival of Captain Cook on his third voyage to the Pacific Ocean. This undertaking was organized in direct reaction to the news of the Spanish expeditions of 1774 and 1775. Both Spain and England felt they had a claim to the northern part of the Pacific Coast of North America, and it seemed time to assert these claims. The Pérez expedition of 1774 made a brief visit to a bay which they called Boca de San Lorenzo and claimed it for the king of Spain. Questions have been raised whether it was truly Nootka Sound where Pérez made his landing. One of his officers, Estevan José Martinez, who later became the commander of the Spanish settlement at Nootka, stated on his return to the area fourteen years later that he was certain he could identify it as the place he had seen on his first voyage. On this statement, the Line of Demarcation, and the apocryphal voyage of Juan de Fuca, the Spaniards laid their claim.

The English claim was no more solidly based than that of the Spaniards. It was founded on Sir Francis Drake, who in 1579 applied the name of "New Albion" to the land when he sailed along the Pacific Coast an unknown distance north of San Francisco Bay. The instructions for Cook's voyage used the term "New Albion" (Beaglehole 1967, p. ccxxl[1]). Cook was instructed to take possession of "convenient situations in the name of the King with the consent of the natives, and in regions that had not been visited by other European nations."

When Cook reached Nootka Sound he initiated a short period when this port became one of the most important and most visited on the

1. References to Cook: the journals will be referred to by writers, e.g. Cook, Burney, Samwell, and reference to the introduction and explanatory material will be referred to as Beaglehole.

Pacific Coast. For this reason, and also because the Nootka are chronologically the first tribe to be well described by many sources, their ethnography as recorded in the eighteenth century will be studied as an example of the Indian life of the central region of the Northwest Coast.

After leaving Plymouth, the Cook expedition sailed around the Cape of Good Hope, south of Australia and Tasmania to New Zealand, to the Cook Islands and Tonga, and then to Tahiti to deliver Omai, a Tahitian who had been visiting in London. From Tahiti they sailed northward, finding and naming Christmas Island on December 25. Next, sailing north and east, they discovered the Hawaiian Islands. Cook wrote that they were agreeably surprised to find that the people were of the same nation as those of Otahiti, meaning that they were similar in appearance and spoke a related language. He named this group the Sandwich Islands in honor of the Earl of Sandwich, first lord of the Admiralty. Early in February 1778, the ships left Hawaii and, sailing north and east, made landfall at a headland which Cook called Cape Flattery because in the fog "there was a small opening in the land which flattered us with the hopes of finding a harbour, but these hopes lessened as we drew nearer, and at last we had some reason to think that this opening was closed by lowland. On this account we called the point of land to the North of it Cape Flattery" (Cook 1967, p. 293). Having missed the entrance to the Strait of Juan de Fuca because of fog and weather, Cook stood out to sea to clear the treacherous breakers. At last on 25 March the weather cleared and he made his way into Nootka Sound, where canoes full of Indians at once came out to the ships, showing no fear or distrust. Exchanges of goods took place, and although the Indians gave whatever they had for anything offered to them they did prefer iron, whose use they knew (Cook 1967, p. 296).

The type of welcome Cook received was commented on in every diary and journal written by a European who visited the Northwest Coast during this period. It exasperated fur traders, who were there for business, and its enthusiasm amused some ships' companies. It was occasionally described with such accuracy that some of the actions can be compared to ethnographic accounts of the nineteenth and twentieth centuries.

Lieutenant King spoke of the wild and savage appearance of the people and said that those in the first canoe eyed them with astonishment; but the second boat with two men in it came closer, and

> the figure & actions of one of these were truly frightful, he worked himself into the highest frenzy, uttering something between a howl and a song, holding a rattle in each hand, which at intervals he laid down, taking handfulls of red Ocre and birds' feathers & strewing them in the Sea; this was followed by a violent way of talking, seem-

> ingly with vast difficulty in uttering the Harshest and rudest words, at the same time pointing to the Shore; yet we did not attribute this incantation to threatening or any ill will toward us; on the contrary they seem'd quite pleas'd with us; in all the other boats someone or other act'd nearly the same way as this first man did. [King 1967, p. 1394]

In one of the larger canoes came a man that seemed to be a chief. King described him thus:

> He stood upright in the middle of the boat, & upon a plank laid across to be more conspicuous; the naked parts of his body & arms were painted with a red, & his face with a whitish paint, his head was wildly Ornamented with large feathers, which were tyed to a stiff string or sinew & fastened to the hair, so that they hung in different directions projecting from the head. [King 1967, p. 1394]

There are many ethnographic accounts of welcome ceremonies on the occasion of potlatches and other feasts. The arriving canoes often had a dancer performing on some planks fastened between canoes, with the occupants of the boats singing as they entered the cove or bay where the host's village was located. At the same time the host and some of his family in ceremonial dress danced and sang on the beach. All the songs and dances for such occasions were inherited family privileges.

Another example of this type of performance is the account of David Samwell, who became surgeon on the *Discovery*. When the ships had been warped into Resolution Cove on Bligh Island, a canoe came alongside and a single individual performed a dance with two masks. Samwell writes:

> The principal or indeed the only performer appeared in a mask which was made of wood, not badly painted in the manner they generally do their faces, of these he had two expressing different countenances which he changed every now and then. Over his body was thrown a fine, large wolfe Skin with Hair outwards and a neat border worked around its edges; thus accoutred he jumped up and down in his canoe with his arms extended, he moved his head different ways and shaked his fingers briskly, while he was acting in this manner all the other Indians sat down in their canoes and sung in concert and struck the sides of their canoes with the but end of their Paddles keeping exact time. [Samwell 1967, pp. 1089–90]

After his dance he continued to sing and "shaking a small box or wooden image of a bird filled with pebbles which made a rattling sound as an accompaniment to the Voice" (Samwell 1967, p. 1090).

The dance involving the two masks was still performed in the 1930s by Charlie Swan, a Makah Indian of Neah Bay, Washington. The Makah are the only Nootkan-speaking tribe in the United States. He described his dance as that of a medicine man or shaman who called on two spirits represented by the masks for help in the cure he was undertaking. Durign his dance he kept one mask concealed under his blanket, and he performed a lightning change while he whirled around.

The masks, which were exhibited in the dances at the greeting ceremonies and later in entertainment when the officers of the ships visited

Fig. 1. Wolf-head mask, Nootka Sound. Cook collection, BM, NWC 71 (Appendix 1:150).

the villages, were never offered for sale or trade. The few that remain in the collections have no references in the texts of the journals giving clues as to where they were acquired. That there are several wolf masks indicates that the Nootka tradition of the wolf was already well established (fig. 1), (British Museum Northwest Coast Collection 71; Appendix 1:150).

The rattles in the form of a bird mentioned by King and Samwell are the most typical among all Northwest Coast tribes (figs. 2–4). A sketch of such a rattle is included in Beaglehole (1967, pl. 40), and a similar one (NWC 29; Appendix 1:194) is in the exhibit with other Cook collection rattles in the British Museum (NWC 27, 28; Appendix 1:192, 193). There is also in Vienna a rattle from Nootka Sound which resembles the others in shape, having a straight front and a head and body like a grouse. The bird's beak is open and there are three wooden pegs at the back of the head which are broken off but which may have represented feathers. The body has no decoration in adze work or paint. The eye is round with a black center and a white ring around it. (Museum für Völkerkunde, Vienna 224; Appendix 1:198).

The rattle in the King collection (National Museum of Ireland, 1882–3659; Appendix 1:197) is also in bird form, representing the seagull. It has an interesting stylistic feature which was carried over into the nineteenth century and persisted as long as rattles were carved—a triangular slit in the throat which has no obvious reason in realism or fantasy for being there. There is a small face on the breast, a feature absent in the British Museum pieces. In the Hunterian Museum at the University of Glasgow there is another bird rattle (E 369; Appendix 1:196) which is like Appendix 1:194 at the British Museum, but with a human face on its breast. The stability of these rattle figures is so amazing that it must be demonstrated with such examples to be believed.

After the dance and the singing, a typical welcome to the ships included an oration lasting an hour or so. When, after traveling halfway around the world, fur traders at last saw the people who had the precious pelts they wanted, then had to stand by and listen to such an oration in an unintelligible language, their patience was sorely tried. Some diaries had harsh words about this custom. But in the Indian culture this was a cordial welcome, and the white feathers spread on the water around the ship were a greeting of friendship. The ships could have been met with a shower of arrows, and this also happened when, after several years of trading, each side had found out the shortcomings of the other.

The way these first explorers and traders reacted to the native peoples often reflected an education which had brought about some tolerance of other cultures; after the first culture shock, they were able to look upon the people they met with some understanding. However, one of the less tolerant members of the Cook expedition, who had seen the people of

Fig. 2. Bird-shaped rattle, Nootka Sound. Cook collection, BM, NWC 28 (Appendix 1:192).

Fig. 3. Bird-shaped rattle, Nootka Sound. Cook collection, BM, NWC 29 (Appendix 1:194).

Fig. 4. Bird-shaped rattle, Nootka Sound. King collection (Cook) expedition, Ireland 1882–3659 (Appendix 1:197).

Tahiti and Hawaii, was conscious of considerable difference in the appearance of these Indians. He wrote as follows:

> When we first entered this Sound at about 5 PM several canoes came of to the ships and In them a set of the dirtiest beings ever beheld—their faces and Hair being a lump of red and black Earth and Grease—Their bodys covered with the Skins of Animals or a kind of garment made Exactly like the *Hahoo* [or cloth] of New Zealand but of a Quality very inferior and differently shaped. In the Canoe that first cam Along side was a Man that stood up and held forth a long while—at the same time pointing to the Sound as if the ship should go further Up—his oratory did not seem to be the best in the world and he appeared to Uter with much difficulty; on his head he wore a kind

> of hat made of cane and in the shape [Cook 1967, p. 295] resembling a buck's head; after having finished his harangue he presented it to Sale as well as several other things, which at once convinced us they were no novices at that business, in return for his hat he had a large Axe and left us quite Content.

This passage is not quoted from Cook's own journal but is a footnote by Beaglehole, quoting Scholfield (1914), who obtained it from the diary of Riou, a midshipman on the *Resolution*. In addition to being very blunt, this account has some incongruities which make multiple records of the same incident very important for gaining a true picture. The paint and grease these Nootka wore in their hair are part of their method of hair-dressing and may be less attractive than the palm oil used by the Polynesians. Wearing skins is not exceptional among primitive peoples, and some of these skins were probably sea otter. If Midshipman Riou was fortunate enough to have gotten any, he could have sold them at Macao the next year for one hundred dollars apiece. Just how he could judge from the deck of his ship that the quality of the woven garments was inferior to those of New Zealand is an open question, unless in their haste to come out to the ship some people may have grabbed old and worn mats or cloaks to wear. It is also rather difficult to judge oratory which one cannot understand, and perhaps the harsh sounds in many Northwest Coast languages seemed to Riou to be difficulties in speech. Finally, if the speaker's hat was made "of cane," meaning basketry, it was not in the shape of a buck's head; but if it was carved of wood it might have been the head of an animal. That he offered it for sale is not surprising, for all tribes on the Northwest Coast were avid traders and the explorers all commented on their shrewdness, which somehow was not expected of "savages."

When quotations from journals and diaries have been used uncritically, such reactions as this have often been quoted alone and not tempered with more favorable comment. Furthermore, as I mentioned before, in using the journals we must keep in mind that the writers often merely made notes which they later elaborated when they were sailing for long periods. Under these circumstances, how accurate were the details of scenes that were new and strange and followed one another in quick succession? These doubts are even more cogent when members of the expedition wrote a whole book without their own notes, as Ledyard did. He is said to have borrowed Rickman's, but they were not even shipmates, and the two ships were not always together.

Cook's journal, as it is now published under the careful editorship of Dr. J. C. Beaglehole, makes the circumstances of the writing on Nootka very clear and simple. First the daily events are published in journal style, and then Cook states:

> Such particulars of the place and its inhabitants, as could be learnt during our short stay and have not been mentioned in the course of the narrative I shall now relate. [Cook 1967, p. 308]

The details of his account of life at Nootka Sound are the basis for the ethnography of these people at the period just before the fur trade started. Throughout, Cook shows understanding and active interest in their customs. Therefore his narrative will be used as a base, just as has been done in the publication of his journal, and other diaries will be used to supplement his contribution.

A new and better harbor was found at Ship Cove (Resolution Cove; Wagner 1937, p. 515) on Clerke Peninsula of Bligh Island. These names clearly show that Cook honored many of his colleagues in naming new places. The site was across Nootka Sound from Friendly Cove, the location of the Nootka village from which the people came to the ships. The Webber sketch of the first anchorage at Nootka Sound shows a rocky shore with no sign of habitation (Cook 1967, plate 33), which is further substantiated by a water color by William Ellis (Beaglehole 1967, plate 34*b*). This brings up a very interesting point about the moorages of the explorers and traders in relation to Indian villages.

At Nootka Sound during the early part of April 1778 the weather was very bad, but the nineteenth was a fair day, so the next morning Cook and a party in two boats went on a trip around the sound. They came to the village of Yuquot in Friendly Cove (Cook 1967, plate 35) where the Spanish later settled. From this village the ships had had a constant stream of visitors, and when Cook and his party arrived they saw familiar faces and were greeted as friends. They were invited into many houses, in each of which several families lived. Mats were spread for the guests, and while they were in one house the owner's share of the day's catch of small fish was brought in for drying. The fish were firts put close to the fire and then were slowly removed until they hung just beneath the roof on racks (Cook 1967, plate 36). From Yuquot they went up Cook Channel to the opening of Kendrick Arm, then across this entrance to Tahsis Inlet, where they saw the ruins of an old village about a mile beyond. The framework of the houses was still standing and some fish weirs were in front of the village. Sailing past this site, they found that they were anchored by an island with many small islands lying off the coast. In his account, Cook does not refer to it by name, but later it appears on his chart as Bligh Island, and the peninsula where they were moored was named Clerke Peninsula, both after members of the ships' companies. They continued the circumnavigation of Bligh Island and stopped at another Indian village where their welcome was not so cordial. In spite of the surliness of the "chief" a few young girls hastily put on their best clothes and sang a song for the visitors. Cook described it as "far from being harsh or disagreeable" (Cook 1967, pp. 304–5). After this visit they returned to their moorage.

On the morning of 22 April, when Cook was preparing to go to the village of Yuquot again, some strangers arrived at his moorage and made a ceremonial circuit around the ships. They had among them Nootka known to the expedition, who acted as middlemen in the trading. Since he was anxious to leave, Cook evidently did not spend much time with them, and it is a pity that no further identity for these people can be established. They may have been Nootka from another village or they may have been Kwakiutl, lured south from Quatsino by their curiosity about the ships. They brought with them some carved wooden heads which they set on the decks of the ships, but were unwilling to sell. Later in the day they took them away, but these heads appeared again in the same way a number of times. Finally the Indians agreed to leave them but wanted no return for them (King 1967, p. 1414). These wooden heads are among the most exciting and interesting pieces in the collections of the eighteenth century. We can assume that they were not made by the Nootka, but that the people who brought them were Kwakiutl from the northern part of the island. The pieces can be related to the Toxuit dance in the winter festival of the Kwakiutl. This dance is always performed by a woman, who allows herself to be killed in many dramatic ways, one of the many sleight-of-hand demonstrations in this series of dances. Among them is a beheading, using a carved wooden head that is a portrait of the dancer bearing the expression of death (fig. 5, Appendix 1:11). This head is held up by the human hair with which it is ornamented. In the firelight, which helps all these demonstrations, it must look much like the dancer. To make it more dramatic a bladder of blood hidden in the neck is pricked at the proper moment so that it streams down to the floor (Boas 1895, figs. 153, 154; pp. 491, 503, 504).

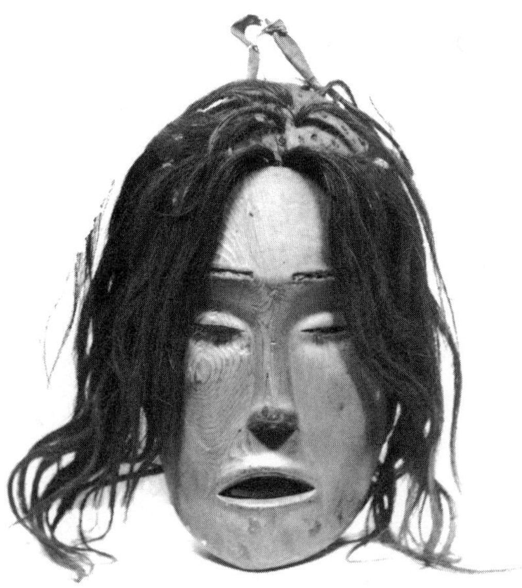

Fig. 5. Carved wooden human head, Nootka Sound. Cook collection, BM, NWC 58 (Appendix 1:11).

There are two of these heads in the Cook collections known at present: one is at the British Museum (BM NWC 58, Appendix 1:11) and is identified only as a human head carved of a block of cedar which seems to have been fixed to a post. It has black human hair, strips of hide as eyebrows, an open mouth, and no teeth. The second one is in a small Cook collection recently found in Capetown. The objects were said to have been left there when the ships were on their way home. I have only seen photographs of this collection, through the courtesy of Mr. Christian Feest at the Museum für Völkerkunde in Vienna.

Cook had plans for a twofold errand on this day, so he started on his way. He wished to give Captain Clerke a chance to gather grass for the livestock on board and he wanted Webber, the artist on the expedition, to have an opportunity to sketch the scene he had seen in the village on his previous visit. Webber had made a sketch of the village as seen from the beach (Cook 1967, plate 35) and one of the interior of the house they visited (Cook 1967, plate 36). The village scene shows the houses facing the water and set in irregular rows, each slightly above the one in front, as the contours of the land allowed. They were built of planks cut from cedar logs with bone or wooden wedges and were rough and without finish. The planks were set horizontally, each row resting on the upper edge of the one below and held in place by slender poles driven into the ground. The roofs were flat, consisting of loose boards which could be moved to control rain and smoke. The houses were set back from the beach, where canoes, as well as the ship's longboat, were drawn up. The sketch shows two groups of people, with the Indians and the ship's party intermingling. The costumes of the Indians were carefully detailed so that the individual garments were recognizable; these will be described later. Between the beach and the houses are some low mounds which might be sand dunes or piles of debris with earth or sand over them. Behind the village is a stand of conifers (Cook 1967, plate 35).

More unusual is the sketch Webber made of the interior of the house they visited (Cook 1967, plate 36). The area shown in the sketch must be one of the larger "apartments" described by Cook. Heavy beams support the roof; two show clearly and a third, which looks squared, is at the far left. At the end of the house these crossbeams are supported by two carved upright posts (Cook 1967, p. 317). Each has a large human face with the mouth rounded as though the figure were calling into the distance. The post on the right has a smaller face carved beneath the mouth, and the other has a horizontal band at his waist through which about a dozen arrows are drawn. The people called the figures *Ackweeks* (Cook 1967, p. 319), but later in his narrative Cook lists them in the vocabulary as *Klumma*, a term used by other Europeans who saw them. Colnett, for instance, mentions the posts and also uses the term *klumma* for the post set up as a mortuary column (Colnett, n.d., p. 58). Martinez wrote (1789) that these figures were not covered as Cook stated, "and as Cook did not see them, it is certain the natives were not as civilised then as today as a result of traffic and communication with the English, for they admit anyone to their houses." Cook laments that he could not get any information about Nootka religion, but he does state that whatever these figures represented, they were not worshiped, by any outward act, nor did he see any offerings laid before them (Cook 1967, p. 322). However, they were often covered, at least partially, with mats.

When Webber started to sketch them, a man who seemed to have some authority covered them further. Webber thought bribery might be effective, so he cut a brass button off his coat and gave it to him. The Indians were very fond of such buttons and had gotten them in trade and as gifts. The figures were uncovered for a short time and then hidden again. Webber gave him another button, and this procedure continued until all the buttons were off the coat; then the figures remained uncovered (Cook 1967, p. 319).

There is a bed platform on the left side of the house on which a number of people are sitting. Behind the platform and above it are large storage chests, smaller wooden boxes, openwork carrying baskets, and matting bags, all household objects of constant use. There is one box with a raised lip on one side of the lid, which is as distinctive of the Nootka and Kwakiutl as the Chilkat blanket is of the Tlingit. Close to the ceiling are racks of fish drying. The floor is strewn with small unidentifiable objects, probably part of the debris mentioned in all the diaries as a constant feature of Indian houses. In the center of the room there is a fire with more small racks on which fish are placed either for drying or for roasting for immediate use. There is also a wooden cooking box by the fire, and one of the Indians sitting beside it holds long wooden tongs with which the hot stones are transferred from the fire into the food box. This method of cooking by heating stones in the fire and then dropping them into the food is almost universal, whether the receptacle is a wooden box or a watertight basket. Webber took great pains to give all the detail he could in his sketches, and it is a joy to see in use so many objects which were collected by this and later expeditions.

A lower platform to the right of the fire is another lounging place. Both the men and the women sitting there wear shredded cedar bark garments which are sketched in the same meticulous detail that Webber used for the household utensils. The same clothing is worn by both men and women, sometimes in slightly different combinations. The sex of the two figures at the cooking box cannot be determined from either their clothing or their occupation, for both men and women cooked. The clothing can be studied not only from the artist's drawings but also from the collections in many European museums—particularly the blankets, cloaks, capes, and skirts made of combinations of cedar bark, wool, and hair. These show the versatility of the Northwest weaver, which was lost in the nineteenth century through the introduction of commercial cloth and European styles of clothing.

The most universal garment is a cape or cloak of shredded cedar bark that can also be used as a woman's skirt. This shape is also used in other materials and for other purposes. It is rectangular with a gentle rounding at the lower edge. The simplest style of wearing it is over the back and tied under the chin or folded double across the chest. This makes it a cloak or cape, used by both sexes. When it is tied at the left shoulder and brought under the right arm, it covers the body except for the right shoulder. It hangs to the knees and is often tied around the waist when the wearer is at work. As a skirt, the woman can bring it up under the arms to make it short, or let it down to the waist for ankle length. This explains why writers sometimes stated that the women were covered from neck to ankles and at other locations said the skirt was short. Whatever the length, the skirt was wrapped around the body and tucked under to secure it. The overlap was always at the center front.

In the Webber sketch of the Nootka interior (Beaglehole 1967, plate 36) there are two men and one woman wearing circular capes, which are pulled over the head and extended to the waistline. The women have some kind of undergarment, which may be the cape just described worn as a wrap-around skirt. One of the men sitting on the bed platform seems to be wearing only the circular cape. The freedom of combinations makes it difficult to distinguish between men and women in some of the sketches. Only men wore the heavy bearskins shown in plate 37 (Beaglehole 1967), and this garment appears to have been widely used on the Northwest Coast, for it is sketched again at Port Mulgrave (Yakutat Bay). The lack of any other garment with the bearskin is characteristic of the Nootka (fig. 9) and the men frequently went completely naked, both indoors and outside.

The discussion so far has centered on the woven garments, partly because the figures in Webber's sketch were all dressed in this fashion, but all accounts also mention skin clothing. Ledyard wrote that the clothing of the Nootka consisted generally of skins, but gave no further description. He was probably referring to the bearskins worn by the men and to the capes or cloaks of sea otter skins sewed together. The later fur traders were much more alert to this use of the skins they had come for, and explained that good cloaks consisted of three skins and poorer ones used two. Some mentioned that the skins were poorly sewn together, but they were just as ready to trade for these as for skins that had not been used. Details of some descriptions are more explicit, stating that a skin covering might be used by women as an undergarment. This will be discussed in the later accounts of the Haida.

The costume of the Nootka was obviously sometimes very meager, but they seldom dispensed with hats. Headgear has flourished on the Northwest Coast because of climate as well as style: in winter hats shed the rain and in bright weather they cut the glare on the water. Hats were worn by men and women, and, as with clothing, there was no sex difference. Cook described the hats as like a flowerpot, but typically they are more conical than this. At Nootka Sound there was a very stylish hat that aroused much comment by travelers (fig. 6). It was shaped essentially like many other hats but had a pear-shaped bulb on top as decoration. Also, the entire hat was woven with an overlaid strand of light-colored bear grass. (*Xerophyllum tenax*) and decorated with scenes of whaling done in dark brown, the most realistic pattern used by the

Fig. 6. Two hats with whaling scene and bulb top, Nootka Sound. BM, NWC 6, 7 (Appendix 1:137, 138).

Nootka. A man at the far left of Webber's sketch wears such a hat (plate 36), and two more are lying on the piled boxes along the wall. These hats were collected by many visitors and occur in the collections at London, Florence, Dublin, Munich, and Vienna. They are also in sketches made by the artists on the Spanish expeditions, and though the Museo Naval in Madrid has records of such a hat in the Malaspina collection it was not on exhibition at the Museo d'América in 1964. In addition to the whaling figures, some of the hats have geometric designs as fillers, similar to the basketry patterns used by the people of southern Vancouver Island, the Fraser Valley, and southward (BM, NWC 7 Appendix 1:138). This type of hat is shown on a woman with a circular cape in Cook (Beaglehole 1967, plate 39*f*). Giglioli describes these hats in his account of the Cook collection in Florence and gives as his sources Ellis (1782, pp. 131, 191) and Cook and King from the French edition (1784, 3:66).

Descriptions of this hat in the early journals often state that the design is painted, but this is an error. Some had seen painted hats in the north, or had observed the hat at such a distance that the fine weaving could not be distinguished. This hat remained in style among the Nootka well into the nineteenth and twentieth centuries, but the pear-shaped bulb is definitely an eighteenth-century decoration, for it was not used later (for technique of weaving see Appendix 2).

Another type of conical hat is shown in a number of Spanish sketches. It appears to be made of vertical slats gathered together at the tip. There are no examples of this type in any collection, and so what seems to be a different weave may only be a quick way of indicating a general texture and should not be taken as an exact representation. The third style of hat, widely distributed on the Northwest Coast, is wider at the lower edge with gently sloping sides and a definite division between the crown and the brim. This type is not represented in any of the Nootka Sound collections and will be discussed with the northern forms.

It is probably too much to expect to find many ornaments described as being worn by the Indians among the objects in collections 190 years later. But the descriptions and the portraits of the Spanish artists are good sources of information. Personal decoration consisted of nose pieces and nose rings, earrings, labrets, body painting, a little tattooing, and bird down and feathers. That grease, red ocher, and bird down were liberally used on the hair is mentioned in many diaries, and from these descriptions of its matted condition it hardly seems necessary to have as many combs as appear in the collections. There are six combs in the British Museum Northwest Coast collection, of which only one is recorded as from the Banks collection and none from Cook (figs. 7, 8). This alone does not totally eliminate their being from Nootka Sound, but the elegant carving of some does make them seem too sophisticated for the general style of Nootka carving. There is one, however (BM, NWC 105 Appendix 1:175) with an incised human face which seems quite in line with other Nootkan carvings and also is comparable to one from Florence (#159, plate III, figs. 64, 65; Appendix 1:180) which is definitely a Cook piece. The second comb in the Cook collection is regarded by Giglioli as possibly coming from the Maori, even though it is placed on the plate with the Nootka Sound objects. The illustration is very small, but even the general design is found not only on the Northwest Coast but also among the Eskimos of western Alaska. The figure is a raven, not often used as far

Fig. 7. Combs, Nootka Sound. BM, NWC 101–6 (Appendix 1:171–75).

Fig. 8. Carved comb, Nootka Sound. Cambridge 25.370 (Appendix 1:179).

south as the Nootka, but it might be from as far north as Norton Sound. In style it certainly belongs to the coast of North America and not to the Maori.

Drucker's ethnography does not mention combs, but does say that in the wolf ritual of Hesquiat the women comb the hair of the novices with their fingers (Drucker 1951, p. 415) and later in the ceremony the novices are seated in a row and their hair is combed ceremonially. In this second combing no implement is mentioned. These facts throw doubt on the specimens in the British Museum (NWC 101, 102, 103, 104, 106; Appendix 1:171–74), some of which are handsomely carved. The point in their favor is that they are all included in the Edge-Partington pictures.

Painting the face with red ocher was common everywhere on the Northwest Coast, and Nootka Sound was no exception. Indians at a later date said that this paint prevented the face from getting painfully sunburned by the glare on the water while fishing, but the addition of blue and white to the red was undoubtedly for aesthetic reasons. For ceremonial occasions they threw a sparkling sand on their faces which adhered to the paint (Haswell 1884, p. 61). Body paint was applied for ceremonial dancing but seldom for daily use.

Although the colors of the face paint do not show in the Webber sketch, one can see on careful examination that some of the Indians he sketched were painted. The woman sitting in front of the carved figure on the right, the standing figure to the right of the fire, and the person sitting at the right of the fire all have dark lower faces, probably complemented with red ocher on the upper part. Ellis, on the Cook expedition, mentions a stamp made of small twigs which was dipped in paint and applied to the face. This is more reminiscent of the tapa stamps used by the Polynesians than the wooden block stamps used by the Tlingit.

Ornaments for the nose and ears were common. The ears were pierced around the entire edge and small shells or just knots of string were tied in the openings for decoration. Nose rings were made of copper (Edgar, n.d.) or cut from pieces of abalone shell. It is interesting that about ten years later a fur trader remarked that many Nootka had their noses pierced but no longer were wearing the nose ornaments formerly used (Haswell 1884, p. 62).

Another form of ornamentation is the bracelet, of which there are two in the Cook collection which are described as being made of a "horny substance." I believe this is the horn of the mountain goat, for they resemble very closely a small group of bracelets collected by George Goodman Hewitt on the Vancouver expedition at Restoration Point on Bainbridge Island in Puget Sound (fig. 53) (Gunther 1960, fig. 4). They are carved with curvilinear designs that would not readily be recognized as coming from the Northwest Coast. The Cook pieces in Florence (Appendix 1:159) and Ireland (1882–3657; Appendix 1:160) are less elaborate. There are occasional bracelets of mountain goat horn in ethnograpic collections, but they are plain or very lightly incised. One from the Tsimshian is also fastened with a simple catch that was later used in the manufacture of silver bracelets. The bracelet in Florence was first cataloged as from New Zealand, but when it is compared with other pieces extant there is no doubt that it belongs to the Northwest Coast (Giglioli, 1895, plate III #68).

Ellis states (1782, 1:119) that bracelets are made of horn and copper. Of the latter there are no examples in any of the eighteenth-century collections, but many have been found in contact archaeology. It is important to have Ellis's statement, for one of the surprises often encountered by the first explorers was the use of copper, and to a lesser degree iron, by people that had not had direct contact with Europeans. The use of native copper and the routes of its trade in the Northwest are the subjects of an excellent paper by Dr. T. A. Rickard (1939, pp. 25–50).

When primitive man wears little clothing his efforts at decoration turn directly to his body and to the use of small ornaments. The Nootka are an excellent example with their interest in adornment, and they extended this interest to adapting the trade goods to further ornamentation rather than utilitarian purposes. A handful of beads bought more than a nail, and if they had to accept a nail it was often used in a necklace instead of as hardware.

One ornament which the Cook expedition did not have an opportunity to exclaim about is the labret or lip plug worn by the women among the northern tribes. All the early travelers spent pages in gruesome description of this decoration. Coming from the south, Cook did not encounter this, but later found chin perforations among the Chugach at Prince William Sound.

While Webber was sketching, Cook had his only opportunity to observe the household goods of the Nootka. Most conspicuous of the household equipment were the wooden boxes which range in size from large chests to small receptacles for cooking and serving food. Cook wrote that their furniture consisted chiefly of a great number of chests and boxes of all sizes, which were generally piled upon each other, close to the sides or ends of the house, and contained their spare garments, skins, masks, and other things they valued (Cook 1967, p. 317). These boxes were also brought out to the ships in their canoes when they came to trade, and from them they produced the skins they had for sale. Both Cook and Samwell mention boxes inverted over each other, with one as the cover. These "telescope" boxes were also included in nineteenth-century collections.

The cooking by the fire (Cook 1967, plate 36) shows one method of preparing food which was used by all Northwest tribes from the Columbia River to southeastern Alaska, a region where the wooden box was a principal container. Cook relates:

> Boiling is performed in a wooden trough like an oblong box, by putting red hot stones into the liquor, a heape of which always compose the fire hearth, they put them in and out of the pot with a kind of wooden tongs. In this manner they boil all kinds of meat and make soups. (Cook 1967, p. 319)

Roasting and broiling directly on the fire was also done, especially for meat and fish. The fish hanging on racks near the ceiling indicate the usual method of preserving. The Northwest Coast tribes could build up food supplies because both salmon and halibut dry well, as do many of the berries. Cook mentions what he calls "caviare" preserved dry on small pine boughs and seaweed (Cook 1967, p. 319). This refers to herring eggs, or spawn, which is collected late in February by laying hemlock boughs on the water in a quiet cove. The spawn collects on the boughs, which are carefully lifted out of the water and dried. When the boughs are dipped in water, the dried eggs fall off and are eaten.

The sketch does not show any spoons, but a number of them appear in collections. The British Museum has three wooden spoons, two of which are marked "Nootka Sound." They are the simplest form of wooden spoon, carved from a solid piece. One (BM, NWC 35; Appendix 1:230) is very plain with a shape characteristic of the southern Northwest Coast area. Another (BM, NWC 32; Appendix 1:225) is very clumsy in shape, with a bowl painted in red. The design is created on the unpainted surface and has an abstract quality found in some eighteenth-century hats. One of the rare records of spoons being used is Captain Cook's statement: "They eat out of the same dish which they never wash, some use wooden or horn spoons" (Cook 1967, p. 318).

Perhaps it would have been more logical to record their methods of fishing before telling how the catch is dried, cooked, and eaten. The Cook expedition visited Nootka Sound too early in the season to witness the principal fishing activities, but there was scarcely any time when the Nootka could not catch some fish, provided the weather was not too stormy. Some fishing demanded moving to coastal villages, and often they were seen in these encampments during the summer. Many journals comment on the Indians' skill at fishing and their specialized gear. All the expeditions bought much fish from the Indians for beads, nails, and so on and they often lamented that they themselves had no luck at fishing. Ledyard did not have much faith in the efficiency of the Indians' fishing gear, even though the ships received much of their food through its use (Ledyard 1783, p. 77). Cook also did not express much admiration for it except for the herring rake, which he described as "an instrument something like an oar; it is 20′ long, and 4-5″ broad and ½″ thick, each edge for about ⅔ of its length (the other third being the handle) is set with bone teeth about 2″ long. This instrument they strike into a shoal of small fish who are caught between or upon the teeth" (Cook 1967, p. 321). A Spanish picture shows a Nootka dressed in a bearskin cape and a steeply conical hat carrying one (fig. 9). Cook speaks of the fish hooks as

Fig. 9. Nootka man with herring rake. Spanish picture.

being "unartificially" put together of wood and bone. In the collection they are not well represented. One, steamed and bent into reversed C shape (BM, NWC, no number), is the characteristic halibut hook used on the southern Northwest Coast.

Although Cook did not see any whale hunting, the gear was to be seen everywhere and some examples are found in the collections still in institutions today. Cook was impressed with the harpoon, whose point was made of half a mussel shell between two pieces of bone, the rear ends of which became barbs. These were fastened with resin, which was also used to fill the hollow side of the shell and to make it smooth (Cook 1967, p. 321). This description fits any whaling harpoon used in the nineteenth century before the iron point came into use. Trevenen, one of the ship's officers, remarks that floats were attached to the harpoon line to slow up the whale's progress after it was hit (Cook 1967, p. 321 n.). The floats were skins of the hair or harbor seal turned inside out and inflated.

The collection includes only several fragments of the whole whaling harpoon, but they are complete enough to demonstrate clearly that the eighteenth-century gear was exactly like that of later times except that a metal blade replaced the shell. There are two pieces in Bern (Appendix 1:111; Appendix 1:101). One consists of a foreshaft with barbs of bone fastened together with a thong and pitch. The original point of shell is missing and has been replaced by the museum for demonstration. The line consists of a bundle of sinew wrapped spirally with cord made of nettle bark (Henking 1955–56, p. 369, fig. 36). These specimens are part of the Webber collection in Bern.

In the British Museum is one of the best documented eighteenth-century pieces, for it still has the handwritten label on it signed "A. Menzies." Archibald Menzies was the botanist on the Vancouver expedition of 1792, but like many of the eighteenth-century travelers this was not his first visit to the Northwest Coast. He was on the *Prince of Wales* with Captain Colnett in Nootka Sound in July 1787 when he acquired this whale harpoon and line, and this is his description: "Fishing line made of a species of Fucus [kelp] by the natives of the west coast of North America. [signed] A. Menzies." Also "The inner bark of the cypressus Thujides [*Thuja plicata*] in its different stages of preparation as manufactured by the natives of the west coast of North America for making mats, garments, etc. From Nootka Sound, July, 1787. [signed] A. Menzies." This label is attached to the line where it is wrapped with cedar bark.

There is no blade in the harpoon, but one can assume that it once had a mussel shell inserted between the bone barbs. There is still resin with which it was once fastened (BM, NWC 15; Appendix 1:112). There is an error in cataloging this object. The number NWC 15 was taken from the piece itself, but that number on the catalog slip is listed as a "bowl-shaped basket."

In addition to this fine specimen, the British Museum also has a harpoon line that is listed as from the Banks collection and from Nootka Sound. This would place it in the group of specimens given to Sir Joseph Banks by one of the eighteenth-century travelers, since they were all anxious to win or retain his favor (BM, NWC 75; Appendix 1:107).

Vienna has a braided line made of finely cut thong, but whether this was strong enough for whaling is questionable. However, smaller harpoons were also used for seals. The item from Florence is cataloged as a harpoon point made of whalebone and can be interpreted as a foreshaft (Florence #306; Appendix 1:103).

The narrative goes on to discuss the tools in use at Nootka Sound. Cook speaks first of "chissels" and knives, both of iron. He was very much surprised to find not only iron in use at Nootka but a Nootkan word for iron and all kinds of metals. He knew that some Spaniards had visited the coast before him from newspaper accounts published in London during May 1776, before he sailed, but he thought that there was too much metal for this brief contact and that it must have been traded from somewhere through other Indian "nations." The iron was a long flat piece, fitted into a wooden handle. The blades of the knives were crooked like a pruning knife and what is ordinarily the back was made into the edge of the blade. They had the breadth and thickness of an iron hoop, which was probably the source of the metal. The fur traders found that the Indians preferred strap iron to finished articles like knives and chisels so that they could shape their tools in their traditional patterns (Cook 1967, p. 321).

One of the first pieces of Indian manufacture Europeans saw was the canoe, for many Indians paddled out to the ships and paraded around them, singing welcome songs. The canoes of the Northwest Coast were the largest made in America and their seaworthiness was admired by many of the visiting captains, Cook among them. He compared them to the Norway yawl, which was square sterned and shovel nosed. The canoes in Webber's drawings show a square stern, but the prow has a long graceful thrust forward ending in a highly stylized head of an animal. The dimensions given by Cook, forty feet long, seven feet broad, and three feet deep, were fairly standard for the smaller canoes, but others extended to sixty to seventy feet long and carried up to fifty persons. The canoe was carved of a single log of red cedar with the sides trimmed down to one to one and one-half inches in thickness. These large canoes were used for traveling to feasts, for other visits, and for war raids. Smaller canoes were made for fishing and local travel from village to village (Cook 1967, p. 316). It is interesting that Cook gives these dimensions for canoes at a period when iron tools were still very scarce. The great impetus in carving during the nineteenth century is always attributed to the spread of the use of iron. Cook's statement shows that Nootka, at least, were capable of making large seaworthy canoes, although it probably took them longer without iron tools. He also describes the paddles as being leaf shaped and about five feet long. With these they handled the canoes with great deftness, for, as is stated in the first edition, although not in Beaglehole, the sail was not used (Cook and King 1784, p. 328). The large canoes were painted on the outside with figures of "bears and fish," and some had broad waving lines in white along the gunwales, according to Samwell (1967, p. 1102), who also confirms Cook's belief that they were not familiar with the use of the sail.

Although they were always surrounded by canoes, they rarely saw weapons in action. Those they did see are listed by Cook as "bows and arrows, slings, spears, short truncheons, made of wood, bone or stone, something like the Patoo patoo of New Zealand and a small pick-axe or Tomyhawk" (Cook 1967, p. 320). Examples of all these are found in various Cook collections as well as in later ones from the fur traders, for weapons would naturally attract the attention of men of action such as all these Europeans were. They also often had to face them.

The bows were about four feet long and were described by Samwell as flat and strung with catgut, which sounds highly questionable. Cook and Ellis both state that the bow was made of yew, which is the same material found in the ethnographies (Ellis 1782, 1:137). The bow was used horizontally, a style found sporadically along the entire Northwest Coast (Samwell 1967, p. 1101). King describes the bow as "indifferently made and weal," but found the Nootka expert marksmen. The bows in the museum collections are not well enough localized to be definitely assigned to any tribe. There are two bows in the Banks collection in the British Museum (NWC 86, 87; Appendix 1:309, 310) and one at Florence which can be counted in this category. One of these is described as "backed with a plaited cord of hair" (Gunther notes), a feature that Drucker's informants deny and which Niblack mentions only for the Tlingit, where he states that it is poorly applied (Niblack 1890, p. 286). His illustrations of bows in the United States National Museum (Niblack 1890, plate 26) include one curved at the ends like the Spanish picture which is assigned to the Haida of Masset and was collected by Swan in the 1870s. The armor worn by the man with the horizontally held bow may not be accurate, but the style might be expected in the north rather than from the Nootka. The best specimen is one in the Florence Museum, which is illustrated on the plate of Nootka objects but cataloged as coming from the South Pacific. Professor Giglioli, however, does not agree with this; he considers the piece Nootkan and compares it with a bow illustrated in Niblack (1890, plate XXVI, fig. 112; Giglioli 1895, p. 115, plate III, fig. 59).

Less controversial are the beautiful examples of arrow storage boxes in the Museum für Völkerkunde in Vienna (fig. 10), a type mentioned by Samwell (1967, p. 1102). One is thirty-six inches long and six inches wide (Vienna 215; Appendix 1:59). The cover, which is not fastened to the box, is carved in very low relief with two primary figures. They are in a style reminiscent of the simpler Salish carving of the south and also of some petroglyph figures. The top figure may be female, for there is an indication of breasts and an x-ray type of stomach. This figure is supported on the upraised hands of the next one, the top of whose head is level with the hands. This figure, the same size, has a chevron-designed rib cage and no indication of breasts, but has the x-ray stomach. The genitals are vaguely indicated, but may be female. Between the legs of this figure is one that looks like a fetus. The legs are drawn up, the head is as large as those of the other figures, and the three faces are alike. This is the most realistic picture of birth I have seen in Northwest Coast art except the woman in labor carved in argillite by the Haida (NMC VII B779). The sides of the box are very shallow and are decorated with a geometric design.

The second box (Vienna 216; Appendix 1:60) has a delicately incised cover showing a bird with a large fish in its mouth and some ducks in flight. These were evidently storage boxes to be used at home or in the canoe, but skin quivers were used for hunting on foot. Samwell mentions both types of arrow storage, the wooden box and the skin quiver (1967, p. 1102). A quiver made of sealskin is at the University Museum, Cambridge (25.380; Appendix 1:67). This may not be a Cook piece, but undoubtedly belongs to the eighteenth century. It came from the collection of the Earl of Denbigh, whose ancestor was Thomas Pennant, a famous scholar and naturalist of the period. Like Sir Joseph Banks, he was the recipient of many artifacts brought to England during that time by explorers. Such a quiver is also shown in a Spanish picture titled "Indio de Nootka." A similar piece is in the collection at Capetown, previously mentioned as seen only in photographs.

The arrows were about two feet long and feathered. The points were of bone and barbed, but there were a few with copper or iron points. The arrow had a range of thirty to forty yards, and Samwell commented that the Indians were excellent marksmen. Spears were used like pikes and were never thrown (Samwell 1967, p. 1102).

The weapon that attracted the greatest attention was one called a "tomyhawk" by Cook (1967, p. 320) and a "tomehawk" by Samwell (1967, p. 1101). Their descriptions agree, so I will quote Cook's:

> The tomyhawk is a stone 6–8″ long, pointed at one end and the other fixed with a handle of wood, the handle resembles the head and neck

Fig. 10. Arrow box (rubbing), Nootka Sound. Cook collection, Vienna 215 (236) (Appendix 1:59).

> of a human figure; the stone is fixed in the mouth as to represent an enormous large tongue. To make the whole appear more like a human head they fix to it human hair. This weapon is called "Taa'wesh" or Tous Kee'ak.

Fig. 11. Ceremonial ax, Nootka Sound. Webber collection (Cook) Expedition, Bern 59 (Appendix 1:322).

These weapons are often called slave killers in the museum catalogs and in the nineteenth-century literature, but I have yet to find this term used in any of the eighteenth-century documents. In the nineteenth century slave killing at ceremonies is often mentioned from hearsay, not observation. Many of the ceremonies took place in the winter and were therefore not seen by the explorers. However, in proportion to other pieces, many examples of these weapons are found in collections; so the Indians must have brought them to the ships. All the pieces in the collections attributed to Cook are also claimed to be from Nootka Sound. By contrast, two pieces are mentioned in the literature which are not in the same class, but still resemble the earlier ones. One, illustrated by Niblack (1890, plate 46, fig. 259), is a poor piece of carving and has a large metal spear or arrow point, instead of a stone blade, protruding from the forehead in place of the stone tongue. This was collected by Swan from the Haida in the 1870s. The other is shown in the wealth of material connected with the winter ceremonies of the Kwakiutl, also with a metal point in the forehead. It is called the club of NuLmaL, the Fool Dancer.

The representative ones which answer the description of Cook are found in the collections at Bern, Florence, Cambridge, Vienna, and the British Museum (figs. 11–13). The first one (NWC 97; Appendix 1:323) is described by Rickman as carried by warriors, together with a knife twelve inches long. A knife of these proportions was not characteristic of the Nootka, at least not at the time of Cook's visit, but this is the type of detail sometimes found in books written by expedition members after they return home. The second piece (NWC 98; Appendix 1:324) is comparable to the one in Florence (Giglioli 1895, plate III, fig. 62) and also to the object from the Klemm collection in the Museum für Völkerkunde in Leipzig (cat. #1004). This is discussed by Dr. Eva Lips (1956) and attributed originally to the Cook collection. The "slave killer" in the University Museum at Cambridge (25. 371; Appendix 1:325) came from the collection of the Earl of Denbigh. Mr. Webber, the artist, also included one of these in his collection at Bern (cat. #59; Appendix 1:372). It is typical and well made. In contrast, the one in the museum in Vienna (211; Appendix 1:327) has all the traditional features but is not well carved. It is called a "war weapon" with no mention of slave killing.

There is also in the collection at the British Museum (NWC 99; Appendix 1:37) one attributed to the Cook expedition that may be Nootkan, but it differs from the standard style which has just been described and resembles a style collected by United States Navy men from the Tlingit, probably in the middle of the nineteenth century (Niblack 1890, plate 46, figs. 257, 258). This consists of a straight club surmounted by a human head, below which a stone blade is set transversely through a hole carved into the handle. The handle is wound with braided cord. In the museum catalog the piece is listed as a "Nootka Tomehawk for killing slaves," and the same caption appears in Niblack.

Another implement which Cook described as "a short truncheon made of bone, wood, or stone" is also included under the term "slave killers" in the museum catalogs. This looks like a lateral hammer which has been cut in half and has had a wedge-shaped lower end added. The whole piece is carved from a single block of stone. The figure on the top is generally a bird face, highly stylized and somewhat reminiscent of Salish carving. (fig. 14) Technically they are well-developed examples of the pecked and polished Neolithic technique of stonework. The two best pieces (figs. 15, 16) are in the British Museum (NWC 93, 94; Appendix 1:352, 353), and a third, simpler one, without the bird-head carving (NWC 95, Appendix 1:354) may be from the Vancouver collections because it is not definitely attributed to Cook (figs. 17, 18). A fine specimen is in the Cook collection in Florence (155) (Giglioli 1895, p. 119–20, plate III, fig. 62) which Giglioli compares to a sketch in *Jacobsen's Reise*

Fig. 12 (*above*). Ceremonial ax, Nookta Sound. Cook collection, BM, NWC 97 (Appendix 1:323).

Fig. 13 (*left*). Ceremonial ax, Nootka Sound. Cook collection, Cambridge 25.371 (Appendix 1:325).

Fig. 14. Stone fighting weapon, Nootka Sound. Cook collection, BM, NWC 95 (Appendix 1:354).

Fig. 15. Stone fighting weapon, Nootka Sound. Cook collection, BM, NWC 93 (Appendix 1:352).

Fig. 16. Stone fighting weapon, Nootka Sound. Cook collection, BM, NWC 94 (Appendix 1:353).

(p. 58) which shows a Kwakiutl version of the same which he calls a "skull crusher." This piece was collected either from Knight's Inlet or Fort Rupert between 1881 and 1883, but it may have been made much earlier. In the ceremonial paraphernalia of the Kwakiutl at the end of the nineteenth century there are copper breakers of the same shape made of wood (Boas 1895, plate 19). It is logical to assume that perhaps these are descendants of the wedge-shaped stone weapons.

In the Vienna catalog a similar object (209; Appendix 1:358) carved of basalt is registered as a copper breaker or a *Schädel Brecher* (skull crusher), with the added statement that it was used for killing prisoners of war.

With so many specimens of slave killers there is still the problem of their prominence in the collections and the absence of any description in the diaries. The majority came from the Cook expedition, with a few from Vancouver, but all are supposed to be from Nootka Sound. If they were slave killers for ceremonial occasions, it is simple to explain the lack of references in the literature by the fact that the ceremonies in which they might have been used were in the winter. Haswell, who was the first mate on Kendrick's ship the *Columbia* on his first voyage to the Northwest Coast in 1787, mentions a slave killing in connection with the ceremony following the capture of the first whale of the season (Haswell 1884; Bancroft 1886, p. 78). Drucker, in his ethnographic study, does not mention any slave killing in connection with the ceremony, but one must remember that he received his information from individuals born in the nineteenth century (Drucker 1951, pp. 177–80). Haswell states that they frequently killed slaves in cold blood and had no hesitation in admitting it. Drucker, however, says that a slave might be killed if a chief's son to whom he was assigned as a guardian should die (Drucker 1951, p. 334).

In their list of weapons both Cook and Samwell include "something like a Patoo patoo of New Zealand," which probably refers to the famous whale bone war club of the Nootka. These clubs are as popular in the collections as the "slave killers." There are seven clubs in the various Cook collections. They are carved of heavy whale bone and range from fifty to sixty centimeters in length. The handle is incised with a profile of a mythical bird, and the two long sides often have a geometric design, such as concentric circles or diamonds connected with straight lines. The grip is often wrapped with thong. These clubs were an important item of trade among the Indians, and parts of them have been found in archaeological sites as far away from Nootka territory as the border of Washington and Idaho. There are three in the Cook collection at the British Museum (NWC 40, 41, 42; Appendix 1:34, 35, 36) and two more in Florence (#18, 19; Appendix 1:42, 43), again first attributed to the Maori of New Zealand, but corrected by Giglioli (1895, p. 117). Vienna also has two (Vienna 212, 227; Appendix 1:44, 45). They are all traditional except one from Florence (#18), which is separated into two short arms at the top instead of the bird's head.

Two of the most beautifully carved war clubs are in remote museum collections containing little else from the eighteenth century. Both are from the Vancouver expedition. One, in the Royal Albert Memorial Museum in Exeter, England (#1275; Appendix 1:40), was collected by Mr. J. W. Scott and given in 1836 to the Devonshire Historical Society by his nephew, Mr. J. Scott Bower (fig. 20). Together with this piece was also an amulet (fig. 21). The other is one of the few pieces left from the Spelman Swaine collection of the Vancouver expedition, which was received from the Wisbech Museum, where it had been deposited in 1842 (fig. 19). These two pieces are among the best documented of any eighteenth-century objects. The war club is numbered #1275 Exeter (Appendix 1:40) and the amulet #332 Exeter (Appendix 1:156).

After such a long description of weapons, something should be said about defensive means. In many Northwest Coast collections there are pieces of armor, but here we must ask whether they were really collected from Nootka Sound, for it is generally supposed that the slat or rod armor was used only farther north. There are two cuirasses in the collection at the British Museum (NWC 72, 73; Appendix 1:1, 2) that are supposed to come from Nootka Sound. They are both made of a combination of slats and rods which fit under the arms. These are woven together by treating each slat as the warp of the weaving and carrying the braided sinew across them horizontally by twining. Drucker states that the customary armor of the Nootka consisted of heavy skin, sometimes folded several times, and that even these were worn only by chiefs (Drucker 1951; p. 335). The notes from the *Sutil* and the *Mexicana* agree with this. There is no armor in the Cook collection in the British Museum that can be definitely assigned to Nootka Sound. Ledyard wrote that the doubled skin jacket was strengthened by having slips of wood sewed transversely to the outside. He demonstrated the power of his musket by shooting holes through one of these jackets (Ledyard 1783, p. 76). There are also statements about ferocious masks worn by warriors, but none have survived in any collections or even illustrations. Warriors painted their faces black, which would not have been necessary if masks were worn. There are also statements that masks were worn in war dances, and this may have been the limit of their use. These dances were seen by some visitors, but there is no record of their having seen any warfare.

With the ceremonious greeting on his arrival Cook heard the first Nootka music to be described by a European. The comments by him and his company vary considerably, from an appreciative interest to cries of horror. Portlock said their war song was the most warlike and awful they

Fig. 17. Stone fighting weapon, Nootka Sound. Hewitt collection (Vancouver), BM, Vancouver 95 (Appendix 1:355).

Fig. 18. Stone fighting weapon, Thurlow's Island. Hewitt collection (Vancouver), BM, Vancouver 96 (Appendix 1:356).

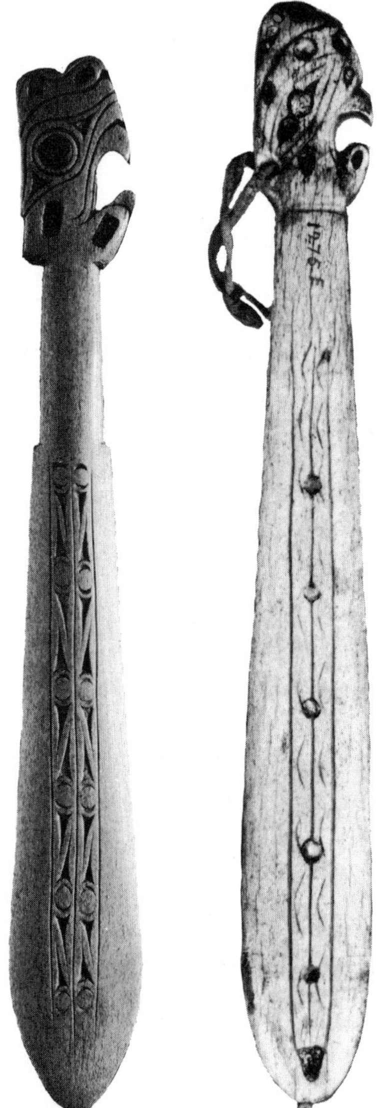

Fig. 19. War club, Nootka Sound. Swaine collection (Vancouver), Cambridge 49.150 (Appendix 1:39).

Fig. 20. War club, Nootka Sound. Vancouver expedition, Exeter 1275 (Appendix 1:40).

had ever heard. Their song leader for more peaceful entertainment was masked and carried a rattle in the form of a bird. He wore a costume with deer hooves hanging from it, which rattled with every motion he made. James Burney, whose father was one of the great musicologists of the eighteenth century, wrote: "Their song was composed of a variety of strange placed notes, all in unison and well in tune, the words were first given out by one Man, as a parish clerk gives out the first line of a Psalm" (Cook 1967, p. 315). Cook compared this singing with that of the Maori of New Zealand, saying that although there is no little resemblance, they do not have the violent motions and hideous contortions of the limbs. Besides the rattle, another instrument, if it can be called such, is a small pea whistle which they put wholly in the mouth to produce a squeaky sound. Cook saw a man in a complete wolf skin using this whistle and assumed that he was hunting by means of a decoy; but Professor Hawthorn of the University of British Columbia, whom Dr. Beaglehole consulted, pointed out that these actions were part of the wolf or shaman's dance, a dramatic performance when novices are inducted into its ritual. Nootkans do not hunt with decoys (Cook 1967, p. 316).

Cook regretted that he could not find out more about the religion and social life of the Nootka and considered the large figures in the house sketched by Webber a real challenge. That they were covered with mats could easily lead one to believe they must have some mysterious meaning. Yet with the proper bribery Webber had the mats lowered so that he could sketch them. Later they were offered for sale and some of the men on the ships bought smaller ones. Cook observed that there was no evidence that they were worshiped since there was no sign of gifts of food around them. In general his observations and those of his company stressed the material features of Nootka culture, because it was scarcely possible to do more when there was such limited communication between the English and the Nootka. In this respect the Europeans who came fourteen years later had the advantage of meeting Indians who had by that time learned a small vocabulary of English and Spanish. The men on the *Sutil* and the *Mexicana* secured much information that the earlier expeditions could not record.

For example, the social structure of the Nootka recorded by the diarists on these ships sheds some light on interpersonal relations and beliefs. The people were divided into two groups, the *taises* or chiefs and their families, and the *michimis* or common people. They even included a myth which has elements found in many Northwest Coast tribes, but whatever term is translated as "God" has been added by the Spanish recorder. The myth as given in the Jane translation is:

> The Nutkenos say that the progation of the human race was brought about in the following manner: God created woman, whom he left

alone in the dark forests of Yucuatl, where lived also deer without horns, dogs without tails and geese without wings. The woman lamented her sad condition day and night without finding solace, until Qautz took pity on her tears and appeared to her, coming over the water in a canoe of copper, which shone brightly, in which many handsome young men were rowing with oars of the same metal. The island maiden was astonished at this sight and remained dumbfounded by the foot of a tree. One of the rowers, however, told her that it was the Almighty who had had the goodness to visit these shores to supply her with that companionship for which she sighed. At these words the sad and desolate maiden cried the more and as the tears trickled down her nostrils, the moisture fell from them to the sand. Qautz then commanded her to look at that which had fallen, and she saw with amazement the tiny body of a child which was entirely formed. By order of Qautz she placed this in a shell suitable for its size, being told to move the child to other shells as it grew larger. When this work had been completed the Creator re-embarked, after having allowed the brute beasts also to experience his bounty, for at the same moment the deer beheld horns sprouting from his forehead, the dog found a tail growing, and the birds rose in the air to make trial for the first time of those wings which they had received. The new-born babe gradually grew, being moved from cradle to cradle until it began to walk. It proved to be a boy, and the first proof which he gave of his manhood was that his mistress conceived by him. Her first-born son is the ancestor of the *taises*, while from her other sons the common people are descended. [Espinosa y Tello 1930, p. 108]

It is quite clear from the style of this myth that it was probably written by one of the chaplains on board the *Sutil* and the *Mexicana*, and it also has elements which are widespread in North American Indian mythology. The manner of birth of the child is the myth called "Mucus Boy," whose miraculous birth and quick growth provides a hero who can perform great deeds. Myths are seldom recorded in this period, and when one can be found it helps in tracing the features of well-known myths to an earlier century. Without written records the history of folktales can be studied only in this way.

The Nootka believe that man's soul is immortal and after death goes on to another life. The souls of *taises* go to join their ancestors in the home of Qautz, the supernatural character that might have been translated by the Spaniards as "God," who also figures in the myth just related. The *michimis* go to another place called Pin-pula, where people of the upper class also go if they live useless lives and are careless about their ritual obligations. A *tais* must offer prayers for the welfare of his people and in times of disaster perform special ceremonies. In the narrative of the *Sutil and the Mexicana* there is a drawing of "the oratorio" of Maquinna, which is a small closet built of planks, just large enough for a person to stand in. The figures painted on it resemble the ones on the painted board also seen by

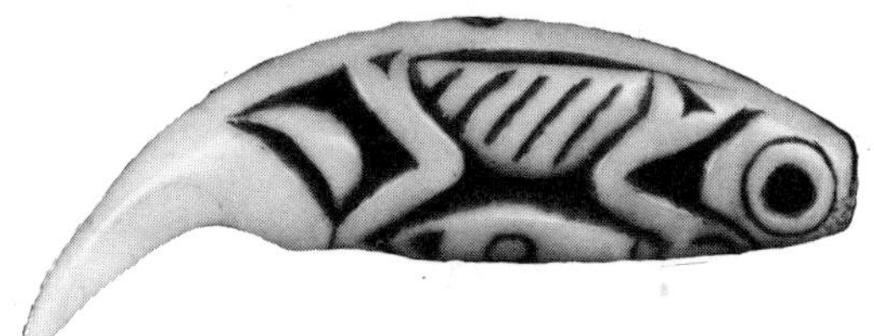

Fig. 21. Amulet, Nootka Sound. Vancouver expedition, Exeter 332 (Appendix 1:156).

Fig. 22. A Nootka couple. Spanish picture.

members of this expedition (Espinosa y Tello 1930, p. 103). The chief must remain continent except during the full moon. The burial of the chiefly class is carried out with much ceremony. The body is laid on a couch of sea otter skins and set into a wooden chest which is hung in the trees. His servants watch over the body until the soul leaves when it has decayed. The common people are buried in the ground (Espinosa y Tello 1930, p. 109).

These customs seem to have disappeared, according to the description in Drucker (1951, p. 147). As they are recorded here they sound rather codified and resemble portraits which the Spaniards made at the same time: some of the clothing was fairly exact, but the faces were definitely not Indian.

On the other hand, there is a description of a girl's puberty ceremony which Maquinna (figs. 23, 24) arranged for his daughter that is much closer to reality. Again, like the few other ceremonies that were witnessed by the eighteenth-century visitors, it is worth reproducing here as it appears in the diary:

> As soon as the first signs of puberty appear in a woman great feasts are given on this account, and her name is also changed; on the same day they are declared princesses, if they happen to be daughter of the principal chief of all the taises. The officers from our station went to congratulate Macuina on the installation of his daughter Istocoti-Clemoc, who had previously been called Apenas. The pomp which dignified this occasion is worthy of description. At one corner of the house, which was placed on the slopes of the woody mountains of Copti, they had set a platform supported by 4 thick pillars, painted white, yellow, scarlet, blue and black, with various badly drawn figures on them and 2 busts at the corners with open arms and hand stretched out as if to signify the munificence of the monarch. In the interior of the house on some freshly strewn rushes there was a couch, where the young princess lay, dressed in the finest cypress threads and loaded with innumerable ornaments. As soon as the appointed hour arrived, Macuina took his daughter by the hand and led her to the platform, placing her on his right and Quatlaza-pe (*his brother*) on his left. The large crowd of natives who thronged the hall and beach remained in the most profound silence. The chief addressing them all, said: "My daughter Apenas is now no longer a girl but a woman; from this time forward she will be known by the name Istocoti-Clemoc," that is "the great princess of Yucuatl." To this all replied with loud shouts of "Huacas, Macuina! Huacas Istocoti-Clemoc" cries equivalent to our "Viva"; the greatest praise among these people is to express friendship, which is signified by the word "Huacas." The taises and other nobles then began to sing and dance, everyone receiving some gift of importance, which Quatlaza-pe scattered from the platform in the name of Macuina and the princess. [Espinosa y Tello 1930, p. 112]

After this the day was spent in wrestling matches and games. Maquinna was greatly pleased that the men from the ships had attended the occasion and gave sea otter skins to the Spanish sailors who joined in the wrestling. Maquinna then led his daughter into the house to a loom and said, "You are a woman now, my daughter, and you must not any longer spend your time except in performing the duties belonging to your sex." She was no longer allowed to visit the ships and not even the commander could persuade Maquinna to bring her with him to dine with the officers (Espinosa y Tello 1930, p. 113).

In modern ethnographies the puberty rites begin with a period of seclusion, a week to a month according to the rank of the girl, and this type of feast is given when she comes out of seclusion. Guests are invited from surrounding villages, and gifts are distributed. This feast signifies that the girl is now ready for marriage proposals.

One more ceremony of the eighteenth-century Nootka which can

Fig. 23. Traditional sketch of Maquinna, chief of Nootka. Spanish picture.

be compared with a known later practice is the self-mutilation the chief inflicts upon himself. He goes with two servants to the shore of a deep lake and taking a piece of the toughest "pine" bark in each hand hurls himself head downward from a rock. When he lifts his face from the

Fig. 24. Sketch regarded as Maquinna. Spanish picture.

water he starts to rub his cheeks with the bark until the blood flows. He repeats this as many times as he thinks proper. Spectators stand by to encourage him. Maquinna's brother did this in the presence of the diarist (Espinosa y Tello 1930, p. 114).

The same type of ceremonial act is carried out when a boy is seeking a guardian spirit or a man wishes to renew and strengthen his relation to his spirit. Bathing in the salt water and rubbing the body with hemlock or fir boughs is done by whalers and others who wish to gain bodily endurance and spiritual strength.

Vancouver was present at another great feast given by Maquinna when the *Venus* with Captain Shepherd found him at Safety Cove on Calvert Island. Captain Shepherd told him that Bodega y Quadra, the Spanish commissioner for settling the claims of the Nootka Sound controversy, was anxiously waiting for him at Nootka Sound and that the storeship *Daedalus* for which he had been waiting was also anchored at the same place. Since the weather was getting too severe for good exploring, Vancouver decided to respond to this call at once and set sail southward, arriving on 28 August at Nootka Sound. He found a very busy port during his stay until 13 October, when he followed Bodega y Quadra to California.

During this period the *Aranzazu* with Caamaño, the *Hope* with Captain Ingraham, the *Columbia* with Captain Gray, the *Jenny* with Captain Baker, and many other ships whose names have been mentioned gathered there for their last rendezvous before sailing for Hawaii, China, or home. The meeting between Vancouver and Bodega y Quadra was not satisfactory, both feeling that they needed more instruction from their governments, but from this contact a warm friendship developed between the two men.

With such a company of friends at hand Maquinna gave a feast in honor of the two captains, and Mr. Bell of the *Chatham*, who probably wrote the *New Vancouver Journal*, gave a glowing account of the hospitality and lavish entertainment that was offered. On entering the house the two captains were led to the places of honor, which were covered with clean, fresh mats. Maquinna's family of four wives and many children, all in their best clothes, were seated in this area to welcome the guests. The captains both brought handsome gifts of copper, blue cloth, and blankets. Although the Nootka house has been described many times, the account by Bell brings in a new feature. The house was very long, but only about thirty yards of it was habitable, because the remainder was not roofed over. Bell and his friends took the opportunity to measure some of the house posts and recorded that there were three beams that ran the full length, the center one being the ridge pole. These were thirty-two feet long and had a circumference of twelve feet. They were supported at each end by posts of equal size which were carved with "strikingly preposterous figures." The beams were solid, without even a knothole, and varied little at the ends.

Bell placed the "royal" kitchen in a corner of the house, which is not its customary location; individual hearths are usually located along the center passage. But because of the many guests and the cooperation of all the housewives living in the group, this change was necessary. The assembled cooks were busy boiling many kinds of oil and preparing stew and fricassees of porpoise, whale, and seal and many delicious meats. And here Mr. Bell relates some strange behavior that showed an unpleasant arrogance on the part of the guests. Captains Vancouver and Bodega y Quadra had decided between them to bring their own kind of food, even though they knew their host was providing a lavish feast. They raised a table of some broad planks from Maquinna's house and spread on them the food brought by Bodega y Quadra and the beverages furnished by Vancouver. The service was as fine as that at the Spanish governor's house.

After the meal the performance commenced, consisting of warlike evolutions by Nootka men. Their costumes were largely drawn from the trade goods, such as woolens and blankets of English manufacture. Maquinna's brother was dressed in a complete suit of stage armor that could once have been used by the ghost in *Hamlet*. Their faces were painted red and black and their hair was perfumed with fish oil, powdered with red ocher, and adorned with down and feathers.

A group of men sat near the door, holding small sticks with which they beat time on a plank in front of them. About twenty men came running in, one after the other, all carrying muskets and making "horrid gestures and hallooing." Each performer was summoned by a signal from the musicians. After each of the twenty had danced individually another twenty came in carrying long spears. When they had all made a circuit around the fire, they gathered at one end of the house and sang "not devoid of harmony," ending with a frightful yell. Then Maquinna entered dancing, dressed in a very rich garment of sea otter skins and wearing a round black hat, a mask, and a "fanciful" petticoat or apron from which were suspended hollow tubes of copper and brass that made a wonderful tinkling sound. Every feature of this costume except the black hat is typical of the dance regalia used in every Northwest Coast tribe. They do not all wear sea otter skins, but some kind of cape and the "petticoat" are traditional not only for dancers but also for medicine men. The jingling copper and brass was preceded by deer hoofs or carved wooden pendants, and sometimes the metal consisted of thimbles after they came into the trade. After Maquinna's dance the group of performers came out again and sang.

Then a man who was probably Maquinna's speaker came forward, holding a sea otter skin, and proclaimed in a pompous voice that it was a present from Maquinna to Captain Vancouver. He went through the ritual a second time, presenting a similar skin to Captain Bodega y Quadra. Mr. Bell wrote that it was apparent that the Indians knew the equal rank and different nationality of the two leaders. After another song the entertainment was over. Mr. Bell finished his account with the statement that this entertainment, in which there was something grand and curious, was well worth coming the distance to see (Bell 1914, pp. 303–5).

In this résumé of Nootka culture after first contact with Europeans, the village of Clayoquot must be included. This community is a short distance south on the west coast of Vancouver Island and is the settlement nearest to Nootka Sound. There was considerable intermarriage and intercourse between these peoples, sometimes friendly, but always with the possibility of attack. Many traders' ships stopped at both villages, but the American ships made it their major port. The first American ships to arrive on the Northwest Coast were the *Columbia* and the *Washington* with Captains John Kendrick and Robert Gray. They sailed from Boston late in 1787 and arrived in the northwest in September of 1788. After stopping briefly at Nootka Sound they moved to Clayoquot Sound, which became their center of operations from 1788 to 1792. The captains exchanged ships and personnel several times. Neither left a journal, but

Fig. 25. Spanish settlement at Nootka Sound. Spanish picture.

several of their companions were prolific writers. The chief mate Robert Haswell and the *Columbia*'s ship's clerk, John Hoskins, observed the Indian life with great interest and recorded many important facts. Another writer, John Boit, who had started on the *Columbia* as fifth officer at the age of sixteen and stayed with this ship on the first American circumnavigation of the globe, was, on his third voyage round the world, commander of the sloop *Union*. It is in the journals of these three men that the happenings at Clayoquot are extensively described (see chap. 3).

Before we leave Nootka Sound, the Spanish settlements should be mentioned. The first was established in 1789 and closed at the end of the same year, having been the seat of the events that led to the Nootka controversy. Little was left of it when the Spaniards returned in 1790 and built a second settlement. This was sketched by Suría on the Malaspina voyage. In 1957 Senor Condoy in the Naval School of Canada painted a scene called "Gran Rancheria de Macuina," naming the vessels the *Sutil* and the *Mexicana*. This is the Spanish settlement and not the native village, and if it represents the Malaspina voyage the ships are the *Descubierta* and the *Atrevida*.

The sketches on the preceding pages are included to show the danger of trusting the printed words in picture captions too far (fig. 25).

3

The Challenge of the Coast South of Nootka: The Strait of Juan de Fuca and the Columbia River

Although the entrance to Nootka Sound was by no means easy for the eighteenth-century navigators, it did offer the first shelter that was visible to those coming north along the coast after completely losing sight of the shoreline in the fog-shrouded area around the Strait of Juan de Fuca. It also offered relief to those fur traders who started their season at Prince William Sound or the Queen Charlotte Islands and then went south to rendezvous with a partner or to refurbish their ships before going across the Pacific to the Hawaiian Islands for the winter or to China to sell their furs. But from this center there was also the lure of finding new areas for trading to the south and the chance of verifying place names that so often proved imaginary on the maps and charts available to them. At this time the Northwest Coast was regarded by the Spaniards as part of Alta California, and in the early 1770s the rumors of Russians in Alaska caused them to send out their expeditions in 1774 and 1775 (see chap. 1). The second voyage north, commanded by Bruno Heceta in the *Santiago*, was notable on two counts: the massacre by Indians of his boat's crew at the mouth of the Moclips River on 14 July 1775 and Heceta's discovery of the Columbia River, which he named Rio de San Roc, on 17 August 1775. For twelve years ships passed the mouth of this river and battled the winds and seas of a shelterless coast until 1787, when Captain Barkley came close to shore and had a similar experience farther north on the Washington coast. Indians killed several members of his crew when they went ashore to get water.

When Barkley's experience became known to the fur traders the interest in the Strait of Juan de Fuca and the need for exploring it was again aroused. This body of water had great fascination and great significance in the late eighteenth century. Even though Cook had declared that a Northwest Passage was impossible, the £20,000 reward posted by Parliament had not been withdrawn, and the chance of finding it still led many to explore hazardous places. They forced their way into narrow passages, but large bodies of water seemed to elude them. Vancouver passed the Columbia River on his way north and ignored the Fraser. Cook passed the entrance to the Strait of Juan de Fuca, named Cape Flattery, when it was shrouded in fog and left the discovery of this entrance to the inland waters of the Northwest Coast to his successors. The passage across the entrance was used by several expeditions before the extent of this strait was realized.

The first of the eighteenth-century navigators to reach the south shore of the strait was Captain Barkley in the *Imperial Eagle*. Having been successful in trading for sea otter skins on the west coast of Vancouver Island, he went south in the spring of 1787 to try his luck there. His diary was lost, and so details of his voyage are not known, but it is recorded that he lost several of his crew when they were attacked by Indians at the mouth of the Hoh or Quilleyute Rivers (Wagner 1937, p. 206). For this voyage southward he is now known as the discoverer, or at least the modern discoverer, of the Strait of Juan de Fuca. Even Meares, who, as Wagner said, was not inclined to give others any credit, acknowledged this claim when he followed the same track the next year.

A few months after Captain Barkley had his unfortunate experience, but knowing nothing about it, Captain Charles Duncan in the *Princess Royal* planned a rendezvous at Nootka Sound with Captain Colnett, his partner in a fur trading expedition. While he was waiting for Colnett he sailed south, starting from Nootka Sound on 1 August 1787, and anchored at the entrance to the Strait of Juan de Fuca on 15 August. As far as the records show, he had no contact with the Indians, but his presence there was verified by a sketch he made at the entrance. He left on 17 August and stood for Hawaii (Wagner 1937, p. 207).

A year later Meares himself, commanding the *Felice*, started out from Port Cox in Clayoquot Sound on 28 June 1788 and the next day came to a large sound where there were several Indian villages. Canoes came out to the ship. The people resembled those at Port Cox and acknowledged Wickananish, the chief of Clayoquot, as their chief. This was probably Port San Juan (Port Renfrew). The next afternoon they arrived at the entrance of a great inlet where there was a small island about two miles offshore and a very remarkable rock almost in the form of an obelisk (Fuca Pillar). Canoes came out from the island with twenty or thirty men in each who looked very savage, with painted faces and sea otter cloaks. They were armed with bows and arrows with barbed bone points and large spears pointed with mussel shell. The group included the chief, Tatootche, whose face was painted black and glittered with sand. Meares's guess about this material was good, but there is a reason to believe that it might have been powdered mica, which was used for this purpose in many places on the Northwest Coast. These men were representatives of the Makah, against whom Wickananish had warned them.

Tatootche told Meares that the power of Wickananish ended here and his territory extended from this point south and east. He would not allow his people to trade with Meares even though he had given the chief a small present. Meares sent his longboat out to look for a suitable moorage, but none was found. When the longboat was near the island many canoes surrounded it, and an Indian jumped into the boat and snatched a few trifles. The men agreed to ignore this since they were outnumbered. Meares was quite certain that Wickananish had an arrangement for receiving skins from these people, because they had trade goods that could only have come from Port Cox or Nootka Sound. One Indian had a complete set of coat buttons. Since Meares realized that he was now across the Strait of Juan de Fuca, he named this body of water after its possible original discoverer (Meares 1790, pp. 152–55).

The next day canoes came again from Tatoosh Island, bringing the chief and about four hundred men. They paddled around the ship, examining it carefully. Then they began to sing, and Meares made the observation, "But offended as we might be with these people, we could not but be charmed by their music." They continued sailing southward to the Bay of Queenhithe (probably the mouth of the Quinault River, Washington), said to have been named by Meares after a place on the Thames River in England, but more likely what "Quinault" sounded like to him. Meares refers to this 1 July 1788. It is likely that it was named by Captain Barkley in 1787. It was once spelled "Queenault" (Wagner 1937, p. 488). In coming here Meares and his crew thought of Barkley's unfortunate experience, probably in the same place, and became very much disturbed when they were temporarily fogged in. When the fog lifted they saw Destruction Island (Green Island) in the distance. They continued south to a place they named Shoalwater Bay, where a canoe with a man and a boy came near the ship. They refused to come aboard with the two sea otter skins they showed, so Meares let down some trifles on a long cord and the boy received them gleefully and showed them to the man. They then tied the skins to the cord to be hoisted back on board. Although this transaction showed their familiarity with trading, there was no sign that they had any European goods or ornaments.

When Gray placed the Columbia River on his map he considered Meares's map showing Shoalwater Bay inaccurate, and since Meares's statements had often been found unacceptable this merely added more doubt of his veracity. However, the bay was explored by Lieutenant James Alden in 1853 and restored to the map (Meany 1923, p. 350). This is discussed by James G. Swan, who lived at Shoalwater Bay in the late 1850s. He also gives his opinion regarding the frequency of deserted Indian villages. During his residence there, he discovered many remains of old houses, canoes, and heaps of shells, which all gave evidence of a large Indian population. As everywhere, the Indians moved closer to the trading centers, and one cannot discount the havoc caused by the early epidemics of smallpox, measles, and other new diseases, including alcohol, to which they had little resistance (Swan 1857, p. 212).

Now Meares thought he was near Cape San Roc, as the Spaniards called the entrance to the Columbia River, and when he could not find it he called it Cape Disappointment and the inlet Deception Bay (Baker Bay). He said emphatically, "No such river exists!"

His annoyance and the thought of the long trip to Nootka made him turn back northward. He intended to go to the first large bay he found after reaching the Strait of Juan de Fuca. This was at Port Cox, which is near the entrance to Barkley Sound, and he wished to see how closely the people there resembled those of Nootka Sound. He put in at Port Effingham and two days later sent Robert Duffin off in a longboat to explore farther into the strait. Duffin had scarcely gone ten miles into the strait when he came to an Indian village (probably Port San Juan), where several canoes promptly came to the boat, while the people stood on the beach watching. The men were armed. They maneuvered the longboat between two canoes and proceeded to attack. This became a hand-to-hand combat, and ultimately almost every man in the longboat was wounded, some seriously. The account mentions one combat between a sailor with a cutlass and an Indian with a stone "bludgeon." When the Indian raised his arm with the weapon in hand the sailor cut off his arm with the cutlass. The Indian, in spite of this injury, jumped overboard and swam ashore. In addition to the assault from the canoes, the watchers on the beach threw stones at the longboat. Meares gives a very graphic account of this conflict, and since he does not mention it again, it can be assumed that all the wounded recovered.

Before leaving the conflict, a word should be said about the "stone bludgeon," because the term so exactly describes this weapon, of which a number of examples are found in several eighteenth-century collections. This, however, is the only instance in the literature where the weapon is mentioned in actual use. In some catalogs they are referred to as slave killers, but this use is never mentioned by the collectors (see figs. 14–18, pp. 42–43). The Vienna catalog states that one piece (209; Appendix 1:358) was "used to kill prisoners of war" who would usually be treated as slaves if allowed to live. Since the Vienna catalog was written a number of years after the collection was acquired in the auction of the Cook collection in London in 1806, it is doubtful that this is anything more than a guess, unless the original label came with the piece. One Vancouver piece (95; Appendix 1:355) is also from Nootka Sound (fig. 17), but the other one is from Thurlow's Island in the Inside Passage, where the inhabitants might have been Salish, but might have acquired the piece in trade or by killing the owner in war (see Appendix 1, weapons).

This was the climax of Meares's attempts to gain further knowledge of the Strait of Juan de Fuca, but the following years brought the seasonal explorers and traders in a continuous procession until in 1792 Vancouver did his customary thorough job by exploring the strait and its many branches to the head of Puget Sound at Olympia.

Approaching the strait from the south, Gray and Kendrick came from the California coast at Cape Mendocino, cruising close enough to the shore to see the Indian settlements and have contact with some. They judged from the number of fires that the shore must have been heavily populated. The Indians appeared hostile and the captains were not inclined to put them to the test. They were carrying bows and arrows and had iron and stone knives. At Tillamook Bay they went ashore to relieve the crew members with scurvy. They visited the houses in the Indian village, which they declared were very unclean. The men wore no clothing except a cape of well-dressed animal skins, and the women wore a short skirt, likened to a Highlander's kilt, made of straw (probably cedar bark). Their canoes were well-shaped, Haswell stated, for any useful purpose. The Indians had no skins for sale, but brought them boiled and roasted crabs, which they sold for buttons. The Indians' effort to entertain the visitors with songs and dances was not appreciated. Haswell wrote that they did a war dance with frightful howls and their music was "something horrid." The following day, when they were digging clams on the beach, Marcus Lapius, or Marcos Lopez, a native of the Cape Verde Islands who was Captain Gray's personal servant, stuck his cutlass into the sand. An Indian snatched it, and in trying to recover it Marcus was killed. The diary mentioned that several men were wounded in the fracas that followed, but it did not state which side they were on (Haswell 1884, p. 28).

Gray and Kendrick continued their separate ways northward, Gray passing the Columbia River, which he later "discovered." On 21 August two canoes came alongside with beaver skins. They had interesting whaling gear in their canoe, but they refused to sell it. This was in the neighborhood of Green Island (Destruction Island), and the Indians came from the Quinault village. Haswell now stated that he still believed the Strait of Juan de Fuca existed, in spite of Cook's denial of its existence. Gray and Kendrick met again, and sailing north entered Clayoquot Sound, where many Indians came with sea otter skins for which they wanted copper. The chief was Wickananish, who was dressed in a "genteel suit of clothes" which he said Meares had given him. He also mentioned the fur traders who had visited him, including Barkley, Hanna, Duncan, and

Douglas. After this brief contact the *Columbia* and the *Washington* went into Nootka Sound and anchored at Ship Cove, where Cook had tied up. Both ships wintered there.

Meares, with his entire party and the ships *Iphigenia* and *Felice*, was also at Nootka, where he built a sturdy garrison around his project. Under the direction of Captain Funter a schooner was being built, for which material and workmen had been brought from China. The local Indians were away at their fishing sites. After Meares had gone, Haswell, Ingraham, and Howe went up the sound for fish oil. There they found that the British traders had forcibly taken all the sea otter skins the Indians possessed and had given them only small pieces of copper in return. They also had taken their dried fish, leaving them without their prepared winter food. As soon as Meares had gone the Indians came to the American ships, and friendly intercourse began. Kendrick stayed in Nootka Sound while Gray went south to the Strait of Juan de Fuca again, but the sea was so rough that it was impossible for him to approach the shore on the south side. He returned to Clayoquot Sound and the *Washington* joined him there.

Soon after they arrived at their new moorage, Wickananish spotted a whale. Haswell does not mention any canoes going out to harpoon it, but relates that he went out with a brother of the chief, who killed the whale. There were ten buoys fastened to the harpoon line. Since this was the first whale of the season there were special ceremonies. When it was brought ashore a slave was sacrificed and the corpse was laid beside the whale's head, which was adorned with eagle feathers (Haswell 1884, p. 51). This is one of the few instances where the actual killing of a slave is mentioned. Boit and Haswell, who were shipmates and may have exchanged information and opinions, are the only eighteenth-century writers who mention cannibalism in any detail. Boit writes that he understood from an Indian that cannibalism occasionally was practiced, but did not specify the reason or purpose. The victim was generally a war prisoner, by which one can assume that he was classified as a slave. It is possible therefore that the "slave killers" in several eighteenth-century collections may be correctly identified, but this does not include the stone fighting weapons (see chap. 2) which are also cataloged in museum collections as slave killers. The club which can be called a slave killer has a wooden handle, often carved with a human head at one end with a stone blade that forms the protruding tongue of the figure. It is usually a handsome piece with beautifully polished stone for the blade. The head is usually decorated with human hair. Its artistic appearance makes one expect that it was used ritually, but either the Indians were reticent or the visiting Europeans did not understand the language well enough to grasp the esoteric details.

Among other features of the Indian culture that came under Boit's sharp observation was the burial of the dead. The body was packed into a box, often dismembered to make it fit, and the container was then lashed to a high position on the trunk of a tree. Cremation, which was practiced farther north, did not occur among the Nootka, according to Drucker (1951, p. 149). Boit also mentioned the myth, shared by many other Northwest Coast tribes, that the eagle creates thunder when he carries a whale from the sea to the mountains to devour it and that lightning is caused by the hissing of a snake. The Indians believed in good and evil spirits and seemed to worship the sun and the moon, a belief attributed to them by many writers, but of which there is no record in the nineteenth-century ethnographies. If this idea had been as central as was believed, some record would have survived the missionary influence of the late nineteenth century.

For the next two years there were many fur traders on the coast, but few went south of Nootka Sound because in this port they were apt to meet many other ships and could exchange information, true and false. After establishing the settlement at Nootka and abandoning it again within a year, the Spaniards started another round of exploring trips, this time sending Quimper to penetrate farther into the Strait of Juan de Fuca. He set out on 31 May from Nootka and made his first contact with Chief Janape in Clayoquot Sound. This chief, Cleaskineh, had exchanged his name with Captain James Hanna of the *Sea Otter* in 1785–86. He was the chief of Ahousit, but he also had been seen in other villages, as was mentioned by Captain Barnet, who found him at Barkley Sound in 1791 (Bartlett 1925, p. 296). Boit writes that he was under the jurisdiction of Wickananish.

On 12 June Quimper stopped at Port San Juan, often called "Poverty Cove" by the fur traders, and the reasons for this name were still holding when Quimper was told that Captain Matthews and Captain Meares in the *Felice* had taken all their furs and given them copper bracelets, earrings, and beads (Wagner 1933, p. 92). Quimper had an uneventful trip in generally pleasant weather during June, cruising along the southern shores of Vancouver Island, naming for saints and Spanish dignitaries locations like Pedder Bay, William Head, and Albert Head which now carry the English names given them by Vancouver. He had no contact with the Indians, though occasionally a small village was sighted from the ship. On 30 June he sent a longboat out with the second pilot, who returned later in the day after planting a cross at the main channel between San Juan Island and Discovery and Chatham Islands. Later that day Quimper himself went ashore at Parry Bay and took possession, planting a cross and burying a bottle with documents (Wagner 1933, p. 107). The next morning some canoes came out from the islands and gave information about the inlets. These people seemed very poor compared with the Indians on the outer coast and had no sea otter skins. It seemed that they had come from elsewhere to provide themselves with food for the winter. On 4 July Quimper stood for the southern shores of the strait to test the information he had received. He came to the neighborhood of Dungeness, and contacts with the Indians increased considerably. A longboat went out to seek information and met Indians in canoes who carried a variety of fish to the ship and bartered them for cask hoops. They had reed mats (*esteras de neda*), which Wagner could not translate completely. *Esteras* means reed mats, but the *neda* is a mystery (Wagner 1933, p. 110). They also had painted woolen blankets, some mixed with feathers (see Appendix 2), and dressed skins of bear, buffalo, and deer. The buffalo was undoubtedly elk. They explained that some of these skins were doubled to form a jacket of armor as protection when they fought their enemies on the north coast. The Indians guided them to two rivers near their village, which may be the two forks of the Dungeness River. They spent the whole day with the visitors and left at sunset, singing and "demonstrating," which was probably some dancing and gesturing in the canoe (Wagner 1933, p. 110). In the vicinity of Dungeness many canoes came to the ship bringing fresh fish, venison, salmonberries, blankets of *neda*, woolen blankets, and mats to exchange (Wagner 1933, p. 111). Quimper's map shows two Indian villages in Dungeness Bay which Quimper named for himself. He planted another cross on a flat piece of land, probably near the present town of Jamestown. So far nothing had been said about the change in language of the Indians, but he made contact with so few that he perhaps did not have a chance to hear their speech. The language was Salish, and he could have heard the same in the vicinity of Esquimault on the north shore. At Dungeness he was in the territory of the Klallam, whose villages were spread along the south shore as far as Clallam Bay, about twenty-five miles east of Neah Bay, two places he soon reached. He sailed eastward along this shore and came to Discovery Bay, which he named Boca de Quadra and which Vancouver renamed, unknowingly, for his ship. Protection Island Quimper called Isla de Carrasco for one of the well-known pilots in the Spanish expeditions.

Quimper now crossed the Strait of Juan de Fuca and came to the Trial Islands, just off the shore near Victoria. At Esquimault Harbor, which he named Cordova, three canoes came to the ship with people he had seen before. They were from Port San Juan and included their chief Janape, who was cordially greeted. They were loaded with seeds which they got at Esquimault and used for food. There is no description from which to guess their identity, Wagner writes (1933 p. 118), and the only guess I could make is very far fetched. It is known that a very choice

Fig. 26. Indian fortification on the Strait of Juan de Fuca. Spanish picture.

variety of seaweed grows in this area, and in the middle 1920s it was being collected and sent to China; but even to an observant stranger it is scarcely possible that this could be confused with seeds. Crossing the strait again, Quimper came to the mouth of the Elwah River, where he found, at the directions of the Indians, some "delicious water." The next day he met a canoe with Chief Tutzi (Tatoosh), who told him that six ships had been to his village to trade, but that they still had some skins. Before reaching the Makah territory the ship stopped at Ensenada de Rojas (Clallam Bay), where there were two Indian settlements. Ten canoes with men and two with women towed his ship to a good anchorage and in return were given small pieces of cask hoops. The Indians also brought fish and salmonberries (Wagner 1933, p. 121). When he approached Neah Bay, several canoes came out and led them to a good anchorage behind Waadah Island. The Indians again brought fish and salmonberries, in addition to a kind of cherry, whose Spanish name, *guinda*, could not be exactly translated. The next morning many canoes came out to barter with goods instead of food. They had woolen cloaks and bearskins, and brought sixteen sea otter skins which Quimper bought with the "king's copper." A number of Spanish expeditions used this term, which may have meant that they had received certain funds from the king's treasury and that the furs received in return were to be delivered to the government. Copper seemed to be the only commodity they had, and sea otter skins were the only product for which it was spent. Usually the "king's copper" was in large sheets, which were cut in appropriate sizes for each transaction.

While they were anchored here Quimper sent some of his men ashore to wash the clothes of the crew. Soon after they had landed and busied themselves at the edge of a creek, the crew on the ship heard screams and saw them chasing two Indian canoes. Quimper sent out another canoe to help them, and it came back with a wounded soldier. He had strayed away from the men at the creek and followed some Indians, who showed him good bushes of the berries he was eating. When they had lured him far enough away they attacked and wounded him. When they saw he was being supported by the men on shore they ran away, leaving their canoes behind. Quimper had the canoes brought alongside the ship to see if the owners would come for them. At ten o'clock at night these Indians came in a small canoe and carried off one of the captured boats. Quimper was forced to fire a swivel gun before they released it and fled. He mentioned again that these people were known for their daring and treachery and that they boasted of killing the captains of two ships that had come to trade. The next afternoon a large canoe arrived, flying an English flag and bringing Tututiaticuz, the brother of Wickananish, the chief at Clayoquot, who came aboard and was feted with wine and biscuit. His manner in accepting this courtesy and in eating showed that he had had considerable intercourse with Europeans. The next morning a canoe came from Tutuzi (Tatoosh) to tell Quimper that the man who had injured the soldier had been punished. In response, Quimper sent back the two canoes he held. On 29 July a canoe came again with the chief, Tutuzi, his brother, and his son. For a small cutlass and a little copper, the son sold the first pilot an Indian girl about eight or nine years old who was a war captive. They also bought twenty sea otter skins. The next day more skins were bought, and a chief called Cuney came from another village. He was considered very treacherous and is supposed to have killed a Captain Mile, which Quimper had heard from Wickananish. This young man was about twenty-four years old, of very light color, and with an agreeable face. Quimper asked him if he had killed Captain Mile, and he began to tremble and tried to flee from the ship; but when Quimper assured him of his friendship he stayed to barter, although he was suspicious and uncomfortable. When he left, the Indians of Tutuzi's village urged Quimper to fire a musket at him; but the captain made them understand that he would not harm anyone. Later in the night a canoe with three Indians came very quietly alongside the ship, but the sentinel fired a shot and they fled. Those on board the ship surmised that it might have been the father of the girl who had been sold, trying to rescue her because she had wept when she was forced to go below deck to a sleeping place assigned to her.

On 1 August 1790, with the usual ceremonies, Quimper named the site he had reached Bahia de Nuñez Gaona, a village now known as Neah Bay, which the Indians called Nisma (Wagner 1933, p. 126). Quimper continued until he came to Koitlah Point, which he called Rada, and then crossed the strait to Puerto San Juan (Wagner 1933, p. 127). This ended the exploration of this strait by Quimper in 1790.

In 1791, Eliza, who became the commander of the port of Nootka when the settlement of the Spaniards was reactivated, sent out several exploring expeditions. One of his pilots, Juan Pantoja y Arriga, left an excellent account of his experiences, covering much of the same area Quimper had mapped the previous year. He was accompanied by Ramon Saavedra and Jose Verdia. After leaving Nootka Sound they stopped first at Clayoquot Sound, where they were greeted cordially by Wickananish, the chief, and his two sons, accompanied by numerous Indians. Wickananish, who had been mentioned many times, was never described until this event. Pantoja said he was about fifty to fifty-five years old, fat and robust, with a pleasing appearance. The sons came aboard, but he refused to. When asked the reason for his reluctance, he explained that when Colnett was there his brother had been invited aboard and had fallen from the ladder and drowned.

By six o'clock the next morning the Indians were around the ships again in great numbers. In fact, Pantoja estimated that there were eighty canoes and about five hundred persons. They traded their sea otter skins and many large crabs. The sons of Wickananish came again in the afternoon and were given two sheets of copper. The next morning Eliza, the commander, the first chaplain, the pilots, and the surgeons went ashore to carry their compliments to the chief. They brought him some Monterey shells (abalone) and a sack of biscuit.

Pantoja's description of the chief's house and his entertainment warrants a complete repetition:

> Having reached the outside of the house we went along a very narrow alley, perhaps some twenty paces long. At the end of this just as we entered the house, which is a huge gallery, is a very large figure, one of the columns or posts which holds up one of the very large main timbers which sustain the roof. The mouth of this figure, only large enough to hold one person, is what serves for a door. As soon as we

entered we saw the captain [chief] in the front. Coming towards us he received us with endearing expression "guacas," that is to say "friends." Then he imperiously ordered some mats to be at once stretched over various chests and made signs to us to sit down on them close to him. Apart from us a great number of Indians did the same. With great seriousness he ordered these to sing. An old man, taking in his hand a string of shells (such as pilgrims use) began the chant which they all continued with such noise and cries that at the end of the song they gave in musical time a roar so loud and terrible that without exaggeration it seemed to make those three huge timbers tremble which sustain the roof of that spacious gallery. The gallery is made of very wide and long timbers. It contains three aisles; the one in the center serves for transit and in the two on the sides the living quarters of both sexes can be seen, but separate, in one the men, and in the other the women and their children, who, as soon as the men had completed their song, began theirs. At 12 we took our leave and embarked in the longboat, accompanied by the sons of Quinquinanis [Wickananish, Spanish spelling] and his father, a venerable old man. All dined with us. In order not to give any cause for suspicion we did not take the dimensions of the gallery, but in view of its length and width and the numerous Indians who assisted at the function I have calculated that it is capable of lodging 900 to 1,000 Indians. By accident I ascertained that the main timbers of the roof are 5⅓ feet in thickness. Each one of the sons has his gallery, but not so large. Besides these there are many others, but all smaller than those mentioned. [Wagner 1933, p. 166].

Verdia, the second pilot, went in a longboat to Haro Strait, where he was surprised by a large body of Indians, with more coming from shore. One Indian went about "animating" the men and distributing arrows. Verdia shot into a canoe when its occupants were trying to attack the longboat with heavy bone spears like harpoons (Wagner 1933, p. 171). The schooner was also attacked by very daring Indians. It is mentioned that these people dressed like the ones at Nootka Sound, but their speech was different. This is an interesting observation, since these contacts were not very conducive to listening for linguistic differences. These aggressive visitors were from the Salish-speaking groups of the Strait of Juan de Fuca and the Gulf of Georgia. This expedition again covered the area that Quimper had mapped the previous year. On 9 September Tutusiasicu, the second son of Wickananish, came from Clayoquot to tell the expedition that Kendrick had sailed ten days before and that Malaspina had been in port for several weeks.

The exploration commanded by Eliza, of which Pantoja so fully recorded his share, ended the major expeditions to the Strait of Juan de Fuca, except for the visit of the *Sutil* and the *Mexicana*. All the principal geographical features had been noted and a fair sampling of the population had been met under various conditions. It was found that the Nootkan-speaking people had a southern boundary and that Salish was also represented on Vancouver Island. The only record of the Spaniards in this area still to be reviewed is the attempted settlement at Neah Bay.

Since the Nootka Sound controversy was not settled, as far as they knew, and they were still seeking a good place for a settlement which could replace Nootka if they were forced to relinquish it, they were looking for a defensible location. This was more important to them than being close to a plentiful sea otter skin trade. For this reason Fidalgo was sent to test the Bahia de Nuñez Gaona (Neah Bay) as a possibility. At Neah Bay he was to erect a respectable fortification and temporary barracks. The spot should be chosen where there was suitable land for sowing crops and getting good water, ballast, and wood. He was ordered to take possession with the customary ceremonies and to treat the natives well, to avoid conflict and persuade them to help with the cultivation. Fidalgo left San Blas on 24 March 1792 in the company of Lopez de Nava, chaplain, Juan de Dios Morelos, surgeon, and Antonio Serrantes, acting first pilot, the whole crew numbering eighty-three men. On 29 May the *Princesa* reached Neah Bay, and Fidalgo began at once building a house for a bakery and an oven; a blacksmith's shop was set up and the trees were cut down within musket range of the site. The longboat was moored close to the shore to permit escape to the frigate, which was anchored in the bay, if there were a strong attack by the Indians. All the buildings were roofed over with grass. I cite these details because during the ensuing summer a number of European ships passing this settlement recorded a variety of observations. Their reactions provide ample reason for not relying on a single report when dealing with the events of history. During the summer of 1792 Joseph Ingraham in the *Hope* was there long enough to invite Fidalgo and his officers for breakfast on his ship. When Bodega y Quadra arrived, he went ashore with him to the settlement, which he stated had "merely a few huts and a tolerably good garden" (Wagner 1933, p. 66). Boit, a mate on the *Columbia*, wrote that he noticed the cross on the beach, about ten houses, and several good gardens (Wagner 1933, p. 66).

The first visitors at the new settlement were the *Sutil* and the *Mexicana*, with Captains Galiano and Valdez. They arrived at the Puerto Nuñez Gaona (Neah Bay) on 6 June and stayed for two days. In contrast to the experience of some of the Spanish explorers in the previous years, the captains found the Indians very friendly and courteous. They observed that the women at Neah Bay were much more attentive to ornament, and this agrees fully with the sketches made by the artist of the expedition. A chief named Taisun, never mentioned elsewhere in the literature, came aboard the *Sutil* and presented the captain with a quantity of sardines. The next day Tetacus (Tatoosh) visited the *Mexicana*. He was served a cup of chocolate, and after tasting it he dipped some bread in it and took it to his wife, Maria, who was in a canoe alongside and refused to board

Fig. 27. Tatoosh and his family. Spanish picture.

the ship. Tetacus examined every part of the ship and ate everything offered him, and recalled the names of the English and Spanish captains who had visited his territory. The next day he asked permission to sail with them to Esquimault, where he had to go on a visit. Maria, his younger wife, again refused to join him on the ship and was supported by the older first wife, so the women traveled in their canoe while Tetacus stayed aboard the ship.

These women have become famous in the literature because their portraits and that of their husband were sketched by Cardero, the artist with the Spanish expedition (fig. 27). Tetacus, like Maquinna, was a leader who became well known to all early explorers and fur traders. In the sketch, he has a very Spanish face, with a formal beard, carefully clipped. He is wearing a hat with whaling scenes and a pear-shaped bulb. He also has a necklace which may consist of small shells, but there is not enough detail for identification. Its entire appearance is an artist's conception; however, the only necklace in the Cook collection in Vienna is

equally strange for the period and setting (Vienna 226; Appendix 1:191).

There are three pictures in the Spanish collection that all represent the wives of Tetacus. One is definitely called the "second wife," and that is probably Maria. The others are referred to only as his wives. All the pictures are very rich in costume and ornamental detail. The "Wife of Tetaku, Chief of Fuca" wears exceptionally long dentalium earrings with small beads at the end of each strand. These may be trade beads. This is also true of her choker necklace of round beads. Beneath this, she has strands of a necklace, possibly made of small pieces of dentalium, that do not show the tapering of the shell, with a small dark bead between which again may be a trade bead. Her hair is shoulder length, parted in the middle of the head and hanging loose. She is wearing a twined cedar bark cape edged with fur. She also has a very Caucasoid face. Another picture shows a woman with a child. The mother looks somewhat like the woman identified as Tetacus's second wife. Her ornaments are similar to those of the others and she is wearing a shredded cedar bark cape edged with fur. The child also has a cedar bark garment, fastened with two bands of patterned weaving. The infant's head is wrapped to deform it in a peaked shape which Boas, when he saw it among the Kwakiutl, called "sugar loaf" form, referring to the cone-shaped package in which sugar was once sold in Europe. Cardero could only have seen this during the last days of the circumnavigation of Vancouver Island by the *Sutil* and the *Mexicana*, because this type of deformation is limited to the Kwakiutl.

The "Second Wife of Tetaku" has many interesting features. Although she also has a very Caucasoid face, she has a thoroughly native ornament—a nose piece. It is a small circular pendant that does not appear to be of native material. It has a serrated edge and resembles the centerpiece of Tetacus's necklace. She is wearing a basketry hat of the same shape as those with the whaling scenes, but instead of the pear-shaped bulb on top there is a cluster of finely trimmed feathers or very thin strips of tanned skin. This type of decoration is also shown in a figure of a man (fig. 30) collected by Vancouver (Gunther 1960, p. 10, fig. 3*b*). The hat also has unusual decoration on its sides, consisting of small pieces of dentalium shell sewn onto the surface in a design which is also not traditional. It seems too complicated for an artist to have devised, so it must have been on his model. She has long earrings, each with three rows of beads that are shaped like trade beads. She is wearing the same kind of many-stranded choker as the others. Her cedar bark cloak has a fringe of skin at the upper edge, and about eight inches below that is a band, possibly of painted skin, with the geometric designs that were used as fillers on the whaling scene hats (BM NWC 7; Appendix 1:137). The design is vaguely reminiscent of a geometric Chilkat blanket (Appendix 2, weaving). Her right shoulder is bare and she wears an armlet of the same texture as her cape, edged with decoration like that on the hat. Her hair hangs loose to the shoulders.

These ladies followed the ships in their canoe, which probably was a large one supplied with enough paddlers to swiftly make the trip to the north shore of the Strait of Juan de Fuca.

When they stopped at Rada de Eliza (Pedder Bay on Vancouver Island), some Indians came alongside with woolen blankets to barter for copper. Vernaci, the officer who was dealing with them, had no copper, so Tetacus took off four well-made copper bracelets he was wearing and gave them to Vernaci to use. Woolen blankets have been mentioned very often in these contacts with Salish groups, and this agrees perfectly with the ethnographies of the nineteenth century. These villages were famous for the large heavy blankets they wove of mountain goat wool, dog wool, duck down, and fireweed cotton (see Appendix 2).

On reaching Esquimault, Tetacus waited for his wives, and when they arrived he took very cordial leave from the ship and went ashore to join them. The canoe in which they came had a large carving of a young eagle at the prow. There is a drawing of such a canoe in the Bauza collection (Museo Naval, plate #12, Book 1, p. 8), titled "Vista del Puerto Nuñez Gaona" (Wagner 1933, p. 242) (fig. 28). The bird is set behind a straight, perpendicular prow, which the Northwest Coast canoes do not have. The straight stern is more plausible, but is found more frequently in the vicinity of the Columbia River. The canoe is full of people, with seven paddlers on one side. A man standing in the center of the boat wears a hat with the traditional pear-shaped bulb that characterizes Nootka hats and a cape over his right shoulder. There are several other hats but only one, on the figure in the stern, clearly has the bulb-shaped top. The landscape is even more difficult to reconcile. The arrangement of the houses on the shore, including the two fenced areas, is identical with a picture of the second establishment at Nootka (Novo y Colson 1884, plate 21). Although Fidalgo states that he set up six guns

Fig. 28. Spanish settlement at Neah Bay (Nuñez Gaona). Spanish picture.

on a small fortification, the gun in the picture is opposite the settlement and would be of no use in an Indian attack on the shore, but the arrangement of the armament does resemble that at San Miguel in Nootka Sound.

Soon after this pleasant excursion, the fate of the settlement at Neah Bay was decided by a conference held on board the *Princesa* in the harbor of Nuñez Gaona. They decided to abandon the settlement attempt because the location was not defensible and their neighbors, the Indians, were not very cooperative, in spite of the friendliness of their chief. Since the buildings were so temporary, no signs of former occupation were left when the next Europeans came to the spot. But in Portage Creek, which is mentioned in the Spanish accounts, some bricks were found which were definitely of Mexican manufacture, and which the Spaniards had unloaded along the banks for future use. One such brick is in the Smithsonian Institution.

On his second voyage to the Northwest Coast, Gray, having gone around the world in returning to Boston from the first, came back to Clayoquot Sound on 5 June 1791. As soon as his ships were refurbished he sailed north and traded in the Queen Charlotte Islands (see chap. 5). On an exploring trip to the mainland, some of his crew were killed by Indians in Portland Canal. He returned to Clayoquot for the winter and, taking a lesson from Meares, built a sloop at his moorage.

While Gray was building the *Adventure*, he and his companions also had an opportunity to observe at close hand the activity of the Indians during this season and to find out many customs that do not readily appear on a short visit in the summer. The area was estimated to have a population of about three thousand, more than that around Nootka Sound. Wickananish's village was about three leagues from Adventure Cove, and Captain Hannah was about nine leagues away but still under the jurisdiction of Wickananish. Pantoja described a Clayoquot house but could not give its dimensions. Boit supplies the dimensions of the main house in the village, belonging to the chief. It was eighty feet long, forty feet wide, and twelve feet high, with a flat roof. The chief's seat was elevated about two feet above the others and had a canopy ornamented with animal teeth (it was probably carved of wood). The furniture consisted mainly of mats and wooden boxes, in some of which they boiled fish with hot stones. Many of the boxes were also decorated with "pearl shells"—probably the opercula of the sea snail. Many boxes were filled with dried fish and stored under the bed platforms on which they slept, rolled in furs, on a stack of mats.

On 1 January 1792, when the visitors arrived, Wickananish was surrounded by a company of about one hundred elderly men. The women had an apartment of their own, where they were weaving the shredded cedar bark garments seen everywhere on the coast. The meal, served in wooden bowls, consisted of fish mixed with berries and seasoned with train oil. The serving was carried out by men "of lower orders." When the men were finished with the meal, the remainder was taken to the women. Polygamy was allowed, but only wealthy men could afford it. From the small number of children around the house, it seemed that the women were not prolific.

The following week a chief from the Strait of Juan de Fuca came to visit. He was married to a sister of Wickananish. They brought many furs with them and he told them that a Spanish ship was in the strait.

Later in the month the ship's officers visited Tatoochkasettle, a brother of Wickananish. They found all the men bathing on the beach early in the morning. That day Wickananish was to give his eldest son his name and take another for himself. About one hundred men were assembled on the beach. They all wore blankets fastened around the loins with a girdle and reaching halfway down the thighs, and their hair was clubbed and tied at the back of the head into a knob decorated with a thick bunch of feathers. Their faces and bodies were painted a dark red, and they wore shredded cedar bark wound around their knees and ankles. They gathered near the water in tiers of four, and at each end of the rows stood women who accompanied the singing with rattles made of copper boxes with small stones in them. The procession moved from the end of the village, the front men "squatting on their hams" and the others standing erect, with the chief's brothers upon their shoulders, who were dancing and running from side to side, in that position, while those under them were in continual motion. The chief stayed in front, giving commands. All their voices kept perfect time with the rattling of the boxes. Such a box rattle, an oblong made of thin wood, is in the Nootka collection at the Thomas Burke Memorial Washington State Museum and was collected by James G. Swan during his residence at Neah Bay in the 1860s.

When they arrived at the chief's house they entered in single file, and Boit, who described the ceremony, wrote, "I followed to see the transaction inside." During the procession the rest of the inhabitants were seated along the beach, viewing the spectacle. When the company moved into the chief's house, they probably also filled all the space left vacant by the dancers. About thirty of the principal actors were seated in a circle and were given a board and small sticks which they used as a drum. The whole company began to sing and dance. Here Boit stopped, just when further description would have been very enlightening to modern ethnographers (Boit 1921, p. 101).

There are a number of ceremonial details here that are recorded in modern studies. Many ceremonies start with a procession from the beach to the house of the chief or wealthy man who is the host. The squatting position is familiar from other Nootkan ceremonies, especially the wolf ritual. Women's shaking rattles and singing is common in many Northwest Coast festivals.

When the sloop *Adventure* was completed Robert Haswell was assigned to take her on a trading trip to the Queen Charlotte Islands to follow up connections that Gray had established there on his previous visits. He left early in March 1792. Gray prepared to leave soon afterward, but before his departure an incident occurred that must be related here. Even though friendly relations existed during the winter months at Clayoquot, a plot was discovered while Gray's ship was beached for repairs. An Indian persuaded a Hawaiian boy in the crew to wet the muskets and steal the bullets to allow the Indians to plunder the ship and kill the crew. The plot was discovered in time and was not carried out.

Boit records the following retaliation in closing his account of their stay at Clayoquot Sound:

> I am sorry to be under the necessity of remarking that this day, March 27, 1792, I was sent with three boats all well manned and armed to destroy the village of Opitsatah. It was a command I was no ways tenacious of, and am grieved to think that Capt. Gray should let his passions go so far. This village was about half a mile in diameter, and contained upwards of 200 houses, generally well built for Indians; every door that you'd enter was in resemblance to a human and beasts head, the passage being through the mouth, besides which there was much more rude carved work about the dwellings, some of which by no means inelegant. This fine village, the work of ages was in a short time totally destroyed. [Boit 1919–20, p. 243]

Requiem for an Indian village! This event was also mentioned by Vancouver (1798, 1:215).

After the *Adventure* departed, Gray took the *Columbia* south, and it was on this occasion that he met Vancouver near the entrance of the Strait of Juan de Fuca on 29 April 1792. He found Gray's Harbor, and on 11 May he found the Columbia River, which he named for his ship. This event is generally regarded as the "discovery" of this great waterway, but it was first seen in 1775 by Heceta, who called it Rio San Roque.

During the years 1775 to 1792, traffic passed the entrance of the Strait of Juan de Fuca, and there were some abortive attempts to explore this body of water, but no one went beyond the section now known as Admiralty Inlet until Vancouver, with his characteristic thoroughness, came in 1792. By this time Gray (1789) had gone as far as Clallam Bay, Quimper (1790) to Port Discovery, Eliza (1791) into the Gulf of Georgia, and the *Sutil* and the *Mexicana* (1792) to the channel between Lummi Island and the mainland.

After the ship had entered the Strait of Juan de Fuca along the southern shore, Puget relates their contact with the natives called the Classet. These Indians were the ancestors of the Makah of today. They came to the ships bringing their fishing gear, implements, and garments which they wished to trade for copper, iron, and yellow buttons (Puget 1938, p. 189). That these were probably brass buttons is substantiated by the entry in the *New Vancouver Journal* where they were called "metal" buttons (Bell 1914, p. 84). In the group was a chief who was conspicuous in a "greatcoat" decorated with yellow buttons in the seams and wherever they would show well. This is the first note of buttons being used in this manner, a style that was widely adopted on the Northwest Coast after pearl buttons came into the trade and were used to outline the applique on woolen blankets. There are many references to the Indians' desire for brass uniform buttons in trade.

Puget's use of the term greatcoat is questionable. It probably was an ample cape of woven shredded cedar bark, which when new is often stiff and looks voluminous. If it was really a greatcoat, it was gotten in trade (Puget, 1939, p. 189). Less detailed entries were made by Vancouver and Menzies, the former noting a small village at Tatoosh Island and a larger one at Neah Bay where the Indians looked like those at Nootka Sound (Vancouver 1798,2:218).

In the records of this part of their survey there are four journals for a period of two weeks. The contributors are Vancouver, Menzies, Puget, and Bell, the author of the *New Vancouver Journal*. The combined observations of these authors provide rich detail about the Indians of this area.

Vancouver mentions that while they were sailing along the coast near Dungeness the Indians who were busy fishing ignored the vessels, and adds that perhaps sailing ships were no novelty to them (Vancouver 1798, 2:225). Others followed the ships to trade skins for copper and clothing with brass buttons, and they also asked for muskets and swords. The large canoes carried household equipment and had bladders of whale oil (Baker n.d., Ad 55/32, ms. No pagination). He noted that the people in these canoes were not Nootkan speaking, which was a correct observation, for they were now among the Salish-speaking Klallam. During this time Puget was out in a longboat looking for a good harbor. He found Discovery Bay, used as an anchorage two years before by Quimper, who called it Quadra's Bay. The expedition moved into this splendid harbor and stayed there for two weeks while longboats were sent out on exploratory expeditions to Admiralty Inlet, Puget Sound, and Hood Canal. In Discovery Bay they found a Klallam village site near an oyster bed that was still remembered by informants in the late 1920s (Gunther 1927, p. 1).

The entry into Admiralty Inlet, as pictured in Vancouver's narrative shows the landscape at its best, with Mount Rainier clearly in sight. In the foreground the artist shows a pole which is one of a pair with a net stretched between them to entangle flying ducks (Vancouver 1798, 2:225).

While the ships were anchored at Discovery Bay the Klallam came daily with fresh fish, which they traded for trinkets. Vancouver and Menzies went to Protection Island, where they commented on the beautiful meadows, which reminded them of English landscape. Vancouver also wrote of the "sportsmen" in the party who hunted with no success, so that their friends were very pleased when the Indians brought venison to vary their fish diet.

These people wore less paint on their faces and bodies than those Vancouver had seen when he was at Nootka Sound with the Cook expedition. They wore ear ornaments but no nose rings. Their clothing included some tanned skins, but more of them wore clothing which they wove of dog wool and the wool of the mountain goat. This is the area where the wool dog was bred, and its fleece was mixed with mountain goat wool, the down of ducks, and the cotton of fireweed to create an unusual blanket for clothing and bedding (Appendix 2). They had no furs to trade (Vancouver 1798, 2:231).

Since their visit to this area extended to about two weeks, they had occasion to see the Indians often and to visit many small villages. Although clothing was worn, there were also times when the men, like the Nootka, found complete nakedness more agreeable. The first two weeks of May were by no means tropical, but with their hardiness they found the weather very pleasant. However, the women seemed very modest and were always clothed, at least in the presence of guests. Many small settlements were found unoccupied, and some appeared to have been left only recently. There were many signs of burials, such as small canoes lashed to the trees and scattered bones on sandspits. There were signs of cremation, but the Klallam of the 1920s staunchly denied ever having had this practice (Gunther 1927, p. 247). Vancouver found a deserted village site that could have been occupied by about one hundred persons in houses of Nootka style, where human bones were lying in the weeds. There were many epidemics of new diseases like measles and smallpox that were not recorded, and a small community could be so reduced in numbers that the survivors fled, leaving the dead unburied.

In addition to bartering fish and other food, the Indians gladly sold their arrows, bows, and fishing tackle, which were always in the canoes. Mr. Hewitt, of the Vancouver expedition, gathered a number of pieces from this general area. Many do not have exact locations, and two or three possibilities within the region are named. He has two composite bows from Port Discovery (BM, Vancouver 6; Hewitt ms. 253: Appendix 1:319) and several arrows (BM, Vancouver 30; Hewitt ms. 249) with barbed bone points that have counterparts elsewhere (see Appendix 1:273, 274).

While they inspected Discovery Bay, Menzies, the botanist, found some trees that had been felled by fire, which he assumed had been used for making canoes. On the following day he found some that had been cut by an ax, which surprised him because he felt certain the Indians had no axes; however, he did not know that Quimper had been there in 1790 (Menzies 1923, pp. 20–21). On 8 May, Menzies, Vancouver, and Johnstone were near Hadlock and each mentioned seeing poles fifteen feet high with human heads on them. Each saw two such poles, and at the same time Puget, who was not far away, saw three poles with human skulls on them. Whether these were the same ones is uncertain, for Puget was not traveling with the others, and although this discrepancy is not important, it makes one realize that these records are not always scientifically accurate (Menzies 1923, p. 25; Vancouver 1798, 2:235; Puget 1939, p. 182). The following day, 9 May, they all agreed that it rained!

The rain brought very "tempestuous" weather, as Puget recorded it, and the place where he encountered it he called Foulweather Bluff. Here he found seventeen Indians, who had no sea otter skins but wanted to sell their bows and arrows and woolen and skin garments. Mr. Hewitt did not mark any purchases as from this place, but it is possible that some of the unlocated pieces may have come from here. Puget gives some excellent details of appearance when he calls attention to the Indians' conically shaped heads and their long hair rubbed with oil and red ocher. He also found a man with a beard. Although wispy beards are sometimes seen in the northern population of the Northwest Coast, facial hair was very uncommon in this southern region. They wore square pieces of shell in their ears, and they also had small rolls of copper, a feature not mentioned elsewhere, but found occasionally in archaeological sites in western Washington. Their skin garments were tied on one shoulder (Puget 1939, p. 183). Vancouver adds that the Indians brought small square boxes of water to the ship but refused to sell the boxes (Vancouver 1798, 2:237).

Although the Indians of this region did not have the more highly developed material culture of the north and were seen principally at their fishing sites, Mr. Hewitt brought away some of the most interesting pieces available from any place the Vancouver expedition visited. Since I have covered this area in an article published in a journal,[1] I will use an excerpt from it here.

The pieces in the Hewitt collection which originated at Port Discovery have more variety and interest than those from the Strait of Juan de Fuca.

1. *Pacific Northwest Quarterly*, vol. 51, no. 1, January 1960.

In the manuscript catalog this material is preceded by sixteen pieces from Nootka Sound, with two blank numbers between. The inventory consists of two composite bows, arrows, a war club, two halibut hooks, a scoop or dipper, a rattle, and a necklace of bird beaks.

Since bows are often mentioned as items of barter, it is strange that only two should remain in the Hewitt collection. These bows, both of which are from the same place, are very short (22½ to 24 inches long) and composite. The description of the longer one in the catalog of the British Museum reads as follows:

> A small recurved composite bow, almost semicircular curve. Flat plano-convex section, broadest at grip where it is bound with thong lashing, near which the wood is entirely broken, leaving the bow supported by the sinew only. The breadth narrows toward the ends, which are nocked and strengthened on concave side by white horn lashed with reddened sinew. At one end both horn and sinew have come away from the wood. The whole concave side [which, when the bow is strung, would be convex] is backed with layers of sinew moulded longitudinally. There is no string.

Many features of these bows are contrary to local conditions. The bows of the Klallam are about three feet long and may be longer if designed for use by a strong man. In the Gulf of Georgia area recurved tips are common.[2] A short bow was probably held horizontally; this fairly universal trait is recorded in many ethnographies.

There are only two arrows in the bundle as represented by Hewitt. One has three feathers, and both have long detachable barbed points of bone. Of these features, the feathers indicate the inner Strait, while the foreshafts link them with the Makah.

Included in the "implements" mentioned in the journals were two bent halibut hooks, a familiar item among all coast Indians who have access to halibut banks. These hooks are described in the ethnography of the Klallam, and so finding them in a collection of 1792 gives this type of hook some historic continuity.[3]

The only household utensil from this point is a scoop or dipper made of horn, probably mountain sheep. The shape is typical of wooden dippers in more recent collections. It is seldom that household pieces occur in these early collections because the trading was generally done by the men and they usually had only their own gear with them when visiting the ships.

Whale bone war clubs generally originated with Nootkan tribes, but

2. Homer Barnett, *Culture element distributions*. IX: *Gulf of Georgia Salish*. University of California Anthropological Records, vol. 1, no. 5 (1939), p. 245.

3. Gunther, *Klallam ethnography*, p. 202.

they are found archaeologically throughout the Northwest. However, the specimen in the Hewitt collection from Port Discovery does not conform to the common type, which is straight and flat; this one is slightly curved.[4] The use of the animal head as part of the handle and the perforation for a wrist thong resemble the standard form, as does the geometric design along the center of the lower part of the blade. The animal head customarily used is that of a bird, but on this club the figure is interpreted as a fish; in fact, the catalog of the British Museum goes on to state that "the back of the blade is ornamented by an incised pattern which seems to represent whales' tails and fishes' eyes conventionalized." The barb at the far end is most unusual. In spite of these deviations, it would be more likely that the piece was traded from the west coast of Vancouver Island than that it was made by the local Klallam. A war club is mentioned in the Klallam ethnography, but it is described as a little over a foot long. It is fastened to the wrist with a thong.

The most important piece in the collection from Port Discovery is a rattle made of mountain sheep horn with a handle of wood.[5] Dalton includes a picture of it,[6] and Franks describes it in the museum catalog as follows:

> Rattle with handle of hard brown wood, carved at the butt end to represent a bird's head. The upper end is oval, and made of horn, perforated where it joins the handle and secured by cord and birch bark; it contains a number of small stones(?). The horn is ornamented with carved designs; on both sides a face is represented, but the two designs are different. Locality: Nootka Sound.

There are two items in this description which must be questioned. The handle is wrapped with two-ply cord of nettle fiber and some pieces of split cedar bark, not birch bark, and the locality attributed to it by Dalton does not agree with the Hewitt catalog, to which Dalton must have had access. Even without this argument, the character of the rattle itself puts it into a Salish rather than a Nootkan setting. The Cowichans, especially, have rattles of this general type, and it might be suggested that this piece came from southern Vancouver Island, for the Klallam are closely related to the Songish and other tribes of that area.

This piece, like all those of the Cook and Vancouver expeditions which have any designs on them, shows a well-developed art which exhibits the principal stylistic features of the Northwest Coast art of the historic period. Both sides of the rattle are deeply carved with a technique that indicates mastery of the medium. The designs differ on the two sides,

4. British Museum Ethnological Document 1126; BM, Vancouver 94.

5. British Museum Ethnological Document 1126; BM, Vancouver 158.

6. Dalton, "Notes," plate 15, fig. 19.

but both are faces. The round eye is often found on coast Salish stone carving, and late in the nineteenth century it was developed in an exaggerated form on the masks of the Cowichan. The nostrils are indicated by two arched lines not deeply cut. The face is filled with designs which may be parts of the creature's body.

The final piece in the group from Port Discovery is a small ornament made of birds' beaks strung on a leather thong. It is too short for a necklace but may have been attached to another thong fastened around the neck. The use of beaks, and claws of birds and animals, is common in this area. It is unfortunate that the bills are not identified.

While anchored in Discovery Bay, Vancouver and his men went on boat expeditions which resulted in several excellent and observant accounts of the Indians they met.[7] The pieces collected during this part of the voyage are listed by Hewitt as from Admiralty Inlet and Restoration Point. The collection from Admiralty Inlet consists entirely of arrows, and these arrows are divided into entries: one entry is for two pieces for which no alternate location is given; the other is for a bundle of ten arrows which might also be from the Columbia River. Two features unify this group, in contrast to those discussed from the Strait of Juan de Fuca: all have three feathers, while the majority of the Strait arrows have two, and the Admiralty Inlet arrows have no foreshafts. The two arrows with no other location have long barbed bone points; six in the bundle of ten have flaked and chipped stone tips; the tips for the remainder are missing. The stone points are triangular in shape. By these definitions, three which are alternately located as Columbia River can be included in the Admiralty Inlet group.

The detailed discussion of the arrows of this collection may be tedious, but it is ethnographically and archaeologically important. These are the only hafted arrows definitely known to have been collected in the eighteenth century in this area. Thousands of arrowheads may be found, both in professional excavation and as surface finds, but the arrowhead is really only half the story. Just as those collected by the Vancouver expedition differ from the ones described by Swan perhaps no more than eighty years later, so modern ethnographic information may also deal with a later style. Furthermore, its validity as far as arrows are concerned is questionable, since as early as 1917 it was almost impossible to find an Indian among the Puget Sound tribes old enough to have used an arrow seriously.

Like the Port Discovery material, the collections from Restoration Point (on Bainbridge Island) offer variety. There are the ubiquitous arrows, a stone hammer, hearths for fire making, a wooden dish, a halibut

7. Vancouver, *Voyage*, 1: 235 ff.; Puget, *Journal*, p. 185.

hook, and, most significant, some mountain goat horn bracelets, a comb, and a small carved wooden figure. Vancouver himself was in the group that visited the Restoration Point village, which he described as consisting of mat shelters and having all the characteristics of a temporary abode. He noted that the Indians were "rooting up this beautiful verdant meadow in quest of a species of wild onions and other roots." For trade they brought their bows and arrows, woolen and skin garments, and a few indifferent sea otter skins. Vancouver wished they had brought more eatables such as venison, wild fowl, or fish, since "our sportsmen and fishermen had little success."

There is no indication that any piece in the Hewitt collection was specifically in this exchange of goods. For trade goods Vancouver's men gave hawk's bells, buttons, and copper. It is disturbing that no reference can be found in the literature to such extraordinary pieces as are listed for Restoration Point in contrast to what had already been secured from this region. Only the rattle obtained at Port Discovery is of the same quality as several of these items, and all can be regarded as gotten in trade from other Indian tribes and not of local origin.

Before we deal with these unusual pieces, the truly local ones should be discussed. Among them are two hearth pieces of fire drills, each with a number of holes on one side. They are made of cedar, a soft wood, and are from five to six inches long. A lateral hammer of dark grey stone, flat at both ends, is typical of those found in this area. There is also a crude fishhook, about eight inches long, made of a branch with very little trimming and no carving.

Among the unusual pieces is a double comb with six teeth at one end and eight at the other.[8] In the center is a carved rectangle which is slightly convex. The carving is deep and well done. It can be interpreted as a face, split down the center, and its details resemble the style of carving on the rattle from Port Discovery. The rattle may have originated among the Cowichan of Vancouver Island, and the distribution of carved wooden combs given by Barnet[9] would make this a possible provenance for the comb as well. The comb also resembles one illustrated by Dalton as part of the collection from Cross Sound, Alaska.[10]

Equally surprising is a small wooden dish representing a man on his back with his knees drawn up and flattened (fig. 29).[11] The body is scooped out; the head is in the form of a mask, concave on the back. The arms are laid along the sides with the hands on the thighs. In general

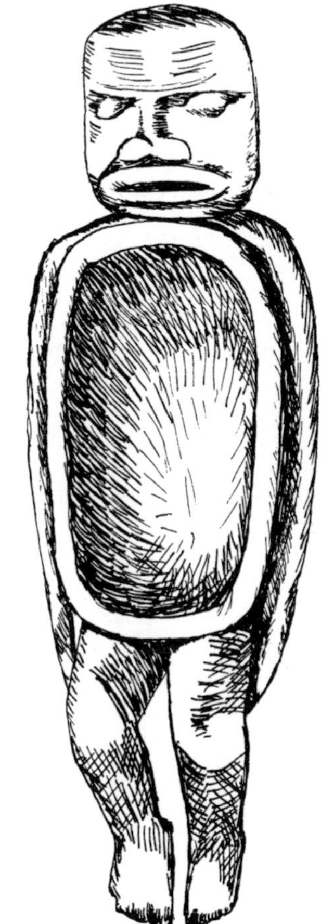

Fig. 29. Food dish, human figure, Restoration Point, Puget Sound. Hewitt collection (Vancouver), BM, Vancouver 161 (Appendix 1:62).

8. British Museum Ethnological Document 1126; BM, Vancouver 219.

9. Barnett, *Gulf of Georgia Salish*, 249.

10. Dalton, "Notes," plate 15, fig. 18.

11. British Museum Ethnological Document 1126; BM, Vancouver 161.

form this piece resembles the Tsonoqwa dishes of the Kwakiutl.[12] It is a well-used grease dish of definitely northern style.

The most extraordinary pieces of the group designated as from Restoration Point are eight mountain goat horn bracelets. Such bracelets are found sporadically throughout the Northwest Coast tribes and probably were much more common before copper was plentiful and before silver and gold bracelets were made, especially in the north. Vancouver frequently noted that the Indians visiting the ships were dressed in woolens "of their own manufacture," by which he can only mean mountain goat wool garments. He mentions the use of dog hair, but since this was always mixed with wool, the Indians must have had more ready access to hunting areas for mountain goat than the informants in modern ethnographies lead one to believe. Therefore, if they had large amounts of mountain goat wool, they could also get the horns used in these bracelets. Along the same line of argument, even though the collections are scanty, it is strange that an occasional mountain goat horn spoon was not found. These spoons, carved or plain, are plentiful in later collections.

Granted that the Puget Sound tribes could get the mountain goat horns, it is difficult to believe that the carving on these bracelets was done in the region where they were supposedly collected. One is a very simple bracelet with the edges delineated by short parallel lines, similar to the designs found on the mountain goat horn spoons which originate farther north in the upper reaches of the rivers—for instance, the Athapascan-made spoons in the upper Stikine. This same edge is used on many silver bracelets which have more elaborate designs in the center. A second bracelet, having this simple edge, has a curvilinear design with spur lines (like those often found in Eskimo carving) running out alternately from the center line.

The other six bracelets are much more formal in design, but they are always within the conventions of the Northwest Coast art, so that no one can doubt the general area from which they come. The eye motif is apparent in all, though it is not developed in its most highly stylized form. On one bracelet the eye pattern is combined with a curvilinear design running through the center of the bracelet, uniting the simpler style just mentioned with the more distinctive Northwest Coast art motifs. The bracelets depend on the spring of the horn to keep them fastened and allow a small overlap with the upper part tapering toward the end. This tapered part is reminiscent of the end of the well-carved mountain goat horn spoon, as one finds it in collections from the northern tribes in the nineteenth century. All together, it is strange that these first examples of well-carved work which fell into the hands of the Vancouver expedition

12. Washington State Museum, Portland Art Museum.

should not have been mentioned in any of the journals. This is true not only of these bracelets, but also of the dish and comb described above and of the small figure which is the last piece in this collection.

This final piece (fig. 30), which is located as from Restoration Point but which in style does not belong there, is a small wooden figure fourteen and one-half inches tall. It is a human figure, standing erect with hands on the breast.[13] The arms are poorly carved and proportioned as is customary in many Northwest Coast figures. The eyes and mouth protrude, with the nose straight and broad at the base, resembling the spirit figure of the Coast Salish. The figure is exceptionally detailed in the back and buttocks. The upper legs are quite cylindrical, and the well-marked knees are bent slightly forward and are flattened on the kneecap. This trait is also common in Northwest carving. In the abdomen is an incision with some fragments of glass imbedded in the sides. The figure wears a conical hat, inlaid with small bits of copper, and out of the top of the crown appear some tassels of leather, a few strung with small beads. This same feature was commented on in the Spanish picture of the second wife of Tetacus.

Through this detail it is possible to find a more plausible explanation for the presence of this figure in a Puget Sound village than it is for any of the other extraneous pieces. The magical and supernatural qualities of crystals recur often in the mythology of the Northwest Coast and are embodied by the Nootka and Kwakiutl in the manufacturing of these figures. They represent spirits and were "sent" as invitations to guests and returned by the latter on their arrival at the feast. In this case the crystals were replaced by glass, at that time a more precious commodity.

It is likely that an important person among the people at Restoration Point had received such a message to come to a feast, for these invitations were sent out a year or two in advance. Since the feast was probably still in the future and the recipient anxious for some of the trade goods which the figure would bring, he may have decided to part with the piece and let the future take care of itself. Or, if this was not the case, he may have bartered the figure from another tribe to whom its meaning, perhaps, was not known or was ignored. The figure does not resemble anything known in Puget Sound culture, for it is not even of the style of the small shaman's figures, best illustrated by Wingert.[14]

This review of part of the Hewitt collection shows its meagerness, but also its importance in any historical reconstruction of the ethnography of

Fig. 30. Small figure of a man, Restoration Point, Puget Sound. Hewitt collection (Vancouver), BM, Vancouver 160 (Appendix 1:10).

13. British Museum Ethnological Document 1126; BM, Vancouver 160, Appendix 1:10.

14. Paul S. Wingert, *American Indian Sculpture*, plates 1–23.

Puget Sound. It deals with objects not found archaeologically and shows the earliest responses to European trade goods. It is significant that metal-tipped arrows were traded back to the expedition so soon after iron became more generally available. The meagerness of the Puget Sound material, with the bulk of it obviously having been traded in, is an important aspect of the cultural level of the area. Modern ethnographic data show that these people were very simple in their material production, but that they placed great emphasis on their guardian spirit cult and shamanistic practices. Unlike other Northwest Coast cultures, they did not produce much in the arts, for their ceremonial gear did not include masks or elaborate costumes.

The Vancouver expedition was unfortunate in the time of year they visited this area, for the majority of villages they saw were "deserted" and the Indians they met were either in temporary locations or on their way to fishing sites. With both parties on the move, the contact was not conducive to detailed study. The material collected as the expedition proceeded northward is richer because there is more in the culture from which to select, again giving the analysis of modern ethnographers a historical depth which archaeology alone cannot supply. The simplicity of the Puget Sound Indians does not seem to be due to an early breakdown of the culture, but rather is of long standing. They did not turn their efforts to making objects, but devoted themselves to the development of religious ideas.

With the careful work of Vancouver and his shipmates, in this instance especially Lieutenant Puget, the survey of the great body of water within the entrance of the Strait of Juan de Fuca was finally completed; and the charts produced are still accurate, except where present-day needs have changed the landscape, such as the filling in of bays and the building of jetties. Now the expedition sailed back to the Pacific Ocean and, turning south, examined the first large bay, Gray's Harbor. They had been preceded there by Gray himself, who named and inspected this bay on 11 May 1792. For this part of Gray's voyage there is only the account of Boit, because at this time the other faithful diarist, Haswell, was in command of the *Adventure* on a trading trip to the Queen Charlotte Islands. Boit records that the Indians appeared in canoes with the men all carrying quivers and bows. The canoes were crudely made dugouts with upright ends. The men were naked and the women wore a small apron made of rushes (probably fringed shredded cedar bark). Boit gives the same description of the Chinook, and while this could be a common style of dress or undress in this region, it might also indicate that Chinook were in Gray's Harbor. They were frequently there during the nineteenth century. Furthermore, Boit comments that, although these people understood a little Nootkan, when they spoke to each other they used a language which he had never heard. This could have been Chehalis, a Salish language, or Chinook.

When Gray entered the mouth of the Columbia River, he crossed the bar and proceeded upstream to a location between Chinook Point and Point Ellice, where a large Chinook village was located, whose chief was named Polack, probably an English corruption of his Chinook name. While they were moored at this point Indian canoes were constantly around the vessel with many furs for trading. The people were very polite and the trading was pleasant and profitable. Boit commented on the fine build of the men and said that the women were pretty, a term that was rarely applied. Like the Chinook seen at Gray's Harbor, the men appeared naked and the women wore an apron that first appeared to be a leaf; but Boit added that some of the gentlemen examined the garment very closely and decided that it was not a leaf, but was of woven material (Boit 1921, pp. 34–35).

In October, Vancouver came into this harbor with the *Daedalus*, the storeship, as part of his expedition. Their crew also helped in the survey. The ships with Lieutenant Whidbey in command entered Gray's Harbor and named all the prominent features of the bay, including Point Hanson for the lieutenant of the *Daedalus*. Whidbey estimated that about one hundred persons lived in the Indian village. He thought they spoke Nootkan, but he was sure it was not their own language. The principal contact between Whidbey and the Indians was trading for salmon, sturgeon, geese, and ducks. Some birds were also supplied by the "sportsmen" in the company, who had better luck here than in the Strait of Juan de Fuca. Whidbey also mentioned the Indians' canoes, but added a feature that either was not in use when Boit saw them or was neglected in his account. In addition to the crudeness of the canoes, Whidbey mentions that they were furnished with rudely cut boards set at each end about three feet above the gunwales. They were perforated and the warriors could shoot arrows through the holes without exposing themselves. Their arrows were pointed with iron, copper, and shell, and some were barbed (Vancouver 1798, 2:79–84). In the Hewitt collection at the British Museum there are five arrows that could be from Gray's Harbor. They all have other designations as well, Admiralty Inlet, and Strait of Juan de Fuca being the most frequent. One feature they have in common is the lack of painting in the feathered area of the shaft. They are all feathered, and all but one have a detachable foreshaft of wood (see Appendix 1).

From Gray's Harbor the expedition moved south to the Columbia River, and Vancouver finally became convinced that it existed and was worth inspecting. He decided that Broughton should take the *Chatham* over the bar at its mouth and investigate the river as far as he considered feasible. This was not an easy task, and the incredible number of sloughs created much difficulty. Broughton left the *Chatham* near the mouth of the river and took longboats for his survey. He traveled about one hundred miles on the river and carefully observed the geographical features along the way. For miles he found no Indians, but he saw deserted houses and many burial sites. These were often on islands. At the point where Gray ended his visit to the river, Broughton named a bay for him. At Puget's Island and Swaine's River they saw four canoes of Indians who were dressed in deerskins and a little sea otter fur. At this point Broughton felt he was approaching a more populated area. The canoes followed him to Mount Coffin, which was surrounded with canoe burials. On the banks of the Rushleigh River there was a large Indian village from which canoes came out; the Indians ordered them to stop and said that if they went farther south their heads would be chopped off. The next day they passed several villages, and about twenty-five canoes with approximately one hundred and fifty Indians came out to join them. That day Broughton took possession of the region, and the Indian chief assisted, drinking to the king! Then the chief and his people accompanied them down the river. They returned to Baker's Bay, which Broughton named for the captain of the *Jenny*, one of the fur trading vessels they had met at Nootka Sound.

Generally the Indians of this region differed only slightly from those they had seen at Willapa (Gray's Harbor). They appeared to use more body paint and more feather ornaments. They all smoked pipes with bowls cut out of hardwood and stems about two feet long. They smoked a mild herb (*Kinnikkinnick*) which was pulverized in a mortar and tasted a little like tobacco. Broughton thought that trading, especially in tobacco, would be very profitable in this region (Vancouver 1798, 2:77). When Broughton returned to the *Chatham* they joined the *Discovery* and sailed to California.

The discovery of this great river was shrouded in mystery for so long that its use can almost better be dated from its "opening" by the two visits in 1792 of Gray and Broughton. After that some fur traders wintered in Baker Bay, which was called at that time Deception Bay and which together with Cape Disappointment reflected the earlier conceptions of the area. This bay is a somewhat sheltered part of the mouth of the Columbia River. There they became acquainted with the Chinook, but unfortunately they left few records. Among them was Captain Charles Bishop, who spent the winter of 1795 there with his vessel the *Ruby*. A short diary of his is extant, but it stops at the beginning of this winter. The activity increased as the eighteenth century came to its end, and the fur trade of the region not only depended on ships but also drew on the products of the interior. In the first decade of the nineteenth century Lewis and Clark spent the winter at Clatsop, on the south side of the river, and soon after that the continental fur trade developed rapidly. In all the diaries written in this period the Chinook villages were mentioned, but few ethnographic details can be gathered. To get a more complete picture of the Chinook it is necessary to go further into the nineteenth century and use the work of Peter Corney. As an officer of a fur trading company, he came to the mouth of the Columbia River in June 1814 in his ship the *Columbia*. First he traded buttons and knives for the bountiful foods which the Indians brought to the ship—salmon, sturgeon, strawberries, blackberries, and raspberries. It is notable that at this late period of fur trading the Indians were satisfied with such simple articles. Perhaps since they gave only food and not sea otter skins this meager return was acceptable. Corney sailed about five miles upstream to the village of Chief Comcomly, or Madsaw, whose name means thunder in Chinook, according to the author. Comcomly was the richest and most powerful man on the lower river. He was elderly, short, and blind in one eye. He had three wives and many children. The eldest son, Cassacas, called himself Prince of Wales and expected to succeed his father. He was strong and well built. At that time he was not well disposed toward the white people, who were beginning to come in greater numbers. His younger brother, Selechel, who called himself the Duke of York, was more favorably inclined toward the newcomers.

Other Chinook villages that Corney visited were Clatsop at Point Adams and one of which Tackum was the chief. The other people near the mouth of the river were called Chickelos, and were said to be Classet, who with their chief, Coalpo, came from Cape Flattery. This is rather doubtful for they are also mentioned as Chinook at Gray's Harbor and they might be Chehalis who mingled with the Chinook at this point (Corney 1896, pp. 59–67).

Before we discuss the details of Chinook ethnography which Corney recorded, a short history of the Comcomly family will give some of their social and political structure, which, if accurately reported, is much better organized or better recorded than any other on the Northwest Coast. Corney mentioned the two sons of Comcomly in 1814 as being young men, but did not assign them any position except their relationship to their father and the amusing names they supposedly had taken on. In 1811 Franchère visited a large village called Thlakalama, which was probably at the location of the modern town of Kalama and whose chief was named Cassino, which he also spells Keasseno. This man was striking in appearance, very intelligent, and a friend of the white visitors. This contradicts the attitude attributed to him by Corney three years later. This same man was also seen by Alexander Ross in July 1811 on the lower Williamette near Saint Helens and is called Kiasno. Alexander Henry, who also saw Cassino, stated that the wife of Coalpo, a Clatsop chief, was Cassino's sister-in-law, meaning that the two men had married sisters. Such marriages outside the village and tribe were very common among the upper-class people of the southern Northwest Coast. Franchère also mentions that another wife was a daughter of Comcomly. Ross, in 1811, also describes the tribes of the lower Williamette River as forming a "nation" known as the Callappohyeass, which was governed by four chiefs, of which the most important was Kayasno. In 1814 Henry reports Cassino as being the chief of the Williamette near the confluence of that river with the Columbia. The editors of the narrative of the life of Ranald McDonald, a grandson of Comcomly, said that Cassino succeeded Comcomly as head chief of the Chinook nation after the old chief's death in 1830. Whether this is the same person mentioned in all these situations is not clear, but this is largely because of the dating, for they all agree on his character and ability. He always acts as a friend of the Europeans who came into the area, in contrast to the attitude Corney gives him in 1814. After this official date of his chieftaincy in 1830, Slacum in 1837 declared that his territory extended from the river "Cowility" to the falls of the Columbia and named him Kassenow. Wilkes in 1842 takes his territory even farther up the river and lists him as chief of the Klackatack, by which he probably means the Klikitat, who lived near the Cascades.

This extended discussion has been given to demonstrate one of the problems of ethnohistory: the recording of Indian words by Europeans, many of whom were not conversant with a variety of European languages and had never faced the difficulties of recording an unwritten language. The diversity of spellings of Cassino's name confuses the issue as much as the fact that he was seen in so many places and that he seemed to be in authority so long before his father's death. However, whether this was always the same man or possibly the grandson of Comcomly, the important issue remains that there was an unusual type of confederacy of villages here that represents a more solid organization than the loose statements by Maquinna, Wickananish, and Tatoosh of territorial power among the Nootka.

Corney's visit was contemporaneous with those of many of the first fur traders and explorers who came into the region early in the nineteenth century. He followed Franchère and Alexander Ross, but saw the Chinook in the same year as Alexander Henry; however, he did not write his book, as far as can be determined, until he settled in Honolulu, and he published it in 1821. The description he recorded gave no indications of the replacement of the essentials of the household by European goods, nor of changes in costume. The following notes show a traditional Northwest Coast culture.

The village of Comcomly consisted of thirty large houses, built of planks resting horizontally on each other and fastened by strips of bark to upright posts stuck in the ground. Some had ridgepoles and rafters, but others had nearly flat roofs which were spread with mats to keep out the rain. Each family—from five to fifteen in one house—had a fire in the center. When they moved, they took the planks and mats with them to make a temporary shelter. The bed platforms were along the sides, about one foot from the ground and covered with mats. Corney wrote that the houses had crude carvings which were called *clamas*, or gods, but he does not tell whether they were house posts like the Nootka had, although he also pointed out that they were not worshiped. If they followed a Salish custom, these may have been house posts, set along the sides of the house and related to the location of each family, that represented the guardian spirit of the head of the family living in that section. There were many boxes and chests of all sizes, which Corney said were "hollowed out from solid wood." The food boxes may have been made this way, but the other boxes and chests were probably made of steamed and bent planks, as all Northwest Coast boxes are. The writer was also aware of the great skill in basketry, which showed in the watertight baskets he saw used in every household for stone boiling.

The division of labor is the customary one, with no observation on who does the cooking. Among the Nootka the men often prepared the food they had obtained from hunting and fishing. Salmon were dried everywhere, and the Chinook liked to combine berries with salmon and seal oil and dry the mixture in the form of a cake. In this region the wapatoo is more plentiful than farther north and is a favorite food, used as the potato would be.

The costumes and appearance of the Chinook are carefully detailed by Corney. He said that the men were stout and hardy, with very little beard. When dressed, they wore a cloak made of the skins of the wood rat sewn together. The use of small skins like the ground squirrel was common on the entire coast, but was seldom mentioned by men whose sole interest was the sea otter. These cloaks were thrown over the shoulders. They were also worn by women, who draped them under the right arm and over the left shoulder and fastened them with a wooden pin or skewer. This left the hands free. With this cloak the women wore the apron or petticoat, as Corney called it, which has already been described. The ears were perforated in many places and dentalium was fastened in with thongs. The nose was pierced and beads or the quill of the goose or swan were pushed through. They anointed their bodies with seal oil and red ocher. The women's hair was worn loosely to the shoulders and cut only when they were in mourning.

The men were expert with bows and arrows, bludgeons, and daggers. The presence of firearms is not mentioned. The bows were of "pine" four feet long and two inches broad in the middle. They were backed with elk sinew, and the bowstring was made of the same. The arrows were light and pointed with bone, stone, glass, ivory, or iron. They used a war club or bludgeon that was handsomely carved of bone and was about two feet long. This description fits the popular Nootka war club perfectly, and they were probably obtained through trade. Pieces of these clubs have been found in some archaeological sites in the area. The dagger was made of flint, stone, or iron. It was double bladed, and like the war club was attached to the wrist with a loop of thong. Their principal tools were chisels of a pine root, axes of stone, and stone mallets. There was no comment on the use of knives and on whether they were locally made of trade iron, which by this time may have been so common that it was not noticed.

Corney's final note was about the canoe, which actually was one of the most important features of their culture. Like all Northwest tribes they were experts in canoe making and in adapting their models to local water conditions. Their model for the large seagoing canoe resembled that of the Nootka, which was general for the southern region of the coast. The large ones were forty feet long and carried at least forty persons with their gear. They were six feet broad and two feet deep and were handsomely ornamented with the teeth of sea otter and wolf. Corney remarks that navigators often thought these were human teeth, and he was probably right. The canoes were also painted, especially at the prow and stern. The paddles were six feet long, of which about two and one-half feet formed the blade. The lower end was forked like a fishtail and the upper end was crutched.

Without Corney's account the literature for the southern region of the Northwest Coast would be very meager. The résumé of the voyages in the region shows that it was not a fur trading area until the interior trappers found their way down the Columbia River and the land-based companies established themselves. The character of those in the trade changed from men who were primarily seamen and merchants because of the maritime approach to their field of action to trappers who brought their harvest to land-based merchants. Without the interest in searching for the Northwest Passage and the mysterious Columbia River, the fur traders who traveled the Northwest Coast would probably never have gone south of the Strait of Juan de Fuca. Their first contacts with the coast of Washington, finding no furs and having their crew members killed, soon convinced them that it was not an area to cultivate; so the Indians there were not exposed directly to the culture changes that occurred elsewhere. They were not left completely out of the extensive trade, however, but continued their old ways of living with just a few additions until the settlers came into the region after the middle of the nineteenth century.

4

The Inside Passage, Where the Spaniards in the *Sutil* and the *Mexicana* Proceed More Slowly and Vancouver Hastens to Establish the Insularity of Vancouver Island

The term "Inside Passage" should technically include only the great welter of islands between the mainland of British Columbia and Vancouver Island, but in the days when many coastal steamers ran northward the term was extended to include the passage through many islands in southeast Alaska, where there is a similar relationship between the near offshore islands and the larger ones of the Alexander Archipelago. Between these two passages, a ship going north went through Queen Charlotte Sound and crossed Dixon Entrance, often not smooth sailing. So the opening of Revilla Gigedo Strait was a welcome continuation of the protection of an "Inside Passage."

The first fur trader to reach the Northwest Coast was James Hanna, who came from China and arrived at Nootka Sound in August 1785. He quickly traded in the vicinity of Nootka Sound and was back in Macao in December 1785, having gone no farther north than the end of Vancouver Island. It is most unfortunate that there is only a meager diary of this first trading venture; for the anthropologist it is doubly frustrating, because the journal ends abruptly when he enters Nootka Sound. His second voyage can be traced only through the records of other traders seeing his ship or hearing of his presence. When Hanna came back to Nootka Sound in August 1786 he found John Mackay, who had been left there by James Strange two months earlier to make friends with the Indians and establish good trading relations. After he had settled Mackay at Nootka, Strange sailed north, and at the end of Vancouver Island he found a group of offshore islands and a cape which he named Scott for one of the partners of his firm. He explored Queen Charlotte Sound but had no conception of its size, though he mentioned noticing a channel to the south which Caamaño entered six years later. Mackay had been sufficiently successful so that when Hanna arrived on his second voyage there was little trade left for him, and in September 1786 Hanna also sailed north. His first trading port was Saint Patrick's Bay (San Josef Bay)[1] and Sea Otter Cove at the northwest end of Vancouver Island. From there he visited the Scott Islands and named one Bruce's Island (Lanz). Hanna then crossed Queen Charlotte Sound, entered Fitzhugh Sound, and anchored at Calvert Island, where he found Peril Rock (Pearl Rock) (Wagner 1937, p. 206). He continued north and named Brown's Island, which Caamaño found on 30 August 1792 and called Arististizabal (Wagner 1937, pp. 373, 434). From there he crossed Dixon Entrance and sailed to Bucareli Bay, which the Spaniards had explored very thoroughly (1774, 1775, 1779), and named Sea Otter Harbour between Noyes and Baker Islands. Like many of the fur traders in future years, he prepared his ship there for the return voyage to China.

Strange was the supercargo on the ships *Captain Cook* and *Experiment*, commanded by Captain Lowrie and Captain Guise. After leaving Nootka Sound, they sailed past the Scott Islands, passed close to Saint James Bay at the southern end of the Queen Charlotte Islands, and, crossing eastward, explored Queen Charlotte Sound, which Strange named. They went far enough south to sight the Princess Royal Islands. The track of these ships was charted by Wedgbrough, commander of the *Experiment*, and compares favorably with the map of James Hanna, also dated 1786 (Newcombe 1914, plates II, III).

In 1787 Captain Charles Duncan in the *Princess Royal*, the consort of the *Prince of Wales* under Captain James Colnett, tried to reach the mainland of British Columbia when trading in the Queen Charlotte Islands was not very successful. He crossed Dixon Entrance and visited some of the nearest islands, which also yielded few sea otter skins. On his return to the Queen Charlotte Islands he and Colnett decided to try the region again together. They sailed as far south as the southern end of Banks Island, where they anchored in Calamity Harbor on 4 September 1787. Here they had trouble with the Indians, who stole tools, nails, and bits of iron from the ships. It was too late in the season to do much exploring, and so the next year they came back together and worked their way through the islands, which Colnett recorded on charts that fell into the hands of the Spaniards when his ship was seized at Nootka Sound in 1789. The Tsimshian they encountered were not accustomed to this type of trading and the contact established with them did not lead to a satisfactory relationship. The two captains returned to the Queen Charlotte Islands and started their trading at Cape Saint James, moving northward. By this time trading had become very active and the Indians were more selective in their choice of trade goods. This forced the traders to look

1. The place names in parentheses are the modern names.

for newer, less sophisticated areas, where goods of little value could be exchanged at greater profit.

Up to this time the Strait of Juan de Fuca and the Gulf of Georgia had not been explored, and this still left the question whether Vancouver Island was a separate piece of land. After the Nootka Sound controversy had been settled, although the official documents had not been signed, both England and Spain decided to send exploring parties for surveys. Vancouver was chosen as the leader of the British expedition partly because he was no stranger to the Northwest Coast, having been a midshipman on the third voyage of Captain Cook. He had his own theory that Vancouver Island was a freestanding piece of land and wanted the honor of proving it.

At the same time, the Spaniards were organizing a similar expedition, but accidents and illness defeated their plans until Malaspina, who was then in Acapulco, suggested that two of his young officers, Captains Galiano and Valdez, lead the survey in two small ships that had just been commissioned, the *Sutil* and the *Mexicana*. It was suggested to Vancouver in his instructions that if the Spaniards were also making a survey cooperation might be possible. He remembered this when the situation arose, but ultimately he preferred to travel alone.

There is always the possibility that an unpublished log may someday reveal that a fur trading ship strayed into the inside passage from the north, where smoother water would permit it to travel farther south than Colnett and Duncan did on their first trip. But if the passage was approached from the south, the narrow waterways and terrific currents would soon discourage a captain.

After completing his survey of the Strait of Juan de Fuca, in the spring of 1792 Vancouver sailed through the American San Juan Islands and anchored in Birch Bay, Washington. Then he continued the same procedure, which had been successful in Washington waters, of sending out the longboats to cover all the promising inlets. From Birch Bay they surveyed as far north as Burrard Inlet, where almost a century later the city of Vancouver was founded. On his way back to the ships from such a surveying party, according to Bern Anderson, Vancouver "was disturbed to see two strange sails anchored near Burrard Inlet." (Anderson 1960, p. 88). These were the *Sutil* and the *Mexicana*, commanded by Galiano and Valdez, surveying as Vancouver was doing. They said that they had been in Nootka Sound and reported that they had met there Don Juan Francisco de la Bodega y Quadra, the Spanish commissioner appointed to deliver to Vancouver, as the English representative, the Spanish territory awarded to Great Britain in the Nootka Sound controversy. At this time Vancouver had not yet received the specific details of this transfer, and therefore was doing his survey while waiting for the storeship *Daedelus* to arrive with the documents. This transfer of territory was also included in his instructions. Since he had been charged with cooperating with the Spanish surveying ships he might meet, he proposed a cooperative survey, but it did not last long. Anderson suggests that perhaps the two groups could not work together because of the contrasts between their methods, the English being thorough and aggressive and the Spaniards more leisurely (Anderson 1960, p. 89). In reading the literature it also appears that Vancouver was ambitious to be first to circumnavigate Vancouver Island and prove that it was not joined to the mainland. And his ships could move faster than the small Spanish vessels.

The best accounts of contacts with the Indians in this region appear in the journal of Menzies, the naturalist and surgeon on the *Discovery*, who went with the officers on many of the survey trips. In going through the Gulf of Georgia they did not see any Indians. It is likely that these islands were used then, as they have been since, primarily for fishing, and the proper season had not arrived. The Indians who moved to the islands brought their planks or mats for temporary shelters and sometimes left the framework of their permanent houses standing. On Whidbey's reconnaissance they found some fireplaces, but no other signs of occupation. Still in this general region on one unnamed island (may be Orcas; Menzies 1923, p. 59) they found four or five families in a temporary shelter, who had either passed the winter there for some reason or had come very early. The survey crew bought some halibut from them. The women were found making mats and large storage baskets. If these two items were of the same material, it must have been split cedar bark. Large storage baskets were made of this material along the major part of the Northwest Coast and the same material was used for mats, principally in the northern area. The Salish of northern Washington and southern British Columbia were on the border line in the use of materials, since they also found tule (cattails) drying on the beach. This is the favorite material for mats in the southern region. In this place they also saw women working on a woolen blanket of a "double twisted woolen yarn" woven with the fingers with "great patience and ingenuity," to create various figures. Menzies stated that he was uncertain from what animal the wool was obtained. He knew about the wool dogs but said this was a pure white, which he knew these dogs did not produce (Menzies 1923, pp. 58–59). Menzies did not know that the Salish beat the dogs' wool with a white diatomaceous earth to remove some of the grease, and this would also whiten the wool a little. They did not see any wool dogs, and all the dogs in the settlement were muzzled. Whidbey reported that on the east side of Whidbey Island "40 dogs in a drove, shorn down to the skin like sheep" were seen (Vancouver 1798, 1:284).

The next day two canoes came; they had nothing to barter, but some bodies were covered up on the floor of the canoes. Since the explorers were not allowed to inspect, Menzies suggests that they may have been dead bodies or women hiding from strangers. Menzies included in his journal a report from Lieutenant Puget, who had been on the surveying party with Captain Vancouver. They cruised past Cape Roberts, at the present boundary of the United States and Canada, and landed near a deserted village (Semiahoo Bay; Menzies 1923, p. 60) for their noonday meal. There were frames of houses enough to accommodate four or five hundred persons. The houses were oblong and were arranged in three rows. The uprights were about fourteen feet high, notched to receive large crossbeams. Here again the people had already gone to their fishing sites and taken the planks of the houses with them for their summer quarters.

It seems that Vancouver, as a sailor of the open seas, did not have much feeling for great rivers. Neither the Columbia—at first—or the Fraser seems to have been of any importance to him. The *Chatham* met the Spaniards, who said they had expected to find a large river, but they found only a deep-reaching shallow bay which was probably the delta of the Fraser (Menzies 1923, p. 56). Vancouver cruised past the delta of the Fraser, and when they reached Burrard Inlet they again met a little group of Indians who bartered some fresh fish for small trinkets. They reacted to a musket shot with such alarm as to indicate that perhaps the surveying party was their first contact with Europeans (Menzies 1923, p. 6). The Indians resembled the people of Admiralty Inlet, and this is quite correct, for they were all small Salish-speaking units.

The expedition continued its survey by sending at least two surveying parties out at a time, each with an officer or two, like Puget and Whidbey or Johnstone. When an area was covered to Vancouver's satisfaction he moved the ships on to another rendezvous, and the parties again went into channels which were unsafe for the large ships. Late in June the ships were moved to Redondo Island, and Vancouver surveyed along the east side toward the mainland in a passage still filled with islands and inlets. There were signs that an Indian population lived here at some time of the year, for there were fish drying racks in the area of Desolation Arm. In the next bay they found a cluster of steep rocky islands with a deserted village in an excellent, inaccessible position. The frames of several houses stood on top, irregularly arranged and very crowded. To make more room several of them were supported by strong scaffolding out over the edge. The village had been occupied not long before, as was indicated by the freshness of the refuse. The place swarmed with myriads of fleas, which were so persistent that the men towed their clothes behind the boats to get rid of them, then steeped them in boiling water after getting back to camp. These vermin were so troublesome that they may have also caused the Indians to leave. At a landing at the base of the rock was a solitary house with painted ornaments on the standing posts and beams. It appeared to be the residence of a chief or of some family of distinction (Menzies 1923, pp. 66–68). There are two items in the Hewitt collection which are marked "Rock Village" and that could have been picked up from the ground rather than gotten by barter. One is a canoe paddle (BM, Vancouver 14; Hewitt ms. 271; Appendix 1:119), and the other is a white bone dagger (BM, Vancouver 91; Hewitt ms. 347; Appendix 1:330). This type of object is often found at a camp or village site.

The area between the southern end of Vancouver Island and the mainland, full of islands and beckoning channels, was the place where the competition between Vancouver and the Spaniards became most obvious; and if they had not all been gentlemen, it might have caused serious trouble. The Spaniards again suggested cooperative efforts, but Vancouver answered that he was responsible for charting the whole coast and therefore felt that he had to have control of everything which was recorded. The Spaniards interpreted this as a lack of confidence in their findings. When Galiano explained to Puget that he had explored a waterway and found it closed, he was rather displeased to see Puget start off in that direction and explore it again. On another occasion Puget met Valdez, who had explored Toba Inlet, and told him that he had seen several fishing stages; but Valdez did not mention the painting he and Galino had found at a village site on another steep rocky island. It is an extraordinary piece which was sketched by the Spaniards (Espinoza y Tello 1930, p. 131), and resembles the style of both realistic and geometric figures found on pictographs and petroglyphs in the region to the south.

While Johnstone was exploring the region around the entrance of Bute Inlet, he met Indians in canoes but did not see the village sites from which they came. They had only bows and arrows to barter. There are so many unidentified bows and arrows in the Hewitt collection that there is no doubt these are among them, but it is impossible from the descriptions in the catalog to place them exactly. From Thurlow Island (there are two, one east, one west) Hewitt acquired a "slave killer" (see discussion of these implements, chap. 2) which, like the pieces from Rock Village, could have been found on the ground. It is a very handsome piece carved of gray stone, with a human face on the top surface and a collar below which defines the handle. The face has a perforated nose through which a thong can be pulled. The lower end is wedge shaped, and in this feature it resembles the copper breaker used by the Kwakiutl in the nineteenth century (Boas 1895, plate 19). This piece is one of the finest specimens in the Hewitt collection (Vancouver 96; Hewitt ms. 419; Appendix 1:356).

After these explorations the Vancouver boats reassembled and the ships moved back to the south end of Quadra's Island at Cape Mudge, where they camped across from the village of Yaculta at the entrance of Discovery Passage. Yaculta, the first Kwakiutl village visited by an exploring or trading expedition, as far as is known, was the largest seen on this journey through the Inside Passage. The village consisted of twelve houses with sides of large planks; some of the planks, especially on the front, were painted with figures. The buildings were quadrangular and had flat roofs. Each was inhabited by several families, the total population being about 350. At the arrival of Vancouver and Menzies, eighteen canoes came to greet them and they counted another seventy lying on the beach. The canoes were small, with projecting prows, all carved of one log. They had four or five thwarts to keep their spread, and the outside was painted in "rude" figures with red ocher. The paddles were short, with pointed blades and rounded handles.

Since this is the first appearance of this important tribe, I will quote Menzies's description:

> Like the generality of Natives we met in this Country these were of a middling stature and rather slender bodied, of a light copper colour: they were awkward in their motions & ill formed in their limbs which no doubt in some measure proceeded from their constant practice of squatting down on their heels in their posture of setting either on Shore or in their canoes: They have flat broad faces with small starting eyes:—Their Teeth are small and dirty; their Ears are perforated for appending Ornaments either of Copper or pearly Shells; the Septum of the Nose they also pierce & sometimes wear a quill or piece of tooth-shell in it; their Hair is streight black & long, but mixed with such quantity of red-ocre grease & dirt puffed over at times with white down that its real colour is not easily distinguishable; they have long black Beards with long Hair about their privates, but none on their Breasts or on the Arm pits.—Some had ornamented their faces by painting it with red-ocre, sprinkled over with black Glimmer that helped not a little to heighten their ferocious appearance.
>
> The women & children did not appear any wise shy or timerous tho we were pretty certain our party were the first Europeans they had ever seen or had any direct intercourse with, nor did they seem to regard us or the vessels with any particular degree of curiousity.
>
> The women were decently covered with Garments made either of Skins of wild Animals or wove from Wool or the prepared bark of the American Arbor Vitae Tree, but many of the Men went entirely naked without giving the least offence to the other sex or shewing any apparent shame at their situation. [Menzies 1923, p. 82]

Their fishhooks were nearly the same as those of Nootka Sound, and fishing nets were drying on the shore. There were sinew-backed bows and arrows as elsewhere, but many had points of mussel shell. This is interesting, because the large mussel shells (*Mytilus californius*) are used by the Nootka on their tremendous whaling harpoons. In this entire region a journal entry frequently found is that "some fish and curiosities" were purchased for "beads and small trinkets," and this arouses curiosity about the "curiosities." What became of the others? No official collection was made, the same situation as on the Cook expedition. Only George Goodman Hewitt, Spelman Swaine, and Menzies seem to have preserved their purchases and recorded them, and yet there are not enough pieces in all these collections to compare with the number of these casual entries. Are they still in some English attic, or have they gone the way of souvenirs generally?

At least two of these "curiosities" have been preserved in the George Goodman Hewitt collection (BM, Vancouver 13; Hewitt ms. 312; Appendix 1:316). One is a bow probably collected at Salmon Cove in Observatory Inlet. The second is a sling (BM, Vancouver 109; Hewitt ms. 348; Appendix 1:332), with the bag and cord of plaited fiber. There is nothing in the manuscript notes except the information in Appendix 1.

The visiting party walked through and around the village, and in the forest at some distance they followed a small path that led them to the burial ground.

> We afterwards walked to the Westward along side of the Channel on a pleasant clear level pasture for near two Miles, where we observed in the verge of the wood their manner of disposing of their dead which was by putting them either in small square boxes or wrapping them well up in Mats or old garments into square bundles & placing them above ground in small Tombs erected for the purpose & closely boarded on every side, but as we saw only two or three of these places they might probably belong to the Chiefs or some Families of distinction. [Menzies 1923, p. 83]

During the days that Vancouver had the ships anchored at Cape Mudge, he sent Johnstone to probe Discovery Passage to see whether it was passable and led to the open sea. Johnstone followed the waterways until he was certain there was an outlet into Queen Charlotte Sound, and after studying the tremendous currents in Seymour Narrows, he taxed his crew to the utmost to get back to the ships and report the good news. This meant that the possible circumnavigation of the island could proceed. Vancouver prepared the ships at once, and on 15 July they started their exciting journey. He awaited the right tide and passed through the Seymour Narrows, one of the most perilous passages on the Northwest Coast. The ships emerged into a strait which Vancouver named for Johnstone. They camped that night at Elk Bay.

Now that the expedition had arrived in Kwakiutl territory, more occupied villages appeared, and an increasing number of Indians came out to the ships in canoes. On the south shore, which Johnstone and his party visited in their boats, they reported an abundance of sea otter skins.

On the evening of 19 July, the ships anchored at the village of Chief Cathlagees. Early the next morning the Indians came to the ships and were very much amused by the crew's eagerness to obtain these skins. Trade was brisk, and it was supervised by the man who called himself their chief. He was very anxious to maintain a good understanding on both sides. The name of the village is not clear in the accounts of this visit. Menzies called it Cathlagees, but that is also the name given for the chief. Vancouver has written it Cheslakees, and when they visited the village they were accompanied by the chief, who called the village Whannoc. The village was on a sloping bank of the south shore where a small creek emptied into the strait. It was sheltered by a dense forest of tall "pines." The houses were regularly arranged, and from the bank their painted fronts were pleasing. When the men came ashore they were received by the Indians, who were assembled on the beach, and were conducted through all parts of the village. The houses were built like those of Nootka Sound, but the village was much neater and better kept than others they had seen. Several families lived in one house, but their sleeping spaces were screened off to give privacy, in a manner not found at Nootka. The women were all busy, some preparing food, others working on mats, garments, or small baskets. Everywhere they asked for presents in such a manner that the visitors were convinced that they were not unaccustomed to such company. Gifts of beads and buttons were handed out so generously that in a short time the men had nothing left. Menzies commented on their modesty and good behavior as well as their friendliness.

When they came to the house of an elderly chief they were entertained with singing, in which everyone joined, beating time on planks or anything else they could find. As they prepared for this they picked up spears, paddles, clubs, and sticks, and the visitors became a little uneasy, for it looked as though they were arming themselves. The old chief gave each visitor a strip of sea otter skin.

They saw many muskets in the houses. The chief himself had at least seven. They appeared to be of Spanish make by their locks and the way the barrel was fastened to the stock. The chief's pieces were in exceptionally good condition. Firearms were the most desired item in their trading, but Menzies commented that they were loath to give them because possession of such powerful weapons would make them too dangerous to neighboring tribes and also make them inclined to be more ambitious in plundering small ships that came for trade.

This village was about twenty leagues away from the entrance of Nootka Sound, but it was obvious that they had commercial intercourse with their neighbors across the ridge of mountains which forms the backbone of Vancouver Island. There were two trails, each along waterways, that allowed portaging of canoes. The first, to the south, went into Muchalat Arm, and the other, starting close to Nimkish village, followed the waterway by that name and came into Tasis Canal, which empties into Nootka Sound. Menzies comments that the skins they brought were of superior quality, but their prices were also high, so that the visitors soon ran out of those goods most desired. The Indians did not care for iron, but wanted copper in sheets and coarse, broad blue cloth, but also were willing to take woolen trousers and jackets. Another indication of their contact with Nootka Sound was a pewter basin which was marked "La Flavie V. Français." This was the French ship *La Flavie*, the last one to come to the Northwest Coast both for trading and to look for the lost ships of La Pérouse (Menzies 1923, pp. 88, 89).

While the *Discovery* was anchored at the mouth of the Nimkish River, Vancouver sent Broughton in the *Chatham* into the region of Knight's Inlet. He found very few Indians, and it was obvious by now that the bulk of the population was concentrated on the south side of Johnstone Strait. Broughton cruised in an archipelago of small islands which Vancouver named for him. Hewitt has a bow from Knight's Inlet in his collection (BM, Vancouver 9, Hewitt ms. 259; Appendix 1:311).

Johnstone returned on 29 July, and soon thereafter the ships commenced their crossing of Queen Charlotte Sound. Vancouver now went out into Queen Charlotte Sound and definitely established that Vancouver Island was indeed an island and not a peninsula of the mainland. He named this newly recognized geographical area Quadra's and Vancouver's Island.

Now it is time to return to the Spaniards, who were working their way northward more slowly, staying closer to the mainland. It is interesting to compare the literature, especially their descriptions of contacts with the Indians. Some of the differences in the journals can be explained by the vagaries of the weather. If a low fog covered the shores it was easy to miss villages, particularly if there were only frames of buildings during the summer desertion. Unless Indians came out in their canoes, there was no sign of life along the shores. On 8 July the Spaniards saw a large village on the west point of the mouth of Bute Inlet, and later that same day Vernaci and Salamanca, in one of the Spanish exploring boats, saw the Indians off Zeballos Island fishing with herring rakes. This is a long flat pole which is set with bone spikes—later, nails—along one side for about the first yard of its length. This pole was dragged through the water and fish were caught on and between the spikes. Nootka Indian in figure 9 is carrying one of these implements, which are used by all Northwest Coast tribes.

At Church House, which is one of the northernmost Salish villages, and still inhabited, three canoes came out to the ships. In the whole area in one day the Spaniards counted about 140 persons, one of the largest gatherings seen in the Inside Passage. The Indians told the Spaniards not to continue in this channel, because bad men who wanted to murder them lived up ahead. This type of warning was often given to explorers and fur traders, sometimes because the Indians wanted no competition in trading or because they believed mythical monsters lived in the mountainous region they had never penetrated.

At this point there were four possible channels: they could go into Ramsay Arm, continue in Bute Inlet, or turn two ways in Cordero Channel. So the Spaniards went to the north side of Stuart Island to an anchorage they called Murfi or Murphy.[2] Here they began to run into swift currents, and the Indians warned them against trying to go through, but showed them by the position of the sun when it would be right to try the rapids. At 3 P.M. the Indians escorted the exploring boats through the narrows and left them hurriedly, to get back before the current changed. One man and one woman in a canoe stayed with them, but finally left because they thought the Spaniards had not taken their advice when they began the maneuver of tacking, which they had never seen. This passage is known as the Arran Rapids, and the current rushes through at the rate of twelve miles per hour. No Indians lived in this area because the roar of the water was too terrifying (Wagner 1937, p. 443).

On 30 July Galiano and Valdez had passed the most difficult waters of the Inside Passage and stopped at Port Neville, where they found some Indians who understood Nootkan. That they were actually Nootka is doubtful, but they may have been from a small Kwakiutl settlement. Their *tais*, or chief, wore a hat which was not described but was said to look like one they had seen at Port Mulgrave (Yakutat Bay). He prized it very much because he had secured it from an enemy in battle. Galiano recorded that they bought it and that it was the only piece they could get. Some of the crews set ashore to get wood and water were surrounded by Indians. When Salamanca went to their rescue and the ship shot off a cannon, the Indians got in their canoes and crossed the channel (Espinoza y Tello 1930, p. 75).

On 1 August two Indians came in a canoe and introduced themselves as Nuchimasis, a different tribe from those who had attacked the day before. The Spaniards' rendering of Indians' names is often difficult to interpret, and this one is a problem. The structure of the word sounds Nootkan. *The Handbook of American Indians* has an entry under *Newchemass* which states:

2. The Irish family name of Murphy is believed to be derived from a Spanish Admiral Murfi who came to Ireland many years ago. This name was used by Galiano, probably because he knew of this story.

> An unidentified tribe mentioned by Jewitt (narr. 77, reprint 1849) as living far north and inland from Nootka Sound early in the 19th century. Their language was different from Nootka but was understood by the Nootka. The people had a darker complexion, were shorter in stature and had coarser hair than the explorers had been seeing. The locality assigned to them corresponds to that of Nimkish.

Reference is made to Galiano, Relacion (*Bulletin*, Bureau of American Ethnology, #30 2:64). Jewitt was at Nootka from 1802 to 1805, and so this is not long after the journey through the inside passage in 1792. The languages of the Nootka and Kwakiutl are dialects of Wakashan. The Nimkish mentioned in the quotation are Kwakiutl living near Nimkish Lake and at the mouth of the Nimkish River. There were also some Nootkan groups who lived primarily in the interior of Vancouver Island and came to the shores for brief periods of fishing. So this "unidentified" group could be one of these closely related peoples.

When they met the Spaniards they carried a musket and a lance with a long iron point. They had large knives with grooves down the middle of the blade like those of the Indians living at 59° to 60° north latitude, which they said they made themselves. They sold nothing because they were only willing to take powder and shot in exchange (Espinoza y Tello 1930, p. 76). A young chief who called himself Canti and who was also a Nuchimasis came to the ship and talked about Maquinna. He offered to bring other chiefs to meet the explorers, and after five days he returned with Sisiaquis, whose companions were all well armed with muskets and had a good supply of ammunition. He offered to entertain the visitors if they would come to his village, because he did all his trading under the guise of exchanging presents. This was a frequent practice among the important chiefs, who said they did not want common barter but offered the commanders of expeditions presents, usually of sea otter skins, and in return expected gifts of equal value. The fur traders did not like this system; it cost them much more than straight barter and of course was to the advantage of the chiefs.

Sisiaquis came on board with two Indians and told the Spaniards that Nootka Sound was to the southeast and could be reached readily by sea. When the visitors came to his village he offered them women, saying that the English always gave large pieces of copper for their favors. The Spaniards had steadfastly refused this form of hospitality and looked down on the English for indulging in it.

The village was large and the houses were set in regular fashion on streets. Many had painted fronts. There were many evidences of luxury, owing to the trade with Europeans. The Spaniards bought sea otter skins and garments made of bark with borders of different colors. It is unfortunate that these objects mentioned by Galiano have never appeared in any public collection.

During their stay at this village the brig *Venus* came by, which the Spaniards had met at Tatoosh earlier in the season. Captain Shepherd brought the news that the Makah had murdered Antonio Serrantes, who was on Fidalgo's ship.

After one more stop in Kwakiutl territory at Hardy Bay the men of the *Sutil* and the *Mexicana* sailed through the Salida Channel and completed their circumnavigation of Vancouver Island, a few weeks after Vancouver. They turned south after rounding the north end of the island and returned to Nootka Sound.

After sailing away from Vancouver Island, Vancouver wished to use the rest of the season of 1792 in exploring northward as far as he could. On 7 August the *Discovery* was driven on the rocks in a storm; she worked loose without damage, but the next day the same misfortune came to the *Chatham*, which took a much harder pounding. One can easily understand why the harbor they found at the southern tip of Calvert Island on 11 August was called Port Safety, named by Captain Charles Duncan in 1788. From here the longboats again went out, exploring Fitzhugh Sound and Burke Channel, where they turned back at Restoration Cove. This was where they began their work at the beginning of the next season. Since it was again on the date of the restoration of the Stuarts to the throne of England, Vancouver named it Restoration Cove to distinguish it from Restoration Point on Bainbridge Island, which he had named on the same date the preceding year.

On 17 August a brig flying English colors entered Port Safety. It was the *Venus* with Captain Shepherd from Bengal. She brought the pleasant news that the storeship *Daedalus* was waiting for Captain Vancouver at Nootka Sound and that the Spanish commander Don Juan Francisco de la Bodega y Quadra, was anxious for Vancouver to arrive. This, together with the worsening weather, caused Vancouver to end his survey for the season and return to Nootka Sound.

While the *Sutil* and the *Mexicana* and the *Discovery* and the *Chatham* were pushing their way slowly through the dangerous waters of the Inside Passage to prove the insularity of Vancouver Island, Jacinto Caamaño was making the final Spanish survey of the southwestern shores of southeastern Alaska. After visiting the Queen Charlotte Islands, he crossed Dixon Entrance again and explored the southern end of Prince of Wales Island and the southern opening of Clarence Strait. Then he returned to Rose Harbor and cruised along the northern shore of Graham Island, visiting Masset Harbor and Virago Sound. Several canoes came to the ship, urging the captain to come to their harbors because they had many sea otter skins and prettier women then Chief Cania (Parry Passage)

(Caamaño 1849, pp. 267–68). Caamaño then ran back to the entrance of Clarence Strait and turned south to the offshore islands of the mainland.

Here he began his most important contribution toward the exploration of the Northwest Coast in tracing the voyage of Colnett and Duncan in 1788 and using their maps. This area had been out of the run of the fur traders and explorers, who, after coming into Nootka Sound for refreshment following their journey from the Orient or Europe or the Atlantic Coast, then started north to the Queen Charlotte Islands or even to Prince William Sound. Caamaño also was now at the north end of the inside passage, which was being surveyed during the same season by the *Sutil* and the *Mexicana* and by Vancouver. He tried to follow Colnett's maps, which had fallen into Spanish hands when his ships were seized by Martinez, but Caamaño found them misleading. He does not mention contact with the Indians until he reached Tuwartz Inlet at the south end of Pitt Island in Nepean Sound, where he states that increasing numbers of Indians were continually coming aboard. This is the first opportunity for gaining any knowledge of the Tsimshian and northern Kwakiutl since Colnett's accounts in 1788, and because of the meagerness of these Caamaño's notes are of special value.

The first contact mentioned was unfortunately not a happy one; when the pilot caught an Indian stealing the candles out of the binnacle, the Indian threatened him with a knife, of the type they all carried slung around their necks. The chief, who was aboard at the time, ordered the man off the ship. This chief had arrived at the ship in his canoe with eight others, including his three wives, in the same style observed at Parry Passage. He wore a long overcoat of blue cloth and over it a cloak of the same material, trimmed with edging of deerskin about five or six inches wide, painted with figures and faces, and two rows of flounces. He had a large cap of black fur with two stiffened ears that stood up about eight inches on each side. From these, gold-colored threads or animal hair hung down his back, and on his shoulders were two large burnished rings of iron twisted in rope fashion.

In spite of the isolation of these people, a number of trade goods were displayed in their ceremonial dress. The twisted-rope iron rings, which had by this time become common, began through the ingenuity of the traders, who found that the Indians would not accept iron except in this form, which could be created on the spot, when demanded, by the blacksmiths who were included in all the ships' crews. When the explorers saw the Indians they were always in ceremonial clothing, and for this they chose their trade goods and used all possible decorative materials. Manufactured woolen blankets replaced the sea otter cloaks they bartered for all these new materials. The combinations of garments they put on looked ludicrous to the Europeans, but they had no models to follow and the clothing given them was highly assorted. In some respects they continued their own cultural tastes; they requested abalone shells and suggested that they should not be exposed to heat in removing the animal. Their quick adoption of European manners is remarkable, but is in keeping with their own culture, for all the Northwest Coast tribes were ceremonious people and were trained to observe mannerly procedure. Since this region had been off the usual waterways, relatively few contacts had been made with foreigners; yet the amount of trade goods in their possession and their knowledgeable behavior were out of proportion to the extent of their intercourse.

When Caamaño explained to the local chief that he was sending his men in longboats to explore the channels running eastward into the mountains, the Indians recited the usual myths that these waters were infested with huge animals that would attack canoes and devour the occupants (Caamaño 1849, p. 275). These myths and their monsters are still active in local folklore.

Early in August the chief and his people left the harbor for neighboring inlets, to go sea otter hunting, Caamaño thought, but Menzies and Vancouver reported large numbers of sea otters in Nepean Sound the following year. While the ship was waiting for the exploring party to return, some of the men took the last galley from the ship and went ashore to wash their clothes. They were attacked by Indians and only with great difficulty were they rescued and brought back to the ship. Helping in the rescue was a brother of Jammisit, the chief, who came aboard to explain that the attackers were visitors from another village whose chief was Gitejon, a recognizable Tsimshian name. In the evening of this day Jammisit and his people set up guards to watch against another attack. Early next morning they came to the ship, dressed ceremonially, chanting "peace, peace." They came aboard and sprinkled white feathers on all who were on deck and presented Caamaño with a sea otter skin. He in turn rewarded them all in proportion to their efforts in rescuing his men. Finally Jammisit gave Caamaño his name in the same type of exchange that had taken place between Cunneah and Douglas (Caamaño 1849, p. 281).

In his survey Caamaño found on Hinton Island an ideal harbor, Puerto de Gaston, and was assured by the Indians that there was an outlet (Grenville Channel) through which they traveled to visit Cunneah on the Queen Charlotte Islands (Caamaño 1849, p. 283). When he was ready to leave, the Indians were so insistent on entertaining him in their village with a feast and dance that he finally yielded, partly because the weather was unfavorable. His description of this event is so excellent that I will quote it completely, because every step in the ceremony is consistent with the proceedings seen by nineteenth- and twentieth-century visitors, which shows the stability of Northwest Coast Indian life in spite of the inroads by Europeans.

> This day [28 August] the S.E.ly wind still held, with frequent squalls, until noon. Jammisit came to visit me in the afternoon, accompanied by upwards of forty of his relatives, all singing and bringing feathers. He, together with his nearest relations, arrived in one of two canoes lashed alongside each other. Jammisit's head appeared from behind a screen formed of brilliantly white deerskin; on it, accordingly as the action demanded or his own particular fancy dictated, he would place various masks or heads of the different animals that he proposed to imitate; the deerskin serving as a curtain by which he was entirely hidden when he wished, unseen to put on or change one of these masks or faces. They remained alongside thus for some time, singing and continuing their antics, until Jammisit with great eagerness explained that he was come to conduct me to his village. Curiosity to see it, as well as the fete for which such extensive preparations were being made, induced me to comply with his entreaties. Accompanied by the master, botanist, and surgeon, I therefore landed in the cutter, at the same time sending nine marines armed with muskets ashore in the pinnace. As we left the ship in the cutter, the five canoes all started to race as fast as they could paddle for the village, intending to be first on shore so as to be able to receive me as I landed. They succeeded in this without difficulty, owing to the extraordinary swiftness of their canoes. By the time we in the cutter reached the strand, there were already six lusty natives carrying a very clean deerskin awaiting me on the beach. These at once dashed into the water up to the waist alongside our boat, making signs for me to sit on the skin to be carried ashore on their shoulders. At first I declined, but they were so vehemently insistent, that I gave in and let them do it; not, however, without considerable apprehension lest I should be dropped upon the ground on my back.[71]
>
> The moment that I placed myself on the deerskin these six fellows hoisted my 150 lb. carcass on to their shoulders and carried me at a run across the shingle and up the pretty steep slope leading from it to the village, whither they brought me at a surprising speed. To pass through the narrow doorway of the chief's house, over which was painted a huge mask,[72] it was necessary to make a litter or hammock of the deerskin. Two of the strongest of the Indians did this, with the other four assisting as best they could, while I was shrinking myself into as small compass as possible (though my bearers were careful enough) to avoid being bumped against the door posts. Once inside, I tried to get on my feet, but this they would not allow before bringing me to the place prepared for my seat, which was to the right of the entrance. The seat was formed of a case or chest, raised higher than those for the others, fitted for only one person, and

71. This custom of carrying a "visitor of standing" ashore was practiced by all our Coast tribes.—W. A. N.

72. This tends to confirm the view of Marius Barbeau, of the National Museum, Ottawa, whose researches among the Tsimshian indicated that house frontal paintings were the forerunners of totem poles.—W. A. N.

covered with a new mat; while a similar one was spread before it. The seats for my officers, ranged on either hand of mine, were made in similar manner; those for my men, were formed of mats spread out on the floor. When we were all (I had left about fifteen seamen and marines in the two boats as a guard in reserve) arranged and seated I noticed that opposite to me and sitting in a seat of the same sort as mine, was the chief named Gitejon; who had not again shown himself on board the frigate since the theft of my men's clothes by his people. This ill-disposed Indian occupied that place of distinction in virtue of his quality as a guest and chief of the other faction. He was wearing a new mantle, of fine blue cloth, edged with leather; on which, as is usual among the chiefs, were painted various grotesque masks or faces.[73] He also wore a breech clout, of the same cloth, but lined with antelope skin, and neatly cut into numerous pendants, about twelve inches deep and perhaps five or six inches wide; oval shaped and hanging from a narrow strap around his hips; thus covering that which otherwise would have been extremely noticeable. So soon as he caught my eye, he arose, straightening his huge stature, bent (though not with years, as he was under 40) by some infirmity or spinal complaint, came over to me and seated himself at my feet. From a small bag made of pine bark, he then produced a quantity of feathers which he proceeded to blow so that they should fall upon myself and my immediate neighbours; followed up this action by other friendly gestures, and then returned to his own seat. By this time, the whole native company, amounting to about eighty people of both sexes, was arranged on the floor. Jammisit, his three wives, and grown family, were in front. Myself, with all my officers and men, were on the right; and only women were allowed behind us. On the left were the remainder from Jammisit's village, and those from that of Gitejon. In this situation, then, Jammisit began to emit piercing howls in a pitiful key; after which, throwing back his head as if about to faint, he sat down, clutching at the collar laces of his cloak, as if wishing to throw it off. Several of his family nearby, who were watching to give him any help that might be necessary, when they noticed this, gathered around him forming a screen so that he might not be seen changing his garments in which some of the others were assisting him.

So soon as he had put on the ones in which he was to show himself, they would break up and sit down out of his way, leaving only a couple of his nearest relations standing by ready to help him as he might require. When he was ready, these also left him, and the actor arose.

On his head was a large well-imitated representation of a seagull's head, made of wood and coloured blue and pink, with eyes fashioned out of polished tin; while from behind his back stuck out a wooden frame covered in blue cloth, and decked out with quantities of eagles' feathers and bits of whale bone, to complete the representation of the bird.[74] His cloak was now of white calico, bearing a blue

73. The behaviour and costume of Gitejon give me the impression that he was a Shaman.—W. A. N.

74. The wooden frame behind the mask also acted as a counterbalance and generally had a string from it to the waist.—W. A. N.

flowered pattern, trimmed with a brown edging. Round his waist hung a deer skin apron falling to below the knee, whose fringe or flounce was made from narrow strips of the same leather, everyone being split into two tails, each of which carried half the hoof of a deer. Over this apron or kilt he wore another, shorter, one, of blue jean ornamented with numerous metal buttons arranged symmetrically, and two rows of antelope hide pendants or tassels, each finished off with an eagle's claw. On his legs were deer skin leggings, tied behind with four laces, ornamented with painted masks and trimmed with strips of hide carrying claws. Clad in this weird rattling rig, he then began to leap and cut capers, reminding one of a rope-dancer trying his rope. He also waved his arms, keeping them low down, in the same manner as that of the blind man at Florida Blanca. After two or three preliminary attempts, he started a song. This was at once taken up by every one inside the house, man or woman, and produced a terrific volume of sound, to whose measure he then began to dance, while a specially chosen Indian beat the time on a large drum. The dance was on the lines I have just mentioned, except that it now took place in the middle of the room, and lasted all the time that the music played; long enough, indeed, to tire the performer. As he finished and sat down, those attending him took off his mantle, and wiped the sweat from his face and body, while others held up a hide to screen his following change of attire from the general view. During this interval, which proved a short one, two tubs or small troughs were brought in, filled with freshly boiled fish for our refreshment though few of us tried it.

The old chief having recovered from his exhaustion due more to his age than the exercise, and being now dressed in the costume for his next performance, the curtain was drawn, and he appeared with a half-length wooden doll on his head.[75]

Two Indians at some distance behind him, who endeavoured to conceal their actions, then proceeded—by means of long fishing rods—to open and close the eyes of the doll, and raise its hands, in time to another tune that was struck up, while the dancer himself imitated the movements of the doll's face, which was sufficiently frightful in appearance, being coloured black and red, and furnished with an owl's beak and nostrils. For this scene, he wore a bear skin cloak, with the remainder of his costume as before. So soon as the music ceased, his attendants again hid him from sight. Before long, however, he again appeared, this time wearing a heavy wooden mask on his head, of which the snout, or upper jaw, was moveable.[76] He also carried a blue cloth mantle, such as distinguishes the chiefs, and the timbrel (or "jingles") that my men had noticed when they were captured. He began by making various weird movements, on which a new tune was started when his gestures and contortions soon worked him into such a state of frenzy, that he reached the point of fainting,

75. These mechanical dolls were used by certain secret societies of the Haida, Tsimshian, and Kwakiutl.—W. A. N.

76. Masks with the upper jaw moveable are a rarity.—W. A. N.

and would doubtless have collapsed, had not the attendants quickly come to his aid. One laid his mouth to the chief's right side uttering loud shouts, while the singers still continued theirs, and laid hold of him, moving and lifting him with his hands as if he were a sack of straw to be stood on end. Others uncovered his breast and one after another sprayed him by squirting great mouthfuls of water from a distance of 10 or 12 feet. These attentions soon revived him, though groaning heavily. He was then led to his seat, his mask and mantle taken off, and the latter exchanged for the one he had earlier worn. He then presented me with a nutria skin and returned to his place, when all the rest of the Indians rose up from theirs. I thereupon did the same, which being seen by my native escort, they at once got ready my coach (the large deer skin as a litter), put me into it, and quickly carried me down to my boat. On the way, I noticed four more houses similar to the one in which we had been entertained. This was about fifty to fifty-five feet in length, and thirty to thirty-five in breadth, with walls and roofs of well-fitted planking. In the middle of the roof was a louver or skylight, placed so as to admit plenty of light, and serving also for the exit of smoke from the hearth (on which a fire is kept constantly burning), but at the same time keeping out the rain. It was cleaner than I had expected to find, and at some time must have been larger, as around and above it stood heavy forked posts with cross timbers. My boat had hardly cleared the beach before the Indians leaped into their canoes and were making for the ship, which they reached simultaneously with us. Here, they asked my leave to come aboard, and when I consented started again to sing with even greater vigour than before. I gave them to eat and drink and towards nightfall they returned ashore with expressions of gratitude and pleasure.

In the morning of the 29th, we had a succession of squalls, with the wind shifting from the southward to the eastward. There were intervals of fine weather during the afternoon of which the natives took advantage to pay us visits. [Wagner and Newcombe 1938]

This is the southern limit of Caamaño's penetration into the northern end of the Inside Passage. He proved to his own satisfaction and that of his government that there is no Estrecho del Almirante Fonte and closed forever the Spanish interest in the Northwest as the farthermost reaches of "Alta California."

When affairs were settled as far as they could be with the lack of some documents, Bodega y Quadra left for San Francisco and Monterey, and Vancouver soon followed him south, where they negotiated again. Then, after arranging for Lieutenant Broughton to go to England for further orders about settling the controversy, he left Monterey in January 1793 and sailed to Hawaii. On his return late in April he came north after a very brief visit to Nootka Sound and started his season from Calvert Island.

They took the *Discovery* into Restoration Cove, where they were visited by three chiefs, Keyut, Comockshulah, and Whacosh, who indicated that they came from a large village on a detached rock in Fisher Channel. They brought skins for sale, including that of an animal from which the Indians secured the wool for their blankets. It certainly was an animal larger than the dog family, for exclusive of head, tail, and legs the skin was about fifty inches long and thirty-six inches wide. The wool seemed to come only from the back and shoulders, where a kind of crest was formed of long bristly guard hairs that came through the wool and also formed the remainder of the covering. The wool was short and very fine (Vancouver 1798, 2:279). All the skins brought in were entirely white or a cream color, but they were so mutilated that it was impossible to reconstruct any picture of the animal. This is the only time in all the accounts used in this study, where the matter of blankets and their weaving has appeared frequently, that the wool has been identified with an animal. That none of the explorers ever saw a mountain goat is not surprising. They stay in the high mountains and wander from one meadow to another as they graze. Hunting these goats was limited to the mountain people, who evidently in the eighteenth century had extensive trade for the pelts, until manufactured cloth and European garments made the hand-woven blankets less necessary (Vancouver 1798, 2:279–81).

Vancouver writes that although he believed these animals were not scarce in this region, he did not see any Indians wearing woolen blankets. It may be the story of the cobbler's child—that the wool was so important a trade item that home consumption was not feasible. When the longboat came the Indians wore sea otter skins or woven garments of shredded cedar bark, some with sea otter fur woven into them and bordered at the sides and along the lower edge with yellow and black wool woven in geometric designs. There are examples of these blankets in many of the Cook collections (See Appendix 1), but none are from the Vancouver expedition. The women wore labrets of well-polished wood in a variety of sizes from 2 to 3¼ inches wide (Vancouver 1798, 2:280).

The area being explored was at the southern point of the Bella Coola tribal territory, which extends along Burke Channel into the Bella Coola River. In the same season that Vancouver was there Alexander Mackenzie reached the mouth of the Bella Coola River, the first white man to cross the continent in this latitude. The mountains are very high in the Bella Coola valley, and the people were the best mountain-goat hunters among the Northwest Coast tribes. They were an interesting tribe which had come to the coast perhaps a few hundred years before they were discovered by Europeans. They drove a wedge between the southern and the northern Kwakiutl and adopted many features of Kwakiutl culture, but they never changed their language, which is a form of interior Salish. From the Kwakiutl they adopted many of their ceremonies, and like any converts they conducted them more strictly than their originators. They were on very friendly terms with the Bella Bella or Heiltsuk, their Kwakiutl neighbors. Many members of these two groups were bilingual, and there was a fair amount of intermarriage. These relationships developed from their joint interest in their ceremonial activities; in fact, the Bella Coola believed that many of their ceremonies were received from the Bella Bella and they respected their superior knowledge. Conversely, they had a very low opinion of the Carriers, who often came down from the cold northeast because they were starving and stayed in the Bella Bella and Bella Coola villages. This contempt was largely due to the Carriers' lack of knowledge of the ceremonies (McIlwraith 1948, pp. 18–20).

In the middle of Fisher Channel lies a large island which Vancouver named for his former shipmate, Lieutenant James King, the officer who brought home the Cook ships after the deaths of Cook and Clerke. Going to the end of this island and heading north, the longboats turned into Dean Channel, where Vancouver also named Point Raphoe after King's father, who was the dean of Raphoe. On this part of the survey the men were so busy combating the elements that Menzies's entries are almost entirely limited to that subject. Vancouver, to whom weather does not seem to matter, gives an excellent description of the houses in the Bella Coola village they saw. The houses again were on a rocky cliff and were cantilevered out on the front and sides with slender poles sixteen to eighteen feet high. The Indians did not want them to enter, but they carried no weapons of any kind to prevent them (Vancouver 1798, 2: 268). At Point Menzies, at the head of the peninsula between Burke Channel and South Bentinck Arm, Johnstone reported seeing another such construction, which was raised about thirty feet from the ground, the whole house occupying an area of thirty-five by fifteen square yards. It was covered with a roof of boards lying almost horizontal. It seemed to be divided into three separate dwelling places, each with access by means of a notched log ladder. Mr. Johnstone was allowed to go up one of these, and after removing a board at the top he found himself on a small platform from which he could look down into the house. But he also found four Indians posted, each bearing a rude iron weapon resembling a dagger. Mr. Johnstone looked in and saw an arrangement similar to all other houses on the Northwest Coast (Vancouver 1798, 2:274).

When they asked for some food, the Indians gave them some "bread" made of the inner bark of the "pine." There is a piece of this type of bread in the Cook collection in the British Museum (NWC 82; Appendix 1:366), which is described as "bread of the pine bark." The bark is probably not pine but spruce. Such cakes were widely used on the Northwest Coast and also were found inland. The shredded bark was pounded together with mashed berries and salmon eggs or herring eggs. It was formed into oblongs and laid out to dry. It is also possible that this was herring spawn that had been gathered on hemlock boughs laid in the water as previously described. The boughs were dried with the eggs on them and the eggs were shaken off when they were wanted for food. The example from the Cook collection came from Nootka Sound and was nine inches long.

In Mathiesen Channel, behind Roderick Island, there was another large dwelling made of broad planks with a nearly flat roof. It was built on top of a precipice against the side of a rocky cliff, with very difficult access. The type of houses in this Inside Passage area is striking, for it certainly points to much intertribal warfare, especially raids on villages (Vancouver 1798, 2:284).

Vancouver now made a long move northward into Nepean Sound late in June and sent Johnstone out again in longboat expeditions, this time visiting the same places where Colnett and Duncan went in 1788 when they named Nepean Sound. Johnstone circumnavigated the island which Caamaño had visited in 1792 and called it Isla de Gil (Vancouver 1798, 2:297). The expedition explored extensively in Douglas Channel and contacted a new group of Indians, the Kitimat, who are the northernmost extension of the Kwakiutl and are also known in modern anthropological literature as the Xaisla. They still occupy the upper reaches of Douglas Channel. Near Gardner Canal the exploring party was visited by two canoes with eight Indians. They brought two salmon weighing seventy pounds and exchanged them for a small piece of iron. Vancouver remarked that they were the best fish they had all season. The Indians followed the explorers, and when they stopped later in the day to dine the Indian party had increased to ten canoes and about sixty persons. The largest canoe, occupied by the chief and his family, had a painted and carved prow. They traded sea otter skins for copper, blue cloth, and blankets. Whidbey invited the chief to eat with them, and he enjoyed grog and bread and sugar. The Indians sang as they paddled away when the surveying party passed Hawkesbury Island and approached Point Cumming. This is their last encounter with the Kwakiutl, for at Hartley Bay the Tsimshian territory begins.

The exploring boats of Puget turned north here and went into Grenville Channel, which separates the mainland from Pitt Island, which is really an archipelago of closely placed islands. They stopped at Point Lambert and then at Raspberry Island, at the mouth of the Skeena River. Vancouver, meanwhile, had been anchored at Fisherman's Cove at the northwest end of Gil Island, and now moved them through Principe Channel between Pitt Island and Banks Island. Coming into Browning Entrance, they sighted the Queen Charlotte Islands when the heavy weather improved. When the fog lifted they saw a whaleboat approaching the ships. The officer who came aboard was from the trading vessel *Butterworth*, which was traveling with two more from the same company, the *Prince Lee Boo* and the *Jackal*, all under the command of Captain William Brown. He led them all to an anchorage, and in gratitude Captain Vancouver named the waterway Brown's Passage. They crossed over to Dundas Island and then sailed into Portland Inlet, which leads into the Nass River and Observatory Inlet (Vancouver 1798, 2:327).

This region is occupied by the Tsimshian, the same people the exploring party found at the mouth of the Skeena River. Since Puget had explored this area, Vancouver passed it by and continued farther north. Considering the distance covered in June and July 1793, very few contacts were made with the Indians; but one must bear in mind that Vancouver's mission was to chart the area and notes on the Indians were incidental. It is obvious that the villages were hidden except when they were situated on steep rocky points, and only a few of these seemed to be inhabited. The frames of houses often seen were only temporarily deserted or unoccupied, for this fits into the pattern of life on the entire Northwest Coast. The custom continued into the nineteenth century, when the first steps toward a wage economy for the Indians made them move for the season to cannery and commercial fishing locations. Later they moved to logging camps and sawmills, and finally to their own larger villages when schools were established there. But many tribes still went back to their old house sites and villages, where they sometimes reconstructed on the old house frames ceremonial houses for their winter festivals.

When the ships were safely anchored at Salmon Cove, the instruments were set up on land and the local exploring parties started out again. Whidbey had examined the continental shore line to Point Maskelyne when he came upon a place where Captain Brown had had a dispute with the Indians, and reverberations of this were felt by the exploring boats in the whole region. The second boat group, consisting of Vancouver, Puget, Swaine, and Menzies, started out with fourteen days' supplies. They soon met a canoe with fourteen Indians, who were well armed with long spears, bows and arrows, and iron daggers. The chief was given bread and dried fish and a glass of brandy. Their language sounded like that of Queen Charlotte Islands, but according to their location they should be Tsimshian. The Indians invited the party to their houses, but when the offer was declined and they saw that these men were not interested in trading, they left.

The next day, at a place where there were no houses, a canoe with fifteen Indians came to join them. These men looked fierce and rejected the small gifts with disdain. The only woman in the party also refused a mirror. The man in the prow of the canoe put on his war garments, put his spears in order, and drew his dagger. All the others followed him. He called "*winnee watter*," the usual call of the Indians when they were asking for trade. When Vancouver left, they followed him, waving sea otter skins. When the surveying party stopped to eat, they came up and traded for the very objects they had refused. When the trade was completed, they left singing and had laid aside their war garments.

In the group of objects collected by Hewitt from "Namakizat," which has not been located, there are two spears that perfectly answer the description of the weapons the Indian arranged so carefully by his side. There are two spears (BM, Vancouver 89, Hewitt ms. 333; BM Vancouver 90; Appendix 1:347, 348; only one was called for in the manuscript, but one can assume they belong together because of their similarity) and a spear point (BM, Vancouver 65; Hewitt ms. 113; Appendix 1:334). "Salmon" is written in the manuscript, which probably indicates that it was used for this kind of fishing.

Their bows (BM, Vancouver 13; Hewitt ms. 312; Appendix 1:316) were well constructed, and they had plenty of arrows, pointed with bone or iron. Their war garments were made of two or three layers of the strongest skin of land animals. They were a kind of poncho with a hole in the center for the head, and the left side was partly sewed up but with enough room for the arm to pass through. The right side was open, which gave plenty of room for action. Over this shirt they wore a cuirass of thin lathes of wood twined together with sinew (Appendix 2).

On their way back on the west shore of the inlet there was a place where all the young trees had been cut down with an ax. Had this been done by other "civilized" people who were there before them? It was interpreted as a certain sign that Russians had been there; but it might also mean that Indians had taken axes in trade, although they generally refused them. A party of Indians came in the evening and said they would return next morning. When they did so they rejected all the trade goods offered them, wanting only firearms. There was a woman in this party, who also steered the canoe. This did not impress Vancouver as much as the fact that "she was a scold with authority and ordered the men to arrange their spears for ready use" (Vancouver 1798, 2:343).

Before we consider the exploration of southeastern Alaska, one other feature of the exploration of the inside passage should be examined—the objects from this region in the Hewitt collection at the British Museum. I have mentioned a few for which specific information is available, but there are a number which have no locations or are from places whose locations cannot be determined. First of all, there were seven pieces located at "Namakizat," which on the British Museum slips is often written in quotation marks. This name does not appear in the Vancouver or Menzies journals or in the Wagner lists of obsolete or current names.[3] The objects are very general Northwest Coast types and have no peculiarities that would place them in a specific subarea of the coast. Three of them are bent hooks, which are widely found in the southern area which includes the lower part of the Inside Passage (BM, Vancouver 128, 129 *a,b;* Hewitt ms. 116; Appendix 1:97, 98). These hooks, usually made of a strong piece of spruce or yew, are steamed and bent. A barb for bait is attached to the straight arm, which is a bone spike on the old ones and a nail after they were available. The shape was so satisfactory that after iron came into common use the whole hook was made of it (Niblack 1890, plate 31). The bait used often was squid. Two more such hooks (BM, Vancouver 135; no Hewitt ms. number, but may be 232), are in the collection with the strange addition of a cluster of bird claws lashed on with "gut" twine.

Another group of "Namakizat" pieces includes a double comb (BM, Vancouver 220; Hewitt ms. 117; Appendix 1:178) with teeth at each end, one end being finished better than the other. It has no decoration, but in general structure it resembles the combs in the Cook collection (Appendix 1:171–77). Another object is a small strip about six inches long made of grayish black feathers twined into four rows of sinew to form a decoration that could have been on a garment. The feathers hang down from the twining and therefore may have been attached to a dancing apron so that the movement would make them flutter. The last piece bearing the Namakizat label is one of the traditional war clubs made of whale bone with a circular eye design joined by a straight line incised on the blade. These clubs were very popular and are found in many places they reached by trade. They were made in Nootka. The club is twenty-three inches long, which is a standard measure (for others of this type see Appendix 1:38–45).

3. There is a slight resemblance between this word and a statement in the account of the sequence of the change of names among the chief's families at Nootka. "The young *Tais* who, at the time of our visit to Nootka in 1792 was called Quicsiocnuc was called Tlupaniapa in his infancy, Namajamitz when he reached the age of puberty, Gugumetazaulz in his early manhood and finally Quicomasis until his marriage." This may sound like a very far-fetched, idea but one must reckon with the spelling of strange names, often by people who were not too certain of spelling in their own language. For example, the Spaniards often wrote Wickananish as Huiqunanichi and Maquinna as Macuina. With these difficult names it is of considerable importance to know the linguistic base of the recorder.

This is also plausible because of the frequent confusion between the name of the chief and the village or location. A relative of this Nootka family may have acquired a chieftaincy on the east coast of Vancouver Island, probably in a Kwakiutl village, and used the same sequence of names. But all these conjectures still do not place "Namakazit" on any map.

Two other Hewitt pieces have locations which do not seem to have been registered by anyone else under the names he used. Two-ho Bay, or "Two House Bay," is the location given for a small box (BM, Vancouver 170; Hewitt ms. 316; Appendix 1:58) that Hewitt called a "buckett." The bent sides were sewn together with "creeper," which was probably his guess for a piece of spruce root. Opposite sides were perforated at the center near the top to accommodate the ends of a handle of twisted cedar bark.

There is also a hat (BM, Vancouver 191; Hewitt ms. 257; Appendix 1:127) in these "lost" pieces which is said to come from "Hawslee." The entry in the British Museum slips refers to "Amerika's Nordwest Kuste" (*Berlin Museum Publication*, plates I and V, and fig. 5), where a similar hat is shown and stated to be called "Keit" by the Koskimo of Vancouver Island. This is a comparative note which can be identified, for this publication contained the material brought back by Boas on one of his first trips to the Northwest Coast. The publication is now very rare. The hat is woven of spruce root and painted. It resembles one in the Cook collection (BM, NWC 5; Appendix 1:134). In the Hewitt manuscript the piece is called a cap, which is very understandable. In the eighteenth century this hat had a very steep and narrow brim and was tied with a chin strap so that it had the appearance of a close-fitting cap. Spruce-root hats are a northern specialty on the Northwest Coast, but they were traded south. They were usually painted on the crown only, whereas the nineteenth-century hats had broader brims and were painted all over.

Another location that cannot be found is Sea Passage, but there is little doubt that it belongs to this area. The object from there is a bow (BM, Vancouver 12; Hewitt ms. 313; Appendix 1:315), a plain one made of yew. It is rather thick, contracted at the grip, expanded in the arms, and contracted again at the tips. It is nocked about two inches from each end and has a string of twisted sinew. At the center for about sixteen inches the grip is covered with lashing that is partly thong and at the ends is of bark. The bow is reddish, and is fifty-five and three-eighths inches long.

Both the ships and the longboat expeditions cruised both sides of Banks Island, but very little has been preserved from the area. There are two very long arrow shafts, slender near the butts and thickest in the center. The butts are nocked and each has three large feathers bound with bark. The space over which the feathers extend is painted with dull red and black rings, with a broader ring near the upper ends of the feathers. There are also three broad red rings near the upper end of the shaft, which is hollowed out to receive a point. No point is left, but the shaft is still wrapped with bark at this place. One arrow has a smaller bark binding twenty-seven inches from the butt end, to which is attached a piece of two-ply cord wound around the shaft. The arrows are fifty-five and one-eighth and fifty-six and three-eighths inches long. If this cord just mentioned were of any length and wound around the shaft, it would resemble the harpoon-arrow type of the very long arrows used by the Eskimo. From Banks Island also came a curved piece of white bone (BM, Vancouver 71; Hewitt ms. 309; Appendix 1:337), with two unilateral barbs nearer the butt than the point. The butt is cut away into a wedge shape for fitting into a shaft and is perforated near the end. It is six and one-half inches long and does not look very convincing. With the perforation, it might have been an amulet or even a heavy awl.

In Brown's Passage, probably on Dundas or Porcher Island, was obtained an arrow (BM, Vancouver 44; Hewitt ms. 310; Appendix 1:290) with a barbed bone point. The shaft was of cedar, and a single feather remained and adhered to two bindings of bark. Under the feathering, as with the arrow discussed above (BM, Vancouver 71), the herringbone patterns were painted in brown on the shaft. The point was detachable and had a single barb. In accordance with its place of origin, it is probably Tsimshian.

From Salmon Cove in Observatory Inlet, the last anchorage before the region which is now Alaska, two bows and a salmon spear are in the collection. One is very fully described (BM, Vancouver 13; Hewitt ms. 312; Appendix 1:316) as being of brown wood, which may be willow. The bow is slackly strung and has a Cupid's bow shape. It looks like a poor copy of a strung convex bow. At the grip, "projecting at right angles a piece of wood is bound, resembling the bridge of a violin" (British Museum slip). Niblack, who shows a bow with this structure (Niblack 1890, plate 26, fig. 115, catalog number 75455), states that it is designed for receiving the blow of the string. He gives as an example one made of willow, which is said to come from the Tinné Indians of the interior of Alaska. It was collected by John J. McLean in the late 1880s.

Another bow, which is not such a problem, is placed here only because it is in the British Museum catalog as Vancouver 13*a*, not mentioned in Hewitt, and follows Salmon Cove. It is of dark brown hardwood, strung with twisted sinew, and on the flat side was once covered with a black gumlike substance which is partly worn off. The bow has hardly any curve.

The last piece from Salmon Cove is listed as a "double headed spear." It is formed of two equal pieces that were originally lashed together (BM, Vancouver 92; Hewitt ms. 130). It is worm-eaten, but what remains is probably the type of salmon spear widely used on the Northwest Coast, of which there are good illustrations in Niblack (1890, plate 29, fig. 138). The piece is labeled "salmon striker," which is a good description of its use.

The Vancouver voyage went on into Alaskan waters, but the problems remained the same: more islands hid the mainland and every inlet beckoned with the possibility of leading to the long-sought Northwest Passage. The Indians came in greater numbers than early in the voyage, and they showed greater aggressiveness. They had met many fur traders with uneven tempers, who had muskets and even small cannons ready for use. These people were not novices at trading, and even when Europeans had not themselves been there, their goods were known through intertribal trade. In 1793 the survey expedition had little contact with Indians; the Indians were away from their villages, and Vancouver was still primarily committed to his survey. Since the season was fast closing, he did not linger and made no effort to seek out Indian villages. The Alaskan survey will continue with the Tlingit (chap. 6).

5

The Haida, the Shrewdest of Traders, Who Set the Style for Demands for Trade Goods

The Haida lived primarily on the Queen Charlotte Islands, but they also had settlements on Dall Island and Prince of Wales Island in Alaska. We know that these Haida migrated from the northwest area of Graham Island, possibly at the end of the seventeenth century. The Tlingit who occupied Prince of Wales Island were pushed north, and once the Haida villages were Kaigani on Dall Island and Sukkwan, Klinkwan, Koinglas, Howkan, and Kasaan on Prince of Wales Island. In the 1870s, with the establishment of canneries and the building of schools, the Haida gradually concentrated around Hydaburg, Craig, and New Kasaan, leaving behind them in the old villages many large wood sculpture houses, especially house frames with carved posts and some totem poles. Many of these villages, especially Kaigani, were considered summer fishing sites and were used by Haida whose winter villages were at the north end of Graham Island. In several diaries of fur traders there are notations that they came to the north shore of Graham Island too late in the spring or too early in the fall, before or after the annual migration.

The earliest trading activities developed around Nootka Sound, but when the ships began to arrive at Prince William Sound and then sailed south, they discovered the trading possibilities on the Queen Charlotte Islands.

The rich descriptions of Indian life at Nootka cannot be matched for the Queen Charlotte Islands, where the fur traders outnumbered the explorers. The latter were observers, but the fur traders came for quick and large profit. The island group was named by Dixon in 1787 for his ship, and not knowing this Gray in 1789 called them the Washington Islands for his ship. When Great Britain established ownership of these islands the name Washington soon disappeared (Walbran 1909, p. 410). Marchand quickly states that he is the second Frenchman to reach this group, the first being La Pérouse in 1786; but since La Pérouse's journal was not published until 1798, this visit was not generally known. His journal only lists the geographic names he gave, mostly on the west side of Graham Island, and Marchand loyally used them; but they do not come into the literature otherwise.

It is interesting to recall here that, except for the unfortunate contact of Chirikof with the Tlingit in 1741, the first Northwest Coast Indians encountered by Europeans were the Haida (see chap. 1). The Spaniards, of course, saw only the northernmost small group on Langara Island, but they again met Haida on Dall Island and at Bucareli Bay, Alaska. The excellent descriptions of these Kaigani Haida left by Crespi and Peña have been discussed, and we have the notes of Camaaño, who visited the area in 1792 after the Indians had had frequent contact with fur traders. As soon as the trade expanded to the Queen Charlotte Islands, Kaigani and Bucareli Bay became a rendezvous for fur traders, where they often stopped to assess their summer's harvest and prepare their ships to make the voyage home, perhaps with a stop in China, or to winter in Hawaii for another season in the Northwest.

After Crespi's and Peña's fine notes there is no mention of the Haida on their main islands until Dixon circumnavigated the group in 1787 and revealed the richness of the fur supply. This opened the floodgates, and every year during the next decade a procession of trading ships came to the islands. Some merely recorded how many skins they received and mentioned the Indians only when they did not act as docile purveyors of the desired goods. When the Indians became dissatisfied with strings of beads and became fickle in their demands, that also became a matter of record. However, there were some visitors who had human interests, and to them present anthropologists and historians are grateful.

Dixon's notes were recorded by W. B. Beresford, who compiled the record of the entire voyage in a series of letters. In his haste to gather sea otter skins before another trader came along, it is questionable whether Dixon himself would have taken the time to write a journal. But even though fur trading was his consuming occupation, he realized that some knowledge and understanding of the people he met was important to his success with them. His limited remarks are the first records of the Haida in the major islands.

Dixon approached the islands from the northwest and thought that they were part of the mainland until he circumnavigated them. He did not know of La Pérouse's visit, because his narrative had not yet been published, and so he renamed many places to which La Pérouse had given French names. In his entire circumnavigation of the Queen Charlotte Islands he never landed, so his observations were made from his contacts with the Indians who came to the ship. He estimated that there were about seventeen hundred inhabitants in these islands and that they had had no contact with any Europeans. They had metal knives and spear points, but these were probably gotten in trade or through warfare.

In the Gold Harbor district Swanton heard a legend that may be a pseudohistorical record of Dixon's ship as it proceeded down the west coast. Swanton was told the story by a Kaisun informant in 1905:

> All the people who moved from Skidegate Inlet to Tc!a'al were dead and their children growing old, when the first ship appeared. When it came in sight, they thought it was the spirit of the "Pestilence," and dancing on the shore, they waved their palms toward the newcomers to turn back. When the white people landed, they sent down to them their old men, who had only a few years to live, anyhow, expecting them to fall dead; but when the new arrivals began buying their furs, the younger ones went down too, trading for axes and iron, the marten and land otter skin cloaks they wore. A youth who was next in succession to the chieftainship at Cumshewa was met by two of the white men who said "Halloo, Gomsiwa"! They mistook him for the "Captain's son" who had been lost. When he became chief the youth called himself "Gomsiwa" because of this circumstance. [This is a Haida jest, the word Gomsiwa is probably Bella Bella *Q!omx.siwa*, "rich at the mouth of the river."] The name of the vessel the Haida recalled as La'lAwai. When one of the white men shot a gun, some of the people said he did it by striking it on the side; another, that he blew through it; and a third, that a little bird sat on top and made it go off. One man purchased kettles, cups, etc. and hung them on his clothing as ornaments. [Swanton 1905, p. 105]

Dixon compared the Haida with the people he had just seen at Norfolk (Sitka) Sound. His first attention was directed toward the labret worn by the women. In contrast to the Sitka Sound tribe of Tlingit, where only the women of high class wore labrets, among the Haida all women seemed to wear them. The Haida men were not jealous of their women and allowed them to go aboard the ship, but not, as the sailors expected, for "amorous entertainment" but to steal what their Haida men wanted. These women wore very interesting complete costumes. First they had a fine tanned skin dress, cut close to the body, which extended from the neck to the middle of the calf. Over this was a cloak or cape which was coarser and sat loose "like a petticoat," tied with leather strings on the shoulders. The picture shows the cloak, but evidently the girl sketched was not wearing the tunic under it (Dixon 1789, facing p. 226).

Through his trading Dixon discovered that there were both village chiefs and clan chiefs, though he did not call them by these names. Only the chiefs did the trading, but if a chief's methods and results were not approved, the people of his village could name a subchief to take his place. Often the trade deal had to be approved by the woman who was head of the family, and stories are told of men being beaten by their wives if the bargain they made was regarded as unsatisfactory. When a party came to trade, they wore ceremonial clothing and sang songs which were introduced by the chief. He wore, among other things, a large coat of tanned elkskin decorated with dried berries and beaks of birds, which rattled when he moved. Dried berries are not mentioned as ornaments in later ethnographies, but the birds' beaks are those of the familiar puffin, or sea parrot, which were used in many ways on costumes and as rattles. The coat of elkskin sounds like the tunic of the same material worn under the wooden cuirass used in warfare. They often heard the Haida singing, and Dixon felt that even this expressed the ferocity of their character. The music had good rhythm, but there was no modulation or harmony.

In May 1787, after a short visit to Prince William Sound, Colnett and Duncan in the *Prince of Wales* and the *Princess Royal* started down the coast and, meeting exceptionally bad weather, crossed over to the Queen Charlotte Islands, where they found people with little iron. They recognized that this tribe spoke a different language and saw large canoes carved of a solid piece of wood. They saw no permanent houses but observed remnants of summer fishing camps. After another attempt at the mainland, Colnett again came to the Queen Charlotte Islands, where he received a letter from Duncan, carried by an Indian chief, asking him to anchor in Saint James Bay. While he was at the south end of the islands he observed an interesting interaction between two local groups. The Indians saw canoes of northern Indians—presumably Haida—and fled to their canoes to put on their armor. This let Colnett see how the wooden helmet was used. Since he does not go into detail, we can assume he referred to a war helmet. Colnett stated that a good-tempered, humorous fellow with a bow and arrow put on a costume of bearskin and performed antics. The entire bearskin, including the head, was sometimes used by shamans, and this "antic" may have been a war dance. Shamans accompanied war parties and gave them courage and protection by their dances and incantations. The chief of each side solicited assistance from the ship's crew. The northern people were old acquaintances, but since the cause of the imminent conflict and the local practices were not known, it seemed best not to respond. The chief, Shelkenance (is this Kansheen of Ingraham at Juan Perez Sound?), advanced in a small canoe and both sides dispatched their women to the shore. The chiefs came close together and were very vociferous; the northern people were the more aggressive and kept their spears ready. But in spite of all this, there was no battle. Since it was growing dark, each party paddled a different way to their homes. A thick fog came in during the night and was heavy all through the morning. Several canoes came from the north, but when they saw the southern Indians alongside the ship they left. Then a storm broke, and Colnett could not keep his rendezvous with Duncan.

The people of these islands, according to Colnett, were the most civilized they had seen and made beautiful utensils. Large spoons were made of mountain sheep horns, which Captain King said weighed as much as twenty pounds. These horns were purchased from Se-ax, a chief living on the east shore of Queen Charlotte Sound. This is the name of a line of Tsimshian chiefs who were great traders between the inland people and the coast (Boas 1916, p. 513). A ladle of this type is in the collection at the British Museum (NWC 34; Appendix 1:222), attributed to the Banks collection. It was given to Sir Joseph by Captain Dixon when he returned from the Northwest Coast on 22 May 1789.

The Tsimshian chief also traded copper, but Colnett did not find out where he obtained it. The year Colnett came to the Northwest Coast for sea otter skins was not a good one, because by that time every Indian had his long knife and his iron spear points and therefore they made no effort to hunt. This attitude toward work still prevails in many areas, and it is difficult for the Europeans, who like to amass wealth, to understand it.

Colnett also commented on the mobility of the population. He found a deserted village and a cemetery where the grave boxes and the houses were in equal stages of decay. He wondered what made the people leave. Poor fish runs? Starvation? In the spring of 1788 he noticed that many people looked poorly nourished, and he wondered if they had had a hard winter. At this boundary between the northern and southern populations of the Queen Charlotte Islands the people were even less stationary. Unattached people who strayed into the region were looking for the winning side. Some Indians who visited the ship promised to bring skins, but they stole a blacksmith's hammer and were afraid to come back. When no other trade goods were available the Haida liked buttons, but it took a great number to buy a skin. They asked for the buttons from the crew's clothing, and when they were told the owners needed them they replied, "not the ones on the back."

Colnett's journal is still in manuscript, although a microfilm is available for study. It has a peculiar personal quality, as if he were writing for his own use and not as an official report. He may have related all these minor incidents to explain the small number of skins they found, which was equally due to very poor weather, the character of the Indians, and the course of events. He came after the first impact, and the Haida had not yet settled down to a continuous trade and responded to the great demand for furs (Colnett 1788; ms. pagination is poor).

When Gray came back to the Queen Charlotte Islands after his journey south of Nootka, Hoskins commented on the clothing worn by the Haida at Rose Harbor, the northeastern point of the islands. He mentioned that a knee-length skin dress the women wore under their cedar bark clothing resembled those worn at Chickleset Bay (in Kyuquot territory of the Nootka). "On their heads they wore a shallow wicker cap tied under the chin." This is again a woven hat of spruce root or split cedar bark with a brim so narrow that it fits close to the head and looks like a cap. Everyone wore glass beads, buttons, and Chinese coins, many of which were sewed on capes made of European cloth. The men carried double-pointed metal daggers in leather cases, slung around their necks. These daggers were always bright and sharp (Hoskins 1941, p. 205).

Gray then crossed over to the southern tip of Alaska, where he saw the Haida at Kasaan Bay, and Hoskins identified the people as related to those on the "Washington" Islands (as Gray had named the Queen Charlotte Islands). No other explorer of that period penetrated so far into Clarence Strait. Orth (1967, p. 720) states that the Haida village was *possibly* established before 1800. Gray's visit in 1792 makes the information certain. Hoskins is again the careful observer, and adds both to the information and to the problem of the eighteenth-century weaving. He stated that the people of Kasaan wore peculiar woolen mantles; some were white, and others had a white background, beautifully patterned with various fancy figures in yellow, green, red, black, and dark brown. These colors were woven into the mantle like pile on velvet, and there were tassels made into little figures that moved when they walked. The top edge was fur and the bottom had a deep fringe. They would not part with them at any price (see Appendix 2, weaving; Hoskins 1941, p. 225).

Ingraham, Captain of the *Hope*, arrived in the Queen Charlotte Islands at Magee's Sound on the west coast of Moresby Island on 29 June 1791, and after celebrating the Fourth of July with roast hog and cheers, started to sail north until he found a good bay, which he named for himself. Walbran believes it was Skelu Bay. At the north end of the islands he arrived at Cloak Bay and met Cow, the chief whose principal village was at the entrance of Cox Strait (Parry Passage). The Indians there did not like his trade goods, for they had gotten plenty from Douglas on the *Grace*, who was there early in 1791, and from Captain Barnet of the *Gustavus III*, who had supplied them with blue jackets and trousers. Cow promised to hunt sea otter for him, as he promised Marchand several weeks later, but neither promise brought any results. Ingraham examined the village and was especially attracted by two carved poles about forty feet high, so designed that one entered the chief's house by stepping through the mouth of the lowest figure. These poles are described in greater detail by Marchand, and these two observers are the first to mention this most distinctive form of carving of the Northwest Coast Indians. Near the village was a crude amphitheater which Ingraham thought was intended for exhibitions of dancing and boxing. He also visited the "fort" which Marchand found and called it a "hippa" from Dixon's name for an island with a similar fortification. Swanton lists a number of "forts" for the T!anu but not for any other Haida groups. He includes the northern end of Graham Island, and so one would expect them to be mentioned if any of importance were there at the beginning of the twentieth century or were remembered by his informants (Swanton 1905, p. 278). Ingraham noticed a large pile of rocks that had been gathered for throwing down. On the shore was a strange rock that looked like a ship, and beyond it was a small island used as a burial place for chiefs. Boxes were set in little houses and before them stood carved poles, a practice which is still found in many places on the Northwest Coast. Only the frames of some of the dwellings were left, which indicates that the houses were probably the traditional Northwest Coast type built with heavy house posts and roof beams completely free from the planks laid vertically or horizontally to form the walls. Often these planks were taken along in the summer to build temporary houses on lighter frames; so the heavy framework that stayed behind did not always indicate a permanently abandoned house. Since the people of this region went to Kaigani for the summer, the village might look different in winter. Vegetation grows so rapidly in this region that an overgrown, deserted look develops quickly.

During his stay here Ingraham was driven to devise new trade goods. Since he had a good supply of iron which the Indians did not want for tools, he put his blacksmith to work making iron collars. These were made of iron rods one-half inch thick, and three pieces were twisted together to encircle the neck. They were polished and weighed five to seven pounds (see Appendix 2). At first these collars were the height of fashion, but in a very few years they began to lose their value. In order to maintain their price Ingraham tried to sell them only for prime skins and only to high-class people. They were worn for ceremonial occasions, and at the death of the owner they were displayed on his mortuary column or at the grave house along with his ceremonial blanket and copper. At the peak of their success each was worth three prime skins that would sell in Canton for forty dollars apiece.

These collars are rarely seen even in museum collections. Emmons found one in a trash pile in an old communal house in Wrangell, and in 1908 Dr. Newcombe knew of four distributed in the Haida villages of Klue and Dadens of North Island and of two from Masset. There is one in the collection at the National Museum of Canada (NMC VII.B.242) which, according to the catalog, was obtained by Dr. Newcombe in the 1890s. It is said to be made of copper, but the piece was on exhibition and therefore could not be handled. This may be one of the four that Dr. Newcombe mentioned, although Ingraham made his of iron.

In his article on the copper neck rings Lieutenant Emmons relates the antiquity of their use to the legend of "the salmon doctor," in which a child goes to the salmon country and is speared when he returns to his river with the salmon. When his mother cuts the salmon open she recognizes it as her son because of the copper neck ring. When the salmon body is placed in a burial chest on the roof of the house, a shaman in full regalia emerges from it (Emmons 1908, p. 647).

Emmons also points out that many ornaments on the Northwest Coast are made by twisting various kinds of material into a ropelike pattern—the great neck rings and head rings of shredded cedar bark, the twisted rope of nettle bark on the halibut hooks, and many other types of cordage which is used decoratively. On all of these two strands are used in the twist, and so it is interesting that for the iron Ingraham used three strands, which is typical of European cord. This may sound very trivial, but it is by such distinctions that an anthropologist can sometimes tell when and where an object was manufactured. In other words, Ingraham was adhering to his own cultural pattern and the Haida seemed willing to accept it because the collars were foreign made (Emmons 1908, p. 647).

When canoes came from the east side of Dixon Entrance, Chief Cow asked Ingraham not to trade with them, because they were "bad." Ingraham did conceal his collars so that he could get rid of his blue jackets and trousers and greatcoats, but the strange chief saw a collar and would trade his last three prime skins only for that. Chief Cow was vexed, said Ingraham.

After finding too much competition at Skincuttle Inlet, Ingraham decided to go to Alaska. But the weather was unfavorable, and so he sailed to the mainland of British Columbia, where he traded in Laredo Sound. Wind brought him back to the Queen Charlotte Islands, this time at the south end in Houston Stewart Channel. While they were traveling he kept his crew busy making blue jackets with bright buttons, and so he had these in addition to his iron collars. He went back to Skincuttle Inlet, but the chief had only indifferent skins. When they were refused, he offered to go and fight for some, not hunt. Plundering each other's villages seemed to be an acknowledged way of getting a supply. This action was not limited to the Indians alone, for many of the fur traders did likewise. Sometimes they would resort to the technique, which Ingraham used at times, of keeping the chief prisoner on the ship until the village had been cleaned out of skins. In many places the chief would not allow any trade until he received a "gift" from the trader. The chiefs also tried to establish reciprocal gift-giving as the system of trading. They were too proud to become commercial!

When his trade goods ran out again Ingraham continued to make collars, but he also set out his Hawaiian feather cloaks and caps for trading. One chief took some, but then tried to recall the bargain. Ingraham stood his ground; so the Queen Charlotte Islands had some pieces that would have sorely confused a visiting anthropologist. Since trading had been poor, Ingraham decided to leave on 15 August and sail to China to sell his skins and acquire more trading material. He left just a week before other visitors appeared—Marchand from France and Gray from Boston. About a week after Ingraham left the north end of the Queen Charlotte Islands, Robert Gray in the *Columbia* arrived at Houston Stewart Channel, where he met Chief Coyac, who is also known as Cunneah, Coneshaw, and Coyah. He had exchanged names with Captain William Douglas of the *Iphigenia* in 1789, and thus is also called Taglas Cania. The name Douglas is still used in the Queen Charlotte Islands by the chief's descendents. This visit is recorded by Boit, one of the officers of the ship, who regarded the people as very savage. The men were naked except for a skin thrown over one shoulder, but the women were entirely covered with a garment made of the bark of a tree (cedar bark). Earlier descriptions of the women's garments usually specified that they were of tanned skin. Whether these were local or seasonal differences or class distinctions cannot be determined. Clothes may have been selected according to weather and occasion. Cedar bark garments were found everywhere, but it is difficult to imagine the structure of a one-piece garment. The Nootka ladies wore a wraparound skirt and a shoulder cape to the waist. This may have been used here and have escaped the notice of the male visitors.

During their stay Boit went to see one of the villages and found a comfortable house where the inhabitants were sitting and eating roasted mussels and singing a warlike song. Since Dixon commented on the vociferousness of their singing, Boit may have inferred the warlike tone. After two weeks of trading they sailed north to Cumshewa Inlet and met Cumshewa himself, a powerful chief mentioned by many of the fur traders (Boit 1921, pp. 280–81).

Marchand sighted the Queen Charlotte Islands on the afternoon of 22 August 1791. The next morning he found an inlet (named Cloak Bay by Dixon) which is part of the channel between Langara Island (North Island) and the northern coast of Graham Island, the larger of the two principal islands of the group. This was discovered by Captain Douglas, but the channel was probably found originally by Gray in the *Washington*. Other than Dixon, Douglas, Duncan, and Gray, no one had attempted to describe the customs of the Indians or the physical characteristics of the region.

When the *Solide*, with Marchand, came into Cloak Bay, no canoes came out to meet her; so a barge was sent out under Captain Chanal with trade goods. Three canoes came to this vessel with about thirty men, women, and children aboard. They came from the north shore of Graham Island, where some houses could be sighted. They had no weapons and only fresh fish and some old skins to barter. On a small island in the bay Captain Chanal found some palisades that looked like an old construction. The enclosure had a platform built out from the rock, supported by several stakes. Entry was by a notched log. There were several wooden boxes without lids (possibly wooden drums). The most extraordinary items were two pictures painted on planks eight to nine feet wide and five feet high, each picture consisting of two planks set edge to edge. The painting was done in red, black, and green and represented parts of the human body. Both were the same. They had been defaced by exposure, and their age could not be estimated. The pictures were called "caniate" or "caniak" in their language, presumably Haida. The enclosure was not a dwelling or a fort. It may have been used for some religious purpose, its discoverers believed, or it may have been refuge when the village was attacked (Fleurieu 1801, p. 395). Adam refers to a "colossal" painting whose discovery he attributes to Swanton. It represents a *qonaqada*, which is the Tlingit word for a monster, a concept present in both their mythology and that of the Haida. I mention this painting because it is done on a house wall and is very large, but it contains only one figure, whereas the paintings mentioned by Ingraham and Marchand are multifigured (Adam 1927, pp. 16, 35).

The Indians bartered only five sea otter skins, some of cubs, and one beaver skin, because they wanted woolen jackets and blankets and there were none on the barge. The Indians offered to hunt if the French would stay a few days. In all, seven or eight canoes came with about sixty persons. This seemed a small part of the population, from the number of "huts" they saw on the shore. The barge returned to the ship to get more trading goods, and while they were waiting for the hunters to return the chief offered to take the party to visit some of the houses on the shore.

We are very fortunate to have an account of the Haida architecture from a Frenchman who had more knowledge and interest in this than the average explorer. Fleurieu has described Haida houses in great detail. They were forty-five to fifty feet wide in front and twenty-five feet deep. Each house had six to ten posts along the front. The house planks were ten inches wide, but he does not say whether they were placed horizontally or vertically. The roof sloped very little and was about ten to twelve feet high at the center, with a smoke hole in the middle. There were small windows in the sides. Inside there were partitions six to eight feet high, presumably between families. The better houses had two stories; the lower one was underground, level with the bases of the posts that supported the roof. This cellar was dug six feet away from the sides and was five feet deep. Beams were laid across and covered with thick planks, and steps down were cut in the earth and encased in planks. The cellar was their winter habitation. The door to the house was oval, raised a foot and a half above the ground, and was part of a huge tree trunk that rose to the height of the house at the center front. The opening, which represented the gaping mouth of a human or a beast, was surmounted with a hooked nose about two feet long. Above this was the figure of a man in the position of a child in the womb, with remarkably small genital organs. Above this was a gigantic figure of a man standing erect, wearing a sugarloaf-shaped cap almost the height of the figure itself. Areas not used for the principal figures were carved with frogs, toads, lizards, and other animals and parts of human beings similar to the figures in the painting at the palisades (Fleurieu 1801, pp. 269–70). Any explanation of these figures was impossible because of the language barrier.

This is one of the earliest and most complete descriptions of the large wood sculptures for which the Northwest Coast is famous and answers the question whether figures in these proportions were made before European contact. With the mortuary columns and the house posts, these frontal poles attached to the house are undoubtedly the forerunners of the large freestanding poles. The arrangement of figures, the combination of animal and human representations, and the filling of vacant spaces all appear in Northwest Coast art in its classic period.

Roblet, the surgeon of the expedition, said that twenty-five families, with five to six persons in each, lived in such houses, but the editor disputes this, saying there would not have been space for that many people to sleep on the floor. Unlike houses in other parts of the Northwest Coast, these have no distinguishable sleeping area like the bed platforms farther south. Cradles were suspended like hammocks. Much gear for hunting and fishing was hung on the walls. All houses had many utensils such as wooden bowls, trays, and dishes, spoons of horn or whalebone, and European goods like iron pots and kettles, frying pans, boilers, and tin basins. Among the tools, metal adzes, joiner's chisels, planes, iron daggers, and lances—all of English manufacture—showed the extent of the fur trade.

Temporary "huts" were scattered and may have been occupied by visitors who had come to trade with the ships. The Haida, like the Tlingit, often carried with them strips of bark, small planks, and stakes to set up shelters when necessary. At some distance from the permanent houses was a graveyard. There were single posts about ten feet high and one foot in diameter, on top of which there was a small platform for the body, covered with moss and stones. Others had four posts on which was placed a coffin covered with carving and sealed. These probably belonged to a chief's family.

Admiring the Indians' taste for architecture, Marchand describes some "large edifices" that did not fit into the Northwest Coast pattern. They did not seem to belong to anyone, and he wondered if they were places of worship. They consisted of an enclosure built of posts six to eight feet high, in the middle of which was a square, uncovered structure built of handsome planks twenty-five feet long and two and one-half inches thick. Sometimes a cave was made in it. This is not clear, but it may have been a pit in which dancers dressed and from which they emerged. The posts could possibly be a house framework from which the outer planks had been removed, a common practice on the Northwest Coast. The inner structure has no parallel in the literature.

In describing the main apartment in the house, Marchand writes:

> Among a great number of figures very much varied, and which at first appeared to me to resemble nothing, I distinguished in the middle a human figure which its extraordinary proportions, still more than its size, rendered it monstrous. Its thighs extended horizontally, after the manner of tailors seated, are slim, long, out of proportion and form a carpenter's square with the legs which are equally ill-made; the arms extended in the form of a cross, and terminated by fingers slender and bent. The face is 12″ [French], from the extremity of the chin to the top of the forehead, and 18″ from one ear to the other; it is surmounted by a sort of cap. Dark red, apple green and black are here blended with the natural colours of the wood, and distributed in symmetrical spots, with sufficient intelligence to afford at a distance an agreeable object. [Fleurieu 1801, p. 280]
> From the description which Surgeon Roblet gives of this picture, it might be imagined that it resembles those shapeless attempts of an intelligent child, who undertakes without principles, to draw the objects which present themselves to his sight; I remark however that the voyagers who have frequented the different parts of the North-west Coast often saw there works of painting and sculpture in which the proportions were tolerably well observed, and the execution of which bespoke a taste and perfection which we do not expect to find in countries where the men seem still to have the appearance of savages. But what must astonish most, and I shall resume this observation in the sequel, is to see painting everywhere, everywhere sculpture, among a nation of hunters. [Fleurieu 1801, p. 281]

The visits of fur traders and explorers to the Queen Charlotte Islands continued through the summer seasons of 1791 to 1795, each venture trying to carry trading goods which would satisfy the Indians. The Indians, on the other hand, had accumulated so much in the way of castoff clothing, blankets, beads, cloth, iron and copper, and household utensils that they became harder to please, and it was difficult for them to absorb this new wealth into their economic structure. Many objects were not of actual use to them, and so they could only be regarded as prestige items and were used in potlatches. The diaries became repetitious except that the frustrations that developed out of these trends brought more violence between the traders and the Indians.

Early in 1791 the trading ship *Gustavus III*, commanded by Captain Barnet, arrived at Forrester Island (Douglas Island at that time). The ship came from China and arrived with a crew partially composed of men who had lost their berths in the sale of the *Massachusetts*, including John Bartlett, whose narrative makes this voyage of great value. Although Forrester Island is now a bird sanctuary, it was then as well populated with Haida as any of the offshore islands, and its leader was Chief Huegar (Ucah, in Ingraham's diary). The people wore sea otter cloaks and had bird feathers in their hair, which was matted and liberally covered with grease and red ocher. They also had a great number of tails and locks hanging from their heads which they acquired by cutting the hair of their victims in war and attaching it to their own. The women wore labrets (Bartlett 1925, p. 298).

Barnet then moved to Cloak Bay, where he found a chief called Conneshaw, who was mentioned by Meares as Blakow Conneshaw, having exchanged names with Captain William Douglas. Since this name does not occur again, it may be that he was a visitor there and that he was Cunneah who exchanged names with Douglas and is often mentioned in the literature as Taglas Cania. Bartlett writes that they were surrounded by about six hundred canoes, and that they found excellent trading with the rather aggressive Haida. On the way to this trading area the captain had his blacksmith make iron collars, but when they arrived they found that the current price for five prime skins was a sheet of copper. These large sheets were used by the Haida to make the famous copper shields which became so important in the potlatches of the nineteenth century. The iron collars were yesterday's fad!

The *Gustavus III*, after sailing along the west coast of the islands and rounding Cape Saint James, went northeast across Heceta Strait and discovered an island which Caamaño found again the next year and named Bonilla Island. Here there was a chief whom Bartlett called Clutiver, but this name never occurs again and it is possible that this was Chief Clue from Tanu, which is more or less west on Moresby Island. Going back to the main islands, they traded with Cumshewa and at Skidegate before returning to Cloak Bay. There they found many men wearing red jackets, showing that Douglas had been trading there. At this point Bartlett added an interesting note to the stone boiling technique practiced by all Northwest Coast tribes: a hole is dug in the sand, which is heated, and the basket of food is set into it to accelerate the rate of boiling. But Bartlett also contributed an observation for which he has become famous in the literature. At Cloak Bay he sketched a house which had a totem pole at the entrance. The visitor walked through the open mouth of one of the figures (Bartlett 1925, p. 306, illustration facing p. 306).

The activities just described were primarily in the major islands of the Haida, but one must not forget the branches at Bucareli Bay and Kaigani in Alaska. In the very busy year of 1792, the Spaniards again turned their attention to the Northwest Coast, with the objective of finding the location for a permanent settlement to replace Nootka Sound, which they expected to surrender as a judgment of the Nootka Sound controversy. While these plans were being developed, Maurelle, who was appointed as commander of the expedition, became very ill, and Caamaño was chosen in his place. On his way to San Blas Caamaño was thrown from his horse and could not immediately accept the appointment. The viceroy was very anxious to get this expedition under way so he turned to Malaspina, who had returned to Acapulco for advice. He offered to lend two of his best officers, Dionisio Alcala Galiano and Cayetano Valdes, to undertake the command which Maurelle and Caamaño could not assume. The two ships, the *Sutil* and the *Mexicana*, which had just been built were assigned to the voyage. Another great asset to the expedition was the appointment of Jose Cordero, a Mexican artist, whose sketches of landscape and people are among the most important documents in the Spanish archives.

Caamaño, when he recovered, was transferred to the *Aranzazu* to make another reconnaissance of the area around Bucareli Bay. This was prompted by the rumor of further Russian settlements in Alaska. Since the Russian encroachment was in the north, it was considered wiser to settle there than to find another spot as far south as Nootka Sound. For the same reason the efforts started at Nuñez Gaona (Neah Bay) were discontinued after a council of the captains of the Spanish ships held in July 1792 decided to abandon the region.

Caamaño left San Blas on 3 March 1792 and arrived at Nootka Sound on 13 June. With little delay he continued to Bucareli Bay and anchored there for extensive exploration with the cutter and pinnace. He and his officers made some interesting observations on the Indians they encountered. They bartered freely with the Spaniards but were very specific about what they wanted. For their sea otter skins they wanted cloth—baize or serge—or other materials for clothing. They would accept small shells provided they were green—probably California *Haliotis* (abalone). They did not ask for iron or copper, for they had undoubtedly received enough from the fur traders who had been in the vicinity for at least five years. Every man carried a knife in a sheath around his neck. This type of weapon, illustrated in Dixon, is a well-shaped dagger with a twelve-inch blade, about four inches wide. The hilt of iron was covered with leather and a thong about seventeen inches long was attached to tie the weapon to the wrist. The pommel inclosed a small knife about six inches long and four inches wide with a blunt end. This was used in fighting to scar the face, and many of the men who came to the ships showed signs of having been in such combat (Caamaño, 1849, pp. 202, 203). (Appendix 2).

These Indians came to the ships, but the exploring expedition did not find any village in Bucareli Bay where the fishing seemed to be poor. They noted that the language spoken by the Indians differed from Nootkan—it was Haida. The women wore labrets and ear and nose ornaments.

Caamaño described the defensive armor of the Indians in great detail, but he did not say whether he actually saw it being worn. It was the rod type which extends from the shoulder to the groin. The cylindrical pieces of wood were woven together with a "hempen thread" which sounds like a fine string of nettle bark. They wore thigh guards of the same material. Over this they wore a shirt of skin, in this instance moose hide traded from the interior. If the translation is correct, wearing the skin shirt *over* the armor is not the usual pattern. In sketches and other descriptions of the use of these two kinds of armor the skin jacket is worn next to the body and the cuirass over it. This withstood all native weapons and stopped a musket shot at moderate range. Caamaño stated that he was told that a helmet was used with this costume, but he did not see one (Caamaño 1849, p. 205).

As was often reported elsewhere, the women were better at bargaining than the men, and if they disapproved of a deal it was called off. Caamaño admired their ability to handle their canoes, though the boats were not as well built as those of the Nootka. He finds the women modestly dressed in tunics of fine deerskin or trade material which extended from the neck to the ankles. The costume was completed with a cape of bearskin, sea otter, or some other fur. Their chief ornaments were rings of twisted iron worn around the wrists and ankles, reminding the visitor of fetters. These were made on demand by the ship's armorer, because the fur traders never were sure what the fancy of the Indians would be. Neck rings of the same style were also worn, especially by the Haida.

The most general dress of the men was typical of the entire coast, a cloak of animal skins or made of the "inner bark of the pine tree." This of course is cedar bark. Caamaño speaks of an unusual tunic he bought that was made, he said, of deerskin dressed white. Newcomb, who annotated this diary, quite correctly suggested that this was caribou skin traded from the interior. The front of the tunic had four fringed rows of the same material, one above the other. These were ornamented with feathers, bits of whalebone, and cedar bark shredded and dyed. Such garments were known in the nineteenth century among the Athapascans in the interior, and specimens can be found in many museum collections. The Indians pointed out that these were their best clothes (Caamaño 1849, p. 206).

Caamaño also obtained a cloak which he describes as made of the "inner wool of the wild goat, spun into a fine thread and well woven. Narrow strips of sea otter fur were worked into this; and are so neatly sewn that the outer side of the garment has the appearance of whole skin, while the fur is not noticeable on the inner side" (Caamaño 1849, p. 207). This description agrees perfectly with a blanket in the museum at Leningrad (2552–4), which was given by the officers of the Cook expedition to Major Behm, the commander of the port of Petropavlovsk, when he was very gracious in repairing and supplying their ships on their return from the coast of Siberia (see Appendix 2, weaving).

When the survey of Bucareli Bay was completed, Caamaño sailed along the west coast of Dall Island and crossed over to the northern end of the Queen Charlotte Islands to relate these two areas to each other in his explorations. In Parry Passage (Puerto de Florida Blanca), four Indians in a canoe came alongside and asked permission to come aboard. When it was granted one man came on the quarterdeck and asked to go to the captain's cabin. He professed friendship and presented Caamaño with a sea otter skin, for which he received gifts of shells, knives, and mirrors. The Indian was joined by another, and after they were assured that the ship was coming to anchor they asked permission to sleep aboard. At supper, which they shared with the captain, they ate heartily, drinking wine and spirits and handling forks and spoons with great skill. All this impressed Caamaño very much and showed the extent of contact they must have had with traders and explorers (Caamaño 1849, p. 215).

In the morning two canoes came from Langara (North) Island, the first carrying the chief of the harbor. He was the chief known to the fur traders as Cunneah Coyac, Coyah, or Coneshow, and also as Taglas Cania, and was the father of one of the Indians who had slept aboard.

Cunneah's canoe contained about forty-five persons, including women and children. They were all seated or kneeling except the coxswain, known by the native word *samoguet*, who stood up to lead the singing to which the paddlers timed their strokes (Caamaño 1849, p. 215). The canoe was fifty-three feet long, had an average beam of six feet, and was about four and one-half feet in depth. In the bow were two men who beat time with the hilts of their paddles, and there was also a large box drum which was struck with the fists. When they reached the ship they dressed themselves, many in native clothes like those of Bucareli Bay, but many also in long frock coats, trousers or loose short breeches, and pieces of cloth as capes, mostly in blue. The coxswain's dress consisted of wide breeches of light blue gray serge and a large cloak of marten, ornamented with extra tails, a distinguishing mark of a village chief. When he came aboard he greeted Caamaño by extending his hand and touching his face with both hands and saying "*Bueno! Bueno!*" All the actions of these people clearly indicated that in five years of contact with Europeans they had learned superficial patterns of behavior. The chief's daughter was judged a good-looking girl, perhaps partly because she did not wear a labret. In the manner of behavior which the chief had probably learned from Europeans, she was offered to the captain and went quickly to his cabin. Caamaño makes no further statement, but does say that when she left with her family she appeared to be displeased with the attention paid to her. A second canoe, smaller than the Cunneah's, arrived with the *tasen*, who seemed to be another chief and who went through similar ceremonies (Caamaño 1849, p. 217).

There was a cluster of seven villages on the north side of Parry Passage on Langara Island that was known later as DAdens, and another settlement opposite on the northern shore of Graham Island known as Kiusta. These Indians brought beautiful sea otter skins to the ship and wanted to exchange them for clothing or for shells—exclusively the rich blue green abalone from Monterey. Furthermore, they instructed the Spaniards that the meat should be extracted from the shell with a knife and not by heat, which damages the surface and discolors it. These shells were used for inlays in carving and other ornaments (Caamaño 1849, p. 218).

The chiefs were dressed in an interesting combination of native garments and newly acquired trade goods. The *tasen* was about fifty years old and wore breeches of flesh-colored silk ornamented with small gold flowers. With these he wore the distinguishing chief's cloak and, Caamaño states, a high hat. This may have been a trade piece, or else it was a native spruce root woven hat with a few potlatch rings on top. Cunneah was about seventy years old, Caamaño guessed, which was an extraordinary age in that culture and time. He wore two loose frock coats of sky blue cloth, one over the other. They were ornamented with Chinese coins, each strung on a piece of sail-making twine along with a light blue glass bead the size of a hazel nut, which was loosely attached to the material. His breeches were also trimmed with coins so that he sounded "like a carriage mule, as he walked." He had a pair of unmatched silver buckles at the bottoms of his trousers, for he wore no shoes. He had a frilled shirt and a headdress similar to the *tasen's*. Since the term headdress is used, another variety of headgear is possible. He may have worn the "chief's" frontlet headdress with the carved plaque, trimmed with ermine. It also looks like a high hat, but it seems that such headgear would have received more description, for Caamaño had been very explicit in his report.

The Indians sang each evening as they left the ship, a practice also mentioned by Dixon when he visited Norfolk Sound. When Caamaño left this group he wrote, "Indeed, along the whole of this coast populated by Indians, I do not believe that one will meet with kinder people, more civilized in essentials or better disposition (Caamaño 1849, p. 220).

Few diaries of this late period show the changes which had taken place among the Indians. Only those entries regarding the Haida will be used here, and many will be mentioned again in other parts of the Northwest Coast where the same men carried on their trade. After a leisurely trip from Boston (29 November 1791) around Cape Horn to the Marquesas Islands, where he built the schooner *Resolution*, Josiah Roberts sailed to Hawaii and from there reached the Northwest Coast in May 1793. His landfall was south of the mouth of the Columbia River, and he prospected along the coast until, after visiting Barkley Sound and Friendly Cove, he went north to the Queen Charlotte Islands. During July 1793 his party traded in this group; the *Resolution*, under Captain Burling went on the east side and Roberts in the *Jefferson* took the west side. The diary relating this voyage was written by Bernard Magee, the first officer of the *Jefferson*, and is still in manuscript form.

The two ships traveled the usual course, staying there two weeks. Increasingly, Roberts and Burling found that the Indians had new desires and that even the iron collars had had their day. The newest demand was for "moose skins" to use as tunics or jackets underneath their slat armor. These skins could be obtained primarily around the mouth of the Columbia River and Gray's Harbor, and were probably elk, since there are no moose in that area. When the ships sailed to Bucareli Bay on Dall Island, Alaska, and found the same demands there, Captain Burling decided to send the *Resolution* to the Columbia River to get these highly desired skins, giving copper in trade for them. Because of bad weather it was impossible to enter the Columbia River, but trading was available in the area.

While the *Jefferson* was in Bucareli Bay they found that the iron collars were still acceptable there, but they could not dispose of iron in any other form. After the *Resolution* went south, the men on the *Jefferson* were fortunate enough to be present during a great salmon run. They fished and smoked a supply of salmon for the following winter. When this work was completed they decided to return to Barkley Sound for the winter.

In the spring of 1794 Roberts again went to the Queen Charlotte Islands. He arrived at North Island, Parry Passage, on 19 May to find that the people were still at their other village, Kaigani on Dall Island. At the end of the month the head chiefs, Cow, Cunneah, Eldarge, and Skilkada arrived, and in six weeks Roberts acquired 1,146 skins. When his store of trade goods was exhausted, he traded everything dispensable on his ship. They made women's dresses of old sails and traded ship's furnishings, dishes, and eating utensils. To ingratiate themselves with the Haida, Roberts and his crew went to the village to plane and smooth a totem pole. Then the crew painted and raised it and finally they carved a figure for the top of the pole. This and Bartlett's picture are the only references to totem poles that are available from the eighteenth century, and so it is especially regrettable that Magee did not include a description of it. This work was followed the next day by a potlatch, another event rarely reported in the eighteenth century on the Northwest Coast. Since this is one of the few accounts, I will quote verbatim from Magee's story:

> The house was thronged with guests and spectators. The scene was then opened by the ceremony of introducing the wives of Cunneah, Enow, two of the chiefs, and the candidates for incision or boring [of the lips for labrets], each coming in separately and backwards from behind the scenes—being saluted by regular vocal music of all present and which had no unpleasant effect. In the same manner the presents were ushered in and displayed to the view of all present and thrown together in a heap being a profuse collection of Clamons [war garments], racoons, and other cutsarks, comstagas both of iron and copper and a variety of ornaments. This being done the spectators were dismissed and the guests placed in order round the house. The incision was performed on the lips and noses of two grown and two small girls. When this ended the distribution of the goods began, the Captain receiving five otter skins and other articles were given among the different chiefs according to their distinction, after which the Captain took his leave and returned aboard. [Magee ms., n.p.]

Roberts stayed in the southern area of the Northwest Coast during the winter of 1793–94, and they had increasing trouble with the Indians at various ports. In May 1794 they returned to the Queen Charlotte Islands, but Magee seemed tired of his diary and only mentioned that they traded and fished in a salmon run at Cunneah's harbor. The demands for trade goods were still unpredictable, and since nothing new was offered to the Indians, the trading lost some of its enthusiasm.

Since the account of helping the totem pole makers is the only mention of totem poles in the literature of the eighteenth century, they probably were not seen elsewhere. It is likely that other diarists would have mentioned them at least briefly. Many believe that the development of Northwest Coast art depended on metal tools. We have seen that the Indians were already acquainted with the use of iron before the first explorers came. That metal became much more common in the late eighteenth century cannot be denied, but the art style was already well established, as can be seen in many of the objects of the period. The more extensive use of the metal increased the rate and scope of production and made larger pieces possible, but it did not change the fine smaller carvings. In fact, many of the tool chests of modern carvers have at least one adze with a stone blade and often a few pairs of beaver teeth.

The Haida probably made greater changes in their clothing than any of the other tribes who participated in the fur trade. They adopted some European manners, and received a few utensils, but the occasional iron pot did not change their way of cooking or discourage the weaving of watertight baskets. The great shock to Haida life came later, in the nineteenth century, with the canneries and white settlement. They were not in the path of Russian expansion; so as the fur trade dwindled and its surplus goods were used up in potlatches, they were left alone until the whaling ships stopped to buy souvenirs and stimulated their argillite carving.

This section on the Haida can be closed at Kaigani, just as it opened there with the Spaniards in 1774. In August 1794 Captain Roberts came to port there to refresh his crew and prepare for the trip across the Pacific. The port had become a rendezvous at the close of the season, as Nootka Sound was the port of welcome. This became especially true when the Queen Charlotte Islands had become an active trading area for sea otter skins, and Kaigani was within easy sailing distance. Here, also, many men changed ships through desertions and legitimate transfer. The season's results were compared, and the tall stories grew as this port took over the function of Nootka Sound to the south.

6

The Aggressive Tlingit, Who Discouraged Vancouver's Surveying and Stood Off the Russians for Half a Decade

The principal villages of the Tlingit were on inside passages, many of which were either hidden from passing ships or were too dangerous for the eighteenth-century vessels to enter without proper charts. The tribe was therefore not well situated to participate fully in the fur trade or to be seen by exploratory expeditions of the period. Ships coming from the south were often blown away from the coast, and if they made a landfall as far north as Alaska, it was more likely to be at Kaigani at the southern tip of Dall Island or at Bucareli Bay to the north of the island. On the 1790–92 voyage, Gray came near Alaska by going deep into Portland Canal until three of his crew were killed by the Indians, but Vancouver was the first to fully explore the southern portion of southeastern Alaska. Knowing that Caamaño had named Revilla Gigedo Channel for the current viceroy of Mexico, Vancouver also gave the name to the adjoining island. From this point he made his thorough survey of the area, which is discussed in its proper chronological order.

During the early years of exploration and discovery in the region now included in Alaska, there were always rumors that the Russians were there, and metals and other trade goods found in the hands of the Indians on the coast were often attributed to their presence. When the Russians could not be found, before there was awareness of the great distances involved, the availability of iron was explained by active intertribal trade, with articles coming ultimately from Hudson's Bay posts. The Spaniards and Cook, in 1774 and 1778, had sailed northward west of the Queen Charlotte Islands, Cook coming nearest to the Alexander Archipelago of southeastern Alaska in the territory of the Tlingit. He named Mount Edgecumbe and Cross Sound without landing and then sailed directly to Prince William Sound. The territory he passed from Dry Bay to Controller Bay had undergone many changes in population in the preceding years, the people from the west and the north moving south and the Tlingit from

Hoonah, Sitka, and Lynn Canal moving northward to the greatest expansion of Tlingit influence.

The Gulf of Alaska coast was once occupied from Controller Bay to the Icy Bay area by Indians, an Eyak-speaking group, but Chugach Eskimo may at the same time have occupied and used Controller Bay during the eighteenth century until they were driven out by the Tlingit or Tlingit-assimilated Eyak. At this time and for a long period before, the general movement of the Tlingit had been to the north and west (DeLaguna 1964, pp. 4 ff.). There are stories that the Chugach raided the Yakutat territory, and these are partially substantiated by the fact that skin boats like those of the Chugach were once used in Yakutat Bay. A sketch accompanying La Pérouse's narrative shows a ribbed framework of such a boat that closely resembles the Eskimo umiak (facing p. 145, Stockdale ed., London, 1798). At Icy Bay is another Eyak group who had migrated from near Chitina on the Copper River. Into this territory came two groups of Tlingit; one was from Southeast Alaska and another group at Dry Bay were Tlingit from Lynn Canal, who had stopped in the southern Tutchone area and intermarried with the Athapascans there. It is difficult to place all these movements chronologically, but some probably occurred in the early eighteenth century. Malaspina recorded a Tlingit vocabulary taken from the chief and his son who probably were Tlingit, whereas the common people were Eyak-speaking (DeLaguna 1964, p. 207).

This is the immediate background of the people La Pérouse was to meet when he made his first Northwest Coast landing at Yakutat Bay to bring another part of this great territory into the orbit of Europeans. He named it Baie de Monti after one of his officers. He was very busy with his ships and left scanty observations about Indian life. On leaving he turned south and entered the most difficult bay on the Pacific Coast. The entrance of Lituya Bay is narrow, and the breakers rise to tremendous heights; but in spite of these dangers this was a favorite Indian hunting ground for sea otters. To people from Chatham Strait to Dry Bay the native name for Lituya Bay was "lake within the point." When La Pérouse arrived he named it Port des Français, and in accordance with his instructions he took possession of it in the name of France. His orders read that when he came to a region in which he did not know of any previous discovery by a European nation, he should claim it for France. As usual, native people did not count.

In 1886 Lieutenant Emmons collected two interesting legends regarding Lituya Bay from Cowee, the principal chief of the Aukqwan, who then lived at Sint-a-ka-heenee on Gastineaux Channel. The first was about *kah-Lituya*, meaning the "man of Lituya," a monster that resented anyone's coming into his domain and captured them as his slaves. They became bears who watched from a tower for approaching canoes. With their master, they grasped the surface of the water and shook it like a sheet, causing tidal waves. The Tlingit dreaded drowning more than any other means of death, because their future depended on the cremation of the body; if it was lost in the water, the spirit wandered forever. This myth has been illustrated in a carving of a wooden pipe (Heye collection before museum numbers) obtained in 1888 from the chief of the Tuck-tane-ton family on Hoonah DAq'dentan; Swanton 1904, p. 399), who claimed this bay as his hereditary hunting ground. The monster is represented as a froglike creature with *Haliotis* eyes, and opposite him is a bear sitting on his haunches; between them is the entrance to the bay, and on it are two brass-covered tidal waves engulfing a canoe with two occupants (Emmons 1911, pp. 294–96).

The second legend relates the meeting between the Tlingit and the La Pérouse expedition.

> Before the coming of the white man natives had no iron; Chilkat and Hoonah made long canoe trips each summer to Yakutat Bay to trade for copper to make knives, spears, ornaments and "coppers" which were exchanged with southern tribes for cedar canoes, chests, food boxes and dishes. One spring a large party of the "worm house" people of the Chilkat started north under the leadership of three chiefs. On entering Lituya Bay four canoes were swallowed and one chief was drowned. The survivors made camp and mourned. While this was going on two ships came into the bay. The people believed they were great black birds with far reaching white wings, like their bird creator, Yehlh, when he assumed the form of a raven. They thought he had returned to earth and they fled in fright. They crept back to the shore, and gathering skunk cabbage leaves which they rolled into crude telescopes and looked through them, for to see Yehlh with the naked eye would turn them to stone. As the ships came in and the sailors climbed the rigging, they thought the large birds had folded their wings and a flock of small black messengers were rising from their bodies and flying about. They believed these were crows and ran away again. One family of warriors put on their armor and launched a war canoe. But scarcely had they cleared the beach when a cloud of smoke rose from the strange apparitions, followed by a voice of thunder which so demoralized them that the canoe overturned and they scrambled ashore as best they could.
>
> Now a nearly blind warrior said his life was far behind him so, for the common good, he would go to see if Yehlh would turn his children into stone. His slaves prepared his canoe and he put on a robe of sea otter skins and they paddled toward the ships, but as they approached the slaves lost heart and all but two deserted him. He climbed aboard, but being hardly able to distinguish objects, the black forms on board still looked like crows and the cooked rice they set before him looked like worms and he feared to touch it. He exchanged his robe for a tin pan and other presents of food and returned. The crowd touched and smelled him, but would not eat any of the

> food. After much thought the old man was convinced that it was not Yelhl but the occupants of the ships were people, so the Indians visited the ships and exchanged their furs for many strange articles. It was said at this time that two boats from the ships were lost and the white men were drowned. [Emmons 1911, p. 298]

Since the entry into Lituya Bay is so very difficult, the Indians told La Pérouse of the tragic event that occurred when seven boats of visitors arrived and only one succeeded in coming through the breakers. The others drowned and their boats were dashed to pieces. In spite of this warning, the same accident happened to La Pérouse's own men when they set out to explore. Twenty-two sailors were lost at the entrance of the bay. Since their bodies were not recovered, a monument to them was erected on an island in the bay which is called Cenotaph Island. This land was sold to the French for this purpose by the chief for several lengths of red cloth, some hatchets, bar iron, and nails. It is difficult to consider deals of this sort binding, for the language barrier makes it impossible for the Indians to comprehend the difference between their concept of land ownership and that of Europeans.

The native visitors who drowned may have been Chugach, and perhaps the framework of the boat mentioned before was the one which reached the shore, or at least one of this type. These conjectures arise because the ribbing of this boat is identical with that of the Eskimo open boat, the umiak, which is used for traveling. The frame was once covered with sealskins sewed together "with such nicety that the best work even in Europe would find it difficult to imitate" (La Pérouse 1798, p. 391). This type of boat is not generally used by the Tlingit, whose principal watercraft is the dugout canoe, known on the entire Northwest Coast. It was mentioned that during the succession of population discussed above a skin boat was sometimes used by the Yakutat.

In meeting the Indians, La Pérouse noticed first that iron and copper were in active use. Every man had an iron knife or dagger hanging around his neck in a tanned skin sheath with a long strap. The blade and handle were of one piece, with the handle rounded off in opposing scrolls. The Indians assured the French that these were used only for hunting and not for fighting. Metals were also common for other uses, such as collars, bracelets, and projectile points. This brings up the question whether Ingraham's manufacture of iron collars was original with him or whether he had seen some in his wanderings on the coast. No collars are visible in the sketches in the La Pérouse atlas, but the bracelets on one female figure appear to be twisted metal. Since the detail in all sketches is so fanciful, we cannot confidently say that these are twisted copper or iron. Of the two metals copper seems to have been more common, but both indicate northern trade, the copper probably being from native sites in the Copper River valley. The Indians seemed to be familiar with forging iron and molding copper, but no description of these techniques is recorded. Probably the procedure was not seen (see Appendix 2).

A cremation site was found where the ashes and preserved heads were wrapped in skin and deposited in a small wooden box set on four stakes. This type of mortuary box is similar to those raised on ten-foot columns, a style of burial widely distributed among the northern tribes of the Northwest Coast. It is interesting to compare this note with the sketch in Malaspina's narrative of the cemetery at Yakutat, which will be discussed later (plate VI in *Publicaciónes del Museo Naval*, vol. 1, Madrid, 1932).

The statement that the Tlingit of Lituya Bay spun the hair of various animals is easily accepted, but one technique described raises the question whether it was actually observed, or if the product was seen and its manufacture surmised. The principal "hair" is the wool of the mountain goat; but they are said to have worked it with a needle into a cloth like tapestry (La Pérouse 1798, p. 370). This is a questionable statement, for no known Northwest Coast textile is made with a needle except the cattail or rush mat. The Chilkat blanket and its predecessors were twilled by hand on warps that hung from a single bar loom. The cattail or rush mat was used by the Salish, Nootka, and Kwakiutl, but it is not used in the north. Their mats are plaited of split cedar bark. That they "mingle" strips of sea otter fur in their weaving is demonstrated in the fine blankets in the Leningrad collection (MAE, 2520–4). However, there is no certainty about where they were collected, and it was probably not from the Tlingit, though they may also have used this technique.

La Pérouse comments that in no part of the world do they make baskets and hats more skillfully. For the art of basketry, the Tlingit are still famous. The baskets are made of spruce root and ornamented with designs woven in with various grasses dyed in bright colors. This type of basketry was so completely analyzed by Emmons (1903) that it is unnecessary to repeat it here. It is interesting that today the northernmost Tlingit at Yakutat are the most skilled weavers. Also, the Chugach and Eyak joined the Tlingit in making the same kind of basketry, which they undoubtedly learned from them. The hats are also woven of spruce root, with twilled self-patterns on the brim, and are painted on the crown. Occasionally one also sees a painted basket. The hats can definitely be traced back to the eighteenth century. Appendix 2 gives an analysis of hat types, designs, and techniques of manufacture.

The clothing of the Tlingit is not described in detail, but it seems in general that they were more fully clothed than the Haida and Nootka, where the men so often were naked. There is a sketch of a young woman wearing a labret whose garment is rather full in the skirt and partially covers her breast. It is tied around the waist, but the upper part shows no fastenings. The garment appears to be made of finely tanned skin, for it drapes fluidly. Another female figure in the group is wearing a similar garment which seems to be covered with a furry cape, waist length and tied under the chin. The older woman is wearing a labret, but the younger seems only to have a slit for one cut in her chin. The men in the sketch have a variety of clothing. Standing is a young man draped in dressed skins in three tiers; all are irregular, and the bottom one has a V-shaped lower edge. His legs are bare from the knees down. His face and hair are not a true copy of a Tlingit, but look European. The dominant figure in the group is a man with an "eared" headdress, which has a headband from which rise two narrow oval pointed pieces, perhaps of rawhide. They are ornamented on the edge with (probably) human hair. Two such headdresses were also seen on the occupants of one canoe in another sketch. Such headdresses with "ears" are widely used on the Northwest Coast. Sometimes the "ears" are actual bears' ears or pieces of fur shaped to simulate them. This man also has a moustache and a small clipped beard. On the right side of the picture, in a group by themselves, are a man and a woman, the man dressed as an Athapascan and the woman in a loose skin skirt and several tiers of fur cape and wearing a labret. The Athapascan costume consists of trousers with feet and garterlike knee embroidery, a shirt with a vague yoke and sleeves, several necklaces, some with claw pendants, and a feather head decoration with some indication of a fur head covering. The barrel of a riflle shows between the man's knees. This could be an example of a Tlingit-Athapascan marriage.

In La Pérouse's text ornaments and bodily decorations are discussed which do not show in the sketches. The men pierce the septum of the nose and the lobes of the ears for hanging ornaments. They make scars on their arms and breast with an instrument which they sharpen with their teeth. Another peculiar custom was this one: the teeth were filed down to the gums by means of a rounded piece of sandstone shaped like a tongue. Such an implement and such a practice have not been recorded elsewhere, and there is nothing even nearly like it to which it can be related. There was tatooing, and they painted their bodies with red ocher and soot, and for ceremonial occasions they added ornaments and clothing received in trade. A simple skin—thrown over the shoulders, with the rest of the body naked—was common for daily wear, and was often accompanied by a small spruce-root hat or cap with horns (perhaps like the headdress just discussed) or eagle feathers. Sometimes the entire head was fitted with a bear's head, mounted on a skullcap of wood. Some had complete shirts of sea otter skins. The head chief wore a shirt which was probably of tanned elkskin. There were no elk in Tlingit territory, but elkskins were traded up the coast all the way from the Chinook at the mouth of the Columbia River. If the shirt was not elk from this source it could be caribou gotten in trade from the interior. In the picture of the boat frame two figures are standing close to it. One man has a caribou skin costume decorated with fringes and porcupine embroidery.

When the Indians first came to the ships they brought fish, which they had been catching in great quantities during the summer. The site where La Pérouse saw the Tlingit was a summer fishing village and consisted of small houses steeply gabled, like the modern A frame, with crude framework, often roped together, as in the sketch with the costumed figures, and covered with broad wooden planks or bark in great slabs. The houses were generally open on the sides not exposed to the wind, and the fish were dried on the house frame where it extended beyond the roof and on drying racks. During inclement weather the fish were hung in the house near the fire. The fishing was done by constructing weirs across streams or with hook and line. Each line was fastened to a large seal bladder and set adrift. One man in a canoe watched about ten or fifteen of them. When a fish was caught it dragged the bladder, and the canoe went after him.

About three hundred Indians gathered in this bay for fishing, and there was a constant change of population, canoes coming and going with the families and all their household gear. Although the Indians go barefoot, their feet are not calloused, showing how much they travel by canoe or by snowshoes in winter.

The editor of the La Pérouse journal stated that the landscape and the people were equally rugged. He says that the Indians seemed to be at war with every animal and killed every living thing. But he does add that every part of the animals they took was used for food or materials. The Indians did not relish vegetable foods, except the berries the women and children ate in the summer. The people constantly quarreled among themselves, or so it sounded to those who could not understand the language and were unaccustomed to their manner of speech. But when they unsheathed their knives during an argument, there could be little doubt of their aggressiveness. La Pérouse stated that with this type of behavior, it would be devastating if alcoholic beverages were ever introduced among them.

It is impossible to discuss the way of life of any Indian group without some reference to their dogs, since they often outnumber the residents in a village. In Lituya Bay there was a small, very savage dog somewhat like a shepherd's dog, but he had no responsibilities. He made a whistling sound like a jackal. Other varieties of dogs are not mentioned, but there can be no doubt that they existed. In many Northwest Coast ports the travelers mentioned the wool dog, but it is very questionable that they saw one. Beyond the area of the Salish in southern British Columbia and Washington they were not known. However, since trade flourished for all rare materials, the wool might have been traded and even the finished blankets could have been in use where the animal was not raised (Howay 1918, p. 83).

This is as much as can be learned about the Tlingit of Lituya Bay from the first European contact. The beads, iron, and copper which they already had came to them through a line of trading, probably from Prince William Sound and other Russian settlements. In the next year, 1787, after parting from Portlock in the north, Dixon came into Yakutat Bay and named the part where he anchored Port Mulgrave. He immediately recognized that the people were different from those at Prince William Sound, especially in the boats they built. Here were the wooden dugout canoes which are typical of the Northwest Coast. Like La Pérouse, he found only temporary fishing settlements which he described as "wretched hovels," a few poles stuck into the ground with no regularity and covered with loose boards. The small canoes, however, were so well made and finished that he bought one and gave it to Sir Joseph Banks. The larger canoes for twelve to fourteen persons were crudely made of a single tree trunk. He saw halibut hooks and commented that the carving on them must have religious significance. The hooks were baited with squid, and each was attached to a bladder like those at Lituya Bay, many being watched by one man in a canoe. The watcher did not take in a line immediately when the bladder indicated a bite, because a large halibut could upset the canoe in his struggles. The fish were killed with a wooden club, often beautifully carved.

All food was cooked by the stone-boiling method, in a basket which Dixon called "wicker." But a wicker basket would hardly hold water, and the Tlingit, like most Northwest Coast tribes, twined an excellent basket of spruce root. Since the basket was damp most of the time, the fibers were always swollen enough to hold water. This method of cooking was used for seal, fish, and porpoise, and the basket was kept closely covered while the food was in it. The Indians preferred this method and were not interested in changing to the kettle which was traded to them. A form of tobacco was mixed with lime and the resinous rind of "pine" (probably spruce) and chewed (Dixon 1789, p. 175).

To return to the main object of his voyage, Dixon notes that trading began very slowly. Indians, four to six in a canoe, came alongside and sat about an hour before indicating that they had something to sell, then showed a few trifles. This continued all the first day. Later Dixon saw that they had beads and iron in the form of knives and spearpoints, all of which looked like those of Prince William Sound. When real trading began he found that they would take blue and green beads for small skins, but wanted "toes" (small wedge-shaped pieces of iron) or pewter basins for the sea otter skins. After this understanding some substantial trading was carried on, and content with this, Dixon then went on to southeastern Alaska, stopping next at Norfolk Sound (Dixon 1789, pp. 165–95).

It is apparent that Dixon had no great interest in the Indians beyond what they could yield in trading. It is very possible that at Yakutat Bay he did not leave his ship and traded only with those who came out in canoes. He carried out this "trade and run" technique on his entire circumnavigation of the Queen Charlotte Islands, and one regrets that when he had such an opportunity to see these people in their first contact with Europeans he was not interested in their way of life.

The next contact in the Yakutat–Lituya Bay area after Dixon left was the Russian team of Ismailov (Ismylov) and Bocherov. The former had been seen by Cook in 1778 at Unalaska, where he was the principal person in the Russian colony. When they arrived on the ship *Trekh Sviatitela* (*Three Saints*) in 1788, they moored in Port Mulgrave, where they had friendly traffic with the Indians. The Russians recorded that these people called themselves Koliuski and lived on the banks of several rivers. Besides an inferior *toion* (*toyon*), they were subject to a superior *toion* whose name was Ilchak. He was visiting this place, traveling in *baidars* (skin boats) with 150 of his subjects, excluding children. He had two sons, Nekcheet and Chirik, and his principal residence was on the coast to the southeast, much farther than the great river Tschitskat (probably Chilkat). His territory bordered on the frontiers of the people called Tschitkanes, who, like the Koliuski, were at enmity among themselves and often assaulted each other. The *toion* ruled over all the Koliuski as far as Yakutat Bay, which was the last of his domains (Coxe 1787, p. 324). This is all repeated in terms used by the Russian visitors. There is no evidence that the Tlingit ever formed a real political confederacy, though groups of towns aligned themselves against one another for short periods, and when the campaign was over they probably started fighting their recent allies.

Ismylov gave Ilchak a portrait of Emperor Paul "at his earnest request," it was said, and decorated him with one of the medals sent out by the governor of Siberia at Kamchatka. Ismylov tried to persuade the Tlingit chief to place himself and his people under the protection of Russia, but it seemed they preferred trade to political alliances. After several days of active trading, Ismylov buried copper plates inscribed "Possession of the Russian Empire."

The Russians left some notes on the Indians which can be added to the brief observations of Dixon. They described the houses, which were square, made of earth on the outside and lined with wood on the inside.

The roof was covered with fir bark and had a square opening for a smoke hole. The wooden part of the building consisted of four poles stuck into the ground about two arshins in height, to which the crossbeams were attached. The sloping roof was made of planks resting on the crossbeams. The entrance was at the side, and mats woven of grass or similar material covered the opening. The house was square, like that Lisiansky described for Sitka in 1804 (Lisiansky 1814, p. 239). The inhabitants had gone fishing in canoes and boats that resembled those of Kamchatka.

It is strange that Ismylov made no mention of Dixon's visit to Yakutat or of La Pérouse's presence at Lituya. Bancroft relates in a footnote that two years later there were no traces of the portrait of the czar, the medals, or the buried copper here or at Lituya Bay, where Ismylov also established marks of Russian possession. The monument placed by La Pérouse to his drowned officers and men on Cenotaph Island may also have been destroyed by this time (Bancroft 1886, pp. 269–70).

Malaspina, on his voyage around the world, came north on the Pacific Coast and was the next visitor to the northern Tlingit, when he made landfall at Cape Engaño (Cape Edgecumbe, which, along with the mountain, was named by Cook in 1778). Malaspina renamed the cape and called the mountain Mount San Jacinto. An excellent group of scientists and artists were with him, and although he did not add much in verbal description of the Indians, his artist, Tomas de Suría, furnished many sketches that are very good and others that are controversial. Suría also wrote a journal which was published as the *Journal of Tomas de Suría*, edited and translated by Henry R. Wagner (1936). It is of special interest because it is an unofficial document and therefore more candid than those sent to the viceroy. Suría was a painter employed by the mint in Mexico City, and because both the original artists left the expedition in Acapulco on account of illness, he filled the position until the Spanish artists designated for this work arrived from Europe. It is his sketches which will be analyzed, together with his journal entries.

The originals of these sketches are in the Museo Naval and the Museo d'América, where the Sala de Malaspina was opened in 1964 as an event for the meeting of the International Congress of Americanists. Previously the collection was known only through two items in the literature. In 1929, Henri A. Lavachery included in *Les arts anciens d'Amérique* a few pieces from the Malaspina collection, and in 1939 Anna Rustow published an extensive article in the Baessler Archiv (vol. 22, no. 4, pp. 173–204, Berlin). She regrets that the collection has been ignored by scholars, but this is not entirely their fault, for I made several unsuccessful attempts to study the pieces and finally had to be content with a brief visit to the exhibit in the Museo d'América in 1964. After discussing Suría's sketches, I will review the article by Rustow.

The picture story of Malaspina's visit to Yakutat late in June 1791 starts with a sketch of his greetings by the Indians (fig. 31). The legend reads: "The Chief of Mulgrave accompanied by other canoes pleads for peace from the goletas [schooners]" (Bauzá collection, 2:22). Malaspina had two ships, but only the stern of one shows here, with no masts or rigging. There are four watercraft in the Indian flotilla. The largest holds eight persons, all appearing to be men except the steersman, who is not wearing a hat and has hair parted in the center. This figure also wears a sleeved coat that covers the knees. This may be a woman, and will be considered as such. Standing in front of her is a large figure, a man with a heavy skin fastened on his shoulders, reaching to the midcalf in back and looped up to his navel in front, where it seems to be tied. He has a beard and is wearing a hat. This is probably the man Suría describes in his journal as follows:

> The chief was an old, venerable and ferocious looking man with a very long gray beard, in a pyramidal form, his hair flaccid and loose on his shoulders. False hair over it in various locks, without any order or arrangement, made him look like a monster. A large lion skin for a cape was gathered in at the waist and left entirely bare his breast, arms, thighs and endowments, very muscular and strong. All gave him somewhat majestic air, which he manifested by speaking but little, assuredly, and with a sound which at times seemed to be the bellow of a bull. At other times it was softer and in speaking to his sons it was sweeter than in conversation. [Suría 1936, p. 249].

Fig. 31. The chief of Port Mulgrave goes to the ships to ask for peace. Spanish picture.

Fig. 32. Detail of the chief's canoe. Spanish picture.

As the footnote by Newcombe suggests, the lion skin was possibly the skin of an Alaskan brown bear.

Four other men in the canoe are wearing painted hats. One has a bearskin cape hanging from his back and another has the same kind of cape pulled up over his shoulders. The third is naked from the waist up, and the last can only be seen wearing a hat. The foremost paddler also seems to be naked. Both the chief and the other standing man have their arms outstretched at shoulder level, and the chief is holding a garment that looks like a pair of trousers in his right hand.[1]

This canoe is also represented in a detailed sketch showing the boat against a background of highly stylized conifer trees (fig. 32). It has some interesting detail which is mentioned elsewhere in the text. The canoe is a dugout, but it has an extra plank fastened to the sides. This is "sewed"

1. A modern Tlingit told me that long ago a man completely bared himself to show that he had no weapons, and that this is the reason for holding up the trousers; but Dr. DeLaguna believes that this picture is one of a series and that here Suría shows the chief returning a pair of sailor's trousers which had been stolen and had caused trouble between Malaspina and the Indians (personal communication).

to the body and seems to lean outward. The four paddles are held against its outer rim. Contrary to this sketch, Suría's journal describes the chief's boat as skin covered (Suría 1936, p. 248). This is entirely possible, for the Eskimo type of larger open boat, the umiak, was used by the Yakutat, though it probably was secured by trade. Although the arrangement of the figures is the same as in the leading boat in the larger picture, the background differs, and the ship without rigging does not show. In the group sketch the canoe just described is nearest the ship and behind it is a kayak with one man. In the right foreground is another canoe with six men, all wearing cone-shaped hats and two wearing bearskin robes. The standing figure is bare to the waist and seems to have a bearskin from the waist down. In the left foreground is a canoe with its stern toward the viewer. There are paddlers on both sides, and a man is standing in the stern, wearing a bearskin and holding his arms outstretched at shoulder level. The background of this picture shows a vague broken shoreline.

A small picture which may or may not belong to this group shows two men in a kayak, each holding a single-bladed paddle (fig. 33). Both are wearing shallow cone-shaped hats; one is naked to the waist and the other has a garment with a gathered neckline and sleeves. This may be a seal-gut rain parka worn by the Aleut and Eskimo. The sketch is not signed and is titled "Piragua de 3M," meaning a small boat (Museo Naval #40).

Another large sketch includes Malaspina's ships with masts, rigging, and flags flying (fig. 34). The scene is a narrow inlet, the background detailed and the foreground showing a ship's boat and two canoes in shallow water along the shoreline. On the background shore, at least three native dwellings show, and the title is "View of the Habitations of the Indians at Port Mulgrave (*Album de Felipe Bauzá*, 1:6).

Fig. 33. A small boat seen in Prince William Sound. Spanish picture.

Fig. 34. Malaspina's ships at Port Mulgrave. Spanish picture.

The sketch at Port Mulgrave which seems to be the most fanciful is printed in the *Publicaciónes* (plate VI) and has as part of the caption "Cardero 1792." According to the literature Cardero, or Cordero, was not with the expedition at this point, and the year Malaspina was at Port Mulgrave was 1791. So the sketch must be by Suría, since the subject could not be from the southern part of Vancouver Island and the Strait of Juan de Fuca, where Cardero was the artist of the expedition of the *Sutil* and the *Mexicana*. The sketch shows several burials. At each side of the picture is a structure with four posts that are cut square with very sharp edges, which could not easily be done with the wood techniques and tools known to the Tlingit at this time. Each structure supports a large box, not in the proportions of the usual Northwest Coast chest, with covers of planks that extend over the front edges. One has a design painted in black, an unsuccessful attempt to copy Northwest Coast style. On the ground inside the square formed by the posts is a chest with a cover, on which are some forms that cannot be distinguished. In the center is a very large wooden figure which looks like a grinning cat but may be a wolf or a bear. It is squatting on its haunches and has a chest on its knees with the tips of its claws resting on the lid. The joint of the wrist is indicated with a small vague face, as in nineteenth-century Northwest Coast art style. The front of the chest is covered with design. This creature has a long tail, very pointed, on which the figure rests, the tail being stuck into the ground. The tail is as long as the height of the people near it. Besides the catlike figure there are five men and a boy with a bow. The child has a cape tied under its chin. Beside him is an Indian with a fur cloak and a spruce-root hat. The next three figures are probably Europeans, and there is another Indian with a bearskin robe on his back. In the foreground between the large figure and one of the elevated coffins is a group of five, with two Indians. One wears a flat hat, a bearskin robe, and a breechclout. The other has his back turned, and his garment looks like a blanket made of small skins sewed together with black tassels sewed into the seams. The garment extends to midcalf. In the background are three Europeans, one of whom is aiming a rifle at a large bird standing on a fallen log. All this takes place in a clearing in the woods (*Publicaciónes del Museo Naval*, #1, plate VI; Rustow 1939, fig. #26).

In the sketches from the Malaspina expedition there is another which represents a burial similar to the type described by Marchand. The chest is set between two poles, and behind and beneath it is a box partially dug into the ground (fig. 35). The box is poorly drawn, but it seems to have a frog's head on it, surmounted by a round pole almost twice as tall as the ones holding the chest. The chest is decorated in the general style of the large storage chests and ornamented with shells set into the wood. The uprights which support it are really not poles but look like square-cut pieces of lumber. They recall the flat dance staffs made by the Tlingit in the nineteenth century, which usually represent the dorsal fin of the killer whale. They are rounded at the top, thus representing the fin more closely, and the outer edge is trimmed with long flowing hair, just like the staffs. The upper end of the pole is painted white, and the remainder of the pole has narrow diagonal bars of red or black on a background of white. The tall round pole on the frog's head is covered at regular intervals by cylinders slightly larger in circumference than the pole itself. They are about one foot in height and resemble the basketry cylinders on the spruce-root hats which indicate the number of potlatches the wearer has given. There are eleven of these. This elaborate piece also stands in the natural setting of a clearing in the trees, which do not grow as closely together as farther south on the Northwest Coast. The people standing beside the sepulcher give some indication of its height, and also show some interesting details of costume. To the left are two Europeans and an Indian wearing a fur cloak and a narrow spruce root hat. On the right are two Europeans

Fig. 35. Burial of the cacique of Mulgrave. Spanish picture.

and an Indian with a wider hat and a bearskin robe which reaches to the middle of the thighs in the front and is longer in the back. The other Indian may be a woman, with a shredded cedar bark waist-length cape and a dress of the same material beneath it, reaching to the ankles. She has some feathers in her hair (Museo Naval, Madrid, Bauzá collection, 2:67). The title of the sketch is "Sepulcro de An-Kau de Mulgrave, anterior a el actual; Muerto, en una Rehierta."

Suría was also the artist of a picture entitled "Hat of the Chief of Mulgrave" (fig. 36), which illustrates how the center post of the sepulcher resembles a ceremonial hat. Although the hat is probably of woven spruce root, this cannot be determined because there is no texture to the surface.

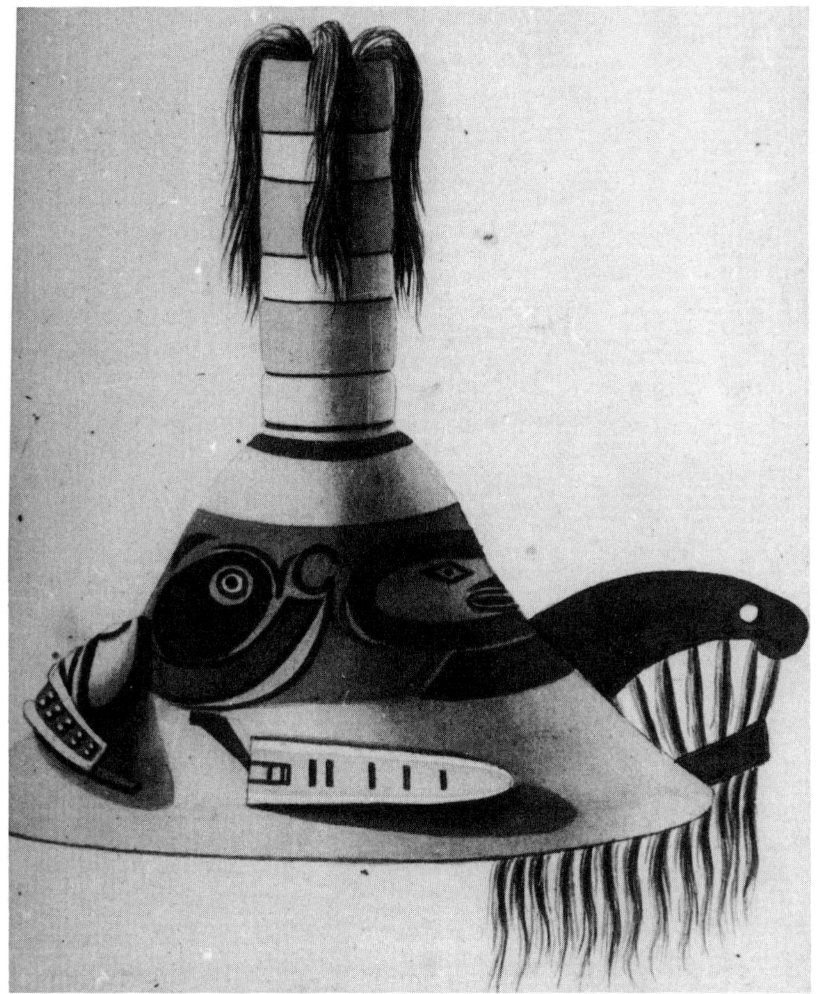

Fig. 36. Ceremonial hat of the chief of Mulgrave. Spanish picture.

The alternative is that it may be wooden, but the adze marks should also show. The rings on this hat might alternate between wooden ones and ones made of basketry. Hair is coming out of the top cylinder and a carved wooden appendage decorated with hair shows at the rear of the picture (*Album de Felipe Bauzá*, vol. #2, part 2, p. 35).

There is one more scene in this collection, showing an altercation between the Spaniards and the Indians (fig. 37). Spaniards with muskets raised are protecting others who are hurriedly boarding the ships' boats. The ship is off to the left, and a puff of smoke on the port side probably comes from a shot just fired. A group of Indians are standing on a low rise at the back of the beach, dressed in bearskin robes and shallow

Fig. 37. Trouble at Port Mulgrave on Malaspina's voyage. Spanish picture.

hats. The situation may have been instigated by some men in the background, who seem to be carrying a large chest away on a litter. The scene is well done and is full of action (*Bauzá collection* "Escene en Mulgrave," 2:9).

There is also a group of sketches representing individuals. There is also a picture of two men, the older, captioned "Chief of Puerto Mulgrave" and the other, "Indio de Mulgrave," a younger man (fig. 38). On some captions he is called the son of the chief. This older man might be the chief shown standing in the canoe asking for peace. He has the beard and shaggy hair shown in the other picture. In this sketch he is wearing a bearskin robe with the right side turned back and a shallow spruce root hat with a row of painting at the top of the crown. The startling feature is his nose pin, which must have a very clever joint at the septum. The younger man also wears a bearskin robe, which he holds close to the neck. His straggly hair shows under a shallow hat with a painted crown and a checkerboard brim. He is captioned "Indio de Mulgrave" (*Bauzá collection*, vol. 2, part 2, p. 45). Another figure of a man merely marked "Mulgrave" (fig. 39) shows him in his bearskin robe, open in the front to the waist and holding in his right hand a dagger that seems poised for stabbing himself. The bare parts of his body are very muscular. He is also wearing a shallow hat with no painting.

Fig. 38 (*left*). Indio de Mulgrave. Spanish picture.

Fig. 39 (*above*). Indio de Mulgrave. Spanish picture.

There are several pictures of women who were certainly not selected for their beauty. One shows a woman standing, holding an infant in a cradle. She is wearing a long dress and over it a cape almost as long. These pieces of clothing do not look like native material. Her hair is shoulder length and is very black. She is wearing a labret. The infant is very small and seems laced into the cradle under a cover that might be tanned deerskin or a piece of trade cloth. The body of the cradle appears to be basketry, like the one more clearly seen in another picture. The woman is barefoot (Ministerio de Marina, vol. 1, plate I [12]; also *Album de Felipe Bauzá*, vol. 2, part 2, p. 49; also *Publicaciónes del Museo Naval*, vol. 1, plate XIII). This picture in the *Publicaciónes* is attributed to Brambila, but on the print received from the Museo Naval is written "Suría." Another woman, standing, is dressed in the same costume; her hair is parted at the center of her head and she also wears a labret. Her hands are almost folded below her waist and she is barefooted. The third picture shows a woman sitting with a cradle in her lap. The cradle is constructed like the one in the first picture in this group and, being larger, is easier to study. The sides of the cradle are carefully textured, but not with any type of basketweaving current in this area. In her right hand she holds a square basket, in twilled technique, such as comes only from the Philippines, southeastern Asia, South America, and the southeastern United States. She is wearing garments that appear to be made of manufactured cloth. Her cape is laced at the neck and may be of finely tanned deerskin. She also wears her hair parted in the middle and hanging shoulder length and has a labret (Ministerio de Marina, vol. 1, plate VI; Museo d'América, Sala Malaspina).

Suría followed the style of Captain Cook by recording the events as they occurred, probably in a daybook, and after the ship sailed he took time on board to write a running description of the people he had just seen. He describes the Yakutat Tlingit as having their eyes set far apart, long and full, sparkling and alive. Their faces are more round than long, with bulging cheeks and a somewhat pointed chin. They have thick hair which in its unkempt aspect looks like a horse's mane. Suría feels sure that if the women did not have so much paint and soot on their faces they would be rather good-looking.

He comments on the poor dwellings, so it must be stated again that he probably saw the people at a fishing site. I cannot agree with Newcombe that the construction was poor for lack of material. Suría also gives another clue to the temporary nature of the houses he saw by his statement that many objects were piled on the roof. This is definitely not a habit in their permanent villages. Since every crumb of information must be gleaned from these journals, it should also be pointed out that among the items on the roof he mentions "canoes, others in skeleton," which agrees with the supposition that the Yakutat used skin-covered boats, but still does not guarantee that they were made there. A skeleton might more likely mean that the skin cover had been removed or destroyed and not necessarily that the boat was in the process of construction (Suría 1936, p. 253).

Suría mentions that on many square wooden boxes "all their ornament is reduced to a mask on the four fronts with the mouth open, badly carved with the teeth inverted and in others by way of ornament they have them placed in a parallel line (Suría 1936, p. 253). This differs considerably from the appraisal of Tlingit art made by Marchand.

Suría describes life in the household, substantiating many facts which have been stated previously and are customary with slight variation among all tribes on the Northwest Coast. Like many other European observers he goes to great lengths in describing the labret worn by the women. Face painting takes the place of the tattooing practiced by the Haida (Suría 1936, p. 254–55).

In this description of the Tlingit, Suría gives a very exact account of the warriors' armor. It has been mentioned before, but the detail included here is important and explains the figure (plate III) in his journal. He says "the fighting Indians wear all their arms," as though this were their constant style of dress; but it seems so cumbersome that perhaps his words should not be taken too literally. This dress consists of a breastplate and back armor and a helmet with a visor. In the Malaspina collection in Madrid there are four suits of armor. One is called a *stabchen Panzer* (Madrid 1287), which can be translated as rod armor, and Suría's illustration may have been made from this piece (Suría 1936, plate III). The piece on the lower left resembles the apron he described (Suría 1936, p. 256). The body of the armor looks more like the rod type than the other pieces, which are called *brettchen Panzer*, or slat armor. This type resembles more closely pictures of eighteenth-century armor in other collections and is more frequently found than the rod type. In these pieces the slats are broad enough for clan or other symbols to be painted on the chest and the back, whereas the rods could not easily be decorated in this way. There are three pieces of slat armor in the Malaspina collection (Madrid 1286, 1289, 1309–26). This armor is worn over a jacket of several layers of heavy skin, preferably elk if it can be obtained in trade from the south. Leggings of skin with the hair outside are worn or else they make shin guards of rods similar to those of the modern hockey player. Suría comments that the apron shown in his sketch makes walking difficult, but that it is not alone in making this armored warrior as immobile as the full caparisoned knight who was hoisted into his saddle by his squires (Suría 1936, p. 255). The helmet was so solid and thick that it weighed as much as if it were made of iron. It always had a great figure in front "like a young eagle or a kind of parrot," the latter probably being a hawk. The author said, "to cover the face they lowered from the helmet a piece of wood which surrounds this and hangs from some pieces of leather in the middle of the head to unite with another one which comes up from the chin." This undoubtedly describes the defensive collar, but other authors have not connected this with the helmet in this way. In the large collection of collars in the museum in Leningrad various holes are drilled in the collars that could be used in such a harness, but there are no thongs to prove it. The collar was laced together at the back and rested on the shoulders.

The warrior carried a lance of yew to which was fastened the blade of a large knife, obtained in trade with the English. It seems that earlier they attached to the lance a copper knife which they obtained in trade with the Athapascans of the interior. The Athapascans used this as a bear spear. It was ten to twelve inches long and grooved throughout its length. The grooves separated at the butt end and curled outward into elegant scrolls. The knife they carry in the belt is like that of the Spaniards. Suría also gives the warrior a hatchet with a head of black stone and a long handle. Newcombe, who so ably annotated this translation, describes it as a "long-handled adze," which serves as a general-purpose tool rather than as a weapon (see Madrid 1229). Suría obtained this detail because an Indian was willing to put on the costume and explain it to the Spaniards with gestures (Suría 1936, p. 256).

Suría finishes his account of the Yakutat with a few notes on features of Tlingit culture that were not apparent to the fur traders, who either never left their ships or were too absorbed in their business. He saw the children playing with dolls that had marble heads (p. 256). The use of white marble in the Tlingit territory is almost as distinctive as the use of argillite by the Haida in the nineteenth century. It is seldom found in large objects, and even the doll heads are rare; so it must be scarce and hard to work. It also shows a phase of Tlingit culture that contrasts with the warrior and the emphasis on belligerence. He also has a few sentences on the principal gambling game of the northern area, among the Tlingit, Haida, and Tsimshian, which is played with bundles of finely carved and painted polished sticks. A handful of these are hidden in two bundles of shredded cedar bark and the opponents must guess which bundle conceals a stick with a certain design or guess the number of sticks in each bundle. If he guesses right he can work his bundle next, but if he misses he loses his wager. Dixon and La Pérouse both mention the games being played at Port Mulgrave (Suría 1936, p. 257). The game is described and the wallets of gambling sticks are shown in Niblack (1890, pp. 344, 345; plate 63). A fuller description will be given later in this chapter.

The lack of information on religion is laid to the lack of communication. Suría wonders whether the Indians worshiped the sun. He then briefly describes a visit to their burial places, which are also described by Marchand. However, the sketches which have previously been described have also been attributed to Suría because he was the only artist with the expedition at that time. The sketches have many fanciful elements, and one wonders whether they were done at the site or later when he was writing his narrative. His writing is so careful that it would be easy to believe some of the flourishes in the sketches are the work of a lithographer, but the supposed originals are in the Museo Naval and the Museo d'América in Madrid. The Spaniards in Mexico were so accustomed to copying the journals and narratives of expeditions in order that the original copy could go to Spain and the copies remain in Mexico that even the so-called originals often cause doubt.

To return to the second contribution of the Malaspina voyage—the collection in the Spanish museums, of which some items have already been mentioned—the work of Anna Rustow reveals its limited quantity and the fact that of the thirty-one pieces listed only eighteen can be definitely placed as Tlingit. Five hats, if they are all the same, are Nootka, and ten pieces are too general to be specifically located. They are marked T and U (unidentified) as an addition to her list, reproduced on page 162 (table 1).

In analyzing the cultural setting of these pieces, it is unfortunate that Rustow did not have a more particularized view of the Northwest Coast, for she seeks to explain designs of the late nineteenth-century Kwakiutl by objects collected in 1791 among the Tlingit. Certain mythological figures have wide distribution on the Northwest Coast, but the specific representation found among the Kwakiutl often cannot be traced far into history. One hundred years of cultural activity and a separation of several hundred miles, with strong cultures like the Haida and Tsimshian between, does not further cultural exchange. Regardless of the theories Rustow proposes, to have any listing of this collection with some illustrations is an important contribution.

Now it is time to pick up again the 1787 voyage of Dixon when he sailed into Norfolk Sound after his visit to Yakutat Bay. This body of water, now Sitka Sound, he named for the Duke of Norfolk. He found a population of about 450 persons, who looked like those of Yakutat Bay but seemed more alert. They dressed in the ordinary clothes that the Yakutat also used, but had exceptional raincoats woven of closely placed rushes (these were probably cattails). One of Dixon's crew who had been with Captain Cook on his last voyage said they resembled those of New Zealand. The Indians painted their faces with a variety of colors and the women wore labrets, but they did not slit the lip until puberty. Although their canoes were similar to those of the Yakutat, they were finished better. They would hold sixteen to nineteen persons (Dixon 1789, p. 191).

TABLE 1

MALASPINA COLLECTION: TLINGIT OBJECTS

Illustration	*Museum Number*	*Object*		*Measurements*	*Materials*	*Colors*
2	1310	Frontlet	(T)	Length: 20 cm; width: 21 cm	Wood, copper, iron, shell	Light wood color; body, blue green
4	1490	Rattle	(U)	Length: 33 cm	Wood	Traces of red
5*a,b*	1185	Flute	(U)	Length: 39 cm	Wood, *Haliotis* shell	Natural color
6	1460	Bird	(U)	Length: 7 cm	Ivory	Natural color
	1458 1459	Two birds	(U)		Wood	Blue green, red, white, dark brown
7*a,b,c* 7*b* 7*c*	192	Hat	(T)	Diameter at crown: 9 cm; at base, 32 cm	Root fibers (spruce root)	Sea green, black, red
8*a,b*	190	Hat	(T)	Diameter at crown: 9 cm; at base, 45 cm	Root fibers	Green, red, black
9*a,b*	191	Hat	(T)	Diameter at crown: 10 cm; at base, 34 cm	Root fibers	Black, red, blue, green
11*a,b*	194	Hat with rings	(T)	Diameter at base: 29 cm; ring diameter: 7 cm; height: 6 cm	Root fibers	Red, black, light green
15	1309/22	Mask	(T)	Length: 22 cm; width: 18 cm	Wood, leather, shell	Light green; lips of red leather
16	1311	Mask	(T)	Length: 15½ cm; width: 15 cm	Wood	Light green, black, light natural wood
17	1290	Helmet	(T)	Length: 36½ cm	Wood	White, red, black
18	1292	Helmet	(T)	Length: 33 cm	Wood	Sea green, white, red, black, brown
	1293	Visor	(T)		Wood, shell	Dark brown
19	1229	Axe	(T)	Height: 48 cm	Nephrite (?), wood, human hair, shell	Green, brown
20*a,b*	1291	Helmet	(T)	Height: 31 cm; thickness: 3–3½ cm	Wood, copper, shell	Natural wood color, green, brown
21	1294	Visor	(T)	Height at center: 13½ cm	Wood	Red, green, black
22	1287	Rod armor	(T)	Height: 51 cm; front width: 56 cm width of rod: 1 cm	Wood, sinew twine, leather	
23	1286	Slat armor	(T)	Height: front, 55 cm; width: 59 cm; width of slat: 2 cm	Wood, sinew twine, leather	Black, red, green on brown wood
13	1289	Slat armor	(T)	Height: 59 cm; width: 56 cm	Same	Red on dark brown, brown
24	1309/26	Slat armor	(T)	Height: front, 58 cm; width: front, 51½ cm	Same	Black, red, green on brown wood

SOURCE: Rustow 1939, pp. 174-75.

It was obvious that they were accustomed to trading, for they refused beads with contempt and wanted pewter basins. Useful tools of iron would bring only small, inferior furs. When trading began each day they would come and sing for half an hour around the ship before starting business. The chief had complete charge of the trade. If another tribe should come alongside while the chief was trading, they would wait until he had finished; and if he told them the prices were good, they would employ him to sell their furs. Sometimes, however, they were very jealous of one another and would not allow their neighbors to see what they had received in trade. At noon they would go ashore to eat. They also left at four o'clock, but not as promptly as at noon. When they left the ship in the evening they would sing again. When the chief had completed a trade he would say "*coo-coo*" quickly three times, and the people in the canoes would answer more or less enthusiastically as they were pleased with the transaction.

Trade brought many exotic articles to the Indians during this period. Dixon tells of a piece of "Sandwich Island" cloth (tapa) which a trading chief saw hanging in the shrouds to dry. The man who owned it was willing to sell it, and the Indian took it away immediately. The next morning he came back with a coat made of this cloth, cut exactly like the skin cloaks, which resembled a waggoner's frock except for the collar and wristbands. The coat fit with all the seams sewn as narrow as the strength of the material would allow (Dixon 1789, pp. 181–89).

There probably were calls from trading ships after Dixon's visit, but the published diaries have no records until 1791, when in August Marchand visited Norfolk Sound, which he called Tchinkitanay, the name he also used for the Tlingit there. In the short time he was there he acquired an unusual amount of detailed information about Indian life. The coastal villages were fishing sites, and the permanent towns were away from the coast. All men had iron daggers, fifteen to sixteen inches long and two and one-half to three inches broad, sharp on both sides. They were carried in a shoulder belt of leather. He speculates that they must have been made of hardwood before metal became available. (They had been made of the leg bone of caribou traded from the interior.) The stone hatchet was replaced with a piece of iron, which was adjusted to the end of a crooked handle like a carpenter's adze. This, of course, was the handle of the standard elbow adze. The Indians still used bow and arrows, although the English had traded muskets to them—a bad policy in Marchand's opinion—but the situation was partially saved because they had little powder.

The men hunted and fished and carried their efforts to preparing and cooking the meat and fish. The women did the final skin dressing and made the clothing. They also cared for the children, who were placed in sitting cradles made of "wicker." This word is constantly used in the translation of Marchand for almost any kind of basketry. In the nineteenth century the Tlingit seldom made a special cradle; they cut some old baskets into broad pieces that were overlapped to strengthen them and formed a sort of shallow tray. They then shaped this to the infant, and after putting in some soft material, woven wool or fur, they laced it up the front. The sketches of the Spaniards at Yakutat Bay show a cradle resembling this type seen by Marchand. It is likely that the sitting cradle, which is not used elsewhere on the coast, was brought from the interior Athapascans by the Tlingit. Marchand states that the child's cover was otter skin, but the sketch does not represent this. Like many other coastal tribes, the Tlingit used moss (sphagnum) as a diaper but, the Frenchman adds, seldom changed it.

The women were highly respected among the Tlingit. They were consulted in trading and often vetoed the choices, to the discouragement of the visiting traders. They ate with the men instead of serving them first, as is the custom in many tribes. It is unfortunate that the language barrier kept Marchand from finding out their place in the social structure of the group. That remained for Krause to report in the 1880s.

Marchand was very much impressed with the art of the Tlingit, saying, "they do various kinds of sculpture and painting and everything announces a long employment of the useful arts. . . . Canoes, chests and all other articles are covered with designs of fish, animals and heads of men." As an example of their artistic skill he describes a ceremonial costume which was put on at his request. He says, amusingly, that it consisted of a sort of grenadier's cap, with the forepart like a miter, placed on the forehead and tied with strings behind the head. The part like a miter was decorated with figures of men, quadrupeds, and birds, and hanging down from the sides and back was long human hair as well as hair of beasts, together with filaments of tree shrub bark (shredded cedar bark) like flax. This whole figure is easily recognized as the frontlet headdress worn by chiefs. The "miter" part is carved and painted, with abalone inlay. The "beasts' " hair hanging down at the sides and back is ermine, and in the nineteenth century the top of the "miter" was decorated with sea lion whiskers and the tail feathers of the flicker. It is the most beautiful and imaginative headdress made on the Northwest Coast and in the nineteenth century was worn with the best type of ceremonial blanket, meaning the Chilkat blanket. This type of headdress is mostly used by the Tsimshian, Haida, and Tlingit and is found in many modern museum collections (Gunther 1962, p. 105).

With this headpiece there was worn, on this occasion, a plastron or cuirass made of material woven of hair, trimmed with slips of skin shaped like the skirts of a corset. This is difficult to interpret, but it may have been similar to the shaman's poncho, except that that is a lozenge-shaped piece of skin, usually slit at the center for the head. The fringed apron he described as the lower part of this dress was probably separate, as dance aprons were, with shells and birds' beaks (puffins) as decorations. The poncho had a design painted on the front, such as he described. With this they wore thigh and knee pieces of the same material, with the knee covered with a grotesque head of a bird with a wooden nose (beak?). Such a costume is not in any currently known museum collection. The dancer carried in his hand a human head made of osier and bark mounted at the end of an eight-inch stick and filled with "sonorous" seeds. This is a round rattle carved of wood (not osier and bark); in the other hand there was a hoop of plaited osier eight to nine inches in diameter, with birds' beaks hanging from it. This is a familiar rattle, still used today and seen in many museum collections. How one wishes that these pieces could have been collected; but Marchand states that the owner would sell no part of the costume.

In addition to the visual arts, singing was a social institution. They sang in chorus at all times, day and night. The chief of the family would start by singing a few measures and then the others would join him. This indicates clearly that the songs are family property, and the pattern of performance is still being carried on. The women sang an octave above the men and beat time by clapping their hands. Paddles were also used to keep time, and this was especially done when they paddled a canoe and sang (Fleurieu, 1801, pp. 226–42).

With the Malaspina sketches and Marchand's observations, the Yakutat and Lituya Bay Tlingit are well represented in the eighteenth-century picture of Indian life. It must, however, be remembered that probably a large section of the population found there in the summer of 1791 were "summer residents" and brought with them the customs that were characteristic of their home villages. In comparison with Lituya Bay, there were probably more permanent families living at Yakutat Bay at that time, and they were the ones that represented Tlingit culture to the Eyak and Chugach of Prince William Sound, with whom they maintained active trade.

Dixon in 1787, and American fur traders beginning in 1790, preceded the Vancouver expedition of 1793 into Southeastern Alaska. Caamaño in 1792 concentrated on Bucareli Bay and made a brief visit to both the north and south shores of Dixon Entrance, but he did not meet any Tlingit. The previous expedition had come into the panhandle of Alaska from the north, but Vancouver, having finished with Observatory Inlet and Portland Inlet, rounded Cape Fox and soon found himself at the entrance of Revilla Gigedo Channel, which Caamaño named during his voyage in 1792. Vancouver entered Behm Canal, which he named for the generous and efficient governor of Kamchatka.

Near the central point in Behm Canal, at Burroughs Bay, a boat expedition found salmon spawning. Soon they came upon a large deserted village, and from nearby some Indians paddled to the boats to trade. They appeared friendly and the canoe that brought them was steered by a woman who wore a large labret. She snatched up the lead line of Vancouver's yawl and lashed it to the bow of her canoe. A young man who seemed to be the chief of the party jumped into the yawl and put on a mask resembling a wolf, which also looked partly human. The first Indian who visited the boat stole a musket. The launch which accompanied the yawl on this surveying party was too far away to be of immediate help; so Vancouver, taking a musket, went up to speak to the chief. He was surrounded by about fifty Indians, who seized their daggers, brandished their spears, and pointed them toward the men in the yawl. The chief told Vancouver to lay down his musket and that they would also lay down their arms, but before any action could be taken the woman who was steersman vociferously urged the Indians on. A ferocious-looking man in the middle-sized canoe seized the yawl's oars so the men could not use them. Puget and Vancouver tried again to persuade them to lay down their arms, but the Indians stepped forward and raised their spears. At this crucial moment the launch arrived within pistol shot. Finally Vancouver fired over their heads and they climbed a steep, rocky precipice and threw stones at the boats. Two men were injured, though not seriously. Vancouver named the entrance to Behm Canal Bettin's Point for one of the injured men.

When they tried to determine the reason for this attack they decided that the Indians might have received defective muskets in a trade; but they soon found out that they were near a deserted village that Captain Brown had cannonaded. This may have been the reason. In reviewing the incident, Vancouver decided he should have been more cautious, but the Indians had changed suddenly from a friendly attitude to a threatening one (Vancouver 1798, 2: 374).

On a short trip to the east shore of Prince of Wales Island, Vancouver named Cholmondely (Chomly) Harbor and anchored at Moira's Sound, where some Indians came from the west shore of Behm Canal. One of them appeared to be a chief and asked to come aboard. He said he knew all the fur traders on the coast and had come from a powerful chief named Ononnistoy, the *U-en* (Ewen) *smoket* or *stikin*, and that his residence was in the northwest branch.[1] He said that if Vancouver would fire a gun this chief would come with salmon and sea otter skins. He then

1. The word *smoket* which Vancouver and Roquefoil used for "chief" is not known in the Tlingit language. *U-en* might be identified with *tlen* meaning "big."

asked whether Vancouver intended to go up Clarence Strait or back to Behm Canal and warned him that in the latter there was no chief and, no skins, and that the people were thieves and very bad. Such warnings were common, but since they were only twelve miles away from Escape Point, where they had had trouble, Vancouver thought there might be some truth to it. He sent the chief some blue cloth in return for the sea otter skin he had received and promised to come later on. After they had moved to a good moorage two exploring expeditions were sent out, one with Baker and fourteen days' supplies and the other, with Johnstone, with supplies for ten days. While they were at this moorage a canoe with seventeen Indians, including Kanaut, their chief, came to the ships at midnight and stayed until dawn, singing. They were in ceremonial dress, with their faces painted and down sprinkled in their hair. They traded very shrewdly but were fair. They acknowledged Ononnistoy as their principal chief. Whidbey met some Indians near Burroughs Bay, and the canoes followed the boats until they landed. They sang in their canoes and came ashore, each carrying a green bough which they laid on the rocks along with a long twist of white wool, which Whidbey interpreted as a peace token. He thought that they were the tribe that had attacked the yawl at Escape Point and that they were trying to make amends (Vancouver 1798, 2: 388).

Farther on a group of seven Indians seemed to be opposed to the boats' landing. Their canoes were close to a miserable hut. After they put on their war garments they advanced to meet the boats, one man carrying a musket and another a pistol. They cocked the guns while the five others picked up their bows and arrows. An elderly man appeared and made a long speech while holding a bird in one hand and plucking out its down with the other. He threw the down in the air at the end of each sentence. The Whidbey party threw some spoons and trifles to the orator, indicating that they would like some food. The old man ordered the armed men to leave and the others brought some salmon. They met some more chiefs, but Ononnistoy did not appear (Vancouver 1798, 2: 389).

Johnstone, on his reconnaissance, was ahead of the ships in Clarence Strait when he commented on the skill with which women handled canoes, large and small. All the women in the canoes wore labrets of various sizes, and so one could study the progress of this "cruel disfigurement."

On 30 August at Port Stewart three canoes came, conducted by two chiefs. Ononnistoy was not one of them. They seemed to be important, so Vancouver made them suitable presents which they almost disregarded. They constantly conversed with each other and ignored the efforts of Vancouver's companions to act as hosts. The following day they returned and brought goods to trade, also enough salmon for both ships. The chief, a fine-looking person, had many scars, probably gotten in war when the iron daggers were used. He came aboard with a few of his people and they were given bread and molasses, which they ate with relish. They brought with them what Vancouver recorded as "stinking whale oil," but found that the Englishmen had no interest in it, except its removal from the deck! During the afternoon a large canoe came, filled with men singing and beating time with their paddles. These new arrivals showed the extreme aggressiveness of the Tlingit. The first party immediately put on their war gear and readied their spears. They advanced slowly on the newcomers, shouting, and passionate speeches were made by both sides. They stopped for a parley and came back peacefully together. When they came close to the *Discovery* one of the chiefs who had been on board drew his dagger from his armor because he seemed irritated by something said in the canoe below. They all picked up weapons again, including pistols and blunderbusses. But again they were reconciled. The chief of the large canoe asked to come aboard and brought another man, not a chief, with him. He turned to him for advice. This may have been the chief's speaker, an official who announces to the public what the chief has to say. Very important chiefs seldom speak themselves. This new highly placed visitor, at last, was Ononnistoy, identified by Kanaut, who came in a small canoe and was received with much ceremony. Ononnistoy and two or three others asked to sleep aboard because they had no houses in the neighborhood. To entertain his visitors Vancouver ordered some fireworks, but the Indians were not impressed; they liked only the water rockets. In the morning Ononnistoy joined the others ashore and all adorned themselves in ceremonial clothes and got into their canoes to sing again. Some of their songs were accompanied by "rude and extravagant gestures" done by all the chiefs in succession. Ononnistoy then asked for trade. He wanted only guns, but these were refused, and so at length he took cloth, files, and tin kettles.

Among these people there was a young man in a blue jacket and trousers who smoked cigars in Spanish fashion and took snuff: in fact, he took the snuff box from the cabin! He was not European, but may have been from New Spain, although he did not understand Spanish. He declined an offer to come aboard the *Discovery*. There is a chance that he might have been a Filipino cabin boy, afraid that the English captain might turn him in as a deserter (Vancouver 1798, 2: 393–95).

Soon after this incident the longboats rejoined the ships. Because of the lateness of the season and the aggressiveness of the Tlingit, which they had faced for several weeks, Vancouver decided to end the survey for 1793 at Cape Decision. As soon as they could prepare the ships they sailed, to return the next spring from Hawaii with their course set for

Cook Inlet. The two ships approached the Northwest Coast separately in April, having become separated as they neared America. They met again at the entrance to Cook Inlet. For the survey in Cook Inlet and Prince William Sound see chapter 7.

Going south in the Gulf of Alaska, the Vancouver expedition came into the Tlingit territory that had been explored eight years earlier by La Pérouse, Dixon, and Marchand, among others. The expedition members' memories of the encounters with the Tlingit in southeastern Alaska during 1793 were still sharp, and it gave Puget considerable relief to find the Russians there, represented by Portoff. This Russian leader had left Cook Inlet about a month before, with seven hundred kayaks and fourteen hundred Indians from Kodiak and Cook Inlet and forty-nine Russians. They assembled in Yakutat (Bering's Bay) as a base for sea otter hunting. Navigation in these waters is very dangerous and this is where Tipping disappeared in the *Sea Otter* after September 1786, where he was last seen by Strange. Puget named the island in Yakutat Bay Knight Island (Orth 1967, p. 533).

Soon after their arrival Puget's ship was surrounded by about fifty kayaks from Portoff's party, and the men purchased white shirts, stockings, and cravats from the officers for bows and arrows, darts, spears, fish gigs, whale gut shirts, and specimens of very neat and curious needlework (Vancouver 1798, 3: 226). The natives were very keen in their bartering. This information is particularly interesting because there are no Yakutat Bay items in the Hewitt collection in the British Museum, but the inventory from Cook Inlet includes many of the items mentioned here (see Appendix 1). According to Portoff, the local Indians were unfriendly and treacherous; but after this visit of the kayaks two local Indians came to the *Chatham* with ceremonial songs and received small presents of iron and mirrors. Although they carefully examined the gifts, they were well behaved.

When the *Chatham* was trying to get into the bay she became grounded. Some Indians came to the ship with salmon and advised Puget that there was no passage from here to Port Mulgrave; so Puget sent out an exploring expedition to test the shoreline to Cape Phipps. Inside the cape they found an Indian village that was accessible only by boat. It looked recently deserted, and about fifty howling dogs were left behind. Puget wondered if Portoff's arrival had caused the Indians to retire into the woods and if that was why Portoff called them treacherous. Portoff denied that the Russians had been harsh or cruel in trying to subjugate them. He said he had met only 30 Indians here in 1787. Dixon that same year counted about 70, and Johnstone, when he was there with Colnett in 1788, reckoned about 150. The difference may have been due to seasonal migration.

Portoff sent a message by one of the Russians that the Indian chief who had slept on board the night before had a gold watch chain with seals hanging on it which he declared was a gift from Puget. Up to that time it had not been missed. Portoff moved his camp to Point Turner because he did not trust the Yakutat, who visited him in a group of about fifty. While Puget was waiting for the *Discovery* he visited Portoff's new camp, where he found a tent set up for him and his weapons. The Kodiak leader had placed two canoes edgewise about four feet apart, laid paddles over the top, and draped the whole with skins, and had put grass mats down as a floor. Many sea otter had been brought in by the Kodiak hunters, and Puget watched the skinning. They drew the skin over the body of the animal without making any incision on the back or the belly. The skins were hung up to dry. The flesh was a delicacy, and some people were scraping the blubber and fat from the carcasses and eating it raw. The rest of the animal was boiled with vegetables gathered in the surrounding woods. The bones of the sea otter were preserved with the greatest care, but Puget could not find out why.

Among many native peoples, attitudes toward certain animals are derived from their status as humans in the mythological period preceding historic times. Many tribes on the Northwest Coast honor the first salmon that comes in the spring; others honor the bear and speak to it either before or after killing it. The sea otter may have been the subject of a similar concept among the Kodiak. In some places the bones of the first salmon were wrapped in mats and carefully laid in the river from which he came so that he could return to the salmon country and start life again. Puget also noted that some of the Kodiak people were engaged in making "curiosities" to sell.

When the canoes sent out with Manby to look for the *Discovery* came back without him, Puget assumed that he had found the ship and boarded it. Late in the evening Portoff sent a message that the *Discovery* was coming around the point, and so they fired a gun and sent Johnstone out; but it proved to be the *Jackall*, whose captain said that they had parted from the *Discovery* the previous afternoon, but that she had been blown eastward in a gale.

On the morning of 5 July all the Indians were gone from Port Mulgrave and had left the Russians in possession of Point Turner. Puget's intercourse with the Indians had been amicable, and before he left they came to the *Chatham* singing and dancing. Several chiefs visited them, and Puget gave them suitable presents. The *Chatham* also now left Yakutat Bay and sailed to Cape Spencer and Cross Sound. At Cape Spencer a dozen Indians came to the ships in one canoe, but they were afraid to come aboard unless a hostage was sent to the canoe. Puget responded and the chief came aboard, bringing a quantity of halibut which was purchased for iron. They were excessively suspicious, probably due to bad experiences with some "civilized" visitors (Vancouver 1798, 3: 237). At Cross Sound some canoes with men, women, and children aboard came out from a cove where they had made a temporary camp. Their numbers increased rapidly, but no one trusted himself on the ship, though they were friendly on shore. They had a great deal of fish but very poor sea otter skins. The diaries again lack information on the bartering, although it produced almost two dozen specimens with more variety than the collection from Cook Inlet, including gambling sticks, spoons, and baskets.

A universal pleasure among American Indians is gambling. Among the Haida, Tsimshian, and Tlingit a game of chance is the most popular form of entertainment and is played whenever a few people assemble. The game is played with thirty-five to sixty beautifully cut and polished sticks of wood about five inches long. These are kept in a bag made of skin or woven cedar bark. One of each kind is in the Hewitt collection from Cross Sound (BM, Vancouver 162; Hewitt ms. 201; BM, Vancouver 163; Hewitt ms. 201, Appendix 1: 121, 122). The sticks in the cedar-bark bag have designs burned into the wood and rubbed with black paint. The ones in the skin bag have painted bands of red and black. One competitor divides his sticks into two parts and works them into two bundles of shredded cedar bark which looks like tow. His opponent must guess which bundle holds the stick with a certain marking. If he is wrong he loses one or more of his sticks and must guess again. If he is successful his opponent loses a number of sticks and must become the guesser. The bets are very high and are made on single guesses or on the whole game, which may last many hours. The playing is often continuous for several days. The game was strenuously objected to by the missionaries, not only because it was gambling but because there was no limit to the amount a player could wager—even his food, his family, or himself. If he lost such a bet he became a slave of the winner. This game is a feature of Northwest Coast Indian culture that has withstood the onslaughts of acculturation, and gambling is still done at many gatherings.

Another type of object secured in Cross Sound or at any of the contacts in the Tlingit territory is the basket woven of spruce root, which is made by many Northwest Coast tribes but highly developed by the Tlingit. These baskets were common household utensils, used for cooking and storing food. They were also examples of women's creativity, and although there were a limited number of designs, they were arranged in a never-ending variety of combinations. For the structure of the baskets see Appendix 2. There are four baskets in the Hewitt collection, all small and of a type which has been a standard "souvenir" since the earliest visits of Europeans. Probably the reason no more appear in these early collections is that the men on the ships were more interested in weapons and fishing gear. These few samples, however, do establish the stability of the shape and the type of weaving and, above all, the continuity of design. They could mingle with late nineteenth-century baskets and not be noticed, for the only feature they lack is the bright colors aniline dyes made possible. But not all the later weavers followed this trend, and baskets in natural colors were still made. For descriptions of individual baskets see Appendix 1, and for the method of weaving see Appendix 2.

Two other pieces of weaving are also registered from Cross Sound, but may come from a wider area. Both are woven of a combination of mountain goat wool and one of the several basket grasses. The larger piece (BM, Vancouver 201, Appendix 1:158) has "white hairs" bound into the twine, which may be the guard hairs of the mountain goat or could even be caribou hair traded from the interior. The piece is thirty-one and one-half inches long and twelve inches wide, and so might have been used as a sash or belt. It has loose ends which could be used for tying. The second piece (BM, Vancouver 200) has six rows of twining with a short fringe along the entire length and is listed as a head ornament. Such headbands with a fringe hanging over the eyes are known.

Household utensils are also very rare in the Hewitt collection, as they are in others, but that may be because Indians seen in the summer, when they are moving from one fishing camp to another, seldom carry more equipment than they need and could not afford to barter any of it. When they were seen in their regular homes, it was possible to pick up such pieces as spoons, ladles, cooking boxes, and small tools. There are two spoons in the Hewitt collection from Cross Sound, a small one made of mountain goat horn (BM, Vancouver 120; Hewitt ms. 207; Appendix 1:228) and a larger one made of wood with a design painted in the bowl in a dull red (BM, Vancouver 119; Hewitt ms. 203; Appendix 1:227).

From the moorage at Cross Sound the exploring expeditions went out in several directions. Whidbey first went south to Cape Decision where the 1793 surveying season closed, and Johnstone headed into Chatham Strait. On 26 July Whidbey returned from a trip into the entrance of Lynn Canal. There was still much suspicion among the Indians there, but he had finally met a chief who presented him with a sea otter skin. He was the most beautifully dressed man Whidbey had seen. His "external robe," as Whidbey described it, was woven of mountain sheep (goat) wool in several colors and reached from his neck to his heels. It was also decorated with little tufts or frogs of wool dyed in the same colors. There are a number of similar blankets in eighteenth-century collections. His headdress was shaped like a crown, made of wood and ornamented with bright copper and brass plates from which hung tails and streamers of wool and fur twisted together and dyed various colors, each terminating in an ermine skin. The whole outfit was very impressive and in very good taste.

During the night a canoeful of Indians came who were very well-armed and appeared unfriendly. The canoe contained seven muskets and some brass blunderbusses. The Indians advanced to the yawl, the leader holding a speaking trumpet in one hand and a spyglass in the other. He had a powder horn slung over his shoulder. Whidbey managed to escape without any conflict, but before he left Lynn Canal he had to face another troublesome party.

On Admiralty Island at Point Parker they saw some new houses being built and noticed some land under cultivation. The plant growing there appeared to be a variety of tobacco, which is also supposed to grow on the Queen Charlotte Islands. It has been well known that the Haida grew some variety of tobacco, but this is the first reference that shows that the Tlingit also planted it. Both groups used it for smoking and chewed it with lime. Occurring sporadically on the Northwest Coast are various wild forms of tobacco or closely related plants which local Indians have used (Drucker 1963, p. 105). In Alaska there was active trade between Eskimo on one side and the Asiatic Eskimo and the Chukkhee on the other, who secured their supplies from the Russians. This trade was most active at Cape Prince of Wales, but spread widely throughout Alaska.

At Hood's Bay the Indians came to barter with salmon and sea otter skins. They preferred to sell the skins rather than the fish, and would take any trifling piece of apparel. This has an important implication. The fish was necessary for the following winter's food and could be gotten in quantity only during the salmon runs. Sea otter can be hunted whenever the weather is favorable, and they were not necessary for a livelihood. So they sold "extras" for "extras," since the clothing they received was generally used only to garnish their ceremonial dress. For their heavy trading in sea otter skins they went to the outer coast where the European ships passed, and there they would take only firearms, not any copper or iron.

On his approach to Cross Sound Whidbey stopped for the night near Port Adolphus, where they saw a box about four feet square on four pillars about six feet high. The box contained a body, carefully wrapped. By its side stood a twenty-foot pole painted in horizontal stripes of red and white. All this looked very fresh and neat. They wondered whether it was the burial of a chief. The description reminds one of the grave sketched by Suría. This closes Whidbey's observations on the Indians of southeast Alaska.

Johnstone was out at the same time and met more Indians than

Whidbey, but he generally did not record much more than their approximate numbers. At one place he feared for the safety of his party. At another place he found a well-constructed platform built out over the edge of the cliff, similar to some structures they had seen on the Inside Passage. Close to this they found many burials in small frame houses of better construction and repair than the dwellings. One was about ten feet high and built around a canoe in which there were four or five bodies wrapped and set in boxes in good repair.

Johnstone and Whidbey met at McCartney Point and together went to Port Conclusion, where the ships were waiting for them. Here Vancouver declared his mission completed, and on 22 August they celebrated with extra rounds of grog. The next day they weighed anchors and started for home.

After the Vancouver expedition left Alaska the Russians were active in developing settlements, and disputes arose between the Lebedef Company and the Russian American Company, of which Baranof was the representative. Meanwhile, both British and American ships came in during the trading season. Baranof continued his attempt to create a settlement in Norfolk Sound (Sitka Sound), and after many misadventures he anchored there on 25 May 1799. He landed at a point known as Old Sitka, about six miles north of the present town. The Sitkan chief, Katlean, met him and asked his intentions. Baranof replied that he had been sent by the emperor of all the Russians to give them his care and protection. He bought a piece of land for beads and other trade goods, and his followers started at once to build.

The following day the *Caroline* with Captain Cleveland arrived from Boston. She looked strange because a screen of hides had been erected around her deck except at the stern, where the captain and his men stood to trade. This precaution was taken because he had a very small crew and did not want the Indians to know. Cleveland was much impressed with the facial painting of the Indians. He went to the village of Hoodnahoo (Killisnoo) and into Chatham Strait to trade, but was constantly afraid of hostility. During his movements in southeastern Alaska in that trading season he encountered the following ships:

Hancock	Boston	Captain Crocker
Dispatch	Boston	Captain Breck
Ulysses	Boston	Captain Lamb
Eliza	Boston	Captain Rowan
Cheerful	England	Captain Beck

Cleveland, according to his diary, had a "linguist" on board who could shout orders to the Indians. He is not described further, so we do not know whether he was an Indian (Cleveland 1842, p. 93). At one place a war canoe came out with twenty-five warriors in war garments. A few years later, Lisiansky described the armor used, which was still basically the same as has been described for elsewhere on the Northwest Coast, with the exception of the *cuada*. First came a jacket of doubled heavy skin, which was fastened around the neck, or a woolen *cuada*, to the upper front of which iron plates were attached to defend the breast from musket balls. These *cuadas* were not made by the natives but were furnished by the traders from the United States in exchange for sea otter skins. Formerly a cuirass of wooden lathes laced with sinew was made and decorated with a coat of arms on the chest (Lisiansky 1814, p. 238, plate 1, fig. *a*). The Indians had firearms, including a small cannon which they also obtained from American traders. Their former use of bows, arrows, and spears had been totally abandoned (Lisiansky 1814, p. 239).

At one point in his cruising in the Tlingit territory, Cleveland observed a steep, inaccessible rock on which a fortified village was perched. This might have been the Chilkat town of Katkwaltu, which means "town on the point of a hill" (Swanton 1904–5, p. 397). It was described as having a spiked fence (*chevaux-de-frise*). People could be seen behind the fence, so it was not one of the many deserted villages seen by the travelers.

Cleveland also went over to the mouth of the Stikine River, where a great chief arrived to visit him in a canoe as long as the ship. He made the captain a present of a sea otter skin, and they commenced trading with greatcoats, cloth, knives, beads, and "China cash." The chief was invited on board and drank half a tumbler of wine. When he left he blew bird down into the air and sang a song to which the Indians paddled in perfect time (Cleveland 1842, pp. 96–97). Soon after this, Cleveland met Captain Beck, who, complaining about the hostility of the Indians, said he had had to shoot into a canoe with a cannon. This probably accounts for some of their behavior.

Rowan, in the *Eliza*, also went to the Stikine River and reported that *Stikine* means "Great River" in Tlingit (Orth, 1967, pp. 919). British and American traders who came to the northern part of the Northwest Coast during the last years of the eighteenth century traded at much higher prices, and so had accustomed the Indians to amounts that Baranof did not want to pay. His system of engaging the hunters for a set wage and taking all their catch could not be imposed on the Sitka as easily as it was on the Aleut.

With this influx of trading ships into Alaskan waters, the calendar eighteenth century ended; but this study will continue into the first years of the nineteenth century because they were a continuation of a historical period. This will allow us to use the important narratives of Lisiansky and Langsdorff, who gave detailed descriptions of the Tlingit of Sitka, at the center of their territory. Without this information we would have only the observations of La Pérouse, Marchand, and Dixon and Malaspina on the more peripheral groups in Lituya Bay and Yakutat Bay, at the northern limits of their distribution.

Lisiansky's voyage covers the period of the Russians' farthest southern extension in Alaska and the beginning of the decline of the sea otter trade because of the severe competition and the extinction of the herds. He came to the Northwest Coast as part of the first circumglobal expedition by the Russians. His objective was to find out whether there was an easier way of delivering supplies to the Russian colonies in Northwest America than the overland route through Okhotsk, Siberia. Krusenstern, the commander of this voyage, also was to take the Russian ambassador to his post in Japan. While he was carrying out this errand, Lisiansky, in command of the *Neva*, sailed to Kodiak Island to make his first contact with North America in the west. He had served as a volunteer in the British navy and had visited North America on the Atlantic side in 1794–95. He traveled from Boston to Savannah and spent a winter in Philadelphia before returning to his ship in Halifax.

Langsdorff was a German scholar who had gone, as many did at that period, to be an adviser at the court at Saint Petersburg. He came to North America on the expedition which brought Resanoff, and the narrative of his four-year voyage is one of the standard works of its period. It was first published in German and then translated into English and published in Carlisle.

When Lisiansky arrived at Sitka he was responding to Baranof's request that he follow him there to help, if necessary, in establishing the second settlement at New Archangel. It was the guns of the *Neva* that forced the Indians to retreat into the forest, even though in this encounter with Baranof they had more firearms than they had had several years earlier. The sale of guns and ammunition is always attributed to the American traders, but by this time the competition had become so keen that it does not seem that others would have refrained entirely from giving them in trade for sea otter skins. The Indians wanted them the most and often held out for them. The siege of the Tlingit lasted four days, and then Baranof started his second building of New Archangel. Soon after the settlement was organized its founders realized that there were not enough supplies of any kind to serve the community. So Baranof bought the American ship *Juno*, from Bristol, Rhode Island, with Captain Wolf in command. This served two purposes: it prevented Wolf from trading with the Indians for sea otter skins and it gave the settlement the food and implements they needed. Captain Wolf was promised passage back to the east coast of America, but from casual inclusion of his name in further accounts of New Archangel, it seems that he stayed there a long time before such an opportunity arose. When Langsdorff arrived with Resanoff they also brought supplies of firearms, rice, linen, woolen cloth, knives, hatchets, axes, kettles, kitchen utensils, and drinking vessels (Langsdorff 1817, p. 279).

After the destruction of their village, the Tlingit settled again in the northeastern part of the Island of Sitka and, still not trusting the Russians, fortified themselves on a high, rocky point of land. Lisiansky has a diagram showing the arrangement of the fourteen houses built there (Lisiansky 1814, plate II) and the type of fence set up across the front. There was only a steep trail up the rock, and this was blocked with fallen trees. There was outward peace and a show of friendship, but both parties stayed on the alert (Langsdorff, 1814, p. 395).

When Lisiansky arrived at Sitka he was favorably impressed with the mildness of the climate and said that oats, barley, and all kinds of European fruits and vegetables could be cultivated. The Sitkans lived on Jacoby Island and Chichagoff Island in settlements independent of each other, but they all spoke the same language and were almost all related through their clan system. All together there were probably about ten thousand Tlingit, of whom about sixteen to seventeen hundred were Sitkans (Lisiansky, 1814, p. 238). They were all grouped together under the name Colushes, or Kolushes, still found in twentieth-century ethnography as Koluschan for the Tlingit language (Swanton 1905, p. 396). Langsdorff also used the term "Koloschain" for the Tlingit, but added that they called themselves G. tinket or S-chinkit (Langsdorff 1817, p. 395).

When the Tlingit came to New Archangel to visit or trade they approached ceremoniously, singing, and the chief delivered an oration about their friendship. The clothes they wore would be a combination of trade goods and their own, or would combine trade goods from various sources. Langsdorff describes a piece of cloth five feet square which was tied around the neck and gathered into a belt around the waist. This could be trade cloth, their own weaving, or made of tanned skins, probably deer or caribou, traded from the interior Indians. They also wore a kind of European carter's frock and often had a garment resembling a shirt but not as large, and with this a pair of short pantaloons. In cold weather they wore dresses of fur, though woolen cloth was more commonly used. The rich wrapped themselves in white woolen blankets, locally made of the wool of wild sheep (mountain goat), which Lisiansky claimed was as soft as Spanish merino. Langsdorff wrote that the animal from which it came was not yet in the natural history of world animals. These blankets were embroidered with square figures and fringed with black and yellow tassels. This description seems to indicate that this is the forerunner of the Chilkat blanket. A person not familiar with the relationship of the design units of the Chilkat blanket would reasonably describe them as "square figures." The tassels of black and yellow are found on many of the early blankets. Langsdorff describes this weaving as "carpetry," and this coincides with many descriptions of Chilkat weaving as "tapestry" (Appendix 2; also De Laguna 1964, p. 180; Osborne in De Laguna 1964, p. 187).

The Indians' favorite colors in the trade woolen goods were blue and red. They seldom used these European materials without some additions of their own; Langsdorff mentions that they added to the carter's frock tassels of ermine skins and eagle tails. He also relates that abalone was always requested and that American traders brought imitation dentalium made in England of porcelain, but could not fool the Tlingit. They used thimbles not for sewing but for jingles on their dance costumes, and Chinese coins were tied or sewn on (Langsdorff 1817, p. 412).

From their descriptions it appears that both Lisiansky and Langsdorff actually visited in the fortified village the Tlingit had built. Langsdorff wrote that the houses were oblong, in various sizes, and set in regular rows, a fair distance apart. Lisiansky called them square and spacious. The sides were of planks fastened to twelve thick house posts driven into the ground. The roof resembled that of the Russian houses; it was covered with large slabs of bark and had an opening about two feet wide along the top to let the smoke out. The houses had no windows and the doorway was so low that a person had to stoop to enter. In the middle of the building was a large hole that served as a fireplace. In the houses of the wealthy this was fenced with boards and the space between the fireplace and the walls was partitioned by curtains (probably split cedar bark mats) so that each family had privacy. A number of related families lived in one house. Lisiansky said there were broad shelves along the sides of the building for domestic purposes. These were probably sleeping platforms with space beneath for storage. Here all the dried foods were stored, and they hung fishing gear, large pieces of clothing, and so on on the walls above the platforms. Langsdorff stated that the entrance, beneath the gable of the roof, was painted in earth colors. He did not mention any carving, such as an entrance pole. He also gave no indication that the house posts were painted or carved (Lisiansky 1814, p. 240; Langsdorff 1817, p. 410).

The houses were built of cedar, and this was also used for their canoes, which were dugouts ranging from sixty feet for war and traveling canoes to the small ones used for fishing and household purposes. The average was about thirty feet. They moved very fast in smooth water and were handled with great skill by both men and women.

Fishing and hunting were essential in providing food for the Tlingit. The collection made by Lisiansky includes a halibut hook with a carved arm, a type widely distributed on the northern part of the Northwest Coast (Lisiansky 1814, plate I *d*). The principal figure in the carving is not clear, but at the sides are the tentacles of an octopus. The fish spears on the same plate (figs. *h*,*k*) are again not peculiar to this group. In hunting not for food but for skins, Lisiansky thought the Sitkans were not as expert as the Aleut. They shot the sea otter only while they were asleep, and since they could not destroy very many in this way, they still abounded in the Tlingit area, whereas the Aleut, who surrounded them in their kayaks at sea, could slaughter a whole herd. Lisiansky stated that from Cook Island to Cross Sound there were scarcely any traces of the valuable animal. Bows and arrows were still used for sea otter hunting, because one gunshot would scatter the herd. Indians could have their guns repaired by the gunsmith, a member of every ship's crew. These men would also buy guns back, repair them, and sell them for new.

The land that Lisiansky described as usable for cultivation produced naturally the abundance of vegetation for which the Northwest Coast is famous. In the spring and summer many varieties of berries were available. They were not named by many of the explorers because they were unfamiliar with these Alaskan plants. The spring also brought the return of the salmon and the spawn of the herring. Many of these products could be dried by the methods developed in Northwest Coast cultures, and the Indians all spent the summer moving from place to place where an abundance of food could be found. The camp sketched in the La Pérouse account is typical of a temporary summer shelter.

Foods like rice, molasses, wheat flour, and tea were secured from traders and incorporated into their diet as their money or tradable goods would afford. Not only the kinds of food but also their cooking methods and utensils changed. Meat and fish were at first roasted on sticks around the open fire, but after trading began these were boiled in iron, copper, or tin kettles. Wealthy people had European stoneware dishes and basins, but the poor continued to use bowls or boxes of wood they made themselves and served and ate with ladles and spoons of mountain sheep or mountain goat horn (Lisiansky 1814, plate III, fig. *f*). Lisiansky calls plate III, figure *e* a spoon, but it is a small grease dish in the shape of a bird. It appears to be one of the pieces he secured in Kodiak Island, since it is almost identical with one in the Museum of Anthropology and Ethnography in Moscow, where the bulk of the Lisiansky material is, and one in the Natural History Museum in Oldenburg, West Germany.

Lisiansky compared the social customs of the Sitkans with those of the people of Kodiak, where he stayed for some time on his way to Sitka. He believed that the Sitkans were much livelier, for they sang and danced more often. They played games, as the bags of gambling sticks in the Hewitt collection indicate (BM, Vancouver 162, 163), and Lisiansky also shows the die for another game. He called it *stopka*, and this word could be Tlingit or Russian. It was played with a single die and the throw counted according to the side it fell on (Lisiansky 1814, plate III, fig. *g*, p. 211). They also sang and danced on all occasions. Langsdorff described a dance, but gave no indication of the occasion.

> They are dressed in a simple garment, or in a sort of carter's frock which they purchase from the merchants of the U.S. of America. In their hands they each hold a tail of a white-headed eagle. The ermine skin round the head, upon the clothes and sometimes held in the hand is a mark of luxury and wealth. The foremost dancer has in his hand a stick ornamented with sea otter teeth, with which he beats time. Some of the dancers have their heads powdered with the small down feathers of the white-headed eagle. The women sit by the dancers and sing: they have the very extraordinary national ornament to the under lip. In the background is a moveable hut of the Koluschians. [Langsdorff 1817, p. 114]

The social system of the Tlingit is very involved and has gone through some changes in the last century and a half. To explain it thoroughly is not pertinent to this material, since few travelers in the eighteenth century stayed long enough or understood the language sufficiently to grasp its intricacies. Therefore, I will merely record the remarks of the two authors used throughout this section. Considering all the difficulties, it is amazing that Lisiansky learned so much. He stated that the Tlingit were divided into tribes, the principal ones assuming titles of distinction from the names of animals they preferred, such as the bear, eagle, crow (raven), porpoise (killer whale or blackfish), and wolf. (These are not tribal but clan or moiety names.) The wolf was called Colqontan (Kagontan; Krause 1885, p. 75) and had privileges over the other tribes. They were the best warriors and were said to be insensitive to pain and to have no fear of death.[2]

The Tlingit commonly had one wife, but polygamy was acceptable among the wealthy. Chiefs often had an older and a younger wife, preferably sisters. At puberty girls underwent a long period of seclusion to prepare them for marriage. The ideal for women was "industry, reserve, modesty, and conjugal fidelity," which Langsdorff states differs from the people to the north (Langsdorff 1817, p. 414). There were many chiefs or *toyons*, often four or five even in small settlements. The right of succession passed from uncle to nephew, except for the chief *toyon*, who acquired his title through his display of importance, strength, and ability and the size of his circle of relationships. He could be despotical and could do much mischief.

2. There are important anthropological studies of the social structure of the Tlingit. In order of publication, they are: Krause 1885; Swanton 1904–5; Stanley 1965; Olson 1967. See bibliography for full citations.

The Tlingit were very easily provoked to warfare, and since non-Tlingit were far away they had many quarrels among themselves. They were extremely cruel to prisoners from any other group, torturing and scalping them. If another Tlingit was captured he became a slave, but if he was an important man he was ransomed by his clan, with payment principally in sea otter skins (Langsdorff 1817, p. 411).

Lisiansky wrote that when the Russians took possession of the new settlement at Sitka they destroyed at least one hundred wooden burial bòxes. The bodies of the dead had been cremated, and the bones that remained, together with the ashes, were put in a chest set on pillars about ten feet high, erected on the edge of the forest not far from the village. The pillars were carved and painted with figures, but unfortunately these are not described. A slave was often cremated with the chief. The reason given for cremation is that the flesh could be used in witchcraft and other harmful practices. Lisiansky noted that this was a ridiculous idea, as was the notion that a shaman's body contained so much evil spirit that it could not be consumed by fire. Shamans were buried (Lisiansky 1814, p. 241). Shamans were feared in their communities, for they had the power to inflict the evil sent by a creator when he was angry. This being could also send disease to the people (Lisiansky 1814, p. 243).

Both authors expressed themselves about the use of the labret and the disfigurement it causes.

This brings to a close the extended information secured about Tlingit in the eighteenth century, and even this brief study clearly reveals that the major material and social characteristics of Northwest Coast culture were well developed in this period. The Tlingit were a large enough group to maintain their way of life, and in spite of their local quarreling they maintained a united front against the Russians. They were the first Northwest Coast people to live with foreign settlers. The fur traders, explorers, and later the whalers came and went. They were interested in their own business, but not in changing the culture of the Indians or offering them new philosophies, like the teachers and missionaries who came later in the nineteenth century. The canneries, logging camps, and miners also were not concerned with the social problems of acculturation; so the Indians were free to use the trade goods in their own ways and come into town when necessary, but to carry on much of their old life, at least during the first half of the nineteenth century.

7

The Northernmost Reaches, with the Chugach of Prince William Sound, the Athapascans of Cook Inlet, and the Aleut and Russians at Unalaska

The Cook expedition left Nootka Sound on 26 April 1778, having been there almost a month. They sailed away from shore in very poor weather and passed the Queen Charlotte Islands on the outside, not seeing them, but conscious that there was an archipelago there. According to his instructions, Cook was to proceed northward along the coast as far as 65° north latitude, taking care not to lose any time exploring rivers and inlets, or upon any other account, until he reached that point. There his real search for a Northwest Passage was to begin. He was expected to arrive there in June (Beaglehole 1967, p. 343*n*).

On 1 May Cook began to approach the shores of southeastern Alaska. He recorded and named Mount Edgecumbe on 2 May and Mount Fairweather on 3 May. He named Cross Sound, but at no place in his diary or in those of King, Clerke, or Samwell was there any mention of an anchorage during these days. This eliminates the possibility that any Tlingit objects were collected on this voyage.

On 10 May Cook came into the Gulf of Alaska between Yakutat Bay and Prince William Sound, which he first called Sandwich Sound in honor of the First Lord of the Admiralty. He continued to honor him by using his personal name for Montague Island and the name of his estate in Kent, Hinchinbrook, for another island in Prince William Sound. Except for Bering's visit in 1741, when Steller went ashore at Kayak Island and saw a recently deserted habitation, Cook was the first European to describe the people, unless there are some records in unpublished and untranslated Russian sources.

The region is of particular interest because it is the meeting place of several cultures, the Northwest Coast being represented by the Tlingit, the Athapascans, the Eskimo, and a small independent group, the Eyak. In the late eighteenth century and probably also in the early nineteenth century, the Tlingit enjoyed their greatest territorial expansion to the north, not always in settlements but sometimes by trading expeditions. At this time the Eyak claimed the lower part of the Copper River Valley, had a town at Cape Martin, and hunted on the offshore islands (Birket-Smith and DeLaguna 1938, p. 2). The Eskimo, represented by the Chugach, lived in Prince William Sound itself, and also used the surrounding territory for hunting. The Athapascans lived in the Copper River valley and to the north. The Tlingit were represented by their trading expeditions, their nearest settlement being Yakutat Bay.

The Cook literature includes many journal entries about the visit to Prince William Sound. All agree that the people differed from those of Nootka Sound, and Cook saw a resemblance to Crantz's Eskimo of Greenland. At Cape Hinchinbrook, Samwell mentions their love of blue and green beads, which were probably gotten from Kamchatka but still left open the possibility of a Northwest Passage. He also noted their ingenious kayak bailer, a tube of wood like a pipette through which they sucked the water out of the kayak (Samwell 1967, p. 1113). Cook described a wooden hat made in the form of a seal's head (fig. 40) which is in the British Museum collection (NWC II; Appendix 1:141) and is marked Nootka Sound, even though Cook's own entry is from Cape Hinchinbrook, Prince William Sound. This piece is sometimes called a helmet or a mask, but it is too light for warfare and does not fit the face well enough for a mask. In 1791 Meares gave another purpose which may be the proper one. Since he wintered at Prince William Sound he had ample opportunity to observe the Chugach at times of the year when the explorers who preceded him were not on the coast. He described seal hunting and mentioned the use of decoys:

> The seal is also an animal very difficult to take, on account of its being able to remain under water. Artifices are therefore made use of to decoy him within reach of the boat; and this is done in general by means of wood in so exact a resemblance of nature, that the animal takes it for one of his own species, and falls a prey to the deception. On such occasions, some of the natives put on these masks, and hiding their bodies with branches of trees as they lie among the rocks, the seals are tempted to approach so near the spot, as to put it in the power of the natives to pierce them with their arrows. Similar artifices are employed against the sea-cow, etc." [Meares 1790, p. 56]

Another example of this headgear is in the Institut für Ethnologie at the University of Göttingen (#820; Appendix 1:141*b*), and the detail carved on this one makes Meares's explanation even more plausible. Meares's statement is also found in Lisiansky for Sitka in 1804, and since these two authors agree at some distance in space and time, this seems the most reasonable explanation for these seal heads, which are definitely from the Cook expedition.

A third example is not from an eighteenth-century collection, though

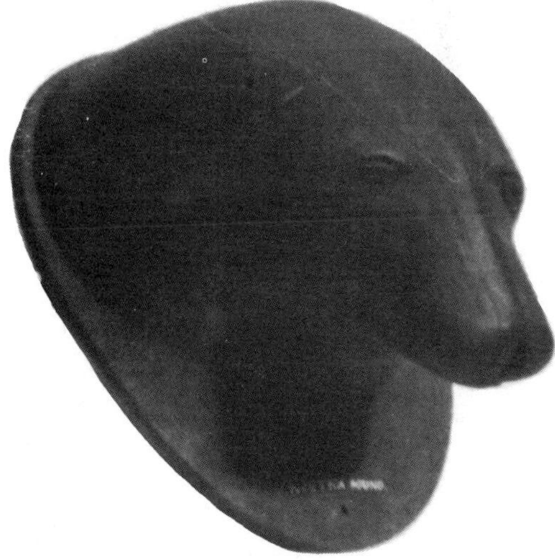

Fig. 40. Decoy hat in the form of a seal's head, Prince William Sound. Cook collection, BM, NWC 11 (Appendix 1:141).

its origin may well date to that period. It is called a "seal mask" and attributed by the National Museum of Finland (no. 46) to the Tlingit. It was collected between 1840 and 1847 by Rear Admiral Arvid Adolf Etholen while he was a member of the governing board of the Russian-American Company. It has the usual realistically carved head of a seal, but at the neckline the front projects into a small visor which makes the use suggested by Meares even more plausible. The visor has a crack in the center which is mended by a simple piece of root, probably spruce root.

The first days in this area gave Cook no glimpse of the inhabitants until Gore went into some inlets near Cape Hinchinbrook and suddenly came upon two canoes carrying about twenty persons. They were not dugouts like those at Nootka Sound, but skin-covered boats like those of the Eskimo farther north (Cook 1967, p. 344). A few days later these boats appeared again, this time at the ships, and were accompanied by many men in one- and two-seated kayaks. Cook did not immediately comment on the difference between these people and those of Nootka Sound. His first reaction was to the disfigurement produced by their variety of labret. Then he related that the Indians differed from those of King George's Sound both in language and in features.

Cook described a visit to the ships by natives in two kayaks, the first with two men aboard and the other with one. Each man carried a stick about three feet long with large feathers and wings of birds attached. When they held them up, the ships decided that "they wished to express peaceable sentiments." Beaglehole adds to this that Bering's records show that at his first meeting with the natives of the Shumigan Islands they threw onto the deck two polished rods with falcon feathers which also were taken as a sign of friendship (Beaglehole 1967, p. 346). There is no mention of ceremonial greetings in Birket-Smith's discussion of the Chugach as he saw them in 1933, but perhaps such rituals no longer are part of the memories of twentieth-century informants.

When the Eskimo came aboard after this greeting, Cook described the chief as wearing a robe of sea otter skins and a cap like those of the Indians of Nootka Sound. The latter part of the statement needs analysis. The Nootka were famous for their hats which had whaling scenes woven into the fabric, not painted as many visitors thought. They also made shallow spruce-root hats which were painted, and because of their narrow brims they could be described as caps, for they fitted close to the head and had a chin strap. There is a hat in the British Museum which might be either in the Cook or Banks collection (NWC 5, Appendix 1:134). It is said to be from Nootka Sound, but this type, with its abstract design, shallow crown, and overall wash of blue, belongs to a northern tribe. Dixon, who was at Yakutat, sent Banks several pieces and may have collected this one also. Its narrowness is correct for the period, and according to Drucker the spruce root hat was not known within the memories of his informants at Nootka (1951, p. 93). Samwell writes in his diary that "some who can afford it have them [the hats] ornamented with beads of different colours" (Samwell 1967, p. 1112). This type of decoration, together with the sea lion whiskers on opposite sides, is characteristic of the northernmost distribution of these hats, perhaps in Prince William Sound (see Appendix 1).

A hat completely conforming to this description is in the Museum of the Institut für Ethnologie at the University of Göttingen (#602, Appendix 1:135), together with several pieces attributed to the Cook expedition. It resembles very closely the one illustrated by Birket-Smith (p. 67, fig. 35) as an example from the Chugach of Prince William Sound, which is trimmed with dentalium shells, small pieces of cloth, and sea lion's whiskers at opposite sides of the crown. This hat was acquired by Jacobsen, a collector who was in Alaska and on the Northwest Coast in 1881–83. It is in

Fig. 41. Hat, woven of spruce root and painted, Prince William Sound. Swaine collection (Vancouver), Cambridge 49.205 (Appendix 1:136).

the collection of the Museum für Völkerkunde in Berlin (IV A 6174). Birket-Smith draws attention to another detail of this hat which bears curious relationship to some other eighteenth-century objects (see Appendix 1:10; also fig. 30). On top are some remnants of tassels which he thinks were made of roots (Birket-Smith 1938, p. 67, fig. 35). These may be compared with a small carved figure of a man wearing a hat with bits of dyed tanned skin still visible in the crown of his hat. This was collected by the Vancouver expedition on Bainbridge Island in Puget Sound, Washington, in 1792. It does not belong there, and has some characteristics that place it among the Nootka, where such figures served as tokens of an invitation to a potlatch (Gunther 1960, p. 10, fig. 6). Another example is a Spanish sketch done in 1791 during Malaspina's voyage, entitled "The Second Wife of Tetaku," who was the chief at the entrance of the Strait of Juan de Fuca and well known to the first explorers (Museo Naval original sketches) (see plate 27*d*). The luxurious plume on her hat may be trimmed feathers, but other feathers drawn by the same artist show a downier edge, so this may be skin, like the hat of the little figure.

Fig. 42. Two baskets in Tlingit style, Chugach, Prince William Sound. Banks collection, BM, NWC 16, 23 (Appendix 1:50, 51).

Another example of the skill of the Chugach and Eyak weavers is the fine basketry, which resembles the Tlingit baskets so closely that it is often thought to be trade goods made by them. In both the ethnography of the Chugach and the reconstruction of Eyak culture by Birket-Smith and DeLaguna the basketry is described with the local names for designs which are also used by the Tlingit, often with other interpretations (Birket-Smith and DeLaguna 1938, pp. 81–87; Birket-Smith 1953, pp. 58–59, 79). The meeting of cultures is well illustrated here, with the Tlingit, Eyak Indians, and Chugach Eskimo all practicing the same type of weaving and even using some of the same designs. If enough were known about the history of these cultures it might be possible to place these common skills in their proper historical period. We know that in the late eighteenth and early nineteenth centuries the Tlingit penetrated far north in their trading activities. Did any Tlingit marry into these groups and teach the art, or did women from the north go to Yakutat, for instance, and learn the weaving to take back to their homes? I mentioned earlier that since the Cook expedition made no landing in Tlingit territory there could be no Tlingit objects in their collections. In view of the close similarities in the baskets in the British Museum that are supposedly from the Cook expedition but are called Tlingit (fig. 42), it seems feasible to consider them as coming from Prince William Sound (BM, NWC 16, 23; Appendix 1:50, 51). The question is, Was the art introduced to these northern people early enough so that they could have gained the technical control of the craft by the late eighteenth century? I am assuming that this type of basketry spread northward, because twined spruce root baskets are also made by the Tsimshian and Haida, the Tlingit's southern neighbors, although without the designs which the Chugach and Eyak share with the Tlingit.

Another object that is probably from Prince William Sound rather than Nootka is a cuirass with wooden slats, two inches wide, across the front and back and rods of the same wood under the arms. Cook speaks of it as defensive armor and adds that the slats are bound together with sinew (Cook 1967, p. 351). Edgar mentions buying armor which is curiouly plaited and fastened at the back like "women's stays" (Edgar ms.). Such a piece of armor is in the British Museum collection (NWC 73, Appendix 1:1), and it may be the piece purchased by Edgar. The armor is also mentioned by Samwell and Ledyard and both of them also place their reference in Prince William Sound. This type of armor was worn by the northern tribes of the Northwest Coast but the literature does not mention it farther south than the Queeen Charlotte Islands (Ledyard 1783, p. 76: Samwell 1967). Drucker states that the customary Nootkan armor was a heavy skin, but a Hesquiat informant told him of armor made of "heavy twigs" (Drucker 1951, p. 335).

Krickeberg, in his analysis of armor in the European museums, agrees with the statement above; he believes this armor is from Prince William Sound and not Nootka Sound. He believes that it was acquired between 12 May and 20 May 1778 from the Tschugatschigmut (Chugach) or from the Ahtena (Krickeberg 1914, p. 678), since he describes an armor jacket made from thin slats from the latter.

On the Pacific coast it is often difficult to identify the exact origin of fishing and hunting gear, for the game varies little and the best method of securing it are almost universally agreed upon. Through the years many parts of this gear have become disassociated, which makes their identity even more uncertain. In the collections in Vienna and Florence there are such pieces which are supposed to come from Prince William Sound, and this provenance is plausible. Niblack (1890, p. 287) draws attention to the similarity between Eskimo and Tlingit hunting arrows. In Florence there are three pieces—a harpoon, an arrow for sea otter hunting with a bone point, and a harpoon cord (catalog numbers App. XII, #2196, 2163, 2102). In Vienna there are also a few pieces of this type—a harpoon with line and bone point (#229; Appendix 1:110), a harpoon without point (#230; Appendix 1:105), and a spear (#228; Appendix 1:349). Such pieces are also well represented in the Webber collection at Bern, where they are in better condition than elsewhere. The collection includes the following: (Bandi 1956, pp. 214–20; Henking 1955–56, pp. 367–78)

1 harpoon point and foreshaft (Al 15) Appendix 1:111
2 harpoons (Al 6*b*, 6*c*) Appendix 1:101
2 sea otter harpoons (Al 6*a*, 6*d*)

1 sea otter harpoon arrow (Al 6*c*) Appendix 1:104
1 spear thrower (Al 4) Appendix 1:360
6 feathered arrows (A2,3,5,6,7,8) Appendix 1:301–6
1 bow (Al 5) Appendix 1:308
1 bird spear (Al 7) Appendix 1:350

It is just as difficult to trace the origin of beads, because they are so easy to trade and carry. DeLaguna states that blue beads of the type Cook described were often found in historic Athapascan and Eskimo archaeological sites when there were no other foreign articles (DeLaguna 1947, p. 33). Osgood mentions blue beads among the Kutchin before white men, and he believes that beads came from the coast. The interior of Canada in Cook's time was a blank, and no one was aware of the great distance across the continent. Jochelson believes that beads came to the Aleut along with iron from the Chukchee and northern Alaska Eskimo or through Chinese, Ainu, and Kamchadal trading before Bering in 1741. The beads cannot be identified as Chinese, but Torii reports some pale blue beads of Chinese manufacture in ancient Mongolian sites. They were traded to Japan about a thousand years ago, and at that time Ainu and Kamchadal influences also began to appear in southwestern Alaska (DeLaguna 1947, pp. 225–29).

The *Resolution* and the *Discovery*, restored by repairs, left Prince William Sound and sailed to Cape Elizabeth at the south tip of the Kenai Peninsula. There they turned south to Marmot Island, changed their course again, and went northward past the Barren Islands and into the entrance of a large body of water which Cook left blank on his chart. He had never named a place for himself. This, however, was called Cook's River, and in 1794 Vancouver changed it to Cook Inlet. About halfway up the inlet two canoes came from shore with the first people they had seen since leaving Prince William Sound. At a point just south of Tyonek, a canoe and several smaller craft came to the ships. The smaller boats were kayaks; one, a single seater, was paddled with a double-bladed paddle. The people were dressed like those of Prince William Sound. They bartered their furs (sea otter) for old clothes, sky blue beads, and small pieces of iron. The expedition went farther up the "river," and after Bligh and King had both gone on exploring expeditions to test the end of the "river" for a Northwest Passage they started back at Turnagain Arm—so named for this action. More natives visited the ships bringing sea otter pelts, and they had knives of copper and iron. Gore describes these in sufficient detail so that they can be traced in ethnographic literature:

> I saw among them a kind of knife or dirk made wholly of iron and neatly manufactured in a manner which I don't think any of Them

> capable, it was nearly a foot and a half long. The Blade Part about one foot, shaped like that of a Boar Spear Thicker in ye middle and more Taper To the point & The Edges very sharp. The Handle part round and below the Grip a Knobb neatly Fluted in a spiral Manner much Like The Head of a Fiddle, Do They send any Such to Hudson's Bay. [Gore, 3 June; in Beaglehole 1967, p. 371]

These knives are undoubtedly the bear spears of the Athapascans, which were hafted to a long strong wooden shaft. The same knife was also used by the Tlingit as a dagger, grooved but without spirals at the grip (Niblack 1890, plate XXX, fig. 108; plate XXVIII, fig. 118). Cook surmised that the metal was secured from the Russians instead of from the Hudson's Bay Company, as Gore suggested, and credited them as well with some of the luxuries such as tobacco. Samwell, who recorded this also devotes some of his attention, as usual, to the women. Many young women came to the ship and sold their favors for a leaf of tobacco. They were very acceptable because of their unusual cleanliness. Also, many notes written in Russian were found among the Indians, but nobody could read them.

When the exploring team came back from Turnagain Arm in Cook Inlet, the Captain began to have serious doubts about the existence of a Northwest Passage; but he still had instructions to search for the Russians. Hoping that perhaps some passage would still open up, he left Cook Inlet and passed along the outside of Kodiak Island. The weather was foggy and stormy, preventing good orientation. When they reached the area of the Shumigan Islands, the *Discovery*, about two miles behind the *Resolution*, fired three guns and signaled that they wished to speak. Cook sent a boat to the ship and it returned with Captain Clerke, who related that three or four Indian canoes had been following them. When they approached the ship one man took off his cap and bowed in a European manner. A rope was lowered to him and he sent up a small piece of wood. He spoke to them in his language, which no one understood, and then all the Indians left. The token they received looked like a bird call, but biting it produced no sound. When the string was released it fell into halves and revealed a folded paper with some Russian writing dated 1778. In the body of the note there was also the date 1776. Many suggestions were made about its purpose—wrecked Russians asking for help, a note to be given to the next Russian ship to pass—but the consensus of the people aboard was that some effort should be made to find the authors of the note. Cook, however, was in a hurry and ignored the suggestions. They discovered afterward that the slip was a receipt for tribute paid to the Russians. It indicated how far east in the Aleutian Islands they had penetrated (Cook 1967, p. 384, with footnote by Bayly, 19 June).

At the Sanak Islands, the end of the Alaska Peninsula, they stopped for some halibut fishing, which was very successful. During the fishing a small canoe came alongside; its occupant bowed and took off his cap. His features were similar to those of the people of Prince William Sound. He wore a pair of green cloth trousers and a jacket of black cloth under his gut parka. He had nothing to barter but a gray fox skin and a few items of fishing gear. He had a lip perforation but wore no ornament and his face was free of paint (Cook 1967, p. 386).

From 22 June the ships traveled through fog and stormy weather until 28 June, when they came to Unalaska and found anchorage at Samganoodha, later called English Bay by Veniaminoff because of Cook's visit there. The first natives that came to the ships were eager to barter some fishing gear for tobacco. These may be the pieces in the collection in Florence. One is a small harpoon made of caribou horn with a point of flint. Giglioli, who wrote on the Cook collection in Florence, quoted Ellis as saying, "We purchased some of their darts, which were about 4′ long, not feathered at the end, and pointed with stone and one or two had four prongs" (Giglioli 1895, p. 130; Ellis 1782, 1:283).

Cook, bound to get to the Arctic in October before it was too late in the season, sailed as quickly as possible to find a passage through the Aleutian chain that would take him northward. He found the passage between Unalaska and Unalga, but it was narrow and dangerous, and so the bay at Samganoodha was welcome. They stayed there long enough to take on water and then hastened north. I will not recount the details of this part of the voyage north, for the little contact he had with the natives involves people beyond the culture area of primary interest. However, he did find here an important clue to the contact with the Russians. An Indian (a term Cook used for all people he met on the North Pacific Coast) brought another note, again written in Russian. Like the former messenger, he bowed in European style and took off his cap. All this assured Cook that there must be Russians in the vicinity.

On his return from the Arctic in October, Cook again anchored in the English Bay, and the crews went ashore. Some picked berries and others fished, thus improving their diet of customary sea rations. On 8 October an Indian named Derramousk (or Yarmousk) brought to the ships two baked loaves, one for Captain Cook and the other for Captain Clerke. These loaves were filled with highly seasoned salmon, and were considered delicious by those who shared them. The presents were accompanied by a note, again in Russian, which no one could read. In response Cook sent Ledyard, with a present of a few bottles of rum, with Derramousk and his party to find the Russians or others and assure them that they were English, and therefore friends and allies. In several days Ledyard came back with three Russians, "seamen or furriers," who lived at Egoochshac Bay where they had a house, storehouses, and a sloop of thirty tons. The men were friendly, but the language barrier prevented them from giving and receiving information. Cook was amazed at their limited knowledge of the local geography. They promised a chart of the islands lying between Unalaska and Kamchatka. Meanwhile, Cook and Webber went visiting to an "Indian village"[1] where they met the tribute collector for the whole Russian colony, Ismyloff (Ismailoff). He arrived in a three-seated kayak accompanied by twenty or thirty smaller ones. After a brief visit Cook invited him to come to the ships the next day and bring his charts with him. From these charts Cook found that Ismyloff was well acquainted with the geography of the North Pacific and knew all the Russian discoveries which changed Cook's current maps. Ismyloff allowed Cook to copy from his charts, especially the one which gave all the Russian discoveries eastward from Kamchatka toward America. They amounted to very little if the voyages of Bering and Chirikof are excluded. The locations of islands did not agree with the Muller map which Cook had, and it would have been difficult at that time to determine which was correct. The Russian assured Cook that none of his people had ever seen any of the continent northward.

Before leaving, Ismyloff gave Cook a letter to Major Behm, the governor of Kamchatka, and the captain gave him a letter to the Admiralty in London, in which he enclosed his chart of the northern coast he had just visited. Ismyloff promised that there would be an opportunity to send the letter to Kamchatka in the following spring and that it would reach Saint Petersburg the following winter.

After discussing the charts which were significant to him, Cook described the Aleut people. His description is so complete and terse that it will be given here in full:

> These people are rather low in stature, but plump and well Shaped, with rather short necks, swarthy, chubby faces, black eyes, small beards, and straight long black hair, which the men wear loose behind and cut before, but the women tie it up in a bunch behind. Their dress has been occasionally mentioned, both Men and Women are made alike, the only difference is in the materials, the Woman's frock is made of Sealskin and the Men's of birdskins and both reach below the knee. This is the whole dress of the Women but over this frock the Men wear another made of gut of which resists water and has a hood to it to draw over the head; some of the men and those of Prince William Sound all wear a kind of oval snouted Cap made of wood, with a rim to admit the head; these are stuck with long bristles of some sea animal on which are strung glass beads, and on the front is a small image or two made out of bone. They make use

Fig. 43. Figure in squatting position, carved of wood, Nootka Sound. Webber collection (Cook), Bern 11 (Appendix 1:5).

1. On this visit it is likely that Webber acquired the interesting little figure (fig. 43) which is in his collection at Bern (Al 11; Appendix 1:5). It is described and a relationship between it and the figures of Ivanov cited.

> of no paint but the Women punctuate their faces slitely and both men and Women bore the under lip to which they fix pieces of bone, but it is as uncommon at Onalaska to see a man with this ornament as a woman without it. Some fix beads in the upper lip under the nostril and all of them have ornaments in their ears. [Cook 1967, pp. 459–60]

The sunshade or "oval snouted cap" is familiar headgear not only in the Aleutian Islands but also along the coast of southwestern Alaska around the mouth of the Kuskokwim River, where they often become very elaborate. The example in the British Museum (NWC 3; Appendix 1:143) is one which Webber sketched. The original drawing, in color, is in the British Museum also, among the originals of Webber, and the reproduction in black and white is plate 48 in the Cook Atlas.

The men's dress made of bird skins is seen in many European collections, for example, in Copenhagen, Göttingen, and Leningrad, and if these do not date to the eighteenth century they are certainly from the very early nineteenth century. They are generally made of tufted puffin skin, which is exceedingly tough. After red cloth came into the trade small tassels made of it were often sewn on the garments. They are very beautiful and nothing brought into the culture could take their place either in appearance or in suitability to the climate.

Cook called the Aleut the most peaceable, inoffensive people he had ever seen and wondered whether this disposition is natural with them or whether it was the result of subjection to the Russians. He said, "Indeed if some of our gentlemen did not misunderstand the Russians, they told them they were obliged to make some severe examples before they could bring them to any order. . . . Each island had its own chief, but they could not find out whether they were tributaries to the Russians" (Cook 1967, p. 459).

Since there is so little ethnographic detail of the precontact period in the literature, it is important to record everything found out about the Aleut, if not in actual precontact times, at least very early in their association with the Russians. As Cook saw them at English Bay, he wrote of a single house that was occupied at three levels of society; the Russians lived at the upper end, the Kamchadals in the middle, and the natives, meaning the Aleut, at the lower end. However, he said, there was little difference in their food or methods of cooking (Cook 1967, p. 450). Their own houses, if they lived away from the Russian settlement, were built on a two-foot-deep square excavation, over which they formed a roof of driftwood covered with sod and grass. Two holes were left in the roof to admit light and let the smoke out. One hole had a notched pole in it which served as a ladder down into the house. Each family had a definite share of the house and the cooking was done communally in the center.

The fire for cooking and warmth was produced by striking two stones (pyrites) together or with a fire drill. Boiling and broiling were the only cooking methods, and in consequence they ate much of their food raw. The lamps for light and cooking were the usual Arctic type: a saucer made of clay or pecked out of stone, with a grass wick (Cook 1967, p. 460). They had bowls and spoons of wood, all neatly carved. Baskets and bags were woven of grass as food containers, and mats of the same sort were used in serving meals. There was an occasional Russian brass kettle or pot. All the Indians used tobacco in the form of snuff, for chewing, and for smoking in pipes, and they valued it so highly that they were willing to barter almost anything for it.

The basketry and the sewing of skin garments were done by the women (see Appendix 2). They also undertook larger projects in sewing the covers of the skin boats, the small kayaks, and the large open boats, used in travel by families. Everything they made was well done, neat, and artistically decorated.

This is as much of the expedition to the northernmost region as can be legitimately included in this study. In each location described so far, only the reports of the earliest contacts have been included. This paragraph in Cook's journal changed the history of the Northwest Coast:

> There is no doubt but a very beneficial fur trade might be carried on with the inhabitants of this vast coast, but unless a northern passage is found it seems rather too remote for Great Britain to receive any emolument from it. It must however be observed that the most, nay the only valuable skins, I saw amongst them was the Sea Beaver, or Sea Otter as some call it; all other skins that I saw were of an inferior kind, the foxes and Martins in particular. [Cook 1967, pp. 371–72]

In spite of these words of warning, when the western Europeans discovered the possibilities of the fur trade—of which the Russians had already known for a quarter of a century—the rush began that changed the Northwest Coast even before the westward movement across the continent. It is interesting that the Spaniards, who saw the area a few years before Cook, did not realize or were not concerned with the mercantile aspect, even though a number of references in the diaries report the acquisition of sea otter skins. It took people from northern temperate climates to see its real value. When the news of this trade spread, expeditions were organized in England, India, and China, and after a little more stabilization of its new government the United States also moved into the race, with ships out of Boston. The first fur trading expedition from the Orient came to Nootka Sound in 1785, and left John MacKay, the surgeon, to become acquainted with the Indians and arrange trading for their return (see chap. 1). Their ships, the *Captain Cook* and the *Experiment*, sailed north, passing the Scott Islands at the northern end of Vancouver

Island and past Cape Saint James at the southern tip of the Queen Charlotte Islands. From there on they saw no land until on 27 August 1786 they came to Snug Corner Cove in Prince William Sound, the harbor used by Captain Cook. Strange, one of the partners of the company sponsoring this voyage, was surprised to find Captain Tipping here, but since he was a member of a rival firm, there was little communication between them. Tipping had been trading successfully in Prince William Sound and mentioned a copper river that the Russians called Mednoi Ostroff (*ostroff* means island). They thought that the copper could be picked up on the beach. After this meeting Tipping and his ship were never seen or heard of again.

Strange comments on the scarcity of population and suggests that the permanent residences are inland. He found one deserted settlement with twelve houses that were better constructed than those at Nootka. They were partially built of six logs each, logs that were long and thick enough to make mainmasts for the largest ship in the British navy (Strange 1928, p. 21). He agreed with Cook's notes and said that even the uncleanliness was not exaggerated. The people were well provided with clothes and ornaments and mats of fur and wool from an animal like a sheep. They wore boots and oil dresses—gut parkas—for wet weather (Strange 1928, pp. 37–43).

Meanwhile, the Russians continued moving east of the establishments which Cook saw in 1778. Delaroff, who later became chief of the Russian colonies, spent the winter of 1783 in Prince William Sound. The period from 1785 to 1794 was well covered by Martin Sauer, the secretary of the expedition conducted by Commodore Joseph Billings, who had been on the Cook expedition and had then joined the Russian navy for this extended voyage. Sauer's excellent description of the appearance and habits of the Aleut on Sedanka Island off the coast of Unalaska is quoted here. There were only five families there, but they were identical in their ways to the people on the larger island, Unalaska.

> They formerly wore a dress of sea otter skin, but not since the Russians have had any intercourse with them. At present they wear what they can get; the women a parka of ursine seal, with the hair outwards. This is made like a carter's frock, but without the slit on the breast, and with a round upright collar, about 3 inches high, made stiff and ornamented with small beads sewn on in a very pretty manner. Slips of leather are sewn into the seams of the dress and hang about 20 inches long, ornamented with the bill of the sea parrot, and beads. A slip of leather 3–4″ broad hangs down before from the top of the collar, covered fancifully with different coloured glass beads, and tassels at the ends; a similar slip hangs down the back. Bracelets of black seal skin are worn round the wrists about ½″ broad, and similar ones round their ankles, for they go barefooted and this is all

their dress. Their ornaments are rings on their fingers, earrings, beads and bones suspended from the septum of the nose, and bones in the perforated holes in the under lip. . . . When they are walking on the rocky beach, they wear an awkward kind of boot, made of the throat of the sealion, soled with thick seal skin, which they line with dry grass. The men wear a parka of birdskin, sometimes, the feathers outward, and sometimes inward. The skin side is dyed red and ornamented with slips of leather hanging down a considerable length; seams covered with thin slips of skin very elegantly embroidered with deer's hair, goat's hair and the sinews of sea animals, dyed of different colours. They also wear tight pantaloons of white leather, and boots as described to be worn by the women at times; the men wear them when they go on foot; but in their baidars or their huts they are without either pantaloons or boots. . . . In wet weather, or when out at sea, they wear a camleey; which is a dress made in the shape of the other, but formed of the intestines of sea animals; the bladder of halibut or the skin off the tongue of the whale. It has a hood to cover the head, and ties close around the neck and wrists so that no water can penetrate." [Sauer 1802, pp. 155–56; see Appendix 2]

Sauer goes into considerable detail about their household equipment and their technical ability in creating it. He speaks of their festivals in the spring and fall, which they celebrate by eating and by dancing with the drum, their only musical instrument. In the spring they wear masks "neatly carved and fancifully ornamented." He relates that a priest burned the collection of masks hidden in a cave and forced the people to allow themselves to be christened. Sauer wrote, "they were not pleased" (1802, p. 160).

In this settlement there were twelve Russians and one Kamchadal, with Tshirepanoff as the leader. They had lived there eight years and expected to go back to Okhotsk that year. They ruled the native people with more despotism than princes; in fact, the people were in abject slavery. The men were sent out on hunting parties and the Russians meanwhile lived with as many women as they chose. The hunting parties went out under a single Russian leader while others stayed near the village and fished. When Billings's expedition visited Trinity Cape in 1790, they found the establishment of Shelikof, where thirteen hundred men and twelve hundred youths were gathered under the supervision of Delaroff, a Greek in the service of the Russians. There were six hundred baidars carrying two or three men each. The women here dried and cured fish, planted gardens, collected edible wild plants, and sewed clothing for their men and the Russians as well (Sauer 1802, pp. 169–71).

They also met Ismyloff, the Russian officer who was collecting tribute when Cook stopped at Unalaska in 1778. Delaroff intended to go to Cook Inlet and set up another settlement. He believed that the climate there was mild enough to grow corn. Billings went on to Afognak, where the

Russians already had a settlement. During July, when the expedition had gone south of Prince William Sound, they came to an island which they tentatively recognized as Cook's Kay Island (Kayak Island). An old man came aboard who said that when he was a little boy a ship had come very close to the island. The people all ran away and hid. When they returned after the ship left they found in their subterranean storerooms some glass beads, leaves (tobacco), and an iron kettle. These were the articles left by Steller when he went ashore during Bering's visit, so Billings's guess that he was on Kayak Island was correct.

The first fur traders from England were Portlock and Dixon, both of whom had been with Cook on his third voyage. They left England in August 1785, wintered in Hawaii, and spent the summer of 1786 in Cook Inlet and the waters near Prince William Sound. They arrived at the mouth of Cook's River (Inlet) on the afternoon of 19 July, and soon heard a gunshot. Remembering the Cook expedition's meetings with the Russians, they assumed that the shot was a signal for them. It was. At Point Bede they found four or five kayaks with one person in each. The captains went in a whaleboat of the *King George* to the Russian "factory," which was a temporary installation for hauling boats ashore. The Russians had come from Unalaska in a sloop, and the people in the kayaks were "Indians" from Codiac (Kodiak). A few days later they sailed into Cook Inlet, where they traded profitably for almost two weeks, and during the latter part of this period there was also a salmon run, which helped provide fresh food for the crews.

Portlock briefly described the people of this area as like those at Prince William Sound, which implies that he considered them Eskimo. According to the distribution of Eskimo and Indian villages in the area given by Osgood (1937, pp. 13–17), this could easily be true, especially since the trading was mainly in the lower inlet. Portlock stated that every boat had a man in authority, and among each boat's occupants there was only one woman, who was treated with great respect.

During the remainder of the season the two ships, the *King George* commanded by Portlock and the *Queen Charlotte* with Captain Dixon, tried to enter Prince William Sound, but being beaten off by weather they continued down the coast, trying Cross Sound with no better results. They finally headed for Nootka Sound, but they did not enter it, sailing directly to Hawaii for another winter (Dixon 1789, p. 73). On their return in April 1787 they came to Montague Island, where they were visited by "Indians" who came in kayaks and suggested that another English ship was there or had been there during their absence. Dixon went on an exploring excursion and was guided to this ship by natives who kept saying "*lally towser*." The ship was the *Nootka* from Bengal, with Captain John Meares in command. He had reached Prince William Sound too late in the season for any activity, and so he decided to winter there. The ship was frozen into the ice and the company suffered great privation and many died. The *Beaver*, their consort ship, was cut off by the natives and none of the crew was ever seen again. Captain Meares had a large Newfoundland dog named Towser, of whom the Indians were very frightened. When they came to the ship to barter they called "*Lally Towser*" and whistled. This strange clue led Dixon to the ship and saved the lives of the ship's company. The captains, even though they represented different trading firms, exchanged supplies and information (Nicol 1925, pp. 129–30).

At this point Portlock and Dixon started southward on the coast, but since the forbidding weather still made it impossible for them to reach land they decided to separate for more efficient trading. Portlock went back to the north, to Prince William Sound and Cook Inlet, while Dixon continued south, where he first visited Yakutat Bay (see chap. 6). Later he went to the Queen Charlotte Islands (still unnamed), and had great success (see chap. 5).

Portlock finally found an opportunity to observe and describe the population of Prince William Sound. He described the people as for the most part short and the men square-made. Both men and women had flat faces with high cheekbones and flattish noses. Their eyes were dark and keen and their sense of smell, which was very good, was sharpened by smelling parched snake root. They were lighter in complexion than many of the southern Indians, and many women had rosy cheeks. Their hair was black and straight and was worn long except when it was cut for mourning. Portlock attributed the ill-shaped legs of the men to their sitting in one position for long periods in kayaks or canoes. This was a customary reason given for the physical build of many Northwest Coast Indians, and only one author took this in a lighter vein. Sproat, in writing about the the Nootka, suggested that a comparable group of Europeans dressed only in breechclouts and shoulder capes would not look much better.

In spite of this supposed handicap, Portlock seemed surprised that they should have "a share of pride and vanity," for they painted their faces and hands red, their ears and noses were bored to receive ornaments, and the chin close to the lower lip was slit for the Eskimo type of labret. Ornaments carved of bone, to which strings of small trade beads were fastened, were used in all these openings (Portlock 1789, p. 249). "But," wrote Portlock, "in all this fancied finery they were remarkably filthy in their persons, and not frequently shifting their garments, they were generally lousy."

Portlock regarded them as friendly to their visitors. They seemed to be very tender and affectionate to their women and children and were pleased when they were given small presents. They were very displeased if any liberties were taken with their women. But as many explorers and traders found almost everywhere, they were inclined to thievery (Portlock 1789, p. 249).

The Chugach shared economic practices with the people of the lower Northwest Coast rather than with other Eskimo, since they lived to a large degree in the same environment. They used all varieties of fish and animals, and like the Eskimo ate heartily when food was available. They ate all the vegetable foods the area afforded and included "an inner 'pine' bark" which helped them recover from scurvy, from which they suffered. The "pine" bark may be spruce, because Captain Cook discovered that "spruce beer" was helpful to his crew in the same circumstances. The Europeans had great trouble identifying the conifers on the Northwest Coast and tried to relate them to trees in Europe (Portlock 1789, p. 251). Portlock also described how the Chugach preserved and prepared food. They dried fish in the sun or roasted it fresh. Meat was boiled in baskets or wooden boxes by putting hot stones in with it until it was "dressed" enough, which did not take long.

We can supplement somewhat the information on their hunting and fishing methods collected by the Cook expedition. A small kind of rock-weed (possibly kelp) which grows to considerable length is mentioned as fishline, and is able to stand great strain if it is kept clear of kinks and properly moistened. Salmon are herded into weirs, where they are speared. Herring are caught in small nets. In the Webber collection in Bern a spear thrower (A14, Appendix 1:360) is included and Portlock must have seen this in action, for he states that darts three to four feet long were thrown from a wooden instrument one foot long (Portlock 1789, p. 254).

The next visitor after Portlock, Dixon, and Meares was James Colnett, who had been at Nootka Sound. He was in command of the *Prince of Wales* and was accompanied by Captain Charles Duncan, commanding the *Princess Royal*. When they arrived at Port Etches they saw many bears and a few natives who fled. After a few days some of them came to the ships in kayaks made of sealskin, which seated two people. Colnett noticed that they used the pipette type of kayak bailer (Colnett n.d., p. 203) which was mentioned by Samwell in the Aleutian Islands (see chap. 7). The men had slits in their chins just below the lower lip and wore interesting pendants in them, made of both native and trade beads. Colnett includes a very delicate and exact sketch of these in his diary. This is typical of the Eskimo and links them with the people of the Bering Sea coast. In trading they always looked for transparent beads, regardless of their color, which they used to decorate their dogs.

After these English fur traders departed, Prince William Sound and Cook Inlet were left largely to the Russians, except for two expeditions by the Spaniards. When La Pérouse visited Concepción, in Chile, in 1785 he showed the Spaniards some Russian maps which had the Russian settlements in Alaska marked on them. These excited the Spaniards more than the news of the prospective fur trade. Orders were sent at once to Mexico to stage another expedition to the north to verify these rumors. Many of the officers who had been leaders in the early exploration of Alaska were now dispersed in Spain's war effort, and it was 8 March 1788 before an expedition set sail under two of the veterans of the earlier voyages. Estevan José Martinez commanded the *Princesa Real*, and Lopez de Haro was captain of the *San Carlos*. Among the officers of the *Princesa* was Estevan Mondofía, who understood a little Russian. On 16 May they were close to Montague Island. They followed Cook's map closely, but they also had Camacho's charts, made during the Arteaga expedition in 1779. In spite of using Cook's map and thereby knowing that he had probably taken possession of the area he surveyed, they took possession again in the name of Carlos III, "King of Spain and the Indians."

After a council of officers Martinez and de Haro disagreed about their course, and when a storm separated the two ships de Haro made no great effort to rejoin his consort. He was near Cape Douglas on the east side of the Alaska Peninsula when he was met by ten canoes filled with Indians who gave him two documents, one in Russian and the other in English, dated 1784 and 1787. The Indians indicated that the Russians had a settlement in the bay. His longboat went toward shore and brought back four Russians, including Delaroff, the Greek commandant. Unfortunately Mondofía was on the other ship, and so communication was very limited. Delaroff told Lopez de Haro that some ships were expected in the next year with supplies to establish a settlement at Nootka, and marked on the map all the Russian settlements already established in Alaska. The two ships met again and proceeded along the Aleutian Islands, remaining there and taking possession by ceremony of planting a cross and burying a bottle of documents. Except for their contact with the Russians they saw no other people. Martinez recorded that at Unalaska they met Potap Zaikop, the governor, who also told Lopez de Haro that a galliot would take possession of Nootka in 1789 to prevent the English from establishing themselves in the fur trade. Abandoning the remainder of his planned voyage, Martinez sailed quickly back to San Blas with this information. He proposed to the viceroy that he be sent back at once to fortify the Spanish claim. The viceroy agreed to the need, but he was reluctant to appoint Martinez because complaints had been lodged against him by his officers. But there was no one else, and so he was sent with orders to set up a formal settlement. He was to admit Russian ships, since Spain allowed them its Mediterranean ports, but the English were to be told that the Spanish discoveries antedated Cook's because Cook had seen an

Indian with two Spanish silver spoons which he said he stole from Martinez in 1774.

The second Spanish expedition at this time was headed by Salvador Fidalgo and went to Prince William Sound. There Fidalgo renamed all the islands and other important geographical locations and took possession for Spain. He also retraced the tracks of earlier expeditions into Cook Inlet, and after turning south and west to Kodiak, he decided the season was too advanced for further exploration. The weather, indeed, justified his judgment, for it became so turbulent that he could not even approach Nootka Sound. In consequence, he sailed directly to San Blas.

In 1791 Malaspina came from Yakutat Bay to the entrance of Prince William Sound but did not enter because of the weather. This left the Russians alone in Prince William Sound except for an occasional fur trader, but no currently known journals were left. During the period, before the organization of the Russian-American Company, there was ruthless rivalry among the Russian fur trading companies. By 1793 Baranof's influence in the area was being felt and the turmoil was slightly reduced. After a winter in California and Hawaii, the crews of the Vancouver expedition came back refreshed and the ships were in good repair to weather a season of exploration even farther north. Early in March 1794 they left Hawaii and set their course for Cook Inlet. On the way they became separated, and after the *Discovery* passed Trinity Island off Kodiak it met the *Chatham* again in Cook Inlet. Off Trinity Island they met two women and a man in a skin canoe (kayak), who greeted them with a European salutation. The man came aboard and ate dinner in the cabin, drank brandy, and accepted presents, of which he preferred the snuff and silk handkerchiefs. He counted with the same words that Cook recorded at Unalaska and Prince William Sound. These people resembled the Kamchadal more than the American natives. Later an Indian approached in a canoe but left without communication (Vancouver 1798, 3:89).

When they entered Cook Inlet they cruised along the west shore and three natives came, single-seated in kayaks, also showing European manners. They asked for snuff and tobacco, ate dinner, drank wine sparingly, as though fully aware of its power. Since they were going up the inlet, their kayaks were taken on the deck and they stayed with the ship until they reached East Forelands, where two more natives came in a kayak and brought a marten skin. One was named Sal-tart. They appeared to be acquainted with the Russians and knew some words of the language. All of these people were well behaved and had no inclination to thievery (Vancouver 1798, 3:103), which must have been a tremendous relief after the last dealings with Indians in southeastern Alaska at the end of the 1793 season.

On 21 April they reached Turnagain Arm and Possession Point, where they found ice. While they were looking for a suitable harbor for the ships, they found on a steep cliff the framework of some houses which seemed to have been deserted for some time. There were four large ones, about twenty-four feet long by fourteen feet wide and ten feet high, built with uprights and cross spars (a seaman is writing!). These had been covered with birch bark. With their perpendicular sides they were shaped like a barn. The walls were nine feet high and the roof was four feet higher in the center and sloped outward. Besides these houses there were two or three hovels that were partly underground. From this description this probably was an Athapascan village, since the Athapascans used birch bark covering and built semiunderground houses as winter residences. All the larger trunks were cut with axes, indicating Russian influence or even Russian work.

A few days later the ships were visited by a young chief, Chatidooltz, who seemed to possess authority. A younger man, Kanistooch, attended him. Their canoe and all eighteen men were taken aboard because the ice was a danger to their fragile craft. At the same time some of the men from the ships met Indians while they were hunting, and they also came aboard. They were from a different tribe but both groups sat down to a hearty dinner of salted meat and biscuits. They slept quietly until morning, when they received snuff, tobacco, iron, chisels, beads, hawks' bells, buttons, and needles. Chatidooltz promised to come back for another visit. Vancouver asked him to bring some meat and fish, but he in turn asked for meat and bread, saying they had little food. By the end of April their winter stocks might well be exhausted, and the heavy ice made hunting and fishing difficult (Vancouver 1798, 3:112).

The violence of the ice drove the expedition out of Cook Inlet. On the way they were met by ten Russians, who told them how they went from Cook Inlet to Prince William Sound, where they had a settlement at Port Etches and another at Kayak Island. They had gone to the end of Turnagain River and crossed fifteen to sixteen versts of mountain trail that led down to an arm of the sea leading to Prince William Sound. They tried to impress Vancouver that all the territory as far east as Kayak Island was Russian possession (Vancouver 1798, 3:115).

When Whidbey was surveying in Turnagain Arm, he looked for the bottle left there by Captain King in 1778, but there was no sign of it. While camping there they fired some muskets which had gotten wet, and this brought fifteen Indians out of the woods. The Indians gave them dried salmon and took the men to their houses, two recently built huts which sheltered the whole group. At North Foreland there was a Russian establishment with a large house about fifty feet long by twenty-four feet wide and ten feet high, in which nineteen Russians lived. They served the visitors fish and cranberries, but the overwhelming smell in the house made it impossible for the guests to eat. Thinking that they could make the food more palatable, the Russians took the cranberries away and beat them up with train oil, which according to English taste did not improve them. They left without eating. Since they were marooned there during several days of bad weather, they invited the Russians to their camp, where they ate heartily. The Russians had been there for four years and dressed and ate like the Indians. They seemed on very intimate terms with the Indians, who also seemed well satisfied. Whidbey was surprised that the Russians had been there so long without cultivating a vegetable garden.

During this same period Lieutenant Puget in the *Chatham* explored the west side of Cook Inlet and found Russians at the southeast point of Point Banks. Moored there was a sloop with eight guns, commanded by Alex "Berrenoff" (Baranof), who wanted to visit the *Chatham*. No engagement was made, however, because Puget did not know where he would be because of the weather. Puget was anxious for the meeting because he wanted to find out about Billings's voyage under Russian authority. Puget and Billings had been shipmates on Cook's third voyage. The Russians either could not understand or would not answer his questions.

North of Cape Douglas twenty-six natives came in small skin canoes with one man leading them. When he was cordially greeted he signaled the others to come. They came aboard and bartered trifles, but had no skins and did not care for copper or iron. Vancouver found that this was universally true in this area of Russian control and surmised that they were not allowed to keep any skins for their own use, even for clothing, but owed everything to the company in return for their living. Many of these people spoke a little Russian and they also seemed to be on very intimate terms with the Russians (Vancouver 1798, 3:130). Closer to Cape Douglas a Russian named Mallacha, who lived with the natives, told Puget that he commanded a sloop with eight guns. Puget gave him a letter to Vancouver, because the two ships were separated at this time. He had little hope of its ever reaching the *Discovery*, because the Russian messenger was intoxicated and it was found that the information he gave was very poor.

A large group of objects in the Hewitt collection were obtained during the exploration of Cook Inlet, but there are no references in the literature to their purchase. Since there is no explanation or description of these except the notes on the British Museum slips, they will be included only in Appendix 1. The area is entered as "Cook Inlet", but many of them may just as well have come from Prince William Sound. It seems that at this time, as in later history, Cook Inlet was occupied by both

Eskimo and Athapascan villages, since they used both kayaks and canoes, though these were also interchangeable in a large surrounding area. The houses found at the end of Turnagain Arm, with their birch bark covering, are a clue to an Athapascan settlement, and this again is in agreement with the distribution of Eskimo and Athapascan sites recorded in modern ethnography (Osgood 1936), the latter being at the far end of the inlet.

After the first week in May the ships left Cook Inlet and sailed toward Prince William Sound, stopping at Fort Dick on the southeast side of the Kenai Peninsula. They saw no ships but were met by many kayaks and canoes. The native clothing now consisted largely of cloaks made of bird skins and skins of small animals, for the expedition had arrived in Chugach territory when they reached Montague Island. From there Whidbey and Johnstone continued their longboat surveys. In June the *Chatham* was sent ahead to inspect Yakutat Bay for a good morage. This brings the expedition into Tlingit territory again, and the final days of the great survey have already been discussed in the chapter on the Tlingit. Vancouver wrote that when they concluded their work and came to Cross Sound they had finished their survey of the "Inside Passage," taking this term to its northernmost extension. But in this study of Indian life I have tried to discuss all the literature on these sections of Tlingit territory when they were on the verge of their first occupation by the Russians.

This review of the eighteenth-century expeditions to the Northwest Coast has attempted to clearly establish the character of the Indian life of the period. It has revealed an amazing stability of culture traits that survived even the crushing effects of later acculturation which have been recorded in the ethnographies written in the late nineteenth and twentieth centuries. In an area where archaeology has not been extensive and where its results have not reached such intangibles as ceremonials and family life, the descriptions of songs and dances, the keen observations of the explorers, and the day-to-day contacts of trading add a century to the culture history of one of the most highly developed Indian cultures of America. The journals have been read by many people, but the attempt to combine these with the objects that expeditions collected has added a new dimension to this study. The objects are all in European museums and are not easy to locate. There is no claim that all have been found, but I hope that this search will be continued, to make the history of this area of America more complete and more appreciated.

Appendix 1
Eighteenth-Century Objects in European Museums

I have included this list so that scholars can pursue research on this material without spending hours finding the objects. I have no doubt that others will be discovered through further study, for there are unlocated and unidentified pieces in many places. In some cases these entries may seem to give repetitious detail. This is especially true for the arrows and harpoons. The arrows compose the largest collection of hafted projectiles assembled for this period and area. Many people have studied projectile points, but these are examples of the entire weapon, which archaeological investigations seldom yield. Many of the descriptions are taken, wholly or in part, from the catalog slips in the Division of Ethnography of the British Museum, and I gratefully acknowledge the privilege of their use.

The museums where these objects were found will be indicated by the following abbreviations:

Berlin-Dahlem—Museum für Völkerkunde, Berlin-Dahlem
Bern—Historisches Museum, Bern
BM—British Museum
Cambridge—University Museum, Cambridge
Edinburgh—Royal Scottish Museum, Edinburgh
Exeter—Royal Albert Memorial Museum, Exeter
Florence—Ethnological Museum, Florence
Glasgow—Hunterian Museum
Göttingen—Institut für Ethnologie, Göttingen
Ireland—National Museum of Ireland, Dublin
Leningrad—Museum of Anthropology and Ethnography, Leningrad
Vienna—Museum für Völkerkunde, Vienna

ARMOR

1. *Cuirass*
Nootka Sound (?) Prince William Sound (?). BM, NWC 72, Cook expedition. The armor is composed of both slats and rods and resembles NWC 73 very closely. It is doubtful that this was obtained at Nootka Sound, and the literature quoted for NWC 73 applies to this as well. Height: 19″; width: 22″.

References: Drucker states that the Nootka wore heavy jackets, but his Hesquiat informant described armor of "heavy twigs" (1951: p. 335). Lisiansky illustrates armor exactly like NWC 72, 73, which is reproduced by Niblack.

2. *Cuirass*
Chugach, Prince William Sound. BM, NWC 73, Cook expedition.

A cuirass made of slats 2″ wide in front and back, with round rods under the arms, is the traditional northern Northwest Coast type. It has a small painted area on the chest. This is worn over a heavy jacket of hide. Height: 22″; width: 22″.

References: Edgar (Cook expedition) mentions buying armor "made of slips of wood fastened together, curiously painted and fastened at the back like women's stays" at Prince William Sound (ms., n.p.); also Ledyard 1783, p. 76.

CARVINGS AND MODELS

3. *Model of house post*
Nootka Sound (?). Berlin-Dahlem IV B 265, Cook expedition (?).
A model of a house post is a very dubious piece.

4. ———

5. *Carving* (fig. 43)
Nootka Sound. Bern Al 11, Cook expedition, Webber collection.

"The old label bore the description 'figure from Nootka Sound.' The small wooden figure of a woman in a squatting position with weakly indicated arm stumps showed a coarsely worked head with a broad nose and weak eye. . . . She is clothed in a costume which is now in very poor condition. It consisted of pieces of quills between strips of leather and remains of a shirt or other coat-like piece of clothing of sealskin. As far as can be determined from these remains it appears similar to one described under the heading 'Unalaska' " (Henking 1955–56, p. 367, #57). It is possible that this could be one of the squatting figures discussed by Ivanov (1949). None share the clothing, but the character of the figure is very similar.

6. *Canoe model*
Nootka Sound. BM, George Goodman Hewitt collection, 1792, Vancouver 148, Hewitt ms. 233.

A model of a canoe is carved of soft wood and has darkened to a deep brown. It has a high bow perforated transversely to receive a cord and a high stern which is almost perpendicular. Length: 27″.

7. *Canoe model*
Nootka Sound. BM, George Goodman Hewitt collection, 1792, Vancouver 149, Hewitt ms. 233.

A canoe model that has a projecting bow, sloping lines and a sloping stern post in which there is a large perforation. It has a rounded bottom. Length: 16½″.

8. *Canoe model*
Nootka Sound. BM, George Goodman Hewitt collection, 1792, Vancouver 150, Hewitt ms. 233.

A very small model has a projecting bow and resembles the beak of a bird. The stern post is almost perpendicular and the canoe is flat-bottomed at the center. Length: 7¾″.

9. *Canoe model*
Queen Charlotte Islands. BM, George Goodman Hewitt collection, 1792, Vancouver 151, Hewitt ms. ?

A canoe model with a plank built up on one side. It is fastened by sewing at intervals. The canoe is painted with totemic designs in red and black on the outside by red transverse bands on the inside.

10. *Carved figure* (fig. 30)
Restoration Point, Puget Sound. BM, George Goodman Hewitt collection, 1792, Vancouver 160, Hewitt ms. 278.

An erect human figure with hands folded on his breast wears a conical hat with a tassel on the top. On his abdomen is an incision containing fragments of broken glass. At the back of the head are tufts of hair. Small bits of copper are inlaid in the wooden hat. Height: 14½″.

Reference: Drucker 1951, p. 369.

11. *Head, human* (fig. 5)
Nootka Sound. BM, NWC 58, Cook expedition, 1778.

A human head carved of a block of cedar seems to have been fixed to a post. The bottom has a hollow square cut in it. The toothless mouth is open and the eyebrows are represented by strips of hide. There is a fringe of black hair above the forehead. This carving is as close as possible in style to the *toxuit* head of the Kwakiutl. King reported its arrival at Nootka: "The natives would sometimes bring strange carved heads and place them in a conspicuous part of the ship and desire us to let them remain there and for these they would receive no return" (King, PRO Adm. 55/122) Height: 11″.

Reference: Boas 1895, pp. 503, 504, figs. 153, 154.

12. *Kayak model*
Cook Inlet. BM, George Goodman Hewitt collection, 1794, Vancouver 152, Hewitt ms. 152.

A one-seated kayak with the figure of a man in it.

13. *Kayak model*
Cook Inlet. BM, George Goodman Hewitt collection, 1794, Vancouver 153, 155, Hewitt ms. 152.

A two-seated kayak with a double prow.

14. *Kayak model*
Cook Inlet. BM, George Goodman Hewitt collection, 1794, Vancouver 154, Hewitt ms. 327.

A one-seated kayak covered with skin and referred to in the manuscript as "Esquimeau"; considered related to those of Greenland.

15. *Kayak model*
Cook Inlet. BM, George Goodman Hewitt collection, 1794, Vancouver 156, Hewitt ms. 152.

One-seated kayak with double prow.

16. *Toggle*
Northern Alaska. BM, Vancouver 166.

An ivory toggle, probably Eskimo, carved to represent a seal. It has a ridge on the back, in which there are two perforations.

CLOTHING.

17. *Blanket or cloak*
No location. BM, NWC 49.

This blanket identifies completely with one in Emmons (*The Chilkat Blanket*, 1907, plate 24, fig. 1) and his description (pp. 331–32). It is cataloged at the British Museum as 1262 or 2262 as well as by the number above. It is a perfect example of the use of wool, dyed yellow and brown, in the border of the blanket. The diamond shape also is a simple version of the Northwest Coast "eye." The sides are roughly fringed, without any braiding. The blanket is loosely woven, with a heavy thread used for the weft. This type of cedar bark cloak is worn by all the figures in Webber's sketch of the interior of a Nootka house (Beaglehole 1967, plate 36).

Reference: Ellis 1782, 1:191.

18. *Blanket or cloak* (fig. 44)
No location. BM, NWC 51, Cook expedition (?).

A blanket woven of a twisted cord covered with white wool (mountain goat wool?). The piece is woven in a diamond pattern. It is described by Ledyard (1783, p. 71) who states that it is made of dog hair (see Appendix 2).

19. *Blanket or cloak*
No location. BM, NWC 53, Cook expedition (?).

This blanket is woven of cedar bark loosely wrapped with mountain goat wool. It has a deep fringe and is painted with a stylized animal design in red. The blanket is shown in Emmons, *The Chilkat Blanket*, 1907, plate 24, fig. 2, with the caption, "cedar bark blanket with painted design and woven ornamental border; from the west coast of Vancouver Island and believed to have been collected by the Cook Expedition." Width: 59″ (without fringe); length: 31½″.

Reference: Inverarity 1950, #8; it is said to be from the Tlingit, but there is no such information on the slips at the British Museum.

20. *Blanket or cloak*
No location. BM, NWC 54, Banks collection #41.

A blanket woven of shredded cedar bark with an ornamental border of zigzag design in black and yellow.

21. *Blanket or cloak*
Nootka Sound. Florence 42, Cook expedition, 1778.

A mantle made of shredded cedar bark woven in a special way, very similar to a textile described as made of phormium from New Zealand. This cape is rectangular on the top and sides, but curved along the bottom. This is the distinction between

Fig. 44. Blanket with diamond design, no location. Cook collection, BM, NWC 51 (Appendix 1:18).

the New Zealand cape and those of the Northwest Coast. Length: 450 mm; width: 820 mm.

Reference: Giglioli 1895, pp. 104–5; Ellis 1782, 2:24.

22. *Blanket*
No location. Ireland, no number, Cook expedition, 1778, King collection.

A shredded cedar bark blanket woven with geometric designs on the top and bottom borders. The upper border has dark brown squares dependent from a horizontal line. The bottom has three rows of alternating dark and light squares. Each row is 1″ wide. It is rather rounded at the bottom. Length: 29½″; width: 53″.

23. *Blanket*
No location. Ireland, no number, Cook expedition, 1778, King collection.

The blanket has a two-ply cedar bark warp with a very hard twist. It is loosely woven with the wefts ½″ apart. There are borders at the top and bottom, worked in a geometric design. There is a braided border at the sides. Length: 40½″; width: 57″; fringe: 7⅞″.

24. *Blanket* (fig. 62)
No location. Ireland, no number, Cook expedition, 1778, King collection.

A soft shredded cedar bark with a twisted cover of mountain goat wool over the warps. The borders have a geometric design, the center of which is the Northwest Coast "eye," which resembles the eye in the Berlin wolf mask. The triangles are dyed yellow with wolf moss (*Evernia vulpina*). The border is proto-Chilkat. Length: 28⅞″; fringe: 15⅞″; width: 52½″; border: 3½″ wide.

25. *Blankets* (2) (fig. 63)
No location. Leningrad 2520–4, 2520–5, Cook expedition, 1778.

Two shoulder blankets of cedar bark warps and mountain goat wool weft with alternate warps made of thin strips of sea otter fur, hide side to the front. The wool side of the blanket is embroidered with rows of concentric rectangles. The black wool left at the end of the largest rectangle in each concentric set is left hanging as a tassel. Length: 101 cm; width: 150 cm.

26. *Blankets* (2)
No location. Leningrad 2520–6, 2520–7.

The blankets are oblong, scarcely curved on the lower edge. They have six rows of horizontal concentric rectangles, six to a row, embroidered in black, with the end of the embroidery yarn hanging down at the right end of the outer rectangle as a tassel. The border design at the top consists of zigzags and along the sides are chevrons. Length: 41¾″; width: 52½″.

27. *Blanket*
Nootka Sound. Vienna 218, Cook expedition, 1778.

A blanket woven of mountain goat wool spun over shredded cedar bark for the warps. It is twined like a cedar bark blanket with the wefts about ¼″ apart. It is braided along the sides and the bottom is slightly shaped. At the top and bottom is one row of design with a face in the center of the top flanked by two vacant spaces and a space at each end consisting of three rows of widely set small squares. At the bottom the same face is used in the center and at each end, with the geometric pattern used above repeated in the spaces beside the center face. In this row the faces are inverted. There was fur around the top of the blanket. It is called a "Chilkat" in the Vienna catalog, but is entered as coming from Nootka Sound. Width: 132 cm; length: 64 cm; fringe: 45 cm.

28. *Cape, circular*
Nootka Sound. Florence 42 ff. Cook expedition, 1778.

A small circular cape of shredded cedar bark with an opening at the top, where it is trimmed with fur. The cape is registered as coming from New Zealand and "is similar to one from Nootka Sound." There is no doubt that this is the one from Nootka Sound. Diam. at top: 280 mm; at bottom, 700 mm; length, including fringe: 350 mm.

Reference: Giglioli 1895, p. 106, plate III, fig. 69. Drucker 1951, p. 94.

29. *Cape, circular* (fig. 61)
Nootka Sound. Ireland 24, Cook expedition, 1778, King collection.

A shredded cedar bark cape which is woven double, like the lining in some hats. It has a heavy fringe and a patterned border at the neckline and above the fringe. It is rubbed with red ocher. This is one of the most remarkable pieces of eighteenth-century weaving. Length: 19″, including fringe; Diam.: top 10″, bottom, 30″.

30, 31. *Skirts* (2)
Nootka Sound. Florence 231, 232, Cook expedition, 1778.

Skirts made of shredded cedar bark hang loosely in strands. They are worn by women.

References: Giglioli 1895, p. 107, #3. Willoughby 1886, p. 269, fig. 2.

CLUBS

32. *Clubs carved of wood* (2) (fig. 45)
Nootka Sound. BM, NWC 37, 38, Cook expedition, 1778.

NWC 37 is a slender club with the figure of an owl carved at the top. NWC 38 is very similar, but the figure of the owl is more carefully done with more detail. Both clubs are too light for warfare and were probably carried in dancing or used to beat time. Both clubs are unpainted. NWC 37, length: 22¼″; NWC 38; length: 24″.

33. *War club carved in wood* (fig. 46)
Nootka Sound (?). BM, NWC 39, Cook expedition, 1778.

The blade is broader than the average whale bone war club, but it is decorated with the same type of geometric design. The handle is carved to represent a human head. The natural wood is unpainted. Length: 21⅛″.

34. *War club of whale bone*
Nootka Sound. BM, NWC 40, Cook expedition, 1778.

These war clubs are a specialty of the Nootka who alone make them and trade

Fig. 45. Two clubs with owls carved at the top, Nootka Sound. Cook collection, BM, NWC 37, 38 (Appendix 1:32).

Fig. 46. War club carved of wood, Nootka Sound (?). Cook collection, BM, NWC 39 (Appendix 1:33).

them to many surrounding tribes. The club is carved of whale bone with a decorated head. The blade broadens toward the far end. The grip is bound with strips of cedar bark.

References: Inverarity 1950, #144; Boas 1927, fig. 298*i*; Force and Force 1968, p. 148.

35. *War club of whale bone*

Nootka Sound. BM, NWC 41, Banks collection #51.

The carving on the blade is inlaid with abalone shell and the grip is bound with plaited cord. The chiefs had ritual names for their war clubs, and they were regarded as badges of office (Drucker 1951, p. 335).

References: Inverarity 1950, #142; Boas 1927, fig. 298*m*.

36. *War club of whale bone*

Nootka Sound. BM, NWC 42, Cook expedition, 1778.

A typical war club, ornamented with a geometric design on the blade. Length: 2¼″.

Reference: Smith 1905, p. 404, fig. 165*a*.

37. *War or ceremonial club*

Nootka Sound. BM, NWC 99, Cook expedition, 1778.

A straight wooden club with a human head mounted on top. Below this is a stone blade passed through the handle horizontally. The handle is wrapped with braided string. The club is described in the British Museum catalog as "a Nootka tomahawk for killing slaves." Length: 22½″; blade: 16″.

Reference: Niblack 1890, plate 46. There are two such clubs, both collected by United States Navy men from the Tlingit. Their presence in Alaska dates after 1867. No Nootka club of this type is listed by Drucker (1949, p. 532). There is such a club at Fort Rupert (Boas 1895, p. 60).

38. *War club of whale bone*

Port Discovery, Admiralty Inlet. BM, George Goodman Hewitt collection, 1792, Vancouver 94, Hewitt ms. 248.

A curved club with a cylindrical handle, with the head carved in the form of a fish's mouth. The blade has a blunt edge along one side, and near the far end there is a deep incision, making the tip resemble a barb. The back of the blade has an incised pattern of joined diamonds. The head is perforated through the fish's mouth for a thong. Length: 21″.

39. *War club of whale bone* (fig. 19)

Nootka Sound. Cambridge, University Museum 49:150, Spelman Swaine collection, Vancouver expedition, 1792.

A handsome war club with a bird's head at the hilt. One of the few pieces still extant from the Spelman Swaine collection, first at the Wisbech Museum and then acquired by the University Museum.

40. *War club of whale bone* (fig. 20)

Nootka Sound. Exeter 1275, Vancouver expedition, 1792; collected by Mr. J. W. Scott.

The club has a well-developed design of a bird at the head. Parallel lines on the blade enclose circles joined by a running line.

Reference: Gunther 1962, #330.

41. *War club of whale bone*
Nootka Sound. Exeter 1275E, Vancouver expedition; collected by Mr. J. W. Scott.

Almost identical with #1275. The circles on the blade appear to have been inlaid with abalone shell.

42. *War club of whale bone*
Nootka Sound. Florence 18, Cook expedition.

A war club having an open semicircle as a handle. Parallel lines are incised along the center of the blade. These war clubs or parts of them have been found in many archaeological sites far from Nootkan territory.

Reference: Smith 1905, p. 404; sketch of club with citation "from Nootka Sound, collected by Capt. Cook, 1778." Giglioli 1895, plate III, fig. 60.

43. *War club of whale bone*
Nootka Sound. Florence 19, Cook expedition.

A club of the same type as BM, NWC 40, 41, 42, with the handle carved in the form of a bird's head. The blade is decorated with split diamond designs connected by a running line through the center. Length: 580 mm.

44. *War club of whale bone*
Nootka Sound. Vienna 212 (241), Cook expedition, 1778.

This club has a solid rounded handle with a faint design incised on it. There are parallel lines along the blade which end in a circle. It is a traditional piece but not as elaborate or well done as many others. Length: 52 cm.

45. *War club of whale bone*
Prince William Sound (probably Nootka Sound). Vienna 227 (242), Cook expedition, 1778.

A typical club with a carved head and a series of diamond-shaped designs on the blade. The head has a hole for a thong. Length: 49.5 cm.

CONTAINERS

46. *Bag*
Nootka Sound. BM, George Goodman Hewitt collection, 1793, Vancouver 163, Hewitt ms. 240.

A bag of split cedar bark, woven in a crossed warp twining technique. Height: 12″; width: 4″.

47. *Bag*
Cook Inlet, Alaska. BM, George Goodman Hewitt collection, 1793, Vancouver 174, Hewitt ms. 163.

A bag of similar structure and material with decorative strips of cedar bark vertically applied.

48. *Bag, flat*
No location. BM, NWC 14, Cook expedition (or Banks collection).

A flat bag woven of the same materials as the Chugach baskets and possibly made by them. The ornamentation is split quills. Cf. BM, NWC 24 and Göttingen 603.

49. *Bag, flat, or mat*
Prince William Sound. Göttingen 603, possibly Cook expedition.

A flat piece of weaving resembles BM, NWC 14, 24, which could be used for both purposes. The designs are identical and so is the shape.

50. *Basket* (fig. 42)
Chugach, Prince William Sound. BM, NWC 16, Banks collection.

This is the Tlingit type of basket that has been adopted by the Chugach, who are Eskimo. The shape is not one used by the Tlingit, but the design and the twined weave are in the true style.

Reference: Birket-Smith 1953.

51. *Basket* (fig. 42)
Chugach, Prince William Sound. BM, NWC 23, Banks collection 13.

A Tlingit style of basket with the design in the upper third of the side. The design is in four horizontal rows and is called "tern's tail" by Emmons (1903, #8). Cf. BM, NWC 16.

52. *Basket*
Cook Inlet. BM, George Goodman Hewitt collection, 1794, Vancouver 173, Hewitt ms. 163.

A small basket twined with strips of cedar bark warp and wefts of grass, some white, some dyed black. The rim is plaited of the bark warps, leaving an open-work band between the edge and the body of the basket.

53. *Basket*
Cook Inlet. BM, George Goodman Hewitt collection, 1794, Vancouver 175, Hewitt ms. 156.

A bucket-shaped basket woven of finely twisted brown root (spruce ?), and very flexible. The bottom is flat. Beneath the rim is a double band of pale, red, and black zigzag pattern with red and black triangles between. It looks like Tlingit work, but this type of basketry was thoroughly adopted by the Chugach and could have also been traded. Height: 5⅜″.

54. *Basket*
Cross Sound. BM, George Goodman Hewitt collection, 1793, Vancouver 176, Hewitt ms. 196.

A small cylindrical basket with cover. It has two rows of a meander pattern.

Reference: Emmons 1903. See also Appendix 2.

55. *Basket*
Cross Sound. BM, George Goodman Hewitt collection, 1793, Vancouver 177, Hewitt ms. 196.

A small cylindrical basket with one band of a "butterfly" pattern woven in yellow, a native color obtained by dyeing the grass with wolf moss. Height: 4⅜″.

56. *Basket*
Cross Sound. BM, George Goodman Hewitt collection, 1793, Vancouver 178*a*, Hewitt ms. 196.

A small undecorated basket with loops of thong on opposite sides, indicating that it was used as a storage container. Many of these household baskets have no decoration except some self-pattern near the rim. Height: 3⅞″.

57. *Basket*
Cross Sound. BM, George Goodman Hewitt collection, 1793, Vancouver 178*b*, Hewitt ms. 196.

A basket similar to Vancouver 178*a*.

58. *Box, wooden*
Two House or Two-ho Bay (50.7° North latitude). BM, George Goodman Hewitt collection, 1793, Vancouver 170, Hewitt ms. 316.

A wooden box with bent sides, sewn together with cedar or spruce root. Opposite sides are perforated in the center near the top to receive the ends of a handle made of twisted bark. It is called a bucket in the manuscript.

59. *Box for arrows* (fig. 10)
Nootka Sound. Vienna 215 (236), Cook expedition, 1778.

A long, narrow box for arrows, which has exceptionally fine design on the cover. The top figure may be female, for there is an indication of breasts; an x-ray type of stomach is indicated. This figure is supported on the upraised hands of the next figure, the top of whose head is level with the hands. This figure is the same size and has a chevron type of rib cage, no indication of breasts, and x-ray stomach. The genitals are vaguely drawn, but may be female. Between the legs of this figure is another that looks like a fetus; the legs are drawn up. The head is as large as the others, and all three faces are alike. This is the most realistic representation of birth I know of in Northwest Coast art except for an argillite carving of a woman in labor, a Haida piece in the National Museum of Canada. The sides of the box are very shallow and are decorated with a small geometric design. Length: 92 cm; width: 15.5 cm.

Reference: Force and Force 1968, p. 185.

60. *Box for arrows*
Nootka Sound. Vienna 216 (235), Cook expedition, 1778.

A second arrow box, delicately incised with designs consisting of a bird with a large fish in its mouth and some ducks or geese in flight. A running curved line passes this design but does not form a border. The box is oblong and very shallow. Length: 98 cm; width: 10.5 cm; depth: 2 cm.

61. *Dish*
Prince William Sound. Vienna 233, Cook expedition, 1778.

A dish made of mountain sheep horn, of the traditional shape with raised ends and no carving on the outside. At the raised ends and at the center of each side are several rows of nucleated circles, some of which are filled with white. Length: 24.8 cm; width: 16.7 cm; depth: 6.4 cm.

62. *Dish* (fig. 29)
Restoration Point, Puget Sound. BM, George Goodman Hewitt collection, 1792, Vancouver 161, Hewitt ms. 277.

A small wooden dish carved in the figure of a man lying on his back with knees drawn up and flattened. The body is scooped out and the head is in the form of a mask, concave in back. The arms are placed along the sides, with the hands on the thighs. In general form, it resembles the Tsonoqwa dishes of the Kwakiutl.

63. *Dish, carved in wood*
Haida or Tlingit. BM, NWC 9, Banks collection, 1789.

A wooden dish with a heavy rim, carved to represent a female figure kneeling when the dish is held upright. The large head is fully carved and the legs from the knees down to the feet are well detailed. Long arms are carved in low relief along the sides. The face has a hawk's-beak nose. This piece may be either Haida or Tlingit, for Dixon, who gave it to Sir Joseph Banks, could have collected it at either place. He was at Norfolk Sound (Sitka Sound) and at many places on the Queen Charlotte Islands. Length: 10½″; width: 5⅛″.

64. *Dish for food* (fig. 47)
Kodiak (?). BM, NWC 13, Cook expedition or Banks collection.

A dish carved in the form of a seal, a common model in the area. It has a flattened rim and extended curved hind flippers. The rim, flippers, and head are inlaid with round shells. This is a type of ornamentation found more among the northern people, such as Eskimo. The flatness of the rim and flippers resembles the dishes collected by Lisiansky at Kodiak and some bowls in Copenhagen, also from Kodiak. Length: 14⅞″; width: 7″.

Reference: Force and Force 1968, p. 172.

Fig. 47. Food dish in the form of a seal, Kodiak (*?*). Cook collection, BM, NWC 13 (Appendix 1:64).

65. *Dish carved in wood* (fig. 48)
Haida, Queen Charlotte Islands. BM, NWC 25, Banks collection, 1789.

A wooden dish similar to NWC 9, carved as a human figure with the body hollowed out in a rectangle. The flattish face and weak arms give it the appearance of Salish sculpture. The arms are carved free from the body and terminate in large hands. The piece was collected by Captain George Dixon.

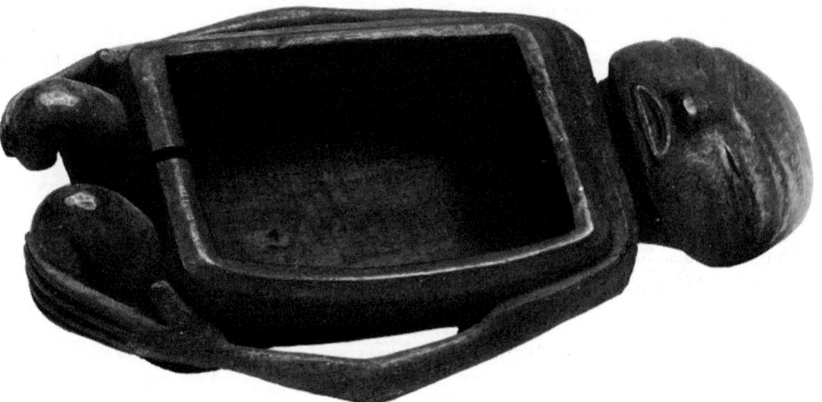

Fig. 48. Food dish in the form of a human, Haida, Queen Charlotte Islands. Banks collection, BM, NWC 25 (Appendix 1:65).

66. *Dish for grease*
Kodiak Island, Alaska. Natural History, Oldenburgh, West Germany.

A small dish in the shape of a crested merganser. It is painted red, with a human face painted and incised on the tail. The rim is flat and horizontal with a highly stylized design painted on it. There is also an eye-shaped design at the point where the neck broadens into the breast of the bird. There is another piece of this kind in the collection made by Lisiansky (1805) in Kodiak.

Reference: Lisiansky, plate III, fig. *f*.

67. *Quiver*
Aleutian Islands (?). Cambridge, University Museum 25.380, Earl of Denbigh collection.

A quiver, made of sealskin. A comparable one is marked as from the Aleut in the Institut für Ethnologie in Göttingen.

FISHING AND SEA MAMMAL HUNTING

Since fish are the basic food on the Northwest Coast, there is great variety and ingenuity in fishing equipment. Few types are localized; most occur wherever their use is feasible. Although individual ethnographies have good accounts for some areas, the best overall reference is Niblack (1890).

68. *Cod hooks* (4)
Mowachut, Nootka Sound. BM, George Goodman Hewitt collection, 1792, Vancouver 136, Hewitt ms. 232.

Hooks which are steamed and bent, similar to ones collected from Neah Bay, Washington (Makah, the southernmost Nootka). Niblack (1890), plate 30, no. 148*a*, *b*.

69. *Fish gig for hauling in fish*
Restoration Point, Puget Sound. BM, George Goodman Hewitt collection, 1792, Vancouver 127, Hewitt ms. 279.

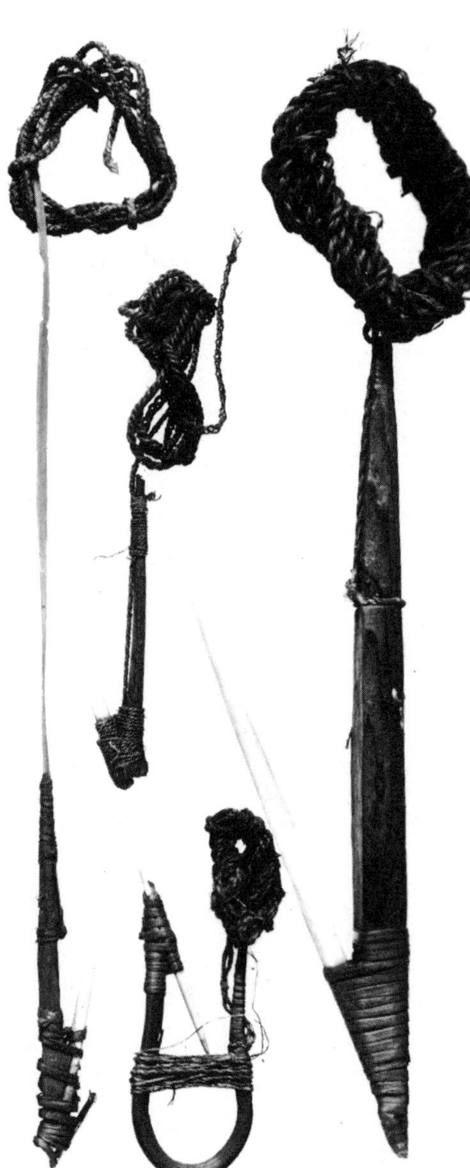

Fig. 49. Fishhooks, Mowachut, Nootka Sound. Cook Inlet. Hewitt collection (Vancouver), BM, Vancouver 122, 117 (Appendix 1:73–77, 83–87).

A fish gig made of the fork of a small branch. Length: 8″.

70. *Head of fish spear*
No location. BM, NWC 81, Cook expedition, 1778.

The head of a fish spear, made of brown wood, bifurcated, each point armed with a bone barb which is fastened by passing a thong through the wood and lashing it with cedar bark. Length: 16¼″.

71. *Hook*
Mowachut, Nootka Sound. BM, George Goodman Hewitt collection, 1792, Vancouver 139, Hewitt ms. 232(?).

The hook has barbs of white bone. Niblack states "for hooking salmon where plentiful" (1890, plate 30, #146).

72. *Hook*
Mowachut, Nootka Sound. BM, George Goodman Hewitt collection, 1792, Vancouver 137, Hewitt ms. 232.

A piece of quill is lashed to the upper end of the shank with sinew binding.

73, 74. *Hooks* (2) (fig. 49)
Mowachut, Nootka Sound. BM, George Goodman Hewitt collection, 1792, Vancouver 140, Hewitt ms. 232.

Two fishhooks are made with shanks of bone and unbarbed points of the same material.

75. *Hook* (fig. 49)
Presumably Cook Inlet. BM, George Goodman Hewitt collection, Vancouver 122, Hewitt ms., no number.

A large hook with a straight wooden shank has two unbarbed points lashed with birch bark (or spruce root), both on the same side. The shank is entirely covered with a casing of interwoven white quill and spruce root, the root horizontal and the quill vertical. A stout thong is attached to the upper shank, which is bound with root.

76. *Fishhook and line* (fig. 49)
No location. BM, NWC 114, Cook expedition.

77. *Hook* (fig. 49)
Mowachut, Nootka Sound. BM, George Goodman Hewitt collection, 1792, Vancouver 141, Hewitt ms. 232.

A fishhook of white bone with one barb.

78. *Hook*
No location. BM, George Goodman Hewitt collection, 1792, Vancouver 123, Hewitt ms. 166.

A gig or snag used for hauling in fish. The wooden shank is straight, expanding toward the butt, where three straight bone points are lashed to it with "creeper" (spruce root). The shank is similarly bound. A thickly painted line is held by the same binding.

79. *Hooks and line*
Mowachut, Nootka Sound. BM, George Goodman Hewitt collection, 1792, Vancouver 138, Hewitt ms. 232.

A group of small fishhooks (see Vancouver 137) attached to a fish-shaped float.

80. *Halibut hook*
Cross Sound. BM, George Goodman Hewitt collection, 1793, Vancouver 124, Hewitt ms. 209.

A large wooden halibut hook carved in openwork represents three land otters, a mother with two young on her back. The large one holds a bar in her front paws. Each side is a row of octopus tentacles. The arms of the hook are held together with wrapping of spruce root, the attached cord is twisted cedar bark rope, and the spike is bone. Length: 12½″.

Reference: Dalton 1897, plate XV, fig. 15.

81. *Halibut hook*
Cross Sound. BM, George Goodman Hewitt collection, 1793, Vancouver 125, Hewitt ms. 209.

A large halibut hook with a carved arm, representing a human figure with a large open mouth, the lower jaw being held by both hands. The hook is carved in wood, with twisted cedar bark rope and a bone spike lashed with spruce root. Length: 12″.

Reference: Dalton 1897, plate XV, fig. 14.

82. *Halibut hook*
Cross Sound. BM, George Goodman Hewitt collection, 1793, Vancouver 126, Hewitt ms. 209.

A large halibut hook of wood, carved to represent an eagle's head surmounted by an unidentified carving in the round. Length: 12½″.

Reference: Dalton 1897, plate XV.

83–87. *Halibut hooks* (5) (fig. 49)
No location. BM, NWC 77, Banks collection 43; BM, NWC 115, 116, 117, and one with no number.

Halibut hooks steamed and bent into a C shape and set with one bone spike each. They are of a timeless pattern which is still current among Northwest Coast Indians from Nootka to Alaska. Length: 9″.

88–98. *Halibut hooks* (9)
Mowachut, Nootka Sound, Port Discovery. BM, George Goodman Hewitt collection, Vancouver 130, 131, 132, 133, 134, Hewitt ms. 232, 250.

These halibut hooks are all steamed and bent into C shapes (see BM, NWC 77).
Halibut hooks (2)
Inside Passage. BM, George Goodman Hewitt collection, 1793, Vancouver 128, 129, Hewitt ms. 116.
Two halibut hooks, steamed and bent; no carving. Length: 7¾″.

99–100. *Halibut hooks* (2)

No location. BM, George Goodman Hewitt collection, 1793, Vancouver 135, Hewitt ms. 232.

Two halibut hooks, steamed and bent without carving. A small bunch of birds' claws is attached with sinew twine.

101. *Harpoon*

Nootka Sound. Bern 63, Cook expedition, Webber collection.

"The point is made of mussel shell. It has a long, oval form with two flaring barbs. . . . In the cut between the barbs the point is fastened. The barbs are made of bone. In front where the point is fastened the barbs are broad and rounded, at the other end they are pointed and flaring. In the center they are wrapped with a broad band of thong. Pitch helps to strengthen this binding so that the two parts are immovable. Under the binding a strong tow line is fastened. This line is made of braided sinew which is wrapped in sinew" (Henking 1955, p. 370; fig. 37).

Reference: Henking 1955, p. 370.

102. *Harpoon*

Chugach, Prince William Sound. Florence 2196.

Giglioli quotes Portlock's description: "The implements with which they kill the sea otter and other amphibious animals are harpoons made with bone, with two or more barbs; with a staff of about six to eight feet long, on which is fastened a skin or large bladder well blown, as a buoy; and darts, of about three to four feet long."

Reference: Giglioli 1895, p. 126.

103. *Harpoon and line*

Nootka Sound. Florence 306.

This piece is registered in the catalog as a harpoon point made of whalebone, but it is actually a foreshaft carrying a point.

Reference: Giglioli 1895, plate III, fig. 67.

104. *Harpoon arrow for sea otter*

Chugach, Prince William Sound. Bern Al 6e.

A harpoon with a detachable point with two unilateral barbs. A line from this point is wound around the shaft.

Reference: Henking 1955, p. 374, fig. 40/68.

105. *Harpoon without point*

Chugach, Prince William Sound. Vienna 230.

A harpoon without a point, shaft only.

106. *Harpoon cord* (2)

Chugach, Prince William Sound. Florence 2102; Vienna 229.

A harpoon line of sinew wrapped with cord.

107. *Harpoon cord, foreshaft, and shell blade*

Nootka Sound. BM, NWC 75, Banks collection.

A stout cord of sinew wrapped with fine string. Attached to it is a bone foreshaft with a shell blade. Length of bone foreshaft: 6¾″; width of blade: 2½″.

108. *Harpoon foreshaft with sheath*
Cook Inlet. BM, George Goodman Hewitt collection, 1794, Vancouver 88*a*, *b*, Hewitt ms. 171.

Foreshaft of white bone, rounded down one side and edged down the other, has two unilateral barbs cut from the latter. The upper end is split to receive a leaf-shaped slate head. The butt is cut away for insertion in the hollow of the shaft. The sheath consists of two pieces of thin wood tied together with twine.

109. *Harpoon head (toggle type)*
Cook Inlet. BM, George Goodman Hewitt collection, 1794, Vancouver 87, Hewitt ms. 170.

Foreshaft of white bone has a leaf-shaped slate head. At the butt end it is hollowed out and cut transversely. Between the butt and the head is a transverse perforation with vertical grooves from it to the butt on each side. Length: 4⅝″.

110. *Harpoon point and line*
Chugach, Prince William Sound. Vienna 229, Cook expedition.

A harpoon with a bone point and line.

111. *Harpoon and line*
Nootka Sound. Bern 62, Cook expedition, Webber collection, 1778.

Two pieces of sperm whale tooth are bound together with thong and resin to receive a point which is clamped between them. The points of the tooth are barbs at the lower end. The line is made of sinew with cord closely wrapped around it. The original point is missing and another has been substituted.

Reference: Henking 1955, p. 369, fig. 36.

112. *Harpoon and line for whaling*
Nootka Sound. BM, NWC 15, Banks collection, collected by Alexander Menzies, 1787.

The label on this piece reads: "Fishing line made of species of Fucus by the natives of the west coast of North America. A. Menzies." In addition, he wrote, "The inner bark of the cypresus Thugides in its different stages of preparation as manufactured by natives of the west coast of N. America, July 1787. A. Menzies." This label is attached to the line where it is wrapped with cedar bark. There is no blade in the harpoon. At this time Menzies was on the voyage of Captain James Colnett on the *Prince of Wales*.

113–14. *Harpoons* (2)
Prince William Sound. BM, NWC 59, Cook expedition.

Two long harpoons with red and black designs painted on the shaft. They have bone points and a bladder float at the butt end.

Reference: Samwell mentions such pieces at Prince William Sound (Beaglehole 1967).

115–18. *Harpoon lines (4 pieces)*
Cook Inlet. BM, George Goodman Hewitt collection, 1794, Vancouver 143, 144, 145, 146, Hewitt ms. 160.

(143) Braided sinew line with a conical "button" formerly ornamented with feathers at one end and a small hank of fine gut threads at the other.

(144) A neatly plaited sinew cord in two patterns with a double loop at one end. The designs are a herringbone and a flat band alternating.
(145) A twisted sinew fishing line; very fine threads.
(146) The same as 145.

119. *Paddle*
Rock Village, Inside Passage. BM, George Goodman Hewitt collection, 1792, Vancouver 147, Hewitt ms. 271.

A canoe paddle of soft wood is painted dark red and the blade is decorated on both sides with totemic designs. The butt is flattened and has a crutch handle. Length: 5′3″.

120. *Salmon spear*
Salmon Cove, Observatory Inlet. BM, George Goodman Hewitt collection, 1793, Vancouver 92, Hewitt ms. 130.

The end of a double-headed spear made of brown wood; it forms two equal pieces which were originally lashed together with root, of which only a small piece remains. One arm is wormeaten and broken. Nine inches from the butt the pieces diverge, expanding laterally and diminishing in size. Near the end each had a single straight bone barb.

GAMES

121. *Gambling sticks with bag*
Cross Sound. BM, George Goodman Hewitt collection, 1793, Vancouver 162, Hewitt ms. 201.

A long bag of woven cedar bark containing about forty small, straight cylindrical sticks of highly polished wood about five inches long. Some have designs burned into the wood and rubbed with red ocher or black soot. Some have checks or painted transverse bands. The upper end of the bag has rough edges, giving the appearance of a fringe.

References: Dalton 1897, p. 237; Niblack 1890, p. 344, plate 63.

122. *Gambling sticks with bag*
Cross Sound. BM, George Goodman Hewitt collection, 1793, Vancouver 163, Hewitt ms. 201.

A skin bag with a long flap and thong fastenings, which holds about forty straight sticks, the same as Vancouver 162. Length of sticks: 5⅛″.

References: Dalton 1897, p. 237; Niblack 1890, p. 344, plate 63.

123. *Spinning top*
Mowachut, Nootka Sound. BM, George Goodman Hewitt collection, 1792, Vancouver 159, Hewitt ms. 236.

A wooden top, whose lower part is globular and ornamented with vertical incised lines. The base has a tin tack as a peg. The upper part has a long vertical rod. With the top comes a bat-shaped handle of wood with several perforations. It is probably a "humming top."

Reference: Reade 1891, plate 11, #7.

124. *Cap, feathered*
Cook Inlet. BM, George Goodman Hewitt collection, 1794, Vancouver 193, Hewitt ms. 164.

A flat, egg-shaped piece of skin with an almond-shaped opening cut in the center. This is ornamented on one side with black skin (seal) with quill work in red and white, following the outline. At the broad end are three pendants of white skin, each with a pair of puffin bills at the ends. Around the edges are traces of hair or bristles.

Reference: caps from Unalaska in Webber's colored drawings.

125. *Hat*
Cook Inlet. BM, George Goodman Hewitt collection, 1794, Vancouver 190, Hewitt ms. 173.

A small brimmed hat, Nootka in shape. The hat is twined of spruce root and has four rings on top into which fine hair is woven. The design is very abstract, almost geometric. It has a label "Cook's River chief's cap."

Reference: cf. hat on man in canoe in left foreground in Webber sketch.

126. *Hat*
Prince William Sound. Cambridge, University Museum 49.205, Spelman Swaine collection, 1794, Vancouver expedition.

A well-woven spruce hat painted around the crown. This hat was secured from the Wisbech Museum as part of the Spelman Swaine collection acquired in April 1842.

127. *Hat*
Hawslee (?) Not located. BM, George Goodman Hewitt collection, 1793, Vancouver 191, Hewitt ms. 257.

A small hat woven of spruce root and painted.

References: cf. BM, NWC 5; *Berlin Museum Publications* part 1, plate 5, fig. 5. A similar hat is figured and stated to be called "keit" by the Koskimo, a Kwakiutl group at the north end of Vancouver Island.

128. *Hat*
Nootka Sound. Florence 185; Cook expedition.

Cook described this hat thus: "Their heads are covered with hats in the form of a truncated cone or in the shape of a flower pot; this hat is of fine matting [plaiting]; a tassel rounded and sometimes painted, or a bunch of skin fringed; it is decorated on the crown and it is tied under the chin to prevent the wind from carrying it off." This type of hat is sketched in a Spanish picture and is worn by the little figure found by Vancouver in Puget Sound (Vancouver 160).

References: Cook 1783, 3:66; Gunther 1956.

129. *Hat* (fig. 58)
Nootka Sound. Ireland, Cook expedition, King collection, 1882–3876.

A conical hat with a whaling scene as decoration; a pear-shaped bulb on top is a singular ornament of Nootka hats limited in production to the eighteenth century.

Reference: Force and Force 1968, p. 145.

130. *Hat*
Nootka Sound. Vienna 219, Cook expedition, 1778.

A small spruce hat with its crown painted in red and black. The design is very simple and more like a modern pattern than the abstract designs of some eighteenth-century hats.

131. *Hat*
Nootka Sound. Vienna 220, Cook expedition, 1778.

A hat woven of spruce, with the crown developed in a self-pattern by the use of a third strand in the twining. The hat is unpainted. Height: 14.5 cm; diameter: ca. 24 cm.

132. *Hat*
Nootka Sound (Clayoquot). BM, George Goodman Hewitt collection, 1792, Vancouver 192, Hewitt ms. 311.

A hat that resembles the one from the King collection in Ireland. It has the pear-shaped bulb on top and whaling scenes on the body. There are seven rows of plain weft twining between the design and the bulb. An old label printed with the word "Clioquat" is still pinned to the piece.

References: Edgar ms., Cook expedition.

133–36. *Hats* (4) (fig. 41)
Prince William Sound. BM, NWC 4, 5; Göttingen 602; Swaine collection, Vancouver expedition, Cambridge 49.205.

These hats should be analyzed together because of their likeness and the conflicting data about them. The one at Göttingen is the only one definitely marked as from Prince William Sound. It compares closely with NWC 4 because of its white beads and abstract design. Since Cook did not actually see the Queen Charlotte Islands, it is vain to include the Haida in this argument. Furthermore, it resembles another (49.205) (plate 42) from the Vancouver expedition. They were at Montague Island in Prince William Sound. NWC 5 has the same characteristics and is shown on a man from Prince William Sound. However, Edgar (ms. 66) on the Cook expedition states that this type of hat was worn by women at Nootka Sound. If these hats are narrow enough they are often pulled down and tied under the chin with straps attached to the brim, making them look like the cone-shaped hats that were more common there. On the basis of this discussion, hats NWC 4 and 5 and Cambridge 49.205 will be regarded as coming from Prince William Sound. They are distinctive from the northern NWC generally in the addition of beads and sometimes sea lion whiskers. They also resemble the identified one at Göttingen which is stated as coming from Prince William Sound. These hats are seen in sketches together with wooden sun visors, and in kayaks as well as canoes.

137–38. *Hats* (2) (fig. 6)
Nootka Sound. BM, NWC 6, 7.

These hats are not included in the Cook collection itself, but they are distinctly Nootka of the eighteenth century, and there are many examples to substantiate this. They are all woven with scenes of the whale hunt and are further distinguished by the pear-shaped bulb on top. As filler in the realistic design the Nootka used geometric designs which are also found on the twined basketry of their southern neighbors, the Salish. This type of hat is shown in Webber's sketch of the interior of a Nootka house and in Spanish sketches of Nootka men and women.

139. *Hat*

Nootka Sound. Florence 193, Cook expedition.

A conical hat in very poor condition, about which Cook said, "We have seen all the operations of the whale hunt painted on their hats." There is no mention of the pear-shaped bulb. Many descriptions say that the design is painted on the hat, probably because they were seen from a distance and many observers had seen painted hats elsewhere; but all those with whaling scenes are Nootka and are woven into the fabric. These hats were worn by both sexes. Diam.: 37 cm; height: 24 cm.

140. *Hat of basketry, with four rings*

Nootka Sound (?). BM, NWC 8, Cook expedition or Banks collection.

A very small hat with steep brim and four basketry rings on top. It is painted blue, green, and red. It is possible that this is not Nootka but is from farther north. In a sketch from Prince William Sound a man in a canoe is wearing such a hat. It is a northern type and compares with one at the Alaska State Museum (954) with the design only on the crown, very steep, with four rings, collected at Sitka in the late 1880s, and with Vancouver 190 BM, which came from Cook Inlet.

141, 141*b*, *c*. *Headgear in the form of a seal's head* (3) (fig. 40)

Prince William Sound. BM, NWC 11, Cook expedition; National Museum of Finland, Etholen collection 46; Göttingen 820.

These three pieces look somewhat like masks, but they have a specific purpose. The wood carving resembles that of the Eskimo rather than the Northwest Coast. The area between the eyes, the raised line in the center, and the two converging lines down the nose also appear in western Eskimo carving. This headdress is worn while seal hunting on land to approach seals sunning themselves on the rocks. The hunter wearing this keeps his body hidden by rocks or shrubs and so can approach the seals closely. The piece is too light for a war helmet and does not fit well as a dancing mask.

References: Cook and King, Atlas, plate 40; Mearses 1791, p. 56; Drucker 1950, p. 234.

141*c*. *Head ornament*

Cross Sound. BM, George Goodman Hewitt collection, Vancouver 200, Hewitt ms. 198.

A woven piece of mountain goat wool, consisting of six rows of twining and a short fringe extending along the entire length.

141*d*. *Sunshade of bent wood*

Cook Inlet. BM, George Goodman Hewitt collection, 1794, Vancouver 194, Hewitt ms. 157.

A hat of thin wood, steamed and bent and painted a brownish red. On the upper edge in the front are sea lion's whiskers, which are threaded with blue and white glass beads. In the center of the front near the top is a small head of a seal carved of white bone. This piece has all the characteristics of Eskimo origin.

142. *Sunshade of bent wood*
Cook Inlet. BM, George Goodman Hewitt collection, 1794, Vancouver 195, Hewitt ms. 157.

Similar to Vancouver 194 except for a beaklike projection of bone tied to the upper rim at the center front.

143. *Visor*
Unalaska. BM, NWC 3, Cook expedition, 1778.

A visor of thin wood bent into shape by steaming. It has a long projecting front and narrows into a strip at the back. The front is painted red and green and is decorated along the upper edge with sea lion's whiskers strung with blue and white glass beads. At the center of the front a small seal head is carved of bone or ivory. Length: 16¾″.

References: Cook and King, Atlas, plate 48; sketch by Webber in color. This is the piece from which the sketch was made. Original sketch in the BM (Add, ms. 23, 921:95) cf. Vancouver 194.

MASKS

144. *Mask* (*wolf?*)
Nootka Sound. Berlin-Dahlem IV B 27, Cook expedition.

A mask classified as "Katz, Schwein, oder Wolf" is a wolf mask with excellent carving. It is made of one piece of wood, natural color with black at the tip of the nose, and the outline for the eye. There is a little white paint left in the eye. It was also probably inlaid at one time. The eyebrows are delicately drawn and the underside of the jaw has a well-designed chevron pattern. Length: 20 cm.

Reference: Force and Force 1968, p. 182.

145. *Mask* (*wolf?*)
Nootka Sound. Berlin-Dahlem IV B 178, Cook expedition, 1778.

The mask is classified as a Haifisch (shark). It appears to be a wolf mask done in simple but controlled carving. It is in two pieces, fastened along the center of the face and to the left of the bottom. Many holes are at the back for cedar bark or feather decoration.

References: Force and Force 1968, p. 182; Gunther 1962, no. 320.

Fig. 50. Mask of a human face, Nootka Sound. Webber collection (Cook), Bern 58 (Appendix 1:146).

146. *Mask, human face* (fig. 50)
Nootka Sound. Bern 58, Cook expedition, Webber collection, 1778.

A wooden mask shows a full, almost square human face. The cheeks are bulging and the chin, under a circular mouth, is weak. Between the large round eyes the nose is a sharp thin line. Originally there was hair on the head and eyebrows. Vestiges of painting are visible. This mask has a "foreign" appearance, though it is regarded as coming from Nootka Sound, but there is another possibility of origin. On returning from the Bering Sea voyage of 1779, the expedition came back along the coast of Kamchatka and Japan. They did not land in Japan, but they might have obtained the mask in Kamchatka. This is only a wild guess, because at that time communication with the outside world was rare for Japanese. The puffed cheeks, the type of eye holes, and the smoothness of the wood are not typical of the Northwest Coast. Height: 26.5 cm.

References: Henking 1955, p. 367, fig. 33; Bandi 1956, p. 215, fig. 4.

147. *Mask in the form of a bird*
Nootka Sound. BM, NWC 55, Cook expedition, 1778.

From the form of its beak, the bird is probably a gull and not a raven as indicated on the label. It has a movable jaw. The design is in black and white and the head is ornamented with flicker tailfeathers. The eye is black, with the white covered with talc and mica and resin worked into it. The surface under the jaw is carved with a sleeping human face. A cluster of limpets hangs inside the beak to rattle during dancing. The carving is an excellent example of the fine work done by the Nootka in the eighteenth century. It is the type of mechanical mask more fully developed in the nineteenth century by the Kwakiutl.

References: Cook, Atlas plate 40 #3; Drucker 1951, plate 4*c*.

148. *Mask of human face* (fig. 51)
Nootka Sound. BM, NWC 56, Cook expedition, 1778.

The mask represents a human face with closed eyes and open mouth. The eyes have strips of hide above them, and there are similar strips on both sides of the mouth. There is no face painting. Above the face is a fringe of long black hair. A similar mask is in the collection at Florence and both resemble the "toxuit" head of the Kwakiutl.

References: Boas 1895, p. 503, fig. 153; Manwaring 1931, p. 115.

149. *Mask of human face* (fig. 51)
Nootka Sound (?). BM, NWC 57, Cook expedition, 1778.

A mask of a human face with eyes of black material covered with talc and teeth of quills fastened to a cord stretched across the mouth. Strips of hide are used for eyebrows. The mask has long black hair fastened along the forehead. Height: 9½″.

150. *Mask in the form of a wolf's head* (fig. 1)
Nootka Sound. BM, NWC 71, Cook expedition, 1778.

A mask in the form of a wolf's head is painted in black, white, and red. The eyes and nostrils are of talc and the forehead is studded with teeth. There is dentalium in the mouth. A broad black skin band hangs over the head and is fringed over the top of the mask. Length: 37″; height of mask: 8″.

References: Inverarity 1950, no. 102: the piece is listed as Kwakiutl, but this could have not been gotten from the Kwakiutl directly, and it is also in very good Nootkan style. Cf. the masks of the Walasaxa, the Kwakiutl wolf masks (Boas 1895, p. 478, p. 493, plate 37).

151. *Mask of human face*
Nootka Sound. Florence 2148, Cook expedition, 1778.

Fig. 51. Two masks of human faces, Nootka Sound. Cook collection, BM, NWC 56, 57 (Appendix 1:148, 149).

A mask carved of wood is ornamented with black hair and closely resembles Vienna 223, especially in the carving of the eyes and mouth.

Reference: Giglioli 1895, p. 121, plate III, fig. 57.

152. *Forehead mask*
Nootka Sound. Florence 2166, Cook expedition, 1778.

The forehead mask is carved of a conifer wood and painted to represent an eagle. Giglioli quotes a passage from the French edition of Cook to the effect that this type of mask was used in hunting. It seems very small for that purpose. Length: 15 cm; height at base: 9.4 cm.

Reference: Giglioli 1895, p. 122, plate III, fig. 58.

153. *Mask of an eagle's head* (fig. 52)
Nootka Sound. Vienna 222, Cook expedition, 1778.

A forehead mask in the form of an eagle's head with a very realistic beak. The eyes are inlaid with abalone shell. Height: 11 cm; width: 16.4 cm.

Reference: Boas 1895, p. 149.

154. *Mask of a human face*
Nootka Sound. Vienna 223, Cook expedition, 1778.

A mask of a human face, very smoothly carved with slit eyes, almost closed, a sharp nose, and a slightly open mouth without teeth. There are three short lines from the center of the chin and at each side of the mouth. The grain of the wood shows in a decorative pattern. Height: 20.7 cm; width: 17.3 cm.

Reference: Boas 1895, plate 49.

ORNAMENTS AND ACCESSORIES

155. *Amulet*
Cross Sound. BM, George Goodman Hewitt collection, 1793, Vancouver 165, Hewitt ms. 195.

Carved in hard wood, a killer whale seems to be swallowing a small seal, which is partially under his body, with the hind flippers in his mouth. Dalton calls it a toggle for a fishline, but it seems more like an amulet. The perforation at the center top is right for suspension and so are the dimensions. Length: 5″.

Reference: Dalton 1897, pp. 222–45.

156. *Amulet* (fig. 21)
Nootka Sound. Exeter 332, collected by Mr. J. W. Scott, Vancouver expedition, 1792.

A small amulet carved of a bear's tooth; probably represents a frog. The eye appears to have been inlaid, perhaps with abalone shell.

Reference: Gunther 1962, p. 14.

157. *Bands of decorated skin* (3)
Cook Inlet. BM, George Goodman Hewitt collection, Vancouver 206, 207, Hewitt ms. 176, 177.

(206) Band of soft skin worked with porcupine-quill embroidery in brown, yellow,

Fig. 52. Eagle's-head mask, Nootka Sound. Cook collection, Vienna 222 (Appendix 1:153).

and white. One edge is fringed and the ends of the fringes are wrapped with quill. It may be a strip at the lower edge of a shirt. Length: 32″.

(207) A pair of narrow bands of buckskin ornamented on one side with geometric designs in red, black, and white dyed porcupine quill. One end is rounded off on each strip. These appear to be the strips on trousers defining the garters. The pattern is similar to the "tree shadow" of Tlingit basket designs. These pieces are almost certainly Athapascan in manufacture. Length: 25″.

158. *Belt or sash, woven*
Cross Sound. BM, George Goodman Hewitt collection, 1793, Vancouver 201, Hewitt ms., no number.

A piece of twined material of a mixture of mountain goat wool and grass (*Xerophyllum tenax*) which is used for the decorative element in basketry. The piece tapers slightly toward the ends, which are the loose threads. From its shape and size it may have been a sash or belt. Length: 31½″; width: 12″.

159. *Bracelet*
Nootka Sound. Florence 81, Cook expedition, 1778.

A bracelet described as being of a "horny" substance; other eighteenth-century pieces suggest that it might well be of mountain goat horn. The one pictured in Giglioli (1895) seems to be carved in the round, representing an animal with a head at one end and a tail at the other. It is certainly different from the ones in the Hewitt collection from the Vancouver expedition. The piece is registered in the catalog as coming from New Zealand.

Reference: Giglioli 1895, p. 110, plate III, fig. 68.

160. *Bracelet*
Nootka Sound. Ireland 1882–3657, Cook expedition, King collection.

A bracelet which seems to be made of mountain goat horn and resembles those of the Vancouver expedition in the Hewitt collection.

161–65. *Bracelets* (5) (fig. 53)
Restoration Point, Puget Sound. BM, George Goodman Hewitt collection, 1792, Vancouver 210, Hewitt ms. 281.

Five bracelets of mountain goat horn, incised and carved with curvilinear designs that have raised, eye-shaped bosses. Each diminishes in breadth at the back, where it may be fastened by passing one pointed end through a perforation at the other end.

166–70. *Bracelets* (5)
Restoration Point, Puget Sound. BM, George Goodman Hewitt collection, 1792, Vancouver 211, Hewitt ms. 282.

Four bracelets of mountain goat horn and one of white bone. The horn bracelets are decorated like Vancouver 210. One bracelet has pieces of shell inlay. They all have the same clasp as Vancouver 210. The bone bracelet has one perforation at each end and a thong is passed through them.

171–74. *Combs* (fig. 7)
Northwest Coast. BM, NWC 101, 102, 103, 104.

Fig. 53. Five bracelets, Restoration Point, Puget Sound. Hewitt collection (Vancouver), BM, Vancouver 210 (Appendix 1:161–65).

These may not all be eighteenth-century pieces, but there is one clue to their age: they are sketched in "Pacific Northwest Artifacts," which establishes them in the period. NWC 101 is marked "Alaska, given by Rev. C. C. Freer," but there is no appropriate number on it.

Reference: Force and Force 1968, p. 157.

175–76. *Combs* (fig. 7)
Nootka (?). BM, NWC 105, Cook expedition, 1778, Florence 60, Cook expedition.

These combs resemble each other very closely. The British Museum piece does not have an entry in the catalog, but it is enough like the Florence comb to assume they may be of the same origin. The only Northwest Coast objects at Florence are from the Cook expedition, another reason for combining them and considering the British Museum piece, at least, also eighteenth century. Both combs have a human face crudely incised; the Florence comb has one on each side. BM length: 8⅛″; width: 4⅝″.

Reference: Giglioli 1895, plate III, fig. 64.

177. *Comb*
Northwest Coast. BM, NWC 106, Banks collection.

A very elegantly carved comb with an arched, grooved handle. It is carved of wood. Length: 5″, width: 2½″.

178. *Comb, double*
"Namakizat." BM, George Goodman Hewitt collection, 1793, Vancouver 220, Hewitt ms. 117.

A comb of brown wood, with ten teeth at one end and seven at the other. The comb has no decoration, but one side is better finished than the other.

179. *Comb* (fig. 8).
Queen Charlotte Islands. Cambridge, University Museum 25.370.

This elegantly carved comb, if the provenance is correct, could not have been in the Cook collection, but it may have been given by Captain George Dixon to Banks or some other gentleman who then gave it to the museum. The carving has Haida elegance. The handle is carved in the form of a raven's beak with a human figure enclosed in it.

180. *Comb*
Nootka Sound. Florence 159, Cook expedition.

A small wooden comb with a little handle carved in the form of a raven. Length: 130 mm.

Reference: Giglioli 1895, p. 113, plate III, #65.

181. *Comb*
Northwest Coast. BM, George Goodman Hewitt collection, 1793, Vancouver 218, Hewitt ms. 204.

A comb of brown wood, carved of a single piece. The handle is twice as long as the teeth and consists of two human figures, back to back, with a right-angle cross between them joining them together. Their hands are folded in front and they are wearing shallow-crowned hats. Their feet stand on the crossbar of the comb. Length: 6⅜″.

Reference: Dalton 1897, plate XV, fig. 18.

182. *Comb, double*
Restoration Point, Puget Sound. BM, George Goodman Hewitt collection, 1792, Vancouver 219, Hewitt ms. 283.

A double comb with six teeth at one end and eight at the other. The central part of the comb is roughly rectangular and ornamented with deeply incised conventional designs.

183. *Labret*
Cook Inlet. BM, George Goodman Hewitt collection, 1794, Vancouver 223, Hewitt ms. 167.

This piece, recorded as a labret, is shaped like a miniature bow. The points have been broken and repaired. The piece is tied into a wooden case made to fit. It is doubtful that this is a labret, especially since it is six inches long. In the picture in Reade (1891) it looks more like a small fastener of a woman's sewing bag, known among the Eskimo as a "housewife." The catalog slip states that it is made of white quartz, which is also doubtful.

Reference: Reade 1891, p. 108, plate XI, fig. 8.

184. *Labret*
Banks Island. BM, George Goodman Hewitt collection, 1793, Vancouver 226, Hewitt ms. 208.

This piece is cataloged as a lip ornament "made of a length of split rush wound round into an oval form and tied around the outer edge with string." The labret is concave on both sides. This may be a temporary form of the labret or one worn when a woman's best one is being saved for other occasions. The material is split cedar bark.

Reference: Dalton 1897, plate XV, fig. 12.

185. *Labret or lip plug*
Rock Village, Inside Passage. BM, George Goodman Hewitt collection, 1793, Vancouver 228, Hewitt ms. 275.

The description of the labret agrees with that given by Dalton for the ones from Cross Sound. Length: 3¼″.

Reference: Dalton 1897, plate XV, fig. 12.

186. *Lip ornaments*
Cook Inlet. BM, George Goodman Hewitt collection, 1794, Vancouver 224, Hewitt ms. no entry.

A pendant of abalone shell crudely carved in the outline of a bird is attached to two very small pieces of white bone. This is an unusual piece because the abalone shell is not often found in this area of Alaska.

187–90. *Labrets or lip plugs* (4)
Cross Sound. BM, George Goodman Hewitt collection, 1793, Vancouver 227, 229, 230, 231, Hewitt ms. 193.

(227) The labret is carved of wood with concave surfaces and edges slightly concave. It has no decoration. Dalton 1897, plate XV, fig. 13. Length: 3½″.
(229, 230) Same as above. Length: 2¾″.
(231) Same as above. Length: 1⅞″.

191. *Necklace of bone pendants*
Nootka Sound. Vienna 226, Cook expedition, 1778.

A necklace of twenty-nine bone pendants all alike. They are strung on cord which is wrapped a number of times around each piece. The cord looks like three-ply and not native. There is a tassel at each end. Length of pendants: 2 cm.

RATTLES

192. *Rattle* (fig. 2)
Nootka Sound. BM, NWC 28, Cook expedition, 1778.

The rattle, in the form of a bird, may represent a sea gull by the shape of its beak. The design on the body is painted in black on an off-white background. It shows the "eye" signifying a joint in the anatomy and on the back its feathers are indicated. The top of the head is flat. The upper and lower parts are tied together with thongs along the sides. Cook describes its use: "He held in his hands a carved bird of wood, as large as a sea pigeon, with which he rattled, as the person first mentioned had done" (Cook 1967, p. 343). Length: 19½″.

References: Cook 1967; Inverarity 1950, no. 112.

193. *Rattle*
Nootka Sound. BM, NWC 27, Cook expedition, 1778.

A rattle, carved of wood in two pieces, held together with thongs along the sides and a wrapped handle. The bill of the bird represented clearly indicates that it is a sea gull. The body is painted an off-white with a design consisting of blocks outlined in black and filled with several black dots. This appears to be the oldest of the three Cook rattles, all of which are the oldest ones from the Northwest Coast. Length: 20½″.

References: Inverarity 1950, no. 111.

194. *Rattle* (fig. 3)
Nootka Sound. BM, NWC 29, Cook expedition, 1778.

The rattle is carved of wood in the form of a bird and is more elaborate than BM, NWC 27 and 28. It has more carving and no painting. The wings are carved partially free from the body, with slight indications of eye-shaped wing joints. The tail is carved in a semiupright position and placed near the ends of the wings, with considerable body area between them and the handle. The underside has a flat carving of a human face, an element which has been continued in bird-form rattles ever since. It also occurs on the underjaw of large Kwakiutl masks. Length: 16½″; height: 8½″.

Reference: Inverarity 1950, no. 113.

195. *Rattle of mountain sheep horn* (fig. 54)
Restoration Point, Puget Sound. BM, George Goodman Hewitt collection, 1792, Vancouver 158, Hewitt ms. 251.

The body of the rattle is made of mountain sheep horn which has been steamed and bent to form both sides. It is tied together on the sides with thong. Each side is carved with a different human face. There is a small geometric border around the faces. The handle is carved of wood with a highly stylized bird's head at the far end and is fastened to the body with twisted cord and a binding of split cedar bark. The body of the rattle contains pebbles. Length: 13¾″.

References: Dalton 1897, plate XV, fig. 19; Gunther 1960, fig. 1*b*.

196. *Rattle* (fig. 55)
Nootka Sound. Hunterian Museum, Glasgow E 369, probably Cook expedition.

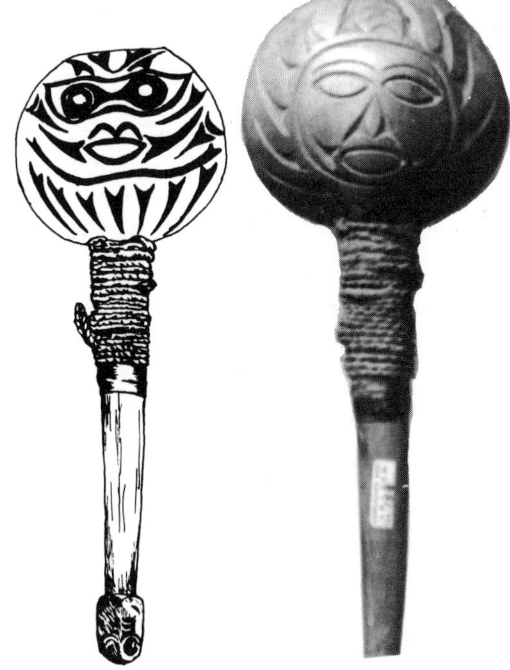

Fig. 54. Mountain sheep horn rattle, Restoration Point, Puget Sound. Hewitt collection (Vancouver), BM, Vancouver 158 (Appendix 1:195).

Fig. 55. Bird-shaped rattle, Nootka Sound. Cook collection, Glasgow E 369 (Appendix 1:196).

A rattle carved of two pieces of wood, is very similar to NWC 29. The beak is longer and more pointed and open, the tail is tilted slightly upward, and the carving of the face on the underside is like the Cook rattle (NWC 29). The adze marks on the surface show good control of the tool. All the design is done in carving; there is no paint on the piece. Length 19½″.

Reference: Laskey 1813, p. 72.

197. *Rattle in bird form* (fig. 4)
Nootka Sound. Ireland 1882-3659, King collection, Cook expedition.

A rattle representing a sea gull with a triangular slit at the throat and a small face carved on the breast. It is recognized as a Cook expedition piece because of a tattered label with "1882" on it, the year the King collection was acquired.

198. *Rattle in bird form*
Nootka Sound. Vienna 224 (312), Cook expedition.

A rattle carved to represent a bird (cormorant ?) is made of alder wood. The hollow cylindrical body is filled with pebbles and is part of a straight round handle. The long beak of the bird is broken. The eyes are round with concentric outlines and at the back of the head were four pegs which have been broken. The inside of the beak is painted red and so were the pegs. The eyes are white outlined in black. The body and handle are fastened together with vegetable fiber and the handle is partially wrapped with cedar bark. Length: 46 cm; body diam.: 9 cm.

TOOLS

199–204. *Bark beaters* (6) (fig. 59)
Nootka Sound. BM, NWC 47, 48, Cook expedition; Bern 61; Cook expedition, Webber collection; BM, George Goodman Hewitt collection, 1792, Vancouver 110, Hewitt ms. 230; Edinburgh 1956-657, Cook expedition; Göttingen 604.

The bark beater is made of whale bone and resembles the tapa beater of Polynesia. It is heavy and well balanced with a grooved surface that breaks up the fibers of the bark. The round handles of all the specimens show long use. This is the only eighteenth-century implement for preparing cedar bark which seems to have been replaced with the large chopper found in later collections. The one in Bern has a deeply cut V at the end of the handle, at the point of which a hole is drilled for a thong. Length: 10¾″–11⅝″.

205. *Hammer*

Restoration Point, Puget Sound. BM, George Goodman Hewitt collection, 1792, Vancouver 111, Hewitt ms. 280.

A small pounder or hammer made of dark gray stone. It is circular in cross section and flat at both ends, with the pounding surface larger in diameter.

206–7. *Hearths of fire-making equipment* (2)
Restoration Point, Puget Sound. BM, George Goodman Hewitt collection, 1792, Vancouver 117, 118, Hewitt ms. 288.

The hearths are made of soft wood and have four and six holes drilled. Length: 6⅝″, 5″.

208–9. *Knives*
Mouth of Yukon River. BM, NWC 67, Banks collection 53; BM, NWC 68, Cook expedition.

The knife from the Yukon River has an iron blade set in a bifurcated handle of bone. The hafting is wrapped with cedar bark. The handle is decorated along the inside edges with a row of nucleated circles (67).
The other knife, NWC 68, is unlocated and has a flaked blade of red stone which is hafted in a handle of wood and bound with cord. Length: 12⅜″.

210. ———

211. *Knife*
Mowachut, Nootka Sound. BM, George Goodman Hewitt collection, 1792, Vancouver 100, Hewitt ms. 231.

Half of a large mussel shell, sharpened on the edge to form a knife. Length: 7″.

212. *Knife*
No location. BM, NWC 69, Cook expedition, 1778.

A chipped stone blade in a wooden handle which is wrapped with cord. Length: 10″.

213. *Knife with an iron blade*
Nootka Sound. BM, NWC 88, Cook expedition, 1778.

The knife has a slightly curved blade of iron and a wooden handle which is bound with strips of hide. Length: 12⅝″.

214. *Knife*
Nootka Sound. BM, NWC 89, Cook expedition, 1778.

The knife has a curved blade of iron and a wooden handle carved in the form of a bird's head. The blade and handle are lashed with strips of hide. Except for the carved handle, it is identical with BM, NWC 88.

215. *Knife*
Nootka Sound. Vienna 214, Cook expedition, 1778.

A knife for wood carving with a short, slightly curved handle and a beaver tooth for the blade. There is no carving on the handle. Length: 16 cm.

216–18. *Paintbrushes*
Cross Sound. BM, George Goodman Hewitt collection, 1793, Vancouver 112, 113, 115, Hewitt ms. 199.

The paintbrushes have very few bristles left but are notable for their carved handles.
(112) The bristles are fastened with a continuous lashing to about half the length of the handle. The end of the handle is carved to resemble an eagle's head, on top of which are the remains of a diminutive squatting human figure. Length: 17 cm.
(113) The bristles are fastened with a cross lashing of split cedar bark. The handle has a human figure draped over the end with his head on one side and the legs on the other. His hands are fastened behind his back; excellent carving. Length: 6½ cm.

(115) The handle is carved to resemble an erect human figure with his hands behind his back, holding his hair to pull his head back, a posture of torture often used on witches. Both this and the figure in 113 are well-known designs used by the Tlingit on large and small sculpture. Length: 17.5 cm.

References: Dalton 1897, plate XV, figs. 16, 17; Niblack 1890, plate 45*a*, *b*.

219–20. *Paintbrush handles*
Cross Sound. BM, George Goodman Hewitt collection, 1793, Vancouver 114, 116, Hewitt ms. 199.

(114) The handle is carved with a human figure, standing erect.
(116) Handle carved to represent a killer whale; only a fragment. Length: 4½″.

References: Dalton 1897, plate XV, figs. 16, 17.

221. *Scraper*
Nootka Sound. Bern 60, Cook expedition, Webber collection, 1778.

An almost cylindrical shaft cut from rough wood is split at one end and an iron blade is inserted and bound with thong. The blade may be reshaped from a plane. Length: 21 cm.

UTENSILS

222. *Ladle* (fig. 56)
Queen Charlotte Islands. BM, NWC 34, Banks collection, 1789.

A ladle made of mountain sheep horn with a deep bowl and long handle that terminates in the head of a waterfowl; It is undecorated except for the carving of this head. The piece was collected by Captain George Dixon and given to Sir Joseph Banks on 22 May 1789. Length: 53 cm.

Fig. 56. Ladle, Queen Charlotte Islands. Banks collection, BM, NWC 34 (Appendix 1:222).

223. *Scoop or dipper*
Port Discovery, Admiralty Inlet. BM, George Goodman Hewitt collection, 1792, Vancouver 121, Hewitt ms. 252.

A scoop or dipper of horn, probably mountain sheep. It has a large bowl and a small vertical handle at one side. Length: 6⅞″.

224. *Spoon*
No location. BM, NWC 31 (not specifically marked Cook expedition).

The handle of the horn spoon (mountain sheep horn?) terminates in a little seated figure of a man with a hat. The bowl is etched with a simple geometric design. Its shape and material are Northwest style, but the face and the hat of the little man have a quality that may be Philippine.

225. *Spoon*
No location. BM, NWC 32 (not marked Cook expedition in the catalog).

The spoon is carved of wood and has a very clumsy shape. The bowl is painted red with a negative design of several abstract figures. There is an eye shape that ties it to the Northwest Coast.

226. *Spoon*
Possibly Cook Inlet. BM, NWC 33, Cook expedition, 1778.

A spoon with a large bowl and a short squared-off handle. It is made of mountain sheep horn. The rim is etched with small groups of parallel lines and the handle is crosshatched. The handle is perforated so that it could be hung with a thong. Length: 9¾″.

Reference: Cf. Vienna 232.

227. *Spoon*
Cross Sound. BM, George Goodman Hewitt collection, 1793, Vancouver 119, Hewitt ms. 203.

An elongated spoon with a ladlelike bowl and a long handle, made of wood. The interior of the bowl is painted with a design in red. Length: 11½″.

228. *Spoon*
Cross Sound. BM, George Goodman Hewitt collection, 1793, Vancouver 120, Hewitt ms. 207.

A curved spoon of one piece of mountain goat horn. The handle is carved to represent a small figure squatting with its hands clasped around its knees and a very small animal. Length: 6″.

Reference: Niblack 1890, plate 41.

229. *Spoon*
Prince William Sound. Vienna 232, Cook expedition, 1778.

The bowl only of a large mountain sheep horn spoon has a design of parallel lines on the underside of the bowl. It appears to be Athapascan in style.

230. *Spoon*
Nootka Sound. BM, NWC 35, Banks collection 20.

A plain spoon carved of wood with no division between the bowl and the handle, which tapers at the end. No decoration. Length: 10¼″.

WEAPONS

231–43. *Bundle of arrows (13)* (fig. 57)
Admiralty Inlet. BM, George Goodman Hewitt collection, 1792, Vancouver 24, Hewitt ms. 129, 287.

A bundle of arrows also marked as Columbia River and Restoration Point; there were fourteen, but one is missing. They are made of unsmooth, pale wood, very slender. All but one have a short foreshaft sharpened at the end to form the point. All are nocked at the butt end. The arrows originally had three feathers bound on with sinew. The part of the shaft covered by the feathers is ornamented with occasional black rings painted above the feathers, and many are smeared with black for several inches.

244–49. *Arrows (6)*
Columbia River. BM, George Goodman Hewitt collection, 1793, Vancouver 25, Hewitt ms. 129.

A bundle of arrows, of which three have short foreshafts of wood, the fourth is hollowed out to receive a foreshaft (missing), and two are of one piece. All are slender and have nocked butts, and the part of the shaft covered with feathers is painted with bands of red, black, and green, sometimes spirally designed. One

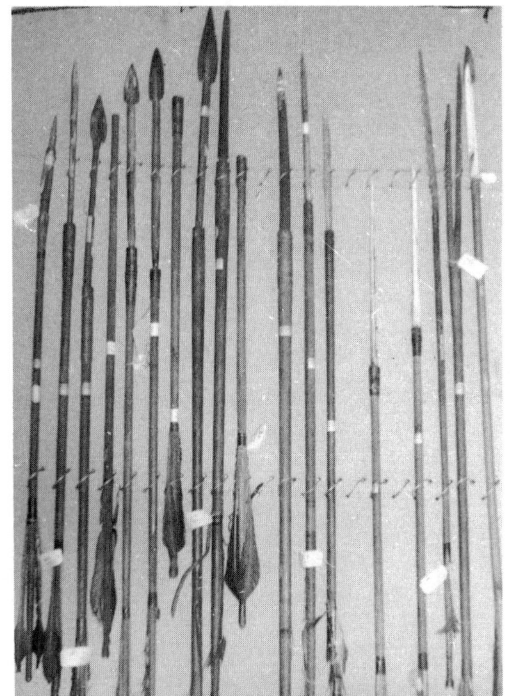

Fig. 57. Arrows, Admiralty Inlet. Hewitt collection (Vancouver), BM, Vancouver 24 (Appendix 1:231–43). (*More on p. 236.*)

with a foreshaft has a triangular point, with lateral indentations secured with cross-binding. The one without a foreshaft has a spiral ornament in red painted near the upper end and a nock for the head.

250–51. *Arrows* (*2*)

Restoration Point, Puget Sound. BM, George Goodman Hewitt collection, 1792, Vancouver 26, Hewitt ms. 287.

Two arrows with no points have shafts of pale wood, slender and well finished. The butts are nocked and each has three feathers. The area covered by the feathers is painted in bands of red and black, the red lines being an imitation of lashing.

252–61. *Bundle of arrows* (*10*)

Admiralty Inlet. BM, George Goodman Hewitt collection, 1792, Vancouver 27, Hewitt ms. 287.

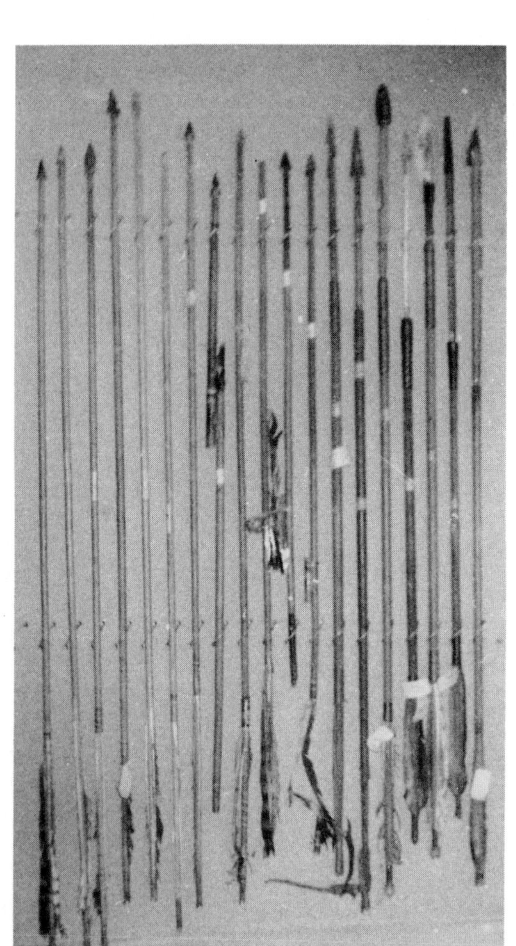

Fig. 57 (*cont.*).

The shafts are of pale wood, well finished, with nocked ends. Three feathers, brown, black, and white, are bound with fibrous material, sinew or shredded cedar bark. Several arrows have the area under the feathers painted with narrow bands of green. Six arrows have triangular heads of gray chalcedony, with deep lateral indentations by which they are bound to the shaft with the same binding. The remainder have no heads, but the cleft is there to receive them. Length: 28¼″ to 34¾″.

262–68. *Arrows* (*7*)

Admiralty Inlet. BM, Hewitt collection, 1792, Vancouver 28, Hewitt ms. 287.

Arrows with well-smoothed shafts and long feathers of brown and white. The spaces between the feathers are painted in bands of brown and brownish red. The heads, which are triangular, are bound to the shafts with a cross-lashing of thin sinew. The heads may be chipped chalcedony, and a small one is a dull red.

Reference: Vancouver 1798, 1:253.

269–72. *Bundle of arrows* (*4*)

Admiralty Inlet. BM, Hewitt collection, 1792, Vancouver 29, Hewitt ms. 287.

Four arrows, very broken and wormeaten, have three feathers each which are intact, bound with sinew, and four points, two of obsidian and two of gray chalcedony. All have lateral indentations for binding to the shaft. The parts of the shaft covered by the feathers are painted spirally in bands of red and black and green, imitating lashing.

273–74. *Arrows* (*2*)

Port Discovery. BM, Hewitt collection, 1792, Vancouver 30, Hewitt ms. 249.

The first arrow has a thick shaft of cedar, nocked at the butt; it has three feathers bound at top and bottom with a strip of cedar bark. The shaft is hollowed out to receive a long detachable point of bone with a circular set of barbs bilaterally placed near the base. The second arrow is similar but has a bone foreshaft with three barbs on one side and two on the other. Length: 31″.

275. *Arrow*

Gray's Harbor. BM, Hewitt collection, 1793, Vancouver 31, Hewitt ms. 342.

The arrow has a detachable foreshaft which is tapered at the end for insertion into lower shaft. The foreshaft has a single barb and is cleft at the upper end to receive a flat, leaf-shaped blade of iron. The blade is perforated near the point and gummed into place. The shaft tapers at the butt end and has two long dilapidated feathers bound at both ends with bark string. Length: 25¼″.

Reference: Vancouver 1798, 1:253, 2:84.

276. *Arrow*
Strait of Juan de Fuca. BM, Hewitt collection, 1792, Vancouver 32, Hewitt ms. 342.

An arrow shaft of soft wood is nocked at the butt and has two long feathers bound with bark. At the upper end it is similarly bound and hollowed out to receive a detachable head of the same wood which has a single long barb and ends in a flat triangular point of shell. Length: 31″.

277. *Arrow*
No location. BM, Hewitt collection, 1793, Vancouver 34, Hewitt ms., no number.

An arrow shaft of soft wood is nocked at the butt end and has two brown feathers bound to it. The upper end is hollowed out to receive a detachable foreshaft with three unilateral barbs and cleft at the upper end to receive a flat triangular blade. Length: 29¾″.

278. *Arrow*
Bella Coola (?); Gray's Harbor (?). BM, Hewitt collection, 1793, Vancouver 35, Hewitt ms. 342.

The shaft of the arrow is nocked at the butt end and has three brown feathers bound at top and bottom with string. It is hollowed out at the upper end to receive a detachable foreshaft with two unilateral barbs and a long row of notches. The upper end is cleft to admit a triangular flat head of whitish shell, kept in place by gum.

279. *Arrow*
No location. BM, Hewitt collection, 1793, Vancouver 36, Hewitt ms. 260.

A slender shaft of pale wood is nocked at the butt and two brown feathers are bound with bark. The upper end is hollowed out and bound with a whipping of bark. In it is inserted a foreshaft of wood with a single barb at half its length and cleft at the upper end to contain a small leaf-shaped blade of shell held in place by resin. The shaft below the blade is also bound with string. Length: 29⅜″.

280. *Arrow with barbed wooden foreshaft, no point.*
Strait of Juan de Fuca. BM, Hewitt collection, 1792, Vancouver 37, Hewitt ms. 342.

A slender arrow shaft is nocked at the lower end, with traces of painted rings above it. Two brown feathers bound with brown bark are in the painted area. At the upper end is a short detachable foreshaft of wood with a long barb that has two ornamented notches below it. The point is lacking but there is some bark binding left on the shaft. Length: 31″.

References: cf. Vancouver 31, 32, 33.

281. *Arrow*
Strait of Juan de Fuca. BM, Hewitt collection, 1792, Vancouver 38, Hewitt ms. 342.

An arrow with a wooden shaft is nocked at the butt end with two brown feathers. The upper end of the shaft is hollowed out to admit a long wooden point, cleft at the top for a blade, which is missing. The shaft below the space for the blade is strengthened by binding and has an irregular row of notches.

282. *Arrow*
Strait of Juan de Fuca. BM, Hewitt collection, 1792. Vancouver 39, Hewitt ms. ?.

Arrow with a thick shaft of cedar with three brown feathers has a foreshaft with two short unilateral barbs. The upper end of the shaft is split to receive a leaf-shaped point of shell with a square base. It is fastened with resin.

283–87. *Arrows* (5)
Mowachut, Nootka Sound. BM, Hewitt collection, 1792, Vancouver 40, Hewitt ms. 238.

Four have foreshafts with points, one has none. The shafts are thick cedar and there are some with two, others with three feathers bound with cedar bark. All are nocked. Three have a single barb and a leaf-shaped point held in place with resin. One head is very long and sharp. The fourth foreshaft has two unilateral barbs and a leaf-shaped blade of mussel shell. Four notches are cut in the lower part.

288. *Arrow*
Nootka Sound. BM, Hewitt collection, 1792, Vancouver 41, Hewitt ms. 238.

A nocked arrow of cedar has one perfect feather and two remnants. Black rings are painted in the feathered area. The upper shaft is bound with bark and has a detachable straight, unbarbed wooden point.

289. *Arrow*

Strait of Juan de Fuca. BM, Hewitt collection, 1792, Vancouver 42, Hewitt ms. 342.

A shaft of soft wood, nocked and bound with bark. There are two feathers and the foreshaft has two unilateral barbs. The point is missing.

290. *Arrow*
Brown's Passage. BM, Hewitt collection, 1793, Vancouver 44, Hewitt ms. 310.

An arrow shaft of cedar is nocked and there remains one feather, adhering to two bindings of bark. The shaft between these bindings is painted in a herringbone pattern. The upper end is hollowed out to receive a long detachable point with a single barb.

291. *Arrow*
Probably Tlingit. BM, Vancouver 45.

A cedar-shafted arrow with a nocked butt with three brown feathers bound with twine. The upper end is hollowed out for the insertion of a point or foreshaft of bone with three unilateral barbs. This end is wrapped with twine.

Reference: Niblack 1890, p. 286.

292. *Arrow*
Probably Tlingit. BM, Vancouver 46.

A cedar-shafted arrow with a projecting nock with three feathers, bound with cedar bark. The shaft has a pair of points, unequal in length, each having a continuous slight ridge of barbs. They are bound with cedar bark. Length: 27⅜″.

293–95. *Arrows* (3)
Probably Tlingit. BM, Vancouver 47 *a*, *b*, 48.

Two arrows with wooden shafts with projecting nocks and two brown feathers bound with cedar bark. The upper ends are inserted with long bone points with ridges of unilateral barbs. The point of one arrow is 7¼″ long, the other 8⅝″ long with only faint ridges on the barbs. Length: 28¾″, 28⅞″, and 29½″.

Reference: Niblack 1890, pp. 286 ff.

296. *Arrow*
Tlingit (?). BM, Vancouver 50.

An arrow shaft with three feathers bound to it with bark at the nocked butt. At the upper end a broad wrapping of bark holds two wooden points of unequal length; the shorter one has six unilateral barbs and the longer has fifteen similar barbs in sets of seven and eight. Length: 35⅛″.

297. *Arrow*
"Alaska, neighbor of Eskimo." BM, Vancouver 51.

The shaft is nocked and has three brown feathers bound with twine. It is hollowed out and strengthened with twine at the upper end to receive a heavy foreshaft of white bone with a single barb at its lower end. In a deep cleft cut in the upper end a triangular head of pale slate is fixed with resinous gum.

298. *Bundle of arrows or darts*
Cook Inlet. BM, Hewitt collection, Vancouver 53–58, Hewitt ms. 168.

A bundle of arrows (17) have shafts of brown wood reddened with red ocher with the upper ends of white bone about six to nine inches long, which at their forward ends are hollowed out and lined with wood to form a circular opening. The points are sharp bone to fit the openings and have two or three barbs each. The points are secured to lines of plaited sinew which are attached to the shaft near the butt end. Each arrow has three brown feathers. The butt is not nocked. These arrows are used for seal and large fish; 55–58 have shafts painted black as well as red.

299–300. *Arrow shafts* (2)
Banks Island. BM, Vancouver 59.

Wooden shafts of very long arrows, most slender near the butts and thickest near the center. The butts are nocked and have three feathers bound to them with bark; the space under the feathers is painted crudely in dull red and black. Each has a broader ring of red painted at the upper end, which is hollowed out and bound with bark. One arrow has a small bark binding bout twenty-seven inches from the butt, close to which is a piece of two-stranded cord bound around the shaft. There are no points. Length: 56⅛″–56⅜″.

301–6. *Arrows, feathered* (6)
Chugach, Prince William Sound. Bern A 2, 3, 5, 6, 7, 8.

307. *Arrow for hunting sea otter*
Chugach, Prince William Sound. Florence 2163.

308. *Bow*
Chugach, Prince William Sound. Bern 5.

309. *Bow*
No location. BM, NWC 86, Banks collection 14.

A bow backed with plaited hair and gut string. It is contracted at the grip and squared at the sides.

310. *Bow*
No location. BM, NWC 87, Banks collection 18.

A bow with convex back; along the face runs a raised ridge ornamented with a transverse black line. The cord is plaited gut. Length: 50½″.

311. *Bow*
Knight's Inlet, B.C. BM, Hewitt collection, 1793, Vancouver 9, Hewitt ms. 259.

A bow of brown wood on the principle of a composite bow, without backing. The grip is lashed with twine under which a brown feather is placed. It has deep nocks at the ends. The edges of the inner side down to the grip from each end is carved with zigzags in low relief and at intervals inlaid with short strips of copper. Length: 34½″.

312. *Bow*
Johnstone's passage or Cape Mudge, B.C. BM, Hewitt collection, 1793, Vancouver 8, Hewitt ms. 315.

A bow of light wood on the principle of the composite bow, but without backing. It is recurved and the tips are well bent toward the concave side (back). The tips are nocked. The bow is lashed with a cedar bark twisted cord at the grip. The string is stout twisted sinew. The locale is written on the bow in ink. Length: 30⅞″.

313. *Bow, plain*
Nootka Sound. BM, Hewitt collection, 1792, Vancouver 10, Hewitt ms. 239.

A plain bow of very dark wood (may be yew) which narrows at the grip and is flat on both sides. It has lateral nocks at the ends. Down the whole "belly" or inner side runs a groove. There is a stout twisted sinew cord. Length: 44⅛″. Reference: Niblack 1890, plate 26.

314. *Bow*
Mowachut, Nootka Sound. BM, Hewitt collection, 1792, Vancouver 11, Hewitt ms. 239.

Similar to Vancouver 10. Length: 48″.

315. *Bow*
Sea Passage, B.C. BM, Hewitt collection, 1792, Vancouver 12, Hewitt ms. 313.

A plain bow of yew (?), nocked laterally about two inches from each end. At the center the grip is lashed with a combination of thong and twisted cedar bark for about sixteen inches. The bow is reddish brown. Length: 55⅜″.

316. *Bow*

Salmon Cove, Observatory Inlet, B.C. BM, Hewitt collection, 1793, Vancouver 13, Hewitt ms. 312.

A plain bow of brown wood, loosely strung. It has a "cupid's bow" shape, each end doubly nocked with string passed over the inner nocks. At the grip, projecting at right angles, is a piece of wood resembling the bridge of a violin, perforated in two places and bound to the bow with thong. The string is twisted sinew. This bow appears to be an unintelligent copy of a strung convex bow, but a similar one is illustrated by Niblack (1890, p. 286, plate 26, fig. 115) as coming from the Tinné Indians of the interior of Alaska, but collected at Sitka where it probably was acquired by trade. Length: 49″.

317. *Bow*

Salmon Cove, Observatory Inlet, B.C. A bow of hardwood (yew ?) is nocked at both ends. The string of twisted sinew is attached at one end. The back is flat and covered with some black gum substance, partly worn off. The bow has hardly any curve. This resembles the bow in the collection in Florence. Length: 49¾″.

Reference: Giglioli 1895, plate III, fig. 59, p. 115.

318. *Bow*

Tlingit (?). Florence 262, Cook expedition (registered as from the South Seas in catalogs of 1822 and 1843).

A bow of the style regarded by Niblack as "general coast type" and compared with plate 26, fig. 112, which is regarded as Tlingit from Sitka. The bow has no groove down the center; it is probably of yew. Length: 1,135 mm.

319. *Bow, composite*

Port Discovery, Admiralty Inlet. BM, Hewitt collection, 1792, Vancouver 6, Hewitt ms. 253.

A small recurved bow, made of brown wood, almost a semicircle when unstrung. The tips are nocked and ornamented with thin sheets of white horn folded over the edges and lashed with sinew. The horn holds the sinew which is molded longitudinally over the concave side of the bow, forming a backing on the outer side when it is strung. The grip is lashed with thong and ornamented with sinew transversely wrapped. Length: 22¼″.

References: Vancouver 1798, 1:253; Puget 1939, p. 183.

320. *Bow, composite*

Port Discovery, Admiralty Inlet. BM, Hewitt collection, 1792. Vancouver 7, Hewitt ms. 253.

Same as Vancouver 6.

321. *Bow and arrows*

Prince William Sound. Bern 64*c*, Cook expedition, Webber collection, 1778.

A bow with sinew backing, reinforced with a small plate of bone held in place with sinew binding. Arrows: copper, slate point, six with unilateral barbs, fore-shaft with three unilateral barbs.

References: Henking 1956, p. 371, fig. 39; Bandi 1956, p. 219, fig. 6.

322. *Ceremonial ax, "slave killer"* (fig. 11)
Nootka Sound. Bern 59, Cook expedition, 1778, Webber collection.

"The blade of gray stone is square in cross section and narrows down toward the cutting edge. The wooden handle is cylindrical and thickens at the end where it gives the blade a powerful base. The handle is carved with the face of a mask with a small nose, long slanting eyes and a wide open mouth in which the blade is fastened in a setting of pitch. In the head of the mask holes are bored for bunches of hair, especially along the forehead. Much of this is still in place" (Henking 1955).

References: Henking 1955, plate 2*c*. Giglioli 1895, p. 177.

323. *Ceremonial ax, "slave killer"* (fig. 12)
Nootka Sound. BM, NWC 97, Cook expedition, 1778.

A club in the form of a human head with a protruding tongue formed of a large polished stone. The head has a fringe of black hair. This is a ceremonial piece supposedly used for killing slaves for sacrificial occasions. There is no record of any eighteenth-century explorer's having seen it in use.

References: Lips 1956; Rickman 1781, p. 224; Inverarity 1950, no. 149.

324. *Ceremonial ax "slave killer"*
Nootka Sound. BM, NWC 98, Cook expedition, 1778.

Another piece exactly like NWC 97, even resembling the Leipzig specimen more closely. It does not have the small human face as a knob at the end of the handle.

325. *Ceremonial ax, "slave killer"* (fig. 13)
Nootka Sound. Cambridge, University Museum 25.371, Earl of Denbigh collection.

This piece closely resembles the one in Bern (59) with the addition of occasional insets of teeth around the mouth where the blade is set.

References: see previous entries.

326. *Ceremonial ax, "slave killer"*
Nootka Sound. Florence 155, Cook expedition, 1778.

This piece also resembles NWC 97, 98. It has a comparatively short handle and much hair on the head. There is a carving on the knob at the end of the handle. Giglioli, 1895, pp. 118–19, plate III, no. 62.

327. *Ceremonial ax, "slave killer"*
Nootka Sound. Vienna no. 211 (240), Cook expedition, 1778.

A club with a human face and a protruding tongue which is the blade of polished stone. It resembles other Cook pieces of the same kind, but does not have fine carving. The catalog calls it a war weapon and does not mention its use as a slave killer. Length: 37.5 cm; blade: 13 cm.

References: Cf. NWC 97, 98; Florence 155.

328. *Ceremonial ax, "slave killer"*
Nootka Sound. BM, NWC 99, Cook expedition (?).

A straight club surmounted by a human head with a stone blade transversely set through a hole near the top of the club. The handle is wrapped with braided sinew string. It is described in the British Museum catalog as a Nootka tomahawk for killing slaves. Niblack (1890) cites two pieces collected by the United States Navy men from the Tlingit in the middle of the nineteenth century (Niblack 1890, plate 46). Such a piece is not mentioned by Drucker (1950, #532), but Boas lists it for the Kwakiutl at Fort Rupert (Boas 1935, p. 60). Length: 12¾″; stone blade: 10″.

329. *Ceremonial club*
Nootka Sound. BM, NWC 100, Cook expedition, 1778.

On one end of this club a human head is carved, and on the other is a wolf holding a human mask in his paw. The wolf's mouth is filled with animal teeth. The masks and the human head have human hair. The former label read "Hand instrument used in war at Nootka." The present label reads: "a warrior's staff." Length: 20¾″.

Reference: Inverarity 1950, no. 140.

330. *Dagger*
Rock Village, Inside Passage. BM, Hewitt collection, 1793, Vancouver 91, Hewitt ms. 347.

A massive dagger of white bone resembling a butcher's steel knife in shape. The grip at the butt end is round and the blade diminishes gradually to a point. Length: 23⅜″.

331. *Dagger sheath*
Cook Inlet. BM, Hewitt collection, 1794, Vancouver 99, Hewitt ms. 159.

A sheath of brown buckskin with a loop of the same. It is covered completely with porcupine quill work, the design consisting of white chevrons on a red background. The side and bottom are fringed with buckskin and porcupine quill alternating. The edges of the loop are also bound with quill. The design resembles the pattern called "fish flesh" in the basket designs of the Tlingit (Emmons 1903). For similar quill work see Vancouver, 176, 177. Length: 13″.

332. *Sling*
Point Mudge, Quadra Island, B.C. BM, Hewitt collection, Vancouver 109, Hewitt ms. 348.

A large sling bag and cord of plaited fiber. The cord is plaited in herringbone design. The edges of the bag are bound with alternate brown and white woolen thread.

333. *Spearpoint*
No location. BM, NWC 70, Cook expedition, 1778.

A point of flaked translucent stone with a hafting of wood, lashed with strips of hide. Length: 8⅞″.

334. *Spearpoint*
"Namakizat." BM, Hewitt collection, 1792, Vancouver 65, Hewitt ms. 113.

A point of wood, brought to a flattened point. The butt is also a point. The word "salmon" is written on it. Length: 9⅝″.

335. *Spearpoint*
Nootka Sound. BM, Hewitt collection, 1792, Vancouver 66, Hewitt ms. 245.

A spearpoint of white bone with five unilateral barbs, the first being three and one-half inches from the point. Length: 10¾″.

336. *Spearpoint*
Nootka Sound.

A spearpoint of bone with three unilateral barbs. It is perforated near the butt.

337. *Spearpoint*
Banks Island. BM, Hewitt collection, 1793, Vancouver 71, Hewitt ms. 309.

A curved spearpoint of white bone with two unilateral barbs. Nearer the butt the piece is cut away into a wedge shape for fitting into a shaft. Written in ink on the spear is "Banks Island." This strange piece may also be an awl. Length: 6½″.

338. *Spearpoint*
Nootka Sound (?). BM, Vancouver 73.

A spearpoint of hollow white bone, cleft for the insertion of a leaf-shaped piece of mussel shell, fastened with resinous gum and wrapped with bark binding from which a short piece of stout cord issues. The butt of the bone is split and expands to a V shape. Length: 4¾″.

339. *Spearpoint*
Nootka Sound. BM, Vancouver 75.

A spearpoint of white bone with a single barb, fitted into a hollowed socket of wood; near its butt is a projection by which the lashing of wild cherry bark binds the socket. Length: 10⅝″.

340. *Spearpoint*
Nootka Sound. BM, Vancouver 77.

A spearpoint with three unilateral barbs; at the upper end a flat iron head is fastened with a wrapping of root. Length: 11½″.

341–42. *Spearpoints* (2)
Cook Inlet. BM, Hewitt collection, 1794, Vancouver 82, 83, Hewitt ms. 78.

Two straight spearpoints of white bone with two large barbs on one side and three very small ones on the other, all cut from a solid piece. Perforated above the butt, which is square. Length (82) 6¼″; (83): 7½″.

343–44. *Spearpoints* (2)
Cook Inlet. BM, Hewitt collection, 1794, Vancouver 84, 85, Hewitt ms. 170.

Spearpoints consisting of a leaf-shaped head of slate with a tang and a foreshaft of driftwood. The lower corners of the head above the tang are cut to form barbs of unequal length. The upper part of the wooden foreshaft is cut away to form a flat triangular point and pared away on one side to fit the tang of the head, which is lashed with twine. The wooden triangular point reaches about one-quarter of the length of the head. Length: 12¾″.

345. *Spearpoint*
Cook Inlet. BM, Hewitt collection, 1794, Vancouver 86, no Hewitt ms. number.

Small bone spearpoint in one piece, leaf shaped. Below the blade it is perforated transversely and below this it is cut away to the butt, which terminates in a beveled ridge with angular corners, with a small groove upon each side. Between the butt and the transverse perforation there is a shallow vertical boring on one side to receive the point of a foreshaft. Length: 3⅛″.

346. *Spear*
No location. BM, NWC 108, Cook expedition.

A beautiful blade of slate in a wooden sheath. Length: 7¼″.

347. *Spear "fighting head"*
"Namakizat." BM, Hewitt collection, 1793, Vancouver 89, Hewitt ms. 333.

A spear with a long bone point which is set in the cleft shaft with wedges to tighten it. The point has a natural groove on one side. Parts of the shaft are decorated with incised designs, which are filled with white. Length: 32½″.

348. *Spear*
"Namakizat." BM, Hewitt collection, 1793, Vancouver 90, Hewitt ms. 333.

A short spear of brown wood with a long straight point of bone, probably femur, with a well-sharpened tip. The shaft is round for a few inches at the butt, then for eight inches it is at its thickest and covered with incised lines deeply cut, with a human face on each side. It is lashed with thong. The head is set with wedges.

349. *Spear*
Chugach, Prince William Sound. Vienna 228 (not in Cook catalog).

A spear with a long point, which according to the label is made of a narwhal tooth. Length: 1.65 m.

350. *Spear (for birds)*
Chugach, Prince William Sound, Unalaska. Bern Al 7, Vienna 228 (also not in Cook listing).

A bird spear with a long central prong and three prongs about two-thirds of the way up from the point.

351. *Spear foreshaft*
Strait of Juan de Fuca.

A wooden foreshaft cut diagonally at the butt end and cleft at the upper end for the insertion of a long bone point with six unilateral barbs. The binding at the insertion is a copper-colored bark. Length: 22⅝″.

352. *Stone fighting weapon* (fig. 15)
Nootka Sound. BM, NWC 93, Cook expedition.

A wedge-shaped weapon, carved of stone, with a convenient round handle above the wedge. A face is carved on a platform above the handle, usually a distorted human face or a bird with bulging eyes. The mouth is always open and is perforated for passing a thong through. In a letter to Martinez, Ingraham mentions this implement and states that it was used only for war, not for splitting wood as Martinez claimed (AGN, Mexico City, Historia Tomo 65,1789). This type of piece is often also mentioned as a slave killer. In later collection the same form appears in wood and is called a copper breaker, illustrated by Boas for the Kwakiutl.

Reference: Drucker 1950, no. 535.

353. *Stone fighting weapon* (fig. 16)
Nootka Sound. BM, NWC 94, Cook expedition.

Another wedge-shaped stone weapon which has a face carved on a flat top. The large eyes are slanting, the forehead is high and curved at the top, and the round mouth is open. It is bored through to carry a thong.

354. *Stone fighting weapon* (fig. 14)
Nootka Sound. BM, NWC 95.

The wedge of stone also has a flat top, which is carved with a figure that might be a frog. It has a small hole for a thong below the figure.

Reference: Force and Force 1968, p. 152.

355. *Stone fighting weapon* (fig. 17)
Nootka Sound. BM, Hewitt collection, 1792, Vancouver 95, Hewitt ms. 234.

A stone weapon that is also called a "slave killer," more in the shape of a hatchet, cut from a single piece of stone. It has a round short handle with a knob at the power end pierced for a thong. The upper end has a blade projecting laterally and surmounted with a head with a face, looking in the same direction as the blade. It has slanted eyes set almost vertically, heavy lips, and a flat nose. It differs considerably from the other weapons of this type. Length: 11½".

356. *Stone fighting weapon* (fig. 18)
Thurlow's Island east of Vancouver Island off mainland shore. BM, Hewitt collection, 1792, Vancouver 96, Hewitt ms. 419.

A wedge-shaped weapon with a distorted face carved on a flat top. The nose is perforated for a thong.

357. *Stone fighting weapon*
Nootka Sound. Florence, no number, Cook expedition.

Resembles NWC 93, 94.

Reference: Giglioli 1895, plate III, fig. 63.

358. *Stone fighting weapon*
Nootka Sound. Vienna 209 (238), Cook expedition.

Resembles the items above, but called a *Schädel Brecher* or skull crusher. It is listed in the Vienna catalog as "for killing prisoners of war as sacrifices." Length: 25 cm.

359. *Stone fighting weapon*
Nootka Sound. Vienna 210 (239), Cook expedition, 1778.

Similar to items above.

360. *Throwing stick or board*
Chugach, Prince William Sound. Bern Al 4.

The upper side of the board is flat and has a bone peg for the butt end of the spear to rest against before throwing. Length: 45.5 cm.

361. *Throwing stick or board*
Cross Sound. BM, Hewitt collection, 1793, Vancouver 104, Hewitt ms. 200.

A throwing board of brown wood is elaborately carved. At one end is a group of three figures, the central one being the largest. The butt end is carved to represent a human figure in the mouth of a large fish; the feet of the figure are carved on the other side. There is the usual hole for the first finger, and at the top of the groove is a small vertical iron pin.

References: Dalton 1897, p. 231, fig. *c;* Niblack 1890, plate 27, fig. 127*a*, *b;* Cf. USNM 7899, a piece collected by Dr. T. T. Minor, U.S. Army, at Sitka.

362. *Throwing stick or board*
Cross Sound. BM, Hewitt collection, 1793, Vancouver 105, Hewitt ms. 200.

A throwing board of wood, largely triangular in cross-section. The angular surface is carved at the upper end with totemic designs, including a human face, and at the lower end is a lizard's head. The hole for the first finger is an open mouth of a grotesque figure. The upper end of the groove has a small vertical peg. Length: 15″.

363. *Throwing stick or board*
Cross Sound. BM, Hewitt collection, 1793, Vancouver 106, Hewitt ms. 200.

A throwing board ornamented with incised designs. It is grooved longitudinally on one side and has a diagonal circular perforation large enough to admit the finger at the lower end of the groove. The butt end is rounded off and the designs are totemic; there is a human face on the back of the upper end. Length: 14½″.

364. *Throwing stick or board*
Unalaska. Vienna 235, Cook expedition (?).

The board is inlaid with ivory and two little figures that look like sea otters are near the finger hole. See also Appendix 1:367.

MISCELLANEOUS

365. *Mat*
Prince William Sound. BM, NWC 24.

If this piece belongs to the Cook collection it is probably from the Chugach of Prince William Sound. It is in the same twined weave as their baskets and has no resemblance in shape to any other examples of this type of weaving. The small geometric designs are the style of such small fillers in Tlingit baskets, which the Chugach also make.

366. *Bread of pine bark*
Nootka Sound.

The tree bark was crushed and the fiber bound together, perhaps with grease. This is used with various kinds of bark in many parts of western America. At Nootka it might also include the herring eggs which are allowed to gather in hemlock boughs. Length: 9″.

367. *Throwing sticks or boards*
Cook Inlet. BM, Hewitt collection, 1794, Vancouver 101, 102, 103, Hewitt ms. 153.

These three throwing sticks are alike. They are made of wood, convex on the ungrooved side, which is ornamented with inlay of pale blue beads. It expands from the upper end, which is almost pointed, to the lower, and the groove diminishes proportionately in depth. The butt end is cut away into a handle with three cavities on the grooved side for the second, third, and little fingers. On the convex side is a round hole for the first finger, just above the handle.

Appendix 2
Technological Processes of the Eighteenth Century

ARMOR

The breast and back armor is described by Suría (p. 255 ff.) as being made of boards "two fingers thick," joined by a thick cord, which after being *berbirlis* by *as* and *embes* (Spanish terms not translated). This description has several familiar points and other points which cannot be explained. Two kinds of units are used in this type of armor; often slats are used across the front and back and round rods are laced in under the arms, probably because they permit freer movement. The slats or boards are not likely to be two fingers thick, but rather two fingers wide, for the former would make this cumbersome and heavy garment almost intolerable.

Regardless of form, they are laced together with string or sinew, and this may be explained by the untranslated words. An excellent diagram of this lacing can be found in Niblack (1890, p. 269) and it may explain what Suría means by the thread taking the opposite direction. Further discussion of this type of armor can be found in Hough (1894). In this article Hough tells that four suits of such armor were obtained by Malaspina, but so far none of these have been shown at the Museo d'América in Madrid where the remainder of his collections are housed.

METALS

Use

The presence of copper and iron among the Indians was often commented on by the travelers and explorers of the eighteenth century, especially when they considered themselves the first Europeans in the area. Rickard traces these materials to both native and foreign sources. Wherever the Europeans contacted Indians, they saw iron or copper or both already in their possession, and they often also had words for these metals in their own language or some other non-European language, pointing to intertribal trade (Rickard 1939, p. 25). Rickard also refers to the fact that the Pérez expedition in 1774 found the Haida on North (Langara) Island in possession of a few pieces of iron. Crespi wrote that a few natives had ill-made iron knives like cutlasses, with wooden handles and sheaths of wood (Crespi, n.d.). In 1775 and 1779 Bodega y Quadra and Arteaga on Prince of

Wales Island saw the Indians with bracelets of copper wire and whalebone and with extremely fine copper wire in their ears. Yet the explorers found nothing that could be regarded as equipment for processing metals. Since no effective technique seems to have been developed, the greatest control of the medium was in the hands of the tribes who happened to live near the outcroppings. Meares mentioned the trade in lumps of malleable copper ore (Meares 1790, p. 113), which had probably come from the Copper River region and was controlled by the Atna Athapascans and their neighbors, the Eyak. Through the Chilkat Tlingit, who traded with these people, copper was dispersed in Southeastern Alaska and along the coast of the Gulf of Alaska. It was handled in very small amounts until the European ships came. They not only brought copper wire and tools, but they also revealed their copper sheathing when they were brought up on the beach for careening. This became a new source, gotten by fair means or foul.

The native copper on the mainland of Alaska is easily derived from the Copper River sources, but the Aleutian Islands are separated from the Alaska Peninsula, and so their most plausible source was Asia. The long iron knives which Bering's expedition saw among them were declared by Steller not to be of European manufacture, which could easily be true, since they might have been secured by the Aleut from the Chukchi with whom they traded in the Diomedes and the Chukchi in turn may have bought the knives from the Russians at Anadyr. At that time copper was also widely used in the Yenesei River region. At each of these exchanges some native work might have been done in reshaping the copper.

A very important and ingenious source of metal for the whole Northwest Coast must not be overlooked, for it required no contact of people. This is drift iron. Rickard explored this source thoroughly in his paper on the subject (Rickard 1939). The following historical facts are taken from this paper. Starting with the iron knives found by Bering on the Shumagin Islands in 1741, Rickard moves to another hint when an iron bolt was found in 1745 and a knife discovered on the coast of northern California in the possession of an Indian who explained that he had made his tool from a spike he found in some wreckage on the shore. Cook commented that the knives he saw among the Indians were of the same breadth and thickness as an iron hoop such as could have been found on stranded casks. This wreckage is brought across the Pacific on the Japanese current which sweeps the Kurile Islands, the Aleutian chain, and the whole western coast of North America. The harvest from this source increased when, after 1714, vessels were built at Okhotsk and their hurried and poor construction could not weather the storms in the North Pacific. Hardwoods from Asia were also included in this drift and it still continues, bringing glass balls and net floats from Japanese fishing gear. Iron had been known for centuries in Japan and Russia, and so no explanation is necessary for its use in shipbuilding. The historical records also supply ample information about the wrecks which took place on the Pacific Coast of America, as well as the occasions when the Indians could not be satisfied with what the ocean currents brought them; when an opportunity came, they sometimes attacked ships for their metal. On the Queen Charlotte Islands a ship which was attacked supplied not only iron but also a number of brass cabin keys. These became treasured items and were worn as ornaments and buried with some chiefs. Occasionally the sea would also bring a Japanese junk with its occupants still alive. The

Japanese were either killed or kept as slaves, and some among them probably knew enough about working iron to help the Indians make their tools. Such a slave could bring considerable wealth to his owner.

In contrast to the natural phenomenon that brought the people and their watercraft from Japan to the western shores of America, another current made it impossible for the Chinese to come. Their wrecks were swept along the Asiatic coast and on to Kamchatka. This drift generally moved on a current at the rate of about ten miles per day.

Technique

The Indians evidently handled metals by a Chalcolithic technique. They had no means of reducing the ore when they found combinations of substances in it (Emmons 1908, p. 645). They occasionally saw a ship's armorer or blacksmith at work with a forge set up on the beach, but they did not copy him, probably because the whole technique was so foreign to them that there was no starting place. However, in a few places some crude manipulating of metals was found. One of Bering's officers found in an Indian (Aleut) house a whetstone which was used for sharpening copper knives. In 1765 Korovin at Unalaska found darts and spears tipped with iron and small hatchets and two-edged knives which were shaped by being rubbed between two stones that were frequently wet with water. Sarytchev in 1801 at Unalaska saw knives and axes gotten from the Russians that were not well used. They fastened a wooden handle to an ax so that they could chip with it as one would with an adze. An ax head was also converted into an adze by attaching a handle at right angles.

Emmons's article includes a statement by Wirt Tassin, chemist of the United States National Museum, about the metallic contents of the copper ring which is illustrated in the text. This ring belonged to a Nishka chief, a Tsimshian, living in Nass Harbor, British Columbia (fig. 142). The report is as follows:

> A qualitative test of the metal shows the presence of silver. Examination of an etched surface shows that the strands are each made up apparently of hammered sheets.
>
> These observations give rise to the following conclusions: the copper is perhaps "native," since silver is a constant constituent of the copper of the Copper River and Lake Superior regions. The sheets composing the individual strands taper from the centers to the ends and vary greatly in thickness at different points, a condition which would arise when hammering a nugget into a sheet with the idea of getting as great a length as possible with a minimum width.
>
> My idea of the method of manufacture is somewhat as follows: The native nugget was heated to a full red and quenched to make it soft and then hammered from the ends to the middle. It was then re-heated and worked in the same manner, except that the work was applied along the edge. These two processes were repeated alternately till the desired flat was obtained.[1]

1. A similar process was observed by Caamaño when he was in the vicinity of Bucareli Bay in 1792. He mentioned that the Indians did not ask for copper or iron and seemed well supplied. The men all carried knives in sheaths slung around the neck. He described them as well-sharpened daggers, twelve inches long, with the pommel enclosing a smaller knife, about six inches long and four inches wide. This was used for scarring the face and body, and many of the men gave good evidence of this use. The iron hilt

> Two of these flats were placed side by side, one end fastened, and both were then twisted together, but not "laid up." When a certain amount of work had been done the twist was heated, cooled and rounded up by hammering, thus forming a strand. Two such strands were thus twisted to form the necklace.

The process described here is relatively simple, and since the necklace is made of copper, which is more malleable than iron, it might have been made by the Indians after they had studied these necklaces for some time and had become more familiar with metals. There is no indication that this is an eighteenth-century piece.

WEAVING

Basketry

Baskets, bags, and mats. The techniques of basketry used on the entire Northwest Coast include almost every process used anywhere else in North America. Coarse checkerboard and twilled plaiting are used on large split cedar bark storage containers by everyone except the southernmost people near the Columbia River. The smaller checkerboard basket is also found almost everywhere, but slightly more frequently in the north. The techniques of these baskets are also used on split cedar bark mats.

Archaeological study does not often reveal samples of basketry, but enough was found at Yakutat so that Dr. DeLaguna and her associates, including Carolyn Osborne, a textile expert, could give some very important statements on the types and possible age of the fragments (DeLaguna 1964, pp. 178–81).

The twined basket is also found throughout the area with the greater concentration in the north, where it has developed into the finely woven self-patterned baskets of the Haida and the beautifully designed baskets of the Tlingit. In the Nootka area a twined basket is also made which differs from the northern ones by the continuous use of a three-ply strand. The decoration is generally geometric, though their hats, woven in the same way, include some realistic patterns. South of the Nootka there is a very strongly developed basketry among the Salish from the southern end of Vancouver Island to the valley of the Fraser River and the coastal tribes of Washington. This will not be discussed because it does not appear in any eighteenth-century literature, though the tribes along the Strait of Juan de Fuca and the inhabitants of Puget Sound and Hood Canal all made it in the nineteenth century, with excellent control of the technique. In scanning the collections, it is obvious that the men on the ships did not care for basketry, though no household they entered could have been without it.

The Tlingit basketry has been so well analyzed first by Emmons (1903) and later by Frances Paul (1944) that there is no need to repeat it here, but a new form of basketry found in the eighteenth-century collections should be noted. In the Cook or Banks collections (BM, NWC 14 or 21) there is a flat bag ornamented with split bird quills. The weave is fine twining similar to that of the Tlingit, and

---

was covered with leather and had a thong for fastening it to the wrist. Caamaño said they were so well made that he did not suspect that they were of native manufacture until he saw the Indians make them by heating the iron in the fire and forging it by beating it with stones in the water (Caamaño 1849, p. 203).

the style of the designs leads one to believe that it was possibly made by the Chugach. The bag has one rounded end and one straight end. There is also such a piece in the Göttingen collection. They both have the Tlingit type of design, the kind used as a "filler" with larger patterns. There is a basket in the Banks collection (BM, NWC 18) which is distinctly Tlingit in style except that it is oblong with rounded ends. This shape was not used by the Tlingit and again can be attributed to the Chugach, because in Cook's voyage he did not stop in Tlingit territory but was in Prince William Sound.

Hats. Hats were a very important part of costume on the Northwest Coast and ranged from the humble rain hat to the elegant ceremonial headpiece trimmed with ermine.

There were two basketry techniques and a choice of materials: in the south the typical hat was the one made by the Nootka, woven of split cedar bark, sedge, and basket grass (*Xerophyllum tenax*). The hat was woven with a liner of split cedar bark that formed a headband, and the body had split cedar bark for the warps and finely split cedar bark for the wefts, which were wrapped in an overlay strand of *Xerophyllum*. The shape of the hat was a truncated cone, and the specialty of the eighteenth century was a pear-shaped bulb on top of the crown. The sides of the hat varied in steepness, and the more shallow ones were decorated by dyeing the third strand of the weft black or dark brown to create the design. The patterns most common were realistic whale hunting scenes with men harpooning the whale or canoes towing the dead animal to shore. Smaller hats were sometimes designed with figures of ducks and small canoes. The top of the crown often did not have the overlay of *Xerophyllum*, but showed the brown cedar bark weft with only dots of the lighter color. The same pattern was followed on the pear-shaped bulb.

These hats were worn by both men and women. They gave protection from the rain and shielded the eyes from the glare of the sea. The hats in the collections are: Vancouver 192; BM, NWC 6, 7; Florence 185; Ireland 1882-3876 (fig. 58). See Appendix 1 for individual descriptions.

Other hats used by the northern tribes of the coast were the forerunners of a standard type used on the entire coast as long as hats were woven. Emmons stated in the early twentieth century that the art of making ceremonial hats had been lost among the northern Tlingit and that they purchased these hats from the Haida and the southern Tlingit (Emmons 1903, p. 256). The brim was coarser than the crown and was woven with a skip-stitch at intervals to form geometric patterns like the chevron. The crown was woven with a three-strand weft which gave a ropelike appearance. If the hat was painted, this was limited to the crown area, with red, black, and blue as the principal colors, and the the design was abstract or geometric. A beautiful ceremonial hat is shown by Emmons (1903, plate 17) with ermine skins at the top of the rings.

The rings on the hat which indicate the status of the wearer are woven with the hat and are shaped around an exact form of partially decayed red cedar. This is very light and is allowed to stay in place, since it will eventually crumble completely (Emmons 1903, p. 257). The ceremonial hats were also cone shaped, but with a different crown, a flat top, and greater flare toward the bottom after the eighteenth century.

Fig. 58. Hat with whaling scene and bulb top, Nootka Sound. King collection (Cook), Ireland, King, 1882–3876 (Appendix 1:129).

Textiles: Cedar Bark

Preparation. Cedar bark was used in many ways, both split and shredded. For mats and storage baskets or wallets, it was split and cut into splints about one-quarter inch wide. Some splints were dyed black by being buried in mineral mud, and both checkerboard and twilled plaiting were worked by combining black threads with the natural ones, producing simple geometric designs. These mats and baskets became very brittle with disuse and are difficult to preserve. Since they were such common household articles, the men on the expeditions were not attracted by them. If any were collected they have not survived the rigors of museums and private collectors.

The shredded cedar bark was put in a steeping tub for six or more days, and when it was thought ready for pounding it was taken out and beaten with paddles of whale bone. There are four of these in the collections studied (see Appendix 1:199–204) (fig. 59). When the fibers had been sufficiently separated, they were carefully washed and made ready for use. This is the only record of this process written in the eighteenth century (Pantoja in Wagner 1933, p. 159). Pantoja says that the prepared fibers were passed on to women who did only weaving, but this is probably correct only for a wealthy household where the weavers were slaves.

The cedar bark was combed to straighten the fibers, and then it was rolled into a loose warp thread, rolled hard on the thigh to make a tighter thread, or rolled with another spun strand to make a two-ply string. This latter was used for warps that were spaced a little apart and would make a stiffer garment.

Weaving process. One of the few references to weaving, which is in the first edition of Cook's *Third Voyage* but not in the current edition of *The Journal* (Beaglehole 1967) described the operation in detail. Garments

> are made of the bark of a Pine tree, beat into a hempen state. It is not spun, but after being properly prepared, is spread upon a stick, which is fastened across to two others that stand upright. It is disposed in such a manner, that the manufacturer, who sits on her hams at this simple machine, knots it across with small plaited threads, at the distance of ½″ from each other. Though, by this method it is not so close or firm as cloth that is woven, the bunches between the knits make it sufficiently impervious to the air, by filling the interstices; and it has the additional advantage of being softer and more pliable. [Cook and King 1784, p. 324]

This description is sufficient to show that the method is the same as the one described by Boas for the Kwakiutl in the late nineteenth century (Boas 1909, pp. 369, 370, 395) and later by Drucker for the Nootka (Drucker 1951, p. 94). By this technique the cloaks, wraparound skirts, and circular capes were made. The weave varied according to the spacing of the twined wefts and whether the warps were spun or twisted into individual strands or used in bunches. If the warps were tightly packed the garments were more impervious to wind and rain. These cloaks or wraparound skirts were oblong, with a rounded lower edge, and fringed. The straight sides often had a braided edge or a short fringe. The top edge consisted of the loops by which the piece was fastened to the loom bar and was often covered with a strip of fur, usually sea otter, which can still be identified even in tattered remnants on museum pieces. A considerable variety in the twining stitch is produced by combinations of warps in the weaving and the relative firmness of

Fig. 59. Cedar bark beaters, Nootka Sound. Cook collection, BM, NWC 47 (Appendix 1:199).

the warp and weft elements. Often the warps are paired so that the first row warps one and two are covered with the same weft and in the next two and three are taken together. These two rows alternate to produce a twilled pattern which is carried over to the Chilkat blanket. An analysis of this type of weaving is excellently done in a paper by Joanne Vanderberg (1953).

Type of garments. The most widely represented garments on the Northwest Coast were made of cedar bark, and they continued to be worn for daily use long after trade goods were adopted for ceremonial regalia. The simplest garment of shredded cedar bark was the woman's skirt (fig. 60), which was most popular in the southern area. For this, strands of shredded bark were taken in a little more than twice the length of the skirt required. A strip of leather or split cedar bark was laid in the middle of the length, serving as a belt, and small bunches of the strands were looped over this. There are two examples of such skirts in the Cook collection in the Ethnological Museum in Florence (Ethnological Museum 231, 232, Appendix 1:30, 31). They were registered in 1822 and 1843 (catalog no. 65) as aprons from Tahiti.

The garment called variously a cloak, a cape, and even a wraparound skirt is the largest one made of cedar bark and certainly the most versatile. The cloak had the oblong shape common to all the pieces which have been mentioned. When it was made specifically for use as a skirt it sometimes was not as rounded at the lower edge. When the explorers described the clothing of the women they sometimes stated that they were covered to their ankles and in other places they said the skirt reached below the knee. This may be accomplished with the same garment by putting it up under the armpits or down at the waist. The garment did not have any ties but was firmly tucked under at the waist.

When the garment was worn as a cloak or cape, principally by men, it could be folded around the waist, leaving the upper body bare. There are many figures in the canoes wearing such capes. Another way of wearing it was to tie it on the left shoulder and carry it under the right arm. This could also be worn by men or women.

The circular cape reached from the shoulder to the waist and was woven from the head opening at the top to the lower edge by constantly increasing the diameter by inserting more warp material. The cloaks and capes were often trimmed with fur around the neck and at the lower edge.

A fine example of the circular cape is one in the King collection at the National Museum of Ireland (Ireland #24; Appendix 1:29; fig. 61). It is woven double of coarsely shredded cedar bark in twining technique with wefts about one inch apart. The yoke is single to about an inch and a half below the neck, and from there on it is double, woven like the inside of a hat. The fringe is made of both warps. The outside is rubbed with red ocher. The cape is nineteen inches long including a four-inch fringe.

Another circular cape is found in the collection in Florence. It is a single weave and therefore more traditional. It is registered there as coming from New Zealand and "resembling a type from Nootka Sound," but it should be the reverse. (Ethnological Museum 42*a*).

Some of the blankets combine cedar bark with a very small amount of wool. If a geometric design is used as a border at the lower edge, it is often woven with a

Fig. 60. Woman of Nootka. Spanish picture.

Fig. 61. Circular cape, double weave, Nootka Sound. King collection (Cook), Ireland, King, 24 (Appendix 1:29).

dyed woolen weft. The colors are generally black, derived from burying the yarn in black mineral mud, white, which is natural, and yellow, dyed with a wolf moss (*Evernia vulpina*). Some experiments were also done by overlaying the outer weft with a very thinly spun bit of mountain goat wool. These might be considered as transitions to the woolen garment or as a frugal use of the mountain goat wool that was available. This method of "stretching" the wool is shown in a blanket at the Museum für Völkerkunde in Vienna (Vienna 218 [1968, 284]). The blanket is called a Chilkat blanket type in the catalog, and it has not only the traditional shape of that type, but also more design than was customary on the blankets from Nootka Sound, where it is supposed to have been collected by the Cook expedition in 1778. Along the top is a border which is divided into five equal areas with a face in the center, a vacant space on each side, and an uneven checkerboard design at each end. This border is repeated at the lower edge with the same face in the center and an inverted face at each end, with the checkerboard pattern in the spaces vacant above. The inverted face is found on true Chilkat blankets as well as on shirts of the same kind of weaving. They also occur on painted dancing aprons.

Generally the cedar bark cloaks were undecorated, except as an individual's fancy was expressed. One example in the British Museum (NWC 53) should be mentioned. The shredded cedar bark cloaks were usually too rough for painting, but this unusual specimen has a complex design painted on it. It compares well with the paintings on the boards found by the men on the *Sutil* and the *Mexicana* when they were circumnavigating Vancouver Island (see chap. 4). The robe is illustrated in Inverarity (1950, no. 8), who attributes it to the Tlingit, but there does not seem to be any evidence for this in the catalog of the British Museum. If it was collected by the Cook expedition, it could not come from this northern territory, for he did not stop there. Inverarity believes it is an early Chilkat blanket, but the general design resembles not only the boards just mentioned but other painting of that period.

More standard in the type of decoration are some blankets that have wool only in the border (BM, NWC 49 or 1262 or 2262). The wool is dyed yellow and brown, and the design is a diamond shape which could be interpreted as the Northwest Coast eye. The blanket is loosely woven with a heavy fringe. This piece identifies completely with one in Emmons (1903, p. 190, plate 24, fig. 1). It has a heavy fringe made of the warps with many strands of twisted cord added. There is also a short fringe along the straight sides. Another British Museum piece, NWC 54, has an allover pattern of diamonds or lozenges, each figure starting at the center with an all-black diamond framed in white, then framed in black. Between these areas are black and white lines which cross each other at the apex of the diamond and join each other at the sharp ends. The patterned area is outlined in a border a little over an inch wide with a black background and zigzag lines of white horizontally placed in it, then an equal band of white and another of black to which white fringes are attached. The fringe on the lower edge does not look as though it had ever been very thick, but now it is very ragged and seems to be largely black. The blanket is almost square and in this respect it resembles the old blankets made by the Salish.

From his descriptions, King was evidently very much interested in weaving technique and materials, for his collection, as represented today in the National Museum of Ireland in Dublin, has a fine assortment of woven blankets. They are all made of shredded cedar bark with a small amount of wool, but it is the character of the weaving and the fine design of the borders which make them noteworthy. These pieces have no recognizable catalog numbers on them, and so they are listed here as Ireland 2, 3, 4, and 5.

The simplest one (Ireland 2) has shredded cedar bark warps and wefts twined at about three-eighth-inch intervals. There is a solid dark brown line at the upper edge with a single row, about one inch wide, of alternating brown and white checks. This same border is repeated at the lower edge with three rows of checks. These borders are in mountain goat wool. At the sides is a band of braiding and a very short fringe. The blanket is well rounded at the bottom and has a fringe about twelve inches long. It is now in very poor condition and very scanty, although it shows evidence of once having been much heavier.

The second blanket (Ireland 3) is also shredded cedar bark with a variation in twining. Instead of one row of twining at intervals, there are two rows close together, giving the effect of a corded material. There is a narrow border at the upper edge and along the sides with a Grecian key pattern. The lower edge has the same design but half again as wide. Below this and under a thin layer of fringe the design is repeated with the figure done in a heavier black. The fringe consists of coarse warps and twisted thread of cedar bark added over the lower border design. This was once a very handsome blanket and fortunately the borders and the fringe are in good condition.

The most elaborate design is on the third blanket of the King collection (Ireland 4), and the blanket is in very poor condition. The blanket is oblong and is straight on the lower edge. The body is loosely twined, with the warp very prominent. The sides are braided and have the tatters of a fringe. This is also true of the lower edge. The borders at both the upper and the lower edges are alike, with the top a little narrower. There are two bands of design which are reversed in their positions at the top and bottom. The upper row at the top consists of broad-based isosceles triangles, alternating in black and white. The second row of pattern is identical with the design on BM, NWC 54.

The last of the King pieces (Ireland 5) (Appendix 1:24; fig. 62) of this type is in very poor condition, but the most important part of its design stands out clearly. It is single row at the lower edge above a long scrawny fringe. Again the broad-based triangles in yellow dominate the pattern on a black background. Between the triangles is a small diamond shape with a black oblong with rounded corners in the center. This is strikingly like the eye of the wolf mask (Berlin IV. B. 178) which is illustrated in the catalog of the Seattle Fair exhibition (Gunther 1962, pp. 43, 97) and is also part of the Cook collection from Nootka Sound. The design represents a very definite Northwest Coast style and can be regarded as a proto-Chilkat form.

Many of the blankets just discussed had a small amount of wool added to the cedar bark. It is not clear whether any blankets in the eighteenth century were

Fig. 62. Cedar bark blanket with border design, no location. King collection (Cook), Ireland, King, no number (Appendix 1:24).

made completely of wool, for they were not always available for close examination. However, the use of wool at least for the complete weft is apparent, and the ingenious way in which it was combined with other materials is another evidence of the technical skill of the eighteenth-century weavers.

Textiles: Wool

Sources. There has been much speculation about the sources of wool, and the information gained from the eighteenth-century accounts is not very helpful because the writers were not familiar with the fauna which might have produced it. They all came from countries where sheep provided the wool, and although they never saw any, they still felt sure that there were wild sheep in the mountains. That the source was a mountain goat was not revealed until much later.

Working backward from the nineteenth century, the Chilkat blanket—the ultimate in Northwest Coast weaving—was consistently made of mountain goat wool for the weft and cedar bark for the warps. Mountain goats must have been more plentiful and their distribution greater in the eighteenth century because it is doubtful that the wide use of their wool resulted from trade alone. In various parts of the long strip of coast other materials were added, ranging from fireweed cotton to the hair and wool of other animals, especially the wool of a local breed of dog, in order to stretch what mountain goat wool was available. These dogs were especially domesticated for wool bearing. They were sheared like sheep, and Vancouver said that the wool which came off was so thick and tight that the whole piece could be picked up by one corner and would not fall apart (Vancouver 1798, 1:85). During the latter part of the nineteenth century, when commercial cloth became easily available, these dogs were no longer segregated and they disappeared into the general "gene pot" that one finds in every Indian village.

The appearance and origin of this particular breed has been a matter of discussion for many years and no acceptable conclusion has yet been reached. In May 1792, at Restoration Point on Bainbridge Island in Puget Sound, Vancouver saw these dogs and described them as resembling the Pomeranian (Vancouver 1798, 1:85), which is of little help today because the Pomeranian of Vancouver's time differed from the small lap dog now known by that name. However, this name is a link which cannot be disregarded. Lieutenant King, on the Cook expedition, mentions dogs in Kamchatka "that in shape are somewhat like the Pomeranian breed but considerably larger."

On an afternoon spent in the library of the British Museum, Natural History Division, I accumulated the following information. Every article consulted in reference to the "wool" dog started with the quotation from Vancouver.

The Pomeranian first appeared in the literature in Carolus Linnaeus's famous classification of animals as *Canis pomeranus* (edition 1788, after Linnaeus's death). It was also mentioned contemporaneously by Buffon. The Pomeranian is a member of the spitz family and was originally quite a large dog, similar to the German *Wolfspitz*. He was bred in temperate climates and far from the traditional home of the group as a whole. The Pomeranian and the Keeshond and all related breeds of old Germania came to central Europe many centuries ago and yet have preserved the characteristics of the group. In 1859 the breed was common in Europe and was called *loup-loup*, recognizing the wolflike side of their ancestry. All this adds to the possibility that this breed may have wandered far enough across Asia with nomadic Germanic tribes that it could have established itself and perhaps joined some of the tribes that came later to America. This is more plausible than any other theory which attempts to account for their presence on the Northwset Coast in the eighteenth century. It is more difficult to determine why this breed should be limited to the lower Fraser River and the region on both sides of the Strait of Juan de Fuca. Nor can the vague pattern of domestication among people who did not practice it on any other animal be explained. They understood enough to segregate them from the other dogs, often by keeping them on nearby islands. Everyone who mentioned them wrote of their curious howl; they did not bark. This description is no solution to the problem but it may be a step forward.

Ledyard, who wrote his book without his diary, said that he saw the dogs, which were almost white and of a domestic kind (Ledyard 1783, p. 71). This may be a lapse of memory or it may be possible that the Nootka traded a few dogs from their Salish neighbors just at that time; but it is doubtful that they continued their breeding. However, regardless of many accounts of white woolen blankets farther north the dog wool probably was not one of the additions. Information about combinations can be gotten from the Salish, who were the most active weavers at the southern end of the Northwest Coast (Gunther 1927, p. 221). The ingredients—fireweed cotton, down of geese and ducks, dog wool, and mountain goat wool—were beaten together with a sword-shaped stick. The mixture was rolled on the thigh and then spun on large spindles with beautifully carved whorls about six inches in diameter. These large spindles were almost essential to handle the texture of these combinations; so possibly the wool was traded already spun, since the Nootka did not have them.

The wool in various combinations gave the weavers a greater opportunity to show their skill, and in addition to the blanket cloak so common in cedar bark, they created a smaller oblong blanket called a shoulder blanket. Excellent examples of this variety are found in the collection of the Museum of Anthropology and Ethnography in Leningrad (2520–4, 2520–5) (Appendix 1:25; fig. 63). These blankets are woven of warps of twisted cedar bark, which are taken two at a time in a twining technique. Between each pair of cedar bark warps a thin warp strip of sea otter fur is introduced, with the fur facing away from the weaver. The weaving is so tight that it scarcely shows in the deep sea otter fur, so that one side appears to be completely fur while the other side shows the mountain goat wool as the weft. This side has six rows of six concentric rectangles embroidered on it. The embroidery starts at the center with the smallest rectangle and ends with the largest, the remainder of the black yarn hanging down as a tassel. The embroidery may be a third strand introduced into the twining or it may be put on separately, since it does not show on the back. The blankets resemble each other very closely.

These two blankets may have had an important place in history. When the Cook expedition, without their commander, returned from their trip to the Bering Sea in the summer of 1779, their ships were sadly in need of repair, so they came into the harbor of Petropavlosk. Major Behm, a German who was a member of the Russian Navy, was commander of the port and was very helpful, supplying everything in his stores which was needed. In gratitude, the officers gave him two blankets they had collected. Their origin is not known, but Nootka Sound is the

Fig. 63. Blanket with rectangular design, no location. Leningrad 2520 (Appendix 1:25).

only place the Cook expedition stopped where such weaving could have been done. Major Behm, who felt these should not be his personal possession, sent them to Saint Petersburg to the Museum of the Czar, and this became the museum where they were found in this century.

Birdskins

There is one more technique of blanket making which is on the borderline of weaving, but perhaps more strictly belongs to netting. This is the use of birdskins in the same way that rabbit skins are used in the plateau region of the United

States. Birdskins with a downy surface are selected, and the heavier feathers are picked off. The usable area is then laid out flat and, starting at the edge, a narrow strip is cut spirally, ending at the center of the piece. This strip immediately twists so that it becomes a cord with down on all sides. These strips are woven into a piece of netting the shape and size of the blanket desired. This technique is used along the entire coast and is also found among the Eskimo of Alaska. The skillful weaver can select the colors of the down carefully so that a blanket can be shaded from black through gray to white. Often the piece is designed in bands of this range of colors.

In the collection in Leningrad there are two birdskin blankets. One (2520–9) is striped dark, white, larger dark stripe, white, and dark. The other one (2520–8) does not have such exact arrangement of the colors. These two blankets are regarded as part of the gift which was presented to Major Behm at Petropavlosk. This guess is based on the fact that all the pieces mentioned have an accession number assigned to Major Behm.

Bibliography

NOTE: Only works cited in the text are included since many excellent bibliographies on the Northwest Coast have been published.

Adam, Leonhard. 1927. *Nordwestamerikanische Indianerkunst.* Orbis Pictus 17. Berlin: Ernst Wasmuth.

Anderson, Bern. 1960. *Surveyor of the sea.* Seattle: University of Washington Press.

Baker, J. n.d. *Log 22 December 1790 to 27 November 1792.* Public Record Office, Ad 55/32. London.

Bancroft, Hubert H. 1886. *Alaska, 1730–1885.* San Francisco: A. L. Bancroft.

Bandi, Hans-Georg. 1956. *Einige Gegenstände aus Alaska und Britisch Kolumbien gesammelt von Johan Wäber [John Webber], Bern/London, wahrend der dritte Forschungsreise von James Cook 1776–1780.* Proceedings, 32d International Congress of Americanists, Copenhagen.

Barnett, Homer. 1939. *Culture element distributions: Gulf of Georgia Salish.* Anthropological Records, vol. 1, no. 5. Berkeley: University of California Press.

Barrington, Daines. 1781. *Miscellanies.* London (Contains Maurelle's journal of the Heceta expedition in 1775).

Barry, J. Neilson. 1930. Broughton's reconnaissance of the San Juan Islands in 1792. *Washington Historical Quarterly*, vol. 21, no. 1.

Bartlett, John. 1925. A narrative of events in the life of John Bartlett of Boston, Mass. in the years 1790–1793 during voyages to Canton, the northwest coast of North America and elsewhere. In *The sea, the ship, and the sailor*, ed. Elliot Snow. Salem: Marine Research Society.

Bauzá, Felipe de. n.d. *Album* (sketches of the Malaspina voyage). Madrid: Museo Naval.

Beaglehole, J. C., ed. 1967. *The journals of Captain James Cook on his voyages of discovery. The voyage of the "Resolution" and "Discovery", 1776–1780.* 2 vols. Published for the Hakluyt Society. Cambridge: At the University Press.

Bell, Edward. 1914. A new Vancouver journal. *Washington Historical Quarterly*, vol. 5, no. 2, 3, 4.

Beresford, William. *See* Dixon, George

Berkh, Vasili. 1823. The chronological history of the discovery of the Alaskan islands; or, The exploits of the Russian merchants in fur trade. Saint Petersburg. Translated by Dimitri Krenov, W.P.A. project 5668; J. S. Richards, sponsor, 1938 (typescript, University of Washington Library).

Birket-Smith, Kaj. 1953. *The Chugach Eskimo.* Nationalmuseets Skrifter, Etnografisk Roekke 6, Nationalmuseets Publikationsfond, Copenhagen.

Birket-Smith, Kaj, and DeLaguna, Frederica. 1938. *The Eyak Indians of the Copper River delta, Alaska.* Copenhagen.

Bishop, Charles. n.d. Commercial journal of the ship "Ruby"; Voyage to the northwest coast of America and China 1794–96. Archives of British Columbia, Victoria.

Boas, Franz. 1895. *The social organization and secret societies of the Kwakiutl Indians.* United States National Museum, report. Washington, D.C.

———. 1905–9. *The Kwakiutl of Vancouver Island.* American Museum of Natural History, memoirs, vol. 8, part 2. Publication of the Jesup North Pacific expedition, vol. 5, pp. 307–516. New York.

———. 1916. *Tsimshian mythology.* Bureau of American Ethnology, report no. 31. Washington, D.C.

———. 1935. Kwakiutl culture as reflected in mythology. Memoirs, American Folklore Society, vol. 28, New York.

Boit, John. 1919–20. Log of the "Columbia," 1790–1792. *Proceedings of the Massachusetts Historical Society*, Oct. 1919–June 1920, vol. 53.

———. 1921. *A new log of the "Columbia" on the discovery of the Columbia River and Grays Harbor*, ed. Edmond S. Meany. Seattle: University of Washington Press.

Bolton, Herbert E. 1927. *Fray Juan Crespi, Missionary Explorer on the Pacific Coast, 1769–1774.* Berkeley: University of California Press.

Broughton, William R. 1930. Proceedings of His Majesty's brig "Chatham" from May 18–25, 1792. *Washington Historical Quarterly*, vol. 21, p. 55–60. Seattle: University of Washington Press. (Original in Library of Royal United Services Institution, Whitehall, London.)

Caamaño, Don Jacinto. 1849. *Expedición de la corbeta "Aranzazu" al mando del teniente de Navio Don Jacinto Caamaño a comprobar la relación de Fonte.* Colleción de documentos ineditos para la historia de España. Por Salva y Barenda 8° Madrid, 15:323–63 Trans., see Wagner and Newcombe 1938.

Cleveland, Richard Jeffry. 1842. *A narrative of voyages and commercial enterprises.* Cambridge: J. Owen.

Colnett, James. n.d. Log of the "Prince of Wales," 1787–1788. Manuscript in Public Record Office, London (microfilm, University of Washington Library).

Cook, James. 1967. In *The journals of Captain James Cook on his voyages of discovery. The voyage of the "Resolution" and "Discovery," 1776–1780*, ed. J. C. Beaglehole. Published for the Hakluyt Society. Cambridge: At the University Press.

Cook, James. 1783. Troisième voyage de Cook; ou, journal d'une expedition faite dans la mer Pacifique du sud et du nord en 1776, 1777, 1778, 1779 et 1780. Trans. de l'anglois. Ed. Versailles, Poincot; Paris, Belin.

Cook, James, and King, James. 1784. A voyage to the Pacific Ocean . . . for making discoveries in the northern hemisphere to determine the position and extent of the west side of North America, its distance from Asia and the practicability of a northern passage. 3 vols. plus folio atlas of plates and maps. London.

Corney, Peter. 1896. *Early northern Pacific voyages*. Honolulu.

Coxe, William. 1787. *An account of the Russian discoveries between Asia and America*. 3d ed. (including a supplement comparing the Russian discoveries with those of Cook).

Crespi, Juan. n.d. Diario de su viage con Pérez en la "Santiago" con el objeto a explorar las costas de las Californias hasta los 60 grados. Original: Archivo General de las Indias, Seville, Spain. Translated by George B. Griffen.

Cutter, Donald C. 1969. *The California coast*. Bilingual edition of documents of the Sutro collection. American Exploration and Travel Series, no. 57. Norman: University of Oklahoma Press (includes the diaries of Crespi and de la Peña).

Dalton, O. M. 1897. Notes on an ethnological collection from the west coast of North America (more especially California), Hawaii, Tahiti, formed during the voyage of Captain Vancouver, 1790–1795 and now in the British Museum. *Internationales Archiv für Ethnographie* 10:225–45.

Dawson, George M. 1878–79. *Haida Indians of the Queen Charlotte Islands*. Appendix A, Geological Survey of Canada. Report of Surveys and Explorations.

Daylton, Margaret Elizabeth. n.d. *Official documents relating to Spanish and Mexican voyages of navigation, exploration and discovery made in North America in the 18th century*. W.P.A. project no. 2799. University of Washington Northwest collection.

DeLaguna, Frederica. 1947. *Prehistory of northern North America as seen from the Yukon*. Memoirs, no. 3, Society for American Archaeology.

———. 1960. *The story of a Tlingit community*. Bureau of American Ethnology, bulletin 172. Washington, D.C.

DeLaguna, Frederica; Riddell, Francis; McGeein, Donald F.; Lane, Kenneth; and Freed, J. Arthur. 1964. *Archaeology of the Yakutat Bay area, Alaska*. Bureau of American Ethnology, bulletin 192. Washington, D.C.

Dillon, Richard. 1951. Archibald Menzies' trophies. *British Columbia Historical Quarterly*, vol. 15, nos. 3, 4. Victoria, B.C.

Dixon, George. 1789. *A voyage round the world, but more particularly to the northwest coast of America . . . in the "King George" and "Queen Charlotte."* London.

Drucker, Philip. 1950. *Culture element distributions: The Northwest Coast*. Anthropological Records, vol. 9, no. 3, Berkeley: University of California Press.

———. 1951. *The northern and central Nootka*. Bureau of American Ethnology, bulletin 144. Washington, D.C.

———. 1963. *The Indians of the Northwest Coast*. New York: McGraw-Hill.

Edgar, Thomas. n.d. Journal of the voyage of the "Discovery." Manuscript, British Museum 521, Egerton 2591; add. ms. 37528.

Edgar, Thomas. 1967. In *The journals of Captain James Cook on his voyages of discovery. The voyage of the "Resolution" and "Discovery," 1776–1780*, ed. J. C. Beaglehole, vol. 2. Published for the Hakluyt Society. Cambridge: At the University Press.

Ellis, William. 1782. *Authentic narrative of a voyage performed by Captain Cook*. 2 vols. London.

Emmons, George T. 1903. *The basketry of the Tlingit*. American Museum of Natural History, Memoirs, vol. 3, part 2. New York.

———. 1908. Copper neck rings of Southern Alaska. *American Anthropologist*, n.s., 10:644–49.

———. 1911. An account of the meeting between La Pérouse and the Tlingit. *American Anthropologist*, n.s., 13:294–98.

Emmons, George T., and Boas, Franz. 1907. *The Chilkat blanket, with notes on blanket designs*. American Museum of Natural History, Memoirs, vol. 3, part 4, p. 329–400. New York.

Espinoza y Tello, José. 1930. *A Spanish voyage to Vancouver Island and the northwest coast of America, being the narrative of the voyage made in the year 1792 by the schooners Sutil and Mexicana to explore the Strait of Fuca*. Trans. Cecil Jane. London.

Fernandez, Justino. 1939. *Tomas de Suría y su viage*. Porrua, Mexico.

Fleurieu, Charles Pierre Claret de. 1801. *A voyage round the world, performed during the years 1790, 1791, 1792 by Etienne Marchand preceded by a historical introduction and illustrated by charts, etc.* Trans. from the French by C. P. C. de Fleurieu. London: Longman.

Force, Roland, and Force, Maryanne. 1968. *Art and artifacts of the eighteenth century.* Honolulu: Bishop Museum Press (sketches made by Sarah Stone Smith in the Leverian Museum, London, in 1780).

Giglioli, Enrico Hillyer. 1895. *Appunti intorno ad una collezione etnografica fatta durante il tèrzo viaggio di Cook*. Archivio per l'Antropologia e la Etnologia, vol. 25, no. 1, pp. 57–147. Florence.

Greenhow, Robert. 1844. *The history of Oregon and California and the other territories of the northwest coast of North America*. Boston.

Grenfell, Harold. Translator of Caamaño, q.v.

Griffen, George Butler. Translator of Crespi and de la Peña, q.v.

Gunther, Erna. 1927. *Klallam ethnography*. University of Washington Publications in Anthropology, vol. 1, no. 5. Seattle.

———. 1960. Vancouver and the Indians of Puget Sound. *Pacific Northwest Quarterly*, vol. 51, no. 1.

———. 1962. Northwest Coast Indian art. *Seattle World's Fair Catalog*. Seattle.

Haswell, Robert. 1884. A voyage round the world on board the ship "Columbia Rediviva" and the sloop "Washington" 1787–1789. In *History of the Northwest Coast*, ed. A. L. Bancroft, vol. 1. San Francisco.

Henking, Karl H. 1955–56. Die Südsee und Alaskasammlung Johann Wäber: Beschreibender Katalog. *Jahrbuch des Bernischen Historischen Museums in Bern.* 35, 36:367–78.

Hewitt, George Goodman. n.d. *Catalogue of the George Goodman Hewitt collection formed on the voyage of Captain Vancouver.* British Museum Ethnological document 1126.

Hodge, Frederick W., ed. 1907–10. *Handbook of American Indians.* Bureau of American Ethnology, bulletin 30. Washington, D.C.

Hoskins, Johns. 1941. Narrative of the second voyage of the "Columbia," 1790–1792. In *Voyages of the "Columbia" to the Northwest Coast, 1787–1790 and 1790–1793*, ed. F. W. Howay. Proceedings of the Massachusetts Historical Society, vol. 79.

Hough, Walter. 1894. *Primitive American armor.* United States National Museum Report for 1893, pp. 625–53. Washington, D.C.

Howay, F. W. 1918. Dog's hair blankets. *Washington Historical Quarterly* 9:83–92.

Ingraham, Joseph. n.d. Journal of the voyage of the brigantine "Hope" from Boston to the northwest coast of North America. Original in Library of Congress, DU 620.H44#3.

Inverarity, Robert Bruce. 1950. *Art of the northwest coast Indians.* Berkeley and Los Angeles: University of California Press.

Jane, Cecil, trans. *See* Espinoza y Tello, Jose.

Jewitt, John R. 1815. *Narrative of the adventures and sufferings of John R. Jewitt.* Middletown, Conn.

Johnson, Margaret Olive. 1911. Spanish exploration of the Pacific Coast. M.A. thesis, University of California at Berkeley.

King, James. n.d. *Journal.* Manuscript adm. 55/122, Public Record Office, London.

King, James. 1967. In *The journals of Captain James Cook on his voyages of discovery. The voyage of the "Resolution" and "Discovery," 1776–1780*, ed. J. C. Beaglehole. Published for the Hakluyt Society. Cambridge: At the University Press.

Krause, Aurel. 1956. *The Tlingit Indians.* Trans. from the German by Erna Gunther (*Die Tlinkit Indianer*, Jena, 1885). Seattle: University of Washington Press.

Krenov, Dimitri, trans. *See* Berkh, Vasili

Krickeberg, Walter. 1914. New collections at the Royal Museum for Ethnography. *Zeitschrift für Ethnologie* 46:678. Berlin.

———. 1925. *Malerein auf ledernen zeremonial-Kleidern der nordwest Amerikaner.* Jahrbuch für Praehistorische und Ethnographische Kunst. Leipzig.

Kroeber, A. L. 1953. *Handbook of the California Indians.* Bureau of Ethnology, bulletin 78. Washington, D.C. (reprint).

Langsdorff, George H. 1817. *Voyages and travels in various parts of the world during the years 1803, 4, 5, 6, 7.* Carlisle.

La Pérouse, Jean François Galup de. 1798. *La Pérouse voyage round the world performed in the years 1785–1788.* Trans. from the French in 2 vols. London.

Laskey, Captain. 1813. *A general account of the Hunterian Museum.* Glasgow.

Lavachery, Henri A. 1929. *Les arts anciens d'Amérique au musée archeologique de Madrid.* Antwerp.

Ledyard, John. 1783. *A journal of Captain Cook's last voyage to the Pacific Ocean, etc. 1778–1779.* Hartford.

Lips, Eva. 1956. *Remarks about several pieces of Northwest Coast Art.* Jahrbuch des Museums für Völkerkunde zu Leipzig.

Lisiansky, Urey. 1814. *Voyage round the world in the years 1803, 4, 5, 6.* London.

McIlwraith, T. F. 1948. *The Bella Coola.* Toronto: University of Toronto Press.

Magee, Bernard. n.d. Journal of a voyage made on board the "Jefferson" 1792–1794. Original in Massachusetts Historical Society, Boston.

Malaspina, Alejandro. *See* Novo y Colson, Pedro de

Manby, Thomas. n.d. The log of the proc (?) of His Majesty's armed tender "Chatham," Lieut. Broughton and Pugget, comm. Sept. 12, 1792–Oct. 8, 1794. Copy of ms. in Provincial Library, Victoria, B.C.

Manwaring, George E. 1931. *My friend the admiral: The life, letters and journals of Rear-Admiral James Burney.* London: Routledge.

Marchand, Etienne. *See* Fleurieu, Charles Pierre Claret de.

Martinez, Estevan José. n.d. Diary of the voyage which I, ensign of the Royal Navy, Don Estevan José Martinez, am going to make to the Port of San Lorenzo de Nuca in command of the frigate "Princesa," 1789. Trans. Wm. Schurz.

Maurelle, Francisco Antonio. *See* Barrington, Dannes.

Meany, Edmond S. 1923. *Origin of place names in Washington.* Seattle: University of Washington Press.

Meares, John. 1790. *Voyages made in the years 1788 and 1789 from China to the northwest coast of America to which are affixed an introductory narrative of a voyage performed in 1786 from Bengal in the ship "Nootka": Observations on the probable existence of Northwest Passage and some account of the trade between the northwest coast of America and China and the latter country and Great Britain.* London.

Menzies, Archibald. 1923. *Menzies' journal of Vancouver's voyage, April to October 1792,* ed. C. F. Newcombe. Archives of British Columbia Memoir no. 5. Victoria.

Mozino, J. M. Suarez de Figueroa. 1913. *Noticias de Nutka.* Mexico. Trans. by Iris Higbee Wilson. Seattle: University of Washington Press, 1970.

Newcombe, C. F. 1914. The first circumnavigation of Vancouver Island. Archives of British Columbia Memoirs no. 1. Victoria.

Niblack, Albert P. 1890. *The coast Indians of southern Alaska and northern British Columbia.* United States National Museum Report for 1888. Washington, D.C.

Nicol, John. 1925. The life and adventures of John Nicol, mariner. In *The Sea, the ship and the sailor*, ed. Elliot Snow. Publication no. 7, Marine Research Society. Salem, Mass.

Novo y Colson, Pedro de. 1884. *Político-científico alrededor al mundo por las corbetas "Descubierta" y "Atrivida" al mando del capitan de navio Don Alejandro Malaspina desde 1789 a 1794.* 1st ed. Madrid. Trans. Carl Robinson. Typescript in University of British Columbia Library.

Olson, Ronald. 1936. *The Quinault Indians.* University of Washington Publications in Anthropology, vol. 6, no. 1. Seattle.
———. 1967. *Social structure and social life of the Tlingit in Alaska.* Berkeley and Los Angeles: University of California Press.

Orth, Donald. 1967. *Dictionary of Alaska place names.* United States Department of the Interior, Geological Survey Professional Paper no. 567. Washington, D.C.

Osgood, Cornelius. 1937. *The ethnography of the Tanaina.* Yale University Publications in Anthropology no. 16. London: Oxford University Press.

Paul, Frances. 1944. *The spruce root basketry of the Tlingit.* Lawrence, Kansas: Education Division of the United States Indian Service, Haskell Institute.

Peña Savaria, Fray Tomas de la. *See* Johnson, Margaret

Pennant, Thomas. 1784. *Arctic zoology.* London.

Portlock, Nathaniel. 1789. *A voyage to the northwest coast of America.* London.

Publicaciónes del Museo Naval, 1932. Vol. 1. Madrid.

Puget, Peter. 1939. The Vancouver expedition: Peter Puget's journal of the exploration of Puget Sound, May 7–June 11, 1792, ed. Bern Anderson. *Pacific Northwest Quarterly*, 30:177–217.

Quimper, Manuel. 1933. Diary of the voyage which the ensign of the royal armada, Don Manuel Quimper, is with the favor of Our Lord about to undertake in the sloop under his command, the "Princesa Real," of four cannon and eight swivel guns, from the Puerto de Santa Cruz de Nuca in lat. 49°35′ N to the Strait of Juan de Fuca which is in the latitude of 48°32′ and in the longitude of 19°35′ from the stated meridian. In *Spanish explorations in the Strait of Juan de Fuca*, trans., ed. Henry Wagner. Santa Ana.

Reade, Charles H. 1891. An account of a collection of ethnographical specimens formed during Vancouver's voyage in the Pacific Ocean, 1790–1795. *Journal of the Royal Anthropological Institute*, o.s. 21:99–108.

Rickard, T. A. 1939. The use of iron and copper by the Indians of British Columbia. *British Columbia Historical Quarterly* 3:25-50.

Rickman, John. 1781. *Journal of Captain Cook's last voyage to the Pacific Ocean on the "Discovery," performed in the years 1776, 1777, 1778, 1779.* London: E. Newberry.

Riobo, Fray Juan Antonio Garcia. 1918. An account of the voyage made by Father John Riobo, chaplain of His Majesty's frigates "La Princesa" and "La Favorita" to discover new lands and seas north of the settlements of the ports of Monterrey and of Our Father, San Francisco, whose missions are in charge of the apostolic missionaries of the College of San Fernando of Mexico. *Catholic Historical Review* 4:222–29. The original is in the archives of the University of Santa Clara, California. Translated and edited by the Very Reverend Walter Thornton, S.J.

Rustow, Anna. 1939. *Die Objekte der Malaspina-Expedition.* Bäessler Archiv, Beiträge zur Völkerkunde, vol. 22, part 4. Berlin.

Samwell, David. n.d. Journal. British Museum ms. 521, Egerton 2591.

Samwell, David. 1967. In *The journals of Captain James Cook on his voyages of discovery. The voyage of the "Resolution" and "Discovery," 1776–1790*, ed. J. C. Beaglehole, vol. 2. Published for the Hakluyt Society. Cambridge: At the University Press.

Sarytschew, Gavrilo. 1806. *An account of a voyage of discovery to the northeast of Siberia and the Northeast Sea.* London (Billings expedition).

Sauer, Martin. 1802. *An account of a geographical and astronomical expedition to the northern parts of Russia, for ascertaining the degrees of latitude and longitude of the mouth of the River Kolyma; of the coast of Tshutski, to East Cape; and of the islands in the northern ocean, stretching to the American coast. Performed by Commodore Joseph Billings in the years 1784-1794.* London.

———. 1803. *Reise nach den nördlichen Gegenden von Russischen Asien und Amerika unter dem Commodore J. Billings, 1785-94.* Weimar.

Scholfield, E. O. S. 1914. *British Columbia from the earliest times to the present.* Vancouver, Canada.

Siebert, Erna, and Forman, Werner. 1967. *North American Indian art.* London: Paul Hamlyn.

Sierra, Fray Benito de la. 1930. An account of the Heceta expedition to the Northwest Coast in 1775. Trans., ed. A. J. Baker. *California Historical Society Quarterly*, vol. 9, no. 3.

Stanley, Samuel. 1965. Changes in Tlingit social organization. Typescript.

Strange, James C. S. 1928. *Journal and narrative of the commercial expedition from Bombay to the northwest coast of America.* Records of Fort George, Madras, ed. A. V. Venkatarama Ayyar.

Suría, Tomas de. 1936. *Journal of Tomas de Suría.* Trans., ed. Henry Wagner. Glendale, California.

Swan, James G. 1857. *The Northwest Coast; or, Three years' residence in Washington Territory.* New York: Harper Bros.

Swanton, John R. 1905. *Haida texts and myths.* Bureau of American Ethnology, bulletin 29. Washington, D.C.

———. 1908. *Social condition and beliefs and linguistic relationship of the Tlingit Indians.* Bureau of American Ethnology, report 26. Washington, D.C.

———. 1909. *Tlingit texts.* Bureau of American Ethnology, bulletin 39. Washington, D.C.

Vancouver, George. 1798. *A voyage of discovery to the North Pacific and round the world . . . performed 1790–1795 with the "Discovery" and the "Chatham" under Captain George Vancouver.* 3 vols. London.

Vanderberg, Joanne. 1953. Chilkat and Salish weaving. M. A. thesis, University of Washington.

Wagner, Henry. 1933. *Spanish explorations in the Strait of Juan de Fuca*. Santa Ana.

———. 1937. *Cartography of the northwest coast of America to the year 1800*. 2 vols. Berkeley: University of California Press.

Wagner, Henry, and Newcombe, W. A., eds. 1938. The journal of Don Jacinto Caamaño. Trans. Harold Grenfell. *British Columbia Historical Quarterly*, July 1938.

Walbran, John T. 1909. *British Columbia coast names, 1592–1906*. Ottawa: Government Printer.

Willoughby, Charles. 1886. *Indians of the Quinaiult Agency, Washington Territory*. Annual report, Smithsonian Institution.

Wingert, Paul S. 1949. *American Indian sculpture: A study of the Northwest Coast*. New York: Stechert.

Woldt, Adrian. 1884. *Capitain Jacobsen's Reise an der Nordwestküste Amerikas, 1881–83*. Leipzig.

Index

Note: The index does not include references to objects in Appendix 1 which are cited with identifying numbers in the text.